William "Baldy" Smith

M000237126

William "Baldy" Smith

*Engineer, Critic and Union
Major General in the Civil War*

STEPHEN NICHOLAS SICILIANO

McFarland & Company, Inc., Publishers
Jefferson, North Carolina

This book has undergone peer review.

Frontispiece:
Major General William Farrar Smith
(Library of Congress).

All maps by Hal Jespersen, www.cwmaps.com.

LIBRARY OF CONGRESS CATALOGUING-IN-PUBLICATION DATA

Names: Siciliano, Stephen Nicholas, 1955– author.
Title: William "Baldy" Smith: Engineer, Critic and Union
Major General in the Civil War
Description: Jefferson, North Carolina : McFarland & Company, Inc., Publishers, 2022 |
Includes bibliographical references and index.
Identifiers: LCCN 2022024209 | ISBN 9781476686134 (paperback : acid free paper) ∞
ISBN 9781476646442 (ebook)
Subjects: LCSH: Smith, William Farrar, 1824-1903. | United States—
History—Civil War, 1861-1865—Campaigns. | United States. Army. Corps, 18th
(1862-1864) | Generals—United States—Biography. | United States. Army—Biography.
| BISAC: BIOGRAPHY & AUTOBIOGRAPHY / Military | HISTORY /
United States / Civil War Period (1850-1877)
Classification: LCC E467.1.S75 S53 2022 | DDC 355.0092 [B]—dc23/eng/20220615
LC record available at https://lccn.loc.gov/2022024209

BRITISH LIBRARY CATALOGUING DATA ARE AVAILABLE

ISBN (print) 978-1-4766-8613-4
ISBN (ebook) 978-1-4766-4644-2

© 2022 Stephen Nicholas Siciliano. All rights reserved

*No part of this book may be reproduced or transmitted in any form
or by any means, electronic or mechanical, including photocopying
or recording, or by any information storage and retrieval system,
without permission in writing from the publisher.*

Front cover image: Major General William Farrar Smith
(National Archives)

Printed in the United States of America

*McFarland & Company, Inc., Publishers
Box 611, Jefferson, North Carolina 28640
www.mcfarlandpub.com*

Table of Contents

Acknowledgments

With any project of this size, its completion was achieved only through the careful guidance and assistance of numerous professors, archivists, librarians, and scholars. Chief Historian Robert K. Krick of the Fredericksburg and Spotsylvania National Military Park and my dissertation committee, Professors Ludwell H. Johnson III, Boyd Coyner, A.Z. Freeman, James Whittenburg, and J. Ward Jones, provided critical guidance and assessment in its initial formulation. The librarians and archivists at the various manuscript collections at the Boston University Library, College of William and Mary Library, Historical Society of Pennsylvania, Huntington Library, Library of Congress, National Archives, New York Public Library, United States Heritage and Education Center, United States Military Academy, Vermont Historical Society, and Virginia Historical Society all provided gracious services and assistance that made the research for the book possible. In particular, I wish to acknowledge librarians Marilyn Blackwell and Paul Carnahan of the Vermont Historical Society and historian and archivist Dr. Richard J. Sommers of the United States Army Military History Institute for their assistance and direction.

I also wish to thank scholars who assisted in providing me additional resources and writing assistance. These include Dr. Mark A. Snell and Dr. Garyn Roberts. In this same way I wish to thank the McFarland reviewers that helped me to improve the work to better prepare it for publication. I also want to recognize Hal Jespersen for his carefully crafted maps that enrich this work.

Finally, I wish to recognize my family for their loving support and encouragement in my study of the American Civil War and my efforts to complete this project. This includes my parents Barbara and Nicholas Siciliano, who sparked my interest in history with my first visit to Gettysburg and continued their support of my lifetime pursuit of the study of history, my wife Peg Poeschl Siciliano, who always believed I could accomplish this work and provided the time for me to do it, and my sons Stephen, Timothy, and Michael, whose encouragement and review helped to finish the work.

Preface

This book began as a dissertation at the College of William and Mary in Virginia. Professor Ludwell H. Johnson III, my dissertation advisor, wisely suggested that a biography was tailor made for the necessary confines of a manageable dissertation topic. I selected this topic as there had not been any scholarly biographies written on Smith. It should be noted, for the sake of transparency, that Professor Johnson's research had led him to a healthy skepticism of the value of political generals within the Federal armies, a belief that was often shared by Smith and ultimately myself.

In my research, I discovered that General Smith, or Baldy Smith as he was commonly known, made important contributions to the Union war effort in two areas. First, he was a critic of the failures of the Federal generalship in the Eastern Theater. His critiques of his fellow officers did not make him popular. But compelled by his care for his men and his desire for victory, he often made his case and took the inevitable negative consequences of speaking one's mind in a culture that expected following orders without debate. The way Smith subsequently was treated illustrated the Union high command's inability to evaluate its own effectiveness in leading the war effort.

Second, on more than one occasion his insight as an engineer and military officer enabled him to offer solutions to challenges faced by his fellow generals. In some cases, his advice was not followed, as in the battles of Williamsburg and Antietam. But when it was followed, as in the battles at Chattanooga, he was recognized for a strategic perspective that helped to save the Union armies from starvation.

Like most generals, Baldy's record of military performance indicates that he too had areas in which to improve. On at least two occasions, had he taken greater risks in confronting the Confederates, he could have either advanced or at least held his own during the battles. But being aware of the fog of war—sometimes quite literally during the battle—Smith's actions overall stand up well in most cases.

The primary sources for this work were found in several manuscript depositories. Three deserve special note. First, the Vermont Historical Society holds the vast majority of Smith's personal papers, writings, and photographs. This collection included two unpublished memoirs. One covers most of his life. The second, shorter one was written for his daughter and focused on his war years. It was edited by Herbert M. Schiller and published in 1990.

The other depositories are the Library of Congress and the United States Army Heritage and Education Center, both of which house several collections of fellow generals. These collections provide a great deal of information on the army politics that surrounded Smith and explain why controversies continued well after the end of the Civil War.

The one regrettable omission from these documents was the near complete absence of Smith's letters to and from his wife, Sarah Lyon Smith. At her request, their letters were destroyed after her death. This limits the book's attention to Smith's role as husband and father. Nonetheless, the book covers Smith's life from his youth, through his war years, and his postwar years as an entrepreneur, political leader, and first-generation Civil War historian.

The other major primary source that was used is *The War of the Rebellion: The Official Records of the Union and Confederate Armies*, which is supplemented by several regimental histories and memoirs. I have used several secondary works on Smith's participation in the war, both in terms of his performance as a commander and as a fellow general. Several modern works on the various battles were used to provide the broader vision of scholarship about these conflicts. These include Stephen Sears' *Lincoln's Lieutenants: The High Command of the Army of the Potomac* (2017) and Gordon Rhea's *On to Petersburg: Grant and Lee, June 4–15, 1864* (2017). Among the secondary works, biographies were often most useful. Mark Snell's *From First to Last: The Life of Major General William B. Franklin* (2002) was among the best, for Franklin was Smith's closest friend in the war, and their correspondence revealed a great deal about Baldy.

Using these works and others, this book attempts to offer the first scholarly account of Baldy Smith's life, making a fair assessment of Smith's contributions to the war and allowing his voice to be heard. At the same time, it also holds him accountable for those times that better judgment would have led to better outcomes for himself and the success of the Union effort.

Introduction

William Farrar Smith, major general in the Union army, played several key roles that aided Federal success in the Civil War. Using his talents and skills as field commander and engineer officer, he twice helped secure the Union army from disastrous defeats. In addition, he offered insightful tactical and strategic plans that could have given the Union greater victories and avoided tragic Federal defeats. These plans were often blocked by his superiors' lack of acumen or by political decisions in Washington. As an important military critic, he showed the tactical incompetence of fellow Union generals Ambrose Burnside, Benjamin F. Butler, and George Gordon Meade. For censuring the failings of his superiors, Smith was ultimately removed from field command. Nevertheless, he continued to demonstrate how blundering generals and meddlesome politicians undermined the Northern war effort. His critique offers a partial explanation of why the North took so long to win the war.

As a boy growing up on his father's farm in northern Vermont, William hoped one day to become an army officer. During his secondary education, Smith developed the talents and skills in mathematics and science that were necessary for admission to West Point. Through the recommendation of his uncle, a Democratic congressman, he was admitted to the United States Military Academy in 1841. At the academy, "Baldy," as his classmates called him, studied engineering as well as military courses. His excellence as a student led him to rank fourth in the class of 1845 and to be appointed to the Corps of Topographical Engineers.

Baldy's engineering training was put to effective use in the years before the Civil War. He helped to survey western Lake Erie in 1845–46 and to establish a practical route between San Antonio and El Paso in 1849. He also reconnoitered the Sacramento Mountains, northeast of El Paso, and participated in two surveys of the Colorado and Rio Grande rivers in 1850. Between 1850 and 1856, he served as assistant to the chief astronomer for the United States–Mexico Boundary Commission, as the engineer officer for the Department of Texas, and as an assistant professor of mathematics at West Point. In December 1856, he became an engineer officer in the Eleventh Lighthouse District at Detroit, where he visited lighthouses, monitored their administration, and inspected their engineering. From 1859 to 1861, as secretary of the Lighthouse Board, he planned the construction of four first-class lighthouses.

In these prewar years, while Smith exhibited his skill and ingenuity as an engineering officer, he also showed a tendency to react intemperately to the faults of his superiors. After a promised leave was denied in 1846, he protested the refusal and won the vacation. During his tenure as an assistant on the Border Commission, his superior made an unjustified, negative reference to Smith. The directives from that superior (the chief astronomer) also showed a lack of confidence in Smith's abilities. The young engineering officer reacted by criticizing the orders and asking to be relieved. The correspondence between the two men became increasingly acrimonious, resulting in Smith's arrest. He was released after he retracted some letters. As engineer of the Department of Texas, he constantly complained about the lack of facilities and blamed the chief engineer for lacking sufficient instruments. Baldy's impatience with the failings of his superiors as well as his engineering skills and military training ultimately characterized his participation in the Civil War.

With the opening of hostilities between the Federal government and the Confederacy, Smith realized that he would be of more service as an infantry commander than as an engineer officer. He succeeded in getting appointed colonel of the Third Vermont on July 23, 1861. Within a few weeks, he was commissioned a brigadier general of volunteers and given command of a brigade. Through regular inspections and constant drill, he held his men to stern discipline; their subsequent performance showed that Baldy trained his troops well. General George B. McClellan, commander of the Army of the Potomac, was impressed by Smith's initial service and promoted him to division commander in September 1861.

During the winter of 1861–62, Smith continued to emphasize the importance of drill to his division. Always concerned about his troops, he wrote to the Vermont governor and testified before Congress about the lack of clothing for his men and the high rate of sickness in his ranks. He also participated in the formation of strategy for the spring offensive. He loyally supported McClellan's Peninsula campaign, which began in late March 1862.

During the 1862 campaigns, he showed his skill as field commander. On April 6, Smith's division found a weakness in the Confederate line on the Warwick River. He directed a brigade to take advantage. But his corps commander blocked his insight and forced Baldy to order his men to return. At Lee's Mill, on April 16, he sent skirmishers across the Warwick River to silence the Confederate artillery. He succeeded in quieting the enemy fire and pushed the skirmishers forward. They gained the first line of the enemy defenses. But a second attack to follow up his initial success proved unsuccessful.

Congress investigated this failure, and some congressmen alleged that Baldy was drunk during the battle. This charge was proven false, but this was not the first time Republican congressmen tried to undermine Smith, who was associated with the most prominent Democratic officer, General McClellan. (During the previous winter, he had been called before Congress to explain his removal of an incompetent regimental commander who was a friend of two Republican senators.) Such partisan actions made Smith a strong critic of political meddling in the war.

The battle of Williamsburg on May 5, 1862, was another example of Smith's insight being ignored by his superiors. Smith's aides found the Confederate works on the extreme right of their line to be unmanned. Realizing that the best method of assisting Major General Joseph Hooker's assault in front was to flank the Confederates, Baldy requested permission to use his division for the flanking movement. Major General Edwin V. Sumner approved the use of only one brigade. However, that one unit, Brigadier General Winfield Scott Hancock's brigade, soon took possession of the enemy's works and threatened their entire line. Yet Sumner refused Smith's repeated requests to reinforce Hancock. By the time McClellan came onto the field and approved Smith's request, Hancock could not push his advantage because of darkness.

Baldy's major service in the Seven Days Battles was as the rear guard that protected McClellan's change of base to Harrison's Landing. His command thwarted several Confederate attacks during the week of fighting. Most important was his stubborn stand at White Oak Swamp on June 30. Despite Thomas J. (Stonewall) Jackson's severe bombardment, Smith fearlessly held his command in position, which helped to keep the Confederates from crossing the swamp in force during the day. His defense enabled the Federals to withdraw safely and concentrate on Malvern Hill. For his service on the Peninsula, Baldy was promoted to major general of volunteers.

The battle of Antietam was still another example of Smith's excellent *coup d'oeil* being nullified by superiors. After deploying his brigades to protect Federal batteries threatened by enemy attack and to connect the Federal center and right, he conferred with his corps commander, Major General William B. Franklin, about a plan to assault the Confederate left. Major General Sumner disapproved of their plan. Later in the day, Smith asked McClellan to allow him to capture a hill that commanded the Confederate left, but the army commander refused. Had Smith's requests been approved, the Federals might have crushed the exhausted Confederate left.

Shortly before the battle of Fredericksburg in December 1862, Smith, who had been promoted to command the Sixth Corps, discussed the coming engagement with McClellan's successor, Major General Burnside. Smith insisted that crossing the army near Fredericksburg would obligate the troops to attack the well-fortified Confederate position on the heights south of the town. Burnside rebuffed such warnings. The day before the battle, Generals Franklin, Smith, and John Reynolds urged an assault by the First and Sixth Corps on the Confederate right flank as the only means of dislodging General Robert E. Lee's forces. Burnside's subsequent orders failed to implement their plan, and the battle that followed was another costly Federal defeat.

In the wake of Fredericksburg, Franklin and Smith wrote to President Abraham Lincoln urging him to abandon the overland strategy to take Richmond and to return to the Peninsula campaign strategy. They suggested moving the army up the James River and placing the men on its north and south sides. Using these two prongs, the Federals would capture Richmond and possibly conquer Lee's army. The James River provided excellent transportation and means for communication, and Lincoln could place the army within twenty miles of Richmond without serious loss. In contrast, the overland route posed difficult problems of communication and transportation; moreover, the Federals would suffer heavy losses in traversing the sixty miles from Fredericksburg to Richmond. Lincoln and War Secretary Edwin Stanton, already suspicious of Franklin and Smith for their association with Democratic General McClellan, rejected this sensible advice and removed Franklin from command. Smith was soon transferred to the Ninth Corps, but he held this command for only a month. The Republicans in the Senate blocked Smith's confirmation as major general, which reduced him to brigadier and relegated him to divisional command. Stanton kept Smith from field duty until mid-June 1863.

In the Gettysburg campaign, Baldy Smith commanded the First Division of the Department of the Susquehanna under Major General Darius Couch. His troops successfully defended Carlisle from General Fitzhugh Lee's cavalry on July 1 and followed the Confederate retreat from Gettysburg. After the invasion ended, Smith's command was dispersed. Meanwhile, Stanton tried to have him arrested for alleged misdemeanors, but Couch supported Baldy's innocence, and the war secretary did not press his groundless charges. With serious duties in Pennsylvania concluded, Smith was relieved of command in late August.

In October, Smith's engineering skill and imagination helped secure the Army of the Cumberland in Chattanooga. On October 3, the army commander, Major General William S. Rosecrans, appointed him chief engineer. After studying the Federal position in Chattanooga with the Confederates occupying the mountains south of the city, he told Rosecrans that the Tennessee River would have to be protected to assure steady supply. Rosecrans rejected this advice, and General Braxton Bragg soon cut off the Union's river supply line. Consequently, on October 18, the assistant war secretary, Charles Dana, reported that the Federals could not hold their position for more than a week without a new route for supplies.

To solve the supply problem, the chief engineer made a reconnaissance on October 19. He found that a narrow gorge in Raccoon Mountain at Brown's Ferry could serve as the focus of a Federal attack, which he believed would result in the capture of the mountains. If this assault were made in conjunction with another Federal attack that seized Lookout Valley, the Confederate threat to the Tennessee River would be ended. He offered the plan to the new army commander, Major General George H. Thomas. Thomas and his superior, Major General U.S. Grant, approved the plan and gave Smith command of the attacking force. His attack on the mountains was executed flawlessly, resulting in Major General Hooker's seizure of the valley and the opening of the river as a supply line for the army in Chattanooga.

The chief engineer also directed the construction of several bridges and supervised the movement of the Army of the Tennessee near Chattanooga. This enabled the Federals to get safely into position and contest the Confederate occupation of Missionary Ridge. He won praise for his engineering achievements from Major General William T. Sherman, and General Grant urged Lincoln and Stanton to promote Baldy to major general and recommended that he be given an army or department command.

Grant's influence was sufficient to get Smith promoted to major general in March 1864. But Republican senators blocked Grant's attempt to date the promotion back far enough to enable an old associate of McClellan to be given command of the Army of the Potomac. Nevertheless, Grant gave the command of the Eighteenth Corps to his chief engineer.

Smith was not given the Army command in part because he still insisted that the overland campaign was based on faulty tactics. In January 1864, he wrote to the Assistant War Secretary Dana urging the occupation of North Carolina to isolate Virginia and break the lines of communication between Atlanta and Richmond. Two months later, he wrote Lieutenant General Grant to persuade him to abandon the overland strategy. Smith offered reasons similar to those he gave to Lincoln in 1862. He warned that the overland campaign would face great logistical problems and cost unnecessarily heavy casualties. The general submitted the North Carolina plan as a superior alternative. Grant had supported this plan, but objections in Washington led him to adopt the overland campaign as the only one acceptable to the administration. Consequently, Smith's firm opposition to such a campaign made him unacceptable as a choice for army commander.

As Eighteenth Corps commander, Smith served under Major General Benjamin Butler, a Massachusetts politician. Both Smith and Major General Quincy Gillmore, commander of the Tenth Corps, were skeptical of Butler's competence. Grant ordered

Butler to capture Richmond by landing the Army of the James on Bermuda Hundred and marching up the south bank of the James River. Smith felt this plan ignored the great opportunity to capture weakly defended Petersburg. After arriving at Bermuda Hundred, Smith and Gillmore asked permission to bridge the Appomattox and capture the city. Butler callously rejected their proposal.

Smith became increasingly anxious about Butler's movement toward Richmond. He warned the army commander about a mile gap between Butler's right flank and the river, which would enable the Confederates to turn the Federal line if the space remained uncovered. To strengthen his position, Smith ordered telegraph wire strung along his lines. In the battle of Drewry's Bluff, the Confederates attacked Smith's right and front. The wire and steadfastness of the Eighteenth Corps repulsed the frontal assaults, but the flanking attack turned the brigade on the extreme right. Reinforcements finally stopped the flanking movement, and Smith rallied the disorganized troops on the right. Nonetheless, Butler ordered the army to return to Bermuda Hundred.

On May 30, Smith was ordered to take his corps and two divisions from the Tenth Corps and join the Army of the Potomac's attack on Cold Harbor. On June 1, his command captured part of the enemy works and several hundred Confederates. Realizing that any subsequent attack needed to be coordinated among the Federal corps, Baldy offered to follow the plan of Major General Horatio G. Wright, the Sixth Corps commander, but Wright decided to make an independent attack. Meanwhile, the Confederates strengthened their fortifications, making them impregnable against attacks in Smith's front. In the attack on June 3, Smith's command gained little ground and suffered staggering losses. When Smith was ordered to continue the attack, he refused to renew the slaughter. Grant sent two engineer officers to examine his lines, and they confirmed Smith's decision to discontinue the assault. Baldy would never forget the disaster at Cold Harbor. It cost his command three thousand casualties.

Smith's force returned to Butler on June 14, and the Army of the James commander ordered Smith to attack Petersburg the next day. Butler told him that the enemy only had weak earthworks that were lightly manned. When Smith arrived at the works, he found that Butler's information was incorrect. Consequently, a careful reconnaissance was done, and Smith concluded that the wide-open space in his front and the scope of the enemy artillery prevented any chance of success by a column of assault. Instead of using columns, he developed the inventive plan of assaulting the works with a heavy line of skirmishers with his artillery fire directed on the enemy salient in his front. The attack began about 7:00 p.m. and soon carried the salient. By 9:00 p.m. six Confederate redans were in Federal hands. At this point, Smith felt a further advance would be imprudent because darkness would disorganize his men and he had received word of enemy reinforcements. After examining the captured Confederate earthworks, Grant and Assistant Secretary of War Charles Dana were pleased with Smith's success. After investigating Butler's command, Grant decided to remove Butler for his tactical incompetence and sought to place the troops of the Army of the James under Smith.

In early July, during a conversation about the Virginia campaign, Smith told Grant that the battle of Cold Harbor was fought in contravention of military principles. Grant was greatly angered by this criticism of his campaign and of Meade's handling of the command of the Army. Insulted by Smith's comments and aware of Butler's important influence in Washington, Grant decided to retain the political general and relieve Baldy. Smith's forthright assessment of the overland campaign ended his active military service.

After his removal as Eighteenth Corps commander, William Farrar Smith showed little inclination to stay silent about incompetent generals and interfering politicians who undermined the Northern war effort. As a special commissioner to investigate the affairs of the Department of the Gulf, Smith determined that the administration was thoroughly corrupt and recommended the arrest of several senior officers, including the department commander. Even after resigning from the army in 1867, Smith continued to demand of others the high standard of honesty, integrity, and competence that he demanded of himself.

During the postwar years, he served as one of the police commissioners in New York City from 1875 to 1881. Here again he fought to establish efficiency and honesty in a police force burdened by widespread corruption. Smith also became active in foreign affairs. He advocated a peaceful settlement in Cuba and participated in efforts to find an equitable solution. After the United States declared war on Spain, he condemned the William McKinley administration for its unnecessary and despotic use of military force to end Spanish rule in Cuba and in the subsequent Filipino war for independence.

Far more important to Smith were his postwar writings on the Civil War. He showed how inventiveness and initiative could bring victory by describing his Brown's Ferry expedition and his assault on Petersburg. His writings also showed how Republican politicians had mishandled the war effort and how the North had won in spite of, rather than because of, the Lincoln administration and its political allies. As during the war, Baldy was condemned for his views. But his determination to offer sensible alternatives to official policy and to speak out against incompetence and corruption, whatever the consequences, enabled him to provide an important critique of military and political decision making in the American Civil War.

CHAPTER I

From Saint Albans to Atlantic Coast Lighthouses

The Making of an Engineer

William Farrar Smith was born in Vermont, on the seventeenth of February 1824. He was the fourth child of Ashbel and Sarah Butler Smith. William's father was a respectable farmer, and the family farm was a short mile from the village of Saint Albans. While still an infant, William moved with his family into the village.[1] At the age of three he started his education in an infant school near his home. Two maiden women taught the children, and he remembered standing at his teachers' knees and going through his lessons. In his early years, Smith was somewhat mischievous. On one occasion, he was sent down into the school cellar for some misdemeanor. The cellar was flooded with enough water to float a large door; the door served as a kind of raft. Young Smith was put on this raft to scare him into being obedient. Instead, Smith managed to get hold of a pushing stick and with boyish imagination pretended he was making a voyage to the ends of the earth.[2]

William's behavior apparently failed to improve when he went to secondary school. At a private academy, his life was filled with punishments which varied from being sent to sit with the girls to flogging. After some years, his father transferred him to a public high school. This was not on account of the youth's behavior, however, since the school master told his father that if the transfer was a question of money, he would be glad to take William without charge. Smith's father seemed to think the academy curriculum of Greek and Latin was unnecessary for a farmer's son.[3]

William's mischievous behavior was also part of his home life. He recalled being whipped for neglecting certain tasks such as weeding the garden beds. His father generally made a point of spoiling the rod (a long apple switch) without sparing the child. His mother would pull off one of her slippers and slap him over the shoulders or put him in a pair of trousers cut off at the knees and then confine him in the loft over the woodshed. Since his younger brother was never flogged, William supposed that he must "have had all the deviltry of the family" in him, or that his father changed his views on corporal punishment.[4]

As a child, Smith received religious and moral training at the village Episcopal church. On Sunday morning, he studied a portion of his catechism, a collect, and a hymn. After these lessons, he went to morning services. These services were followed by a mid-day meal, afternoon Sunday-school, and afternoon services. Late in the afternoon, he repeated extra lessons to his mother, for whom he always tried to be a commendable pupil.[5]

His greatest pleasure as a boy was hiking up one of two rocky mountains that flanked his village. Once at the summit, he would lie in the shade and enjoy the beautiful view of Lake Champlain, the lake islands, and the village below. In a small New England village where everyone knew almost everything, Smith's excursions created sympathy for his father since it was apparent that the Smiths' had a lazy son. Young Smith did not think this criticism to be true at that time, but in the light of later years came to agree with his elders.[6]

In 1837, when William was thirteen, the Smith family moved to a farm about a mile and a half south of the village. There William learned to ride and developed a great capacity for training animals. During the same year, an insurrection broke out in Lower Canada. The popular Canadian leaders, Joseph Papineau and William L. Mackenzie, were frustrated by the Imperial government's unwillingness to give the French Canadians a responsible government and resorted to rebellion. The fighting lasted for over a year, and since much of it was near Montreal, the excitement in Vermont, just across the border, was intense. To preserve the neutrality laws, the Federal government ordered troops to the border, and a company of artillery was stationed in Swanton near the frontier. When Smith visited this village to see his old aunt, a company was being drilled on an adjoining lot by a young lieutenant from Saint Albans who had gone to West Point. Smith went to see the soldiers and was so pleased with their uniforms that he at once took up the idea of going to West Point. This idea was reinforced when the young drill-master remembered Smith from Saint Albans and spoke with him. During the chat the lieutenant asked Smith what he intended to do for a living. He promptly replied, "Go to West Point and be a soldier."[7]

Meanwhile, William's uncle, John Smith, who was a lawyer and a ten-year member of the state House of Representatives, publicly supported the rebel forces in Canada. Despite Vermont being a strong Whig state, John Smith, a staunch Democrat, was elected to Congress in 1838 because of his stand on the Canadian rebellion. During his first and only term, the new congressman found that he was entitled to nominate a person for admission to West Point.[8]

In December 1839, John Smith had his nephew placed on the register of applicants for admission to the Military Academy. However, William was not admitted to the academy in its annual selection in March 1840. Despite his embarrassment at making a second request for the admission of his nephew, the congressman renominated William on January 20, 1841. The academy swiftly admitted William, and he accepted the appointment with his father's endorsement on January 30, 1841.[9]

Part of the reason for William's selection was his improvement as a student in his later years of secondary education at the Franklin County Grammar School. His principal, Almon Lawrence, in a letter to Congressman Smith in November 1839, praised William's scholastic ability and supported his admission to West Point. In a November 1840 letter to the secretary of war, Lawrence renewed his effort on behalf of William. The principal stated that William "has ever shown those scholar-like and gentlemanly habits that I feel a pleasure in recommending him to you as a worthy person to enter the Military Academy." Lawrence believed William's natural talents and acquired abilities far exceeded the prerequisites for admission. Specifically, Lawrence wrote, "As to his knowledge of Arithmetic, I may say he understands the whole works. He is also well acquainted with the first five books of geometry and with Algebra as far as through quadratic equations. He has studied chemistry and natural philosophy to some extent and is continuing his studies still."[10]

With Smith's appointment came orders to report to the Academy on June 1, 1841. In the intervening months, Smith anxiously prepared for the entrance examination. He left his home and arrived at West Point on May 25. His journey from Saint Albans was a delightful undertaking for a youth who had never before been fifty miles from his native village. Upon arrival at West Point, Smith was sent to the sutler to obtain two blankets and a naked pillow. He and three other candidates slept on the floor of a small room and washed at the pump outside the barracks until after they had passed their exams.[11]

Initially Smith suffered from the strains of the drills and the pain of homesickness. By the middle of June, his spirits improved after the fourth class arrived in camp. Life at camp was pleasing at first from the novelty but soon became monotonous. When the summer was over, the new cadets were delighted to march to the barracks at West Point. The barracks that Smith and the other cadets found were not ideal accommodations. Cadets lived in crowded quarters where four or five cadets occupied a twelve-by-twelve room that was hot in the summer and poorly heated in the winter. On beginning its recitations, the class was arranged in alphabetical order. Shortly afterward, however, the cadets' work was examined weekly, and their rankings changed according to their grades. As the year progressed, rank changes became less frequent. Smith's class started with 125 cadets, but after the first major exam on January 1, severe academic attrition began. The greatest academic challenge for cadets was mathematics. Fortunately, Smith had a strong background in mathematics and exceeded in this subject.[12]

During his first year of study, Smith pursued just two subjects—mathematics and French. His math study included algebra, geometry, and trigonometry. In general merit, he ranked fifth; in math, third; and in French, thirteenth. His work kept him busy, but he had some time for recreation, including a half-day on Saturday that he generally spent roaming the hills, visiting Fort Putnam and Crow's Nest for the views, and wandering around the plain. Sometimes he and other cadets would go on picnics. Smith's behavior, like the behavior of other students, was assessed by West Point's demerit system. His small number of demerits during his first year placed him in the upper quarter of the best-behaved cadets. His major transgressions were throwing bread in the mess hall at supper and being absent from tattoo and reveille roll calls.[13]

In his second year, he studied mathematics, French, drawing, and English grammar. His mathematics pursuits included analytical geometry and calculus. His drawing course dealt with the human figure and topography. In general merit he was ranked fourth; math, fourth; French, sixth; drawing, thirty-second; and English, sixth. Despite a reduction of demerits from his first year, Smith still enjoyed his occasional prank. Not unlike other upperclassmen at the Academy, Smith engaged in a bit of hazing of the fourth class cadets. Given some of the types of "devilment" as they called hazing at the time, however, his type was relatively mild. For instance, Smith was detailed to drill a squad, which signified that he was on the list for promotion to corporal. He came close to losing this promotion. One day as he advanced the squad to musket drill, he remembered how it tired him the year before to hold the musket aimed at a target. Once on the drill field, he tortured the squad by holding them in that position until their arms were exhausted, and their muskets began to wobble. He became so convulsed with a desire to laugh that he could not give the command to recover arms. Smith saw an inspector coming towards him and recovered his composure so quickly that he escaped censure. He tried no more tricks as squad teacher. His rank of corporal kept him from walking post. Also, during his second year, Baldy roomed with Richard "Dick" Howard and future

Confederate General Edmund Kirby Smith. Baldy worked to push Howard through, but Howard failed his science exams and left the academy in 1844; Howard would later work with Baldy in Texas. Ultimately, Smith was glad to see his examinations for his second year finished and glad to get his furlough for the summer. Although his pay was only twenty-eight dollars a month, and he had to pay his mess bills, books, clothes, and washing, he was able to save enough to pay for his furlough—a trip home and back.[14]

On returning for his third year, Smith found that he had been made a color-sergeant; there were three color-sergeants who, with three corporals, formed the rear rank of the color guard. Fitz-John Porter, who for over half a century and to the day of his death was an intimate friend of Smith, was the ranking sergeant of the color guard at this time. Smith stated of Porter that he was "the most prominent member of his class during his service in the army up to the time of his persecution."[15] As members of the color guard, they carried the colors when they were out on parades or reviews.[16]

In his third year at the academy, Smith's subjects of study were natural and experimental philosophy, chemistry, and drawing. His philosophy course apparently was a physics course which included mechanics, electricity, magnetism, optics, and astronomy. His drawing course dealt with sketching landscapes and topography. He ranked fourth in general merit, philosophy, and chemistry. His conduct seemed to decline slightly as his transgressions included being absent from morning drill, laughing during a recitation, not wearing a sword at supper mess parade, and having lights on after taps.[17]

In his fourth year at the Military Academy, Smith advanced to the rank of cadet lieutenant. At this time, his courses were engineering and science of war, ethics, infantry tactics, artillery tactics, and mineralogy and geology. In his engineering and ethics courses, he ranked fifth; in artillery tactics and mineralogy, sixth; and in infantry tactics, seventh. His conduct rank continued to slide, falling into the third-quarter of the cadets. He was demerited for being absent from morning drill, wearing pants out of uniform, being in bed during study hours, being absent from quarters after taps, leaving his seat without permission during his engineering class, coming into his engineering class "redolent of tobacco smoke," and having a messy room.[18] Yet Smith's deteriorating behavior did not affect his graduation. Smith, or "Baldy" as his cadet friends called him, ranked fourth in his graduating class of forty-one members behind three college graduates. At commencement, many regrets were expressed concerning the separation of friends, but the sorrow was overshadowed by the freedom of the summer.[19]

Smith lived at home for a month. Then on July 11, 1845, the colonel of the Corps of Topographical Engineers, John J. Abert, notified him that he was attached to the corps and had the usual leave for graduates. If Smith wished to waive the leave, he would have it the next winter and was to report to Lieutenant Colonel James Kearney in Buffalo to assist the survey of the upper lakes, particularly Lake Erie, where the surveying force was shorthanded. Flattered by this request from the colonel of the corps, Smith consented at once. On July 21, Smith accepted his appointment of brevet second lieutenant in the United States Army. He proceeded to Buffalo and spent some days there waiting for a steamer and enjoying a very pleasant time with the officers of the garrison. He finally got a steamer and landed on Kelley's Island in the western part of Lake Erie. He spent three months hard at work surveying the shoreline and making soundings a mile or so from the shore. On October 7, with stormy autumn weather approaching, the survey team returned to Buffalo for the winter. On October 15, Smith applied for his promised leave of absence, which was disapproved by Kearny and promptly refused by Abert.

Smith was enraged at such a breach of contract and protested, giving a copy of the letter which had been written to him promising the two months of unexpired leave on completion of his duty. Smith's protests resulted in Abert granting him a three-month leave starting November 1.[20]

During the winter 1845–46, many of Smith's classmates had been ordered to Texas; these classmates urged him to get orders to join them. He applied for such orders on May 18, 1846, but his application was refused. Another year was spent surveying Lake Erie. While doing his survey duty, he received a request from Professor Albert E. Church at West Point to come to the academy to serve as an acting assistant professor of mathematics. Smith accepted the appointment and was promptly ordered to West Point. With full-scale war going on between the United States and Mexico, Smith again applied for war duty on August 6, 1847. Again, he was refused. Baldy was intensely anxious to be where classmates were winning honors and could not understand why he was not with them. He was content enough at West Point where the duties were pleasant and where he had many warm friends, but he wanted to be in the war. He applied a second time to leave West Point to go to war on October 25, but his application was refused since his teaching duties could not be curtailed mid-term without serious inconvenience and injury to his students.[21]

Knowing that officers who had refused to go to church at the academy were always relieved from duty there, Smith began consistently missing church services. His absence soon was noticed by the superintendent of the academy, Captain Henry Brewerton. As Smith expected, the superintendent sought to have Baldy replaced. Before Smith's replacement arrived, however, the war ended. Smith was relieved of his teaching position at the academy on September 1, 1848. Abert ordered Smith, however, to temporary duty at West Point to aid Captain Thomas J. Lee in the observatory there. This duty lasted from September 7 until December 2 when Smith was ordered to report to Lieutenant Colonel Joseph E. Johnston in Washington. Smith had tried to get relief from his temporary duty on October 24 by applying for duty under Colonel Persifor F. Smith on the Pacific coast, but this was denied.[22]

In Washington, Baldy gathered surveying and astronomical instruments and reported to Colonel William J. Worth at the headquarters of the Department of Texas at San Antonio de Bexar. Worth greeted Smith affably and told him to get an office from the quartermaster and wait for orders. In a few days, Smith came under the command of Second Lieutenant William Henry Chase Whiting, who had graduated first in Baldy's class and who was a roommate in his last year. Smith was also reunited with Dick Howard, who had moved to Texas to become a surveyor and scout. Not long after the arrival of Whiting, Worth sent for Whiting, Smith, and Howard and ordered them, on February 9, 1849, to organize a party to go to El Paso del Norte on the Rio Grande and find a road that the Third Infantry could use to reach the Rio Grande above El Paso.[23]

Neither Whiting nor Smith had the slightest experience with this kind of service, so they relied on Howard as one of their escorts and to help them "fit out" the party. The group also was to be escorted by some Texas rangers (hired by the day) and was to be equipped with animals, saddles, and arms. The entire party comprised Whiting, Smith, Howard, thirteen rangers, and a young Mexican American scout named José Policarpio Rodriguez.[24]

On February 12, they were ready to start and began packing the mules. The mule with their mess kit was so badly packed or inexperienced that soon after starting, it stampeded, bucked, and kicked, until its load was strewn for a mile over the country-side. Out of the wreckage, they managed to save a cup apiece, three plates, and the coffee pot. The group held a "council of war" and concluded it would be sign of weakness to go back—so they continued on their way.[25]

Their route lay through Fredericksburg, and thence partly by the old Pinta trail to the headwaters of the south fork of the San Saba River. After leaving Fredericksburg on the twenty-first, they were in Indian country and had to take that circumstance into account in their daily marching and camping. At the close of each march, if possible, they camped in the open, near water, and in good grass, which was abundant for half their journey. When they reached the San Saba River, they ascended the high table-lands, where they rode for three days and four nights without water before they arrived at Live Oak Creek, a tributary of the Pecos. They had some difficulty in crossing the Pecos because of the nature of this river's banks, and there were some amusing scenes of men and mules floundering and being helped out with ropes. After the crossing, a dry wind enabled the party to withstand the intense heat of the sun. Everyone searched for a line of trees to indicate a water-course, or for the light green leaf of the cottonwood—an unfailing sign of water.[26]

On one occasion, the party found two cottonwood trees. While investigating the area around these trees, Smith found a shallow cave filled with beautifully clear water. Before his cup reached the water, a snake sprang at him from the rear of the spring with a venomous hiss. Baldy jumped back, and the snake retreated to its cover. Once more, Smith sought to fill the cup, but again the hiss and fiery eyes of the snake caused Smith's quick retreat. After this last attempt, Smith decided that thirst was only a disease of the imagination, and he moved to where the other men were drinking.[27]

While traveling over the flat lands to the Davis Mountains, Smith amused him-self by killing rattlesnakes that came out in the early morning to sun themselves. As they were approached, these snakes would spring their rattles and coil themselves for a strike. Smith got quite accustomed to shooting off their heads, always protruding above the coil. The party reached the foothills of the mountains on March 17. With Smith and two other men in the advance, the party went through a narrow valley between the mountains. Suddenly, Smith noticed that Native Americans were moving down on the main body of the group. The advance, unable to make the main body understand its pre-dicament, hurried back in time to be surrounded by 125 Native Americans. The Native Americans were of two bands—the Mescalero Apaches and the Northern Apaches. The Mescaleros did not see much plunder in the small party and were convinced by the expedition's interpreter that their party was supported by a large force only a short dis-tance away. The Northern Apaches were more hostile and willing to attack if the Mes-caleros would agree to join them.[28]

Despite Whiting's parley with the chiefs of the bands, Smith felt the Native Amer-icans would soon attack, and he attempted to secure the best obtainable position for defense. Taking all the pack mules, he tied their heads together with bridles and lari-ats so that they could not be stampeded. The first mule that fell would anchor the oth-ers. Some of the men went up the slope to prevent the Native Americans from getting behind them. The interpreters were in front of the party at close range. Smith sat down and loaded the empty chambers of his revolver. This was immediately noticed, and the Native Americans hastened their preparations for a fight. Some were armed with lances and others with bows, but very few had firearms. This tense position lasted for half an hour with the men selecting the Native Americans that they would shoot first. Whiting cooled hostilities in his talk with the Native Americans, but the party waited for darkness and then quietly put their packs and saddles in the four corners of a square so as to afford some protection from a rush of horsemen. In the Native American powwow that night, the Mescaleros forced the Northern Apaches to give up the attack. The next day, the Mescaleros guided the expedition through the mountains and indicated the shortest route to the Rio Grande.[29]

On March 24, the party reached the Rio Grande at Fort Seaton across the river from the Presidio del Norte. They refitted at Seaton and on March 30 started on their trip up the river. The group moved between the valley of the Rio Grande and the mountain trails until reaching El Paso on April 12. There they entirely refitted, and on April 19 they started back with some reinforcements.[30]

The lack of water on their journey to El Paso prompted them to choose a different road. They travelled near the San Pedro River on their return trip until they struck the Woll Road, near the head of the Leona River, which led them to San Antonio. The major difficulty now was traveling through the narrow San Pedro River valleys. The expedition also suffered from a violent hailstorm and had their animals stolen one hundred miles from San Antonio. The group figured that the closest fort was seventy-five miles away. Fortunately, they came upon an army working party after marching only four miles. They learned that since they had left San Antonio, a cavalry post had been established on the Leona River about ninety miles west of San Antonio. When they reached this post, they were all right. Despite their difficulties, this new route was vastly superior to the old one because it was shorter and had more available water. This reconnaissance was a clear improvement over former efforts and provided an important means of supplying whatever posts would be erected in the Indian country along the Rio Grande. In Smith's report of May 25, 1849, he estimated the distance between San Antonio and El Paso by this route to be 645 miles, and he determined the approximate latitudes of nine strategic points along the route—a significant start toward a map of the area.[31]

On returning, Smith found that Lieutenant Colonel Joseph E. Johnston had been ordered to Texas as the senior officer of Topographical Engineers. Johnston's assignment was to test the new route. By marching the Third Infantry to El Paso, he would determine whether the route was practical for provision trains. Using Howard, Rodriguez, and Baldy as guides, Johnston's expedition commenced on June 13. Common laborers assisted Captain Samuel G. French's quartermasters and Johnston's engineer in making the route functional. Captain John H. King's company from the First Infantry served as their escort. The road finally established by the expedition deviated only twice from the Whiting-Smith route: one time between the lower ford of the San Pedro and the Pecos; the other below Eagle Mountain to avoid the mountains in the approach to the Rio Grande. The arrival of the expedition on September 8 provided a confirmation of the existence of a practical road.[32]

While recruiting the teams for the return march, Johnston sent Smith on a reconnaissance to ascertain if there was an available pass in the Sacramento mountains. Smith carried out the reconnaissance between September 21 and October 3 but found that the possible passes were either too difficult for wagon trains to travel or had no water supply. On October 11, the party began their return march. In order to examine the country between the Rio Grande and the heads of the Colorado and Brazos, Johnston's party took the northern route. But in the middle of October, the autumn became

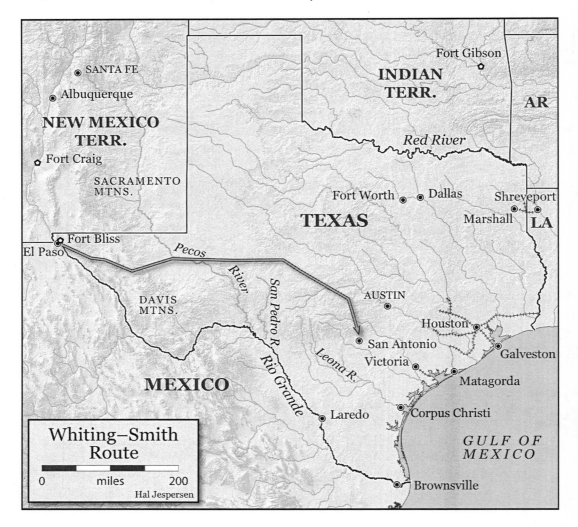

Whiting-Smith Route.

severe enough to force the party southward. They marched along the southern road to San Antonio where they arrived on November 23.[33]

Smith spent the winter in San Antonio making maps and reports. On January 16, 1850, he was promoted to second lieutenant of Topographical Engineers. It was during the long trip to El Paso and back and the winter in San Antonio that Smith came to know Johnston well, and the two engineer officers grew to deeply respect each other's ability and skill. This respect led to a life-long friendship.[34]

During the winter of 1849–1850, the Federal government desired information on the possibility of removing a large raft of logs and other debris obstructing the Colorado River. Johnston ordered Smith to accompany Captain Henry Cheatham in a reconnaissance of the river. The government was primarily interested in the availability of the river as a means of military supply to the interior chain of forts. However, the reconnaissance also fostered the supply of information to civilian groups interested in the commercial possibilities of the river up to Austin. Based upon Smith's examination,

Johnston's report listed three sorts of obstructions to navigation: a 3,509-yard long raft of logs, fifty-four clusters of snags, and several large overhanging trees. He assessed the cost of the removal of the obstructions at about $56,000, but the improvement of the river would reduce the annual expense of transporting supplies in the military department by at least $20,000. Consequently, after three years, the annual financial benefit would exceed the initial expense of removing the obstructions. Should the government remove the raft of logs, Johnston assured the Topographical Bureau, the inhabitants of the Colorado valley would complete the opening of the river.[35]

In the spring of 1850, Johnston directed Smith and Second Lieutenant Francis T. Bryan to go to El Paso del Norte to survey and examine the river from that point to Presidio del Norte. Smith was directed to combine a military reconnaissance with his survey of the river. Accompanied by Bryan, Smith left San Antonio, on April 14, 1850, and reached El Paso on May 27. From that time until June 15, they were occupied in preparing boats for the survey. On June 15, they left El Paso with Bryan in charge of the land survey and Smith in charge of the river survey.[36]

At the time Baldy and Bryan entered the Rio Grande, the river was exceedingly high and the current rapid. The intricate channels of the river were separated by sand bars and frequently choked by fallen trees. About five miles from the starting point, the two provision boats, which were poorly manned, were upset and sunk. Only one was recovered. The accident detained the expedition until June 24. They started again and reached San Elisano in three and one third hours, having travelled twenty-four miles. Smith made daily reports on the condition of the river including its depth, rate of current, obstacles, straightness and width, and the condition of the riverbanks. He also noticed that the land on either side showed evidence of Native American trails and water holes, and he suggested that a military post be established close to a crossroad near Eagle Spring. The survey ended seven miles from Presidio del Norte. Smith's and Bryan's final camp near Fort Seaton was 377 miles from El Paso. The river, Smith reported to Johnston, contained several rapids and dangerous rocky bends that could not be improved without enormous expense.[37]

On September 25, 1850, Smith requested a six-month leave of absence. Both Colonels Johnston and Abert approved the application. During his leave, Baldy finished his report on his recent survey of the Rio Grande. (While he was on leave, his commander, Colonel Johnston, wrote Colonel Abert that Smith's knowledge of the geography of Texas made his service particularly valuable on the frontier.) On March 31, 1851, Smith was ordered to report to Lieutenant Colonel James D. Graham at Indianola, Texas, where he was to assist Graham with his duties on the Mexican Boundary Commission. Smith regretted leaving Johnston but soon felt that Graham was a delightful man to serve. The Boundary Commission went beyond El Paso, crossing the Rio Grande at the boundary line above El Paso, and wintered at Santa Rita del Colbre. Here a violent quarrel broke out between Graham and Commissioner John R. Barlett; Graham was replaced by Major William Emory.[38]

Emory had graduated from West Point in 1831 and was appointed a first lieutenant of topographical engineers in 1838. He was breveted twice for gallantry during the Mexican War. Since the war, Brevet Major Emory had served as the chief astronomer of the Boundary Commission.[39]

On December 15, 1851, Emory ordered Smith to select a position and erect a temporary observatory to receive the Ristor and Martin transit. Smith was also to select a position inside the walls of the Presidio for a substantial structure that might become the principal observatory. In the temporary observatory, Smith began a series of observations of the moon and the culmination of the stars to determine the local time and, by the use of flashes, the difference in longitude between that point and the headquarters at Frontera. He was also ordered to direct Charles Wright's survey of the river opposite San Ignacio. Smith proceeded with the survey, selecting the northwestern angle of the Presidio for the site of the observatory and hiring men to put up the walls and piers for the transit building. During this time, he actively engaged himself in erecting the observatory, making observations for time, and obtaining the approximate latitude and direction of the meridian of the observatory.[40]

Smith's relations with Emory were markedly different from the excellent relations he had with his former commanders. When Emory first arrived at the commission, a party was held in his honor. At the party, Emory stated that if Smith did not want to work for the commission, he would be relieved. Since Baldy's relationships with his other commanders were favorable and he never expressed regret for serving Graham in the commission's work, he considered Emory's remark as so unwarranted and prejudicial as to indicate that Emory desired to relieve him. Smith had not requested duty at the commission, and Emory's remark made Smith regret even more his current assignment. Such personal differences led to conflicts over duty in the commission's work.[41]

Personal differences with Emory would mark the beginning of several quarrels Smith would have with his superiors. Smith had a high opinion of his own ability. This belief was reinforced by his West Point performance and by the opinions of his other superiors, and he was beginning to feel that he must unremittingly press for redress of any real or imagined grievance made by his superiors. Baldy's demands for justice often bordered on insubordination, although he rarely meant disrespect in his actions. He generally was correct in his demands for redress, but under military rules of discipline he often endangered his future as an army officer. That he never placed his own personal position above his honestly-held views was commendable, but his often tactless way of objecting to his superiors made him at times foolhardy.

On January 15 and 16, 1852, Emory gave Smith detailed instructions to check Wright's surveying work. He also told the young engineering officer to have the surveyor note the topography of the valley, including the width of the valley for agricultural purposes, the woods, grasses and character of the soil, prominent peaks, sources of all tributaries, and most importantly, the adaptability of the valley to wagon or railroad travel. The surveyor was also to check the breadth, depth, and velocity of the river, and its capacity for navigation. If Wright's survey, upon examination, was unsatisfactory, Emory suggested the valley be resurveyed by another surveyor named Mauritz von Hippel.[42]

Baldy reacted vehemently to Emory's orders on January 20. First, he denied responsibility for the surveyor who, by his own admission, was entirely unfit for the assignment. Smith did not have the time or means to oversee his operations. Second, he felt the extremely detailed instructions indicated Emory believed Smith was incapable of performing his engineering duties without extra instruction. Baldy felt that if such an order was seen in Washington, it would unjustly reflect his ability. Third, he took exception to comments made by Emory concerning Smith's health. An attack of neuralgia had prevented him from meeting with Emory on January 8. Smith argued that Emory's reference to Smith's "continued indisposition" wrongly inferred that Smith had been unfit for duty for some time.[43]

Emory replied to Smith's objections. First, he insisted that Smith supervise the surveyor's work. Second, Emory stated:

> I must be permitted to give such instructions as are deemed proper and necessary and I cannot permit them to be criticized by officers under my command. At the same time, I acknowledge the right of any officer or man to complain against me for any act of injustice of impropriety and I will cheerfully forward the same to the authorities at Washington when requested to do so.

He told Smith that copies of his instructions were never designed to be sent to Washington and were only intended for Smith's use. Third, Emory said he was "very glad to learn that in this [Smith's illness] I was misinformed." Nonetheless, he cited correspondence from Smith's assistant indicating Smith was ill for several days and discussing Smith's absence from dinner on January 2 and from the meeting of January 8 due to illness. Emory stated that such illness, however, did not indicate that Smith was unfit for duty since Emory's instructions showed that he considered Smith in charge of the observatory and its construction. Emory added that he would "consider no service here as profitable unless it is willing service." He concluded that if Smith still felt mistreated, Emory would try to have him withdrawn from the commission duty.[44]

Smith answered Emory's letter by denying that his criticisms had overstepped his position and violated military discipline. He requested relief from duty on the United States and Mexican Boundary Commission and an order to report to the bureau in Washington. Smith wrote, "I have been doing duty in the state of Texas for the last three years and am extremely anxious to change stations if it is compatible with the Public Service. The duty I am now engaged on was unsought by me, has been disagreeable from the first and has become extremely so of late."[45] Emory complied with Smith's request and applied for Smith's relief to the adjutant general. Meanwhile, Smith would continue under Emory's command.[46]

The heated differences between Smith and Emory came to a climax over a minor matter of control over a wagon and a team. On February 23, Emory wrote Smith: "In the present reduced state of the transportation it may be necessary to take your wagon and mule team in short notice." Smith answered Emory on March 2: "The wagon and team at present under my control was [sic] furnished me [as a] consequence of a written agreement made between the Commissioner and your predecessor (Colonel Graham), and I think I should only be deprived of it only by the joint action of the Com. and yourself." Smith reminded Emory of the commissioner's promise to leave the wagon and train with Smith. Smith added: "If the wagon and team are to be taken from me for your own use I have of course nothing to say." But Smith warned Emory: "if they are to be given to any Pet-Familiars I protest against it because I rank them all and am therefore entitled to the preference because a mule team is absolutely required here to afford necessary transportation to the members of the Commission."[47]

On March 7, Emory wrote a letter of reprimand that warned: "You cannot be permitted to use with impunity offensive language to me and make insinuations and unfounded charges against one your senior in years and rank and your commanding officer."[48] Emory, feeling a written reprimand was insufficient, decided to put Smith under arrest. On March 31, he notified Smith that he would be charged with writing disrespectful letters to his commanding officer, but that he would not be put under arrest immediately since there would be considerable time before a court could convene at Frontera for the trial. Smith was placed under arrest on May 12, and turned over, to his assistant, all instruments, books, notes, and public property. He was ordered to report in person to Colonel Abert. Emory's charges were sent to the department commander and chief of engineers. On June 9, Smith asked and obtained Emory's permission to withdraw the disrespectful letters, and then Emory released him from arrest and withdrew charges against Smith. Nevertheless, Smith did not regret his actions. In responding to the adjutant general's inquiry about the matter, Smith wrote in December: "I intended no disrespect in my communications but simply to notice in plain terms a series of acts of injustice committed against me by Major Emory and which I am quite prepared to prove." Smith was relieved from duty on the Mexican survey in June and ordered to report to Johnston at San Antonio for duty.[49]

On December 1, 1852, Smith was in New York City awaiting approval for a six-month leave. The application was denied, and on December 4, he was ordered to report to Captain Campbell Graham or the senior officer of the corps at Fort Brook, Tampa Bay, Florida. He would assist in the canal survey at Fort Brook. On December 13, Smith reported to Abert that he had not proceeded to Florida because he was summoned to appear before a United States Senate committee investigating charges against the commissioners of the United States–Mexican Boundary Commission. Despite his summons, Smith was never called before the committee. With Congress adjourned, Smith was ordered to duty in Florida on February 28, 1853, under the command of Second Lieutenant Martin Luther Smith.[50]

Smith's relations with his new commander were amicable and very pleasant. In Florida, he made some reconnaissances from Tampa Bay along the western coast to Charlotte's Harbor and to the mouth of the Caloosahatchee River near Fort Myers, an artillery post. He also participated in surveying a possible route for a ship canal across the state. On May 1, Smith was promoted to first lieutenant. On July 4, with his work completed, he joined the headquarters at St. Augustine. As the working season was over, he enjoyed a comparatively relaxing summer. In late August, M.L. Smith left St. Augustine and directed Baldy to open all public communications addressed to his commander and answer those which required immediate attention.[51]

On October 7, 1853, William Farrar Smith was ordered to report to Brevet Major General Persifor F. Smith in San Antonio. Smith gained approval of the adjutant general to delay his trip to Texas until early November because of the prevalence of yellow fever along the route. Upon his arrival in Texas, Baldy was appointed the topographical officer in the staff of the general commanding the Department of Texas. Smith suffered from a lack of funds for his engineering duties and continually complained to the Topographical Bureau in Washington that he was unable to do his work because of a lack of an office and necessary instruments.[52]

On December 22, he requested a long list of surveying instruments, animals, forage, provisions, and funds to hire men but was told that no funds existed for the necessary instruments. Finally, in June 1854, Smith was informed that the instruments were being sent in two boxes.[53] On June 16, Smith requested funds for an office and an assistant. The new instruments would need space, and Smith lacked a place to work. During June, Smith worked on compiling a map of a portion of Texas. Nevertheless, on August 3, Smith restated his former complaints: he did not have the necessary funds to do his work, he still did not have the necessary instruments, he needed an office, and he desired equal footing with other staff officers in the department. In responding to a request for a copy of the map he was drawing, Smith wrote on August 17 that since he did not have an office or instruments, the bureau's request for the maps was unexpected. He understood that his request for instruments had been refused.[54]

The bureau assured Smith that the June shipment was on its way. Colonel Abert sent a statement of policy to Smith from Secretary of War Jefferson Davis that the men, transportation, and subsistence necessary to execute military reconnaissances and surveys under orders from the headquarters of that department could be furnished in the same manner as for any other military duty. The instruments and other articles, not being military supplies, had been or would be furnished by the Topographical Bureau.[55]

Baldy got a four-month break from this frustrating situation when General Smith in mid–August had his topographical officer accompany him on a tour to El Paso and Presidio del Norte. Lieutenant Smith turned over his engineering work to the adjutant general of the department and eagerly joined General Smith's expedition. After selecting mules for wagons and ambulances, and a squadron of the Mounted Rifles for an escort, the expedition started on the Whiting-Smith route to El Paso. They got into camp about an hour before sunset and dined, and then everyone felt like getting to bed after the fatigue of a long day. On October 1, Smith reported that his work consisted of measuring the distances with an odometer and making two or three observations for local time at El Paso. As General Smith believed that he had neither men nor subsistence to employ in a topographical reconnaissance or survey, Lieutenant Smith presumed he would not likely "be placed in a position to do any duty of any importance" any time soon.[56] On the trip to and during the stay at El Paso, General Smith established two posts: Fort Davis at Wild Rose Pass and Fort Bliss above El Paso. On their return on November 21 to Corpus Christi, Baldy found that a yellow fever epidemic had taken some of his friends, including the department surgeon.[57]

With his return to his topographical duties at Corpus Christi, Baldy's former problems of missing and delayed instruments and no place to work continued. So, on November 27 he made more requests for instruments. Because the requested barometers and thermometers could not be sent safely, Smith was ordered to New Orleans to purchase them. He was also told to open all the shipment boxes before he made more requests. Apparently, his superiors believed he had more resources available to him than he knew.[58]

However, Smith's time was not entirely occupied establishing his office and completing his report. During the late winter of 1855, the rather monotonous life was varied by fishing excursions to the coast where he would catch red-fish and by a trip into the interior for wild geese. Also, during this period, Smith served as a groomsman at General Smith's wedding in Corpus Christi.[59]

In the spring of 1855, Baldy Smith was hit with a severe attack of malaria. The doctors bled him (an acceptable medical practice of the day) and gave him 120 grains of quinine in two doses—one in the evening and the other in the morning. This treatment warded off the dangerous chill. He supposed he was very ill, for one or the other of his professional friends was with him every minute for two weeks. Wives of officers ministered to his feeble appetite, and the officers kept him amused with their stories and gossip. On May 5, Smith reported himself sick and enclosed a special order from General Smith granting him a leave of absence for thirty days with permission to apply for an extension of five months for the benefit of his health. Smith left his instruments in the care of the Quartermaster when he went on his leave. On June 6, he enclosed a surgeon's certificate to the Adjutant General with a request to extend his one-month leave another five months. In his certificate, Dr. Levi H. Holden stated Smith would be unfit for duty for a least six months. He reported that, during the last month, Smith had several attacks of cerebral congestion complicated by vertigo, dizziness, numbness of the extremities, and other alarming symptoms. As these conditions might be precursors of something more serious, Holden thought that timely attention should be given to their causes. All exposure to the heat of the sun, all severe bodily or mental exertion, and anything that might induce a vascular excitement of the brain were to be avoided.[60]

On his sick leave, Smith traveled from the hot climate of Texas to Washington, D.C. There he was examined by Dr. Richard H. Coolidge and told to go to the mountains. So, Smith traveled to the White Sulphur Springs of Greenbrier County, Virginia. The country was beautiful and the climate ideal. Smith recovered somewhat physically but could not read without painful headaches. Arriving back in Washington, Smith found orders to go to West Point as an assistant professor of mathematics. Smith felt this was a most honorable position carrying with it extra pay, but he knew he was in no condition to undertake the duties. He went to Coolidge for a certificate of disability. Coolidge refused to give the certificate and told Smith to try the duty. Smith believed that Coolidge refused because he knew that Secretary of War Jefferson Davis had selected Smith for the teaching post in order to replace a professor who had been at West Point for many years. Smith also thought that Coolidge, as an army doctor, feared Davis' reputation of ordering any officer who thwarted his plans to the most disagreeable post in the army.[61]

Smith wrote to the adjutant general on August 30 and requested that the order sending him to West Point be suspended until the first day of October. He made the request for the benefit of his health, which had not yet entirely re-established itself. Davis blocked this application because the academic courses commenced on September 1. Smith also went to the adjutant general's office, where he found his friend Captain Seth Williams, who seemed almost afraid to speak to him and urged him to leave town that night, as Davis was making inquiries as to whether or not Smith had yet reached West Point.[62]

Upon arriving at West Point, Smith found many friends, among them Captain Henry F. Clarke, later commissary-general of the Army of the Potomac. Clarke and Smith took a cottage together near the gate and had a comfortable home. Smith worked hard to restore his health. He bought a horse and rode fifteen to twenty miles a day, but he continued to suffer from painful headaches. The labor of teaching made his condition so much worse that he was becoming melancholy. When he completed grading his cadets' June examinations, he had to tell the professor of mathematics that he was unable to continue his duties to his own satisfaction and that the academy ought to have a better man. However, the students felt differently. One of Smith's pupils, James Harrison Wilson, failed to discover any lack of knowledge or perspicacity on the instructor's part. To the contrary, Smith impressed his students as a very clear-headed professor with remarkable powers of mind and great aptitude as a disciplinarian and teacher.[63]

Smith was given the customary leave of an assistant professor at the academy, but this proved insufficient. On August 28, 1856, Smith enclosed a medical certificate to the adjutant general of the Military Academy with his request of a two-month leave for health reasons. In his certificate, Dr. Samuel Moore recommended less intellectual labor, more physical exercise, and approval of a two-month leave. According to Moore, Smith's illness included painful headaches and "derangement of digestive organs." The doctor reported that Smith contracted the disease in the South and was in poor health upon arrival at the school. The doctor continued that because of the stress of his instructorship, Smith's condition had worsened during the winter. He lost partial use of his mental ability and had periods of partial paralysis of his right side and tongue. Davis accepted the doctor's recommendation and Military Academy Superintendent John G. Barnard's favorable endorsement and had Smith relieved from duty at the Military Academy on September 6. Davis ordered Smith to send monthly reports on his health. In October and November, Smith sent the requested reports to the adjutant general accompanied by medical certificates which reported that Smith suffered from numbness in his lower extremity, from local paralysis and was unfit for duty.[64]

At this time, Captain William B. Franklin was appointed engineer secretary of the Lighthouse Board, and through him, in December 1856, Smith was detailed as engineer of the Eleventh Lighthouse District with headquarters at Detroit. Smith's duties included visiting lighthouses in the district and inspecting their engineering. He kept out of doors as much as possible, and this finally began to improve his health. In April 1858, Smith and Captains Horatio G. Wright and George G. Meade were appointed as a board to examine the channels of the St. Mary's River in Michigan. In February 1859, Smith and Captain A.W. Whipple were ordered to form a commission to examine and report upon the location of the railroad and depot on the military reservation at Fort Gratiot that was located at the junction of the St. Clair River and Lake Huron. On July 12, 1859, Smith was promoted to captain to take effect from July 1. On November 2, Smith was assigned to duty as engineer secretary of the Lighthouse Board and ordered to report to the secretary of treasury. Smith filled Franklin's spot when Franklin was put in charge of the new Treasury building.[65]

Baldy found his duties as secretary the most pleasant that he ever had. During the years 1859 and 1860, Smith planned and began four first-class lighthouses: one at Ponquogue on the south shore of Long Island, two at the Highlands of Navesink—as guides to Sandy Hook, and one at Cape Canaveral in Florida. Since the position at the Navesink Highlands commanded the entrance to New York Harbor, Smith thought the light should be housed in something more than an ordinary, simple tower. He built a square tower and a round one, connecting them by the keepers' houses and offices in such a way as to give approaching ships the appearance of a large castle with battlements and defensive towers. Owing to financial troubles at the beginning of the war, the building was not completed until 1862.[66]

William Farrar Smith's childhood, tenure at West Point, and work in the antebellum regular army revealed two themes that would be significant during the Civil War. The first was his talent as an engineer. This had been illustrated by several varied experiences from the Southwest to the Atlantic Coast. His intelligence and ability were recognized by most of his superiors and would be reflected later as a tactical commander in the war. The second theme was Smith's determination to hold others to the same high standards as he held himself. Smith was quick to point out his commanders' failures to measure up on small or large issues. The Civil War would provide him with ample opportunities for such criticism. Unfortunately, such critiques ultimately would end Smith's field service well before the end of the war.

CHAPTER II

Smith Prepares for War

The Making of a Brigade Commander

During 1860, Baldy Smith was faced with the growing sectional divisions resulting from the divisive presidential campaign. Like most military officers, Smith did not participate in partisan politics. When Abraham Lincoln's election in November led to the secession of the Lower South in the winter of 1860–61, however, Smith reacted on both personal and professional levels. Smith and many of his old army friends looked forward to the coming conflict with keen regret since a civil war to them meant more than it did to most others. The army ties and the comradery of West Point would be snapped, and friends, who would had risked their lives for each other, would be found in hostile camps.

During the secession winter, Smith was much occupied with correspondence about the strife that was threatening the nation. He wrote primarily to two of his classmates from West Point. One was William Henry Chase Whiting, who served with Smith in Texas and ranked first in their class. Whiting was a native of Mississippi and had married into a North Carolina family. Smith tried to convince Whiting to support the North, but his letters had no effect. Whiting would die as a Confederate major general in 1865.[1]

The other classmate was Barnard E. Bee of South Carolina, stationed at the time in Utah as a captain of infantry. Bee was Smith's best friend. Smith said their friendship "was of that quality that carried such perfect confidence that a support to any extent was ready at anytime in any difficulty." During the winter, Bee wrote Baldy that they were drifting into a civil war brought on by politicians who on both sides were looking to the West Pointers to pull their chestnuts out of the fire. He urged that they not be parties to any such conflict and suggested that the two should go down to far western Texas where his brother had a million acres of land. Both being acquainted with frontier life, they could raise cattle and earn their own living there and be out of the accursed war. To this Smith replied that he felt sure Bee would be compelled to go with his people, and that Smith's duty was with the flag. Bee lost his life as a Confederate brigadier leading a victorious charge at First Bull Run. Smith felt that Bee, given the chance, would have been as great as Thomas J. Jackson or James Longstreet. He never ceased loving Bee's memory.[2]

While Smith was busy in his unsuccessful attempts to keep his West Point friends loyal, he was also involved in protecting Federal property in the South. Smith feared that the Southern members of President James Buchanan's cabinet would use their powers to cripple the Federal government and reduce its effectiveness against the secession movement. He was most concerned about the lighthouses in Southern waters, which were of the utmost value to the navy. Some of the lights on the eastern coast of Florida were built on coral reefs some distance from the mainland, and their destruction would be an irreparable loss to the navy in the navigation of the Gulf stream. Since Georgian Howell Cobb was treasury secretary under whom the Lighthouse Board served, and Alabaman Raphael Semmes was the other secretary of the board, Smith could not make a move or utter a word officially, as it might cause the catastrophe that Smith hoped to avoid.[3]

Smith sought out loyal members of the board to talk over the subject. Dallas Bache, head of the Coast Survey, concurred in the importance of the matter and suggested that Smith advise Brigadier General Joseph Totten, chief of engineers. Totten also saw the importance of taking steps to prevent the lights' destruction and referred Smith to Commodore William Shubrick, the chairman of the board. Shubrick told Smith, "If those people wish to destroy or capture the lights, let them go." Smith was forced to give up his idea of forceful protection. The situation changed when Major General John Dix replaced Cobb, and Semmes resigned. As soon as the change occurred, Smith visited the new treasury secretary to urge lighthouse protection. On broaching the subject, Dix asked Smith to wait a minute, went into his inner office, and returned with a paper which he read as a copy of a dispatch he had just sent to the captain of a revenue cutter in New Orleans, saying, "If any man offers to pull down the American flag, shoot him on the spot." Smith asked him if he had any idea if the message would ever reach the captain. Dix said possibly not, but it would have an effect on the North. Dix then listened to Smith's arguments for protecting the lights on the Florida reefs from destruction by the Rebels. Dix gave him carte blanche to turn out and appoint as many keepers as were necessary to protect the lighthouses on the reefs.[4]

On February 9, 1861, Dix requested the war secretary's permission for the steamer that was leaving New York for Texas to land Smith at Fort Jefferson and for the ordnance officer at Fort Columbus, New York, to sell to the Lighthouse Board certain arms and ammunition. Smith departed with his instructions and a large number of rifles and ammunition in the *Daniel Webster*. This steamer had been chartered to go to Texas to bring back troops that had been surrendered by the department commander and had been paroled.[5]

Smith had a most tempestuous voyage to Key West. On landing at Key West, he found the Confederate flag flying over the custom house and the collector of the port acting for the Confederate government. As Florida had seceded from the Union, the local citizens already thought themselves out of the jurisdiction of the United States. Smith turned over his arms, ammunition, and powers to Naval Commander Charles W. Pickering, the lighthouses inspector, to protect the lighthouses in two districts. Smith was soon deep in conference with Captain John M. Brannan, who commanded a company of artillery, and Captain Edward B. Hunt of the Engineers, in charge of the fort there. Brannan told Smith that, knowing the disloyalty of Secretary of War John B. Floyd of Virginia, he had not asked instructions to move from the barracks into the fort, fearing it would trigger a coup and the seizure of the fort by the Confederate volunteers from Key West and the mainland. He had, however, kept one third of his force in the fort under the pretense of practicing at the heavy guns, and when the engineers had stopped up a big hole in the wall at which they were hard at work, he would move his whole company in and report his actions by a private letter to Lieutenant General Winfield Scott.

One clerk in the custom house was a loyal man and came to Smith every night and reported everything he could gather in regard to the sentiments and acts of the people. Brannan carried out his plan and occupied the fort before anyone suspected his intentions. Thus, he saved a naval station that would have caused an irreparable loss had it been seized by a Confederate force, for the location was an important strategic position at the entrance to the Gulf of Mexico.[6]

With the outbreak of the Civil War, Smith was given an additional duty while still serving as engineer secretary of the Lighthouse Board. The adjutant general ordered him to New York City to muster volunteers into government service.[7]

While on muster duty, Smith married Sarah Lyon of New York on April 24. He had met her two years earlier and had been engaged for some time. They had planned to marry in October, but the outbreak of the war caused them to push up the date of the wedding. They took a short wedding trip to Smith's native state of Vermont. The Smiths would be life-long partners facing the hardships of frequent separation through the war years. They had five children during their marriage, but only two would survive to adulthood. The Smiths lost at least one of their young children during the war.[8]

During the wedding trip, Smith offered his service to Governor Erastus Fairbanks. The governor promised Smith that as soon as the Third Vermont was called for, the command would be offered to him.[9] Smith hoped to gain command of an infantry regiment because he felt he would be more effective in leading such a command than remaining as an engineer officer on the Lighthouse Board. Yet he also did not relish beginning the war as a captain when so many non-professional men were entering as colonels. On April 29, Smith applied to the new secretary of the treasury, Salmon P. Chase, for relief from his duties on the Lighthouse Board to take command of a Vermont regiment. Assistant Treasury Secretary George Harrington favorably endorsed the request. Captain W.B. Franklin wrote on Smith's behalf to the War Department on May 8: "Capt. Smith is very anxious that his request may be favorably acted upon by the Department, as he believes that he can do better service to his Government as Colonel of the Vermont Regiment than as a Captain of Topographical Engineers."[10] Major Hartman Bache wrote on behalf of the Topographical Bureau to the adjutant general on May 18, that the Governor of Vermont had tendered Smith a command of a regiment of volunteers and that Smith be allowed to accept the command. Nevertheless, the War Department initially blocked approval of Smith's request to join the volunteer service. Instead, Smith was relieved of his muster duty in New York City and was assigned as a topographical officer under Major General Benjamin F. Butler at Fort Monroe, Virginia. Smith arrived at Fort Monroe in early June and took up residence with an old army friend Captain Alexander B. Dyer, chief of ordnance.[11]

Among the standing orders at Fort Monroe was one requiring all staff officers to report at the quarters of the commanding officer whenever the long roll was beaten. One night, three or four days after Smith's arrival, the long roll was beaten, and Smith made ready to go to headquarters, despite Dyer jeering Smith for his "plebishness." Smith went to Butler's house and found everything quiet and dark. As there was no answer to his ring, Smith rang again and again, determined to make somebody in the house pay attention to the standing order which he was obeying. At last, looking through a side window, he saw a figure in a long white single garment, carrying in his hand a lighted candle, come slowly down the stairs. It was Butler. Presently, the major general opened the door, and his candle went out. Smith stated his name and rank and the reason for his presence. Butler said, "Inasmuch as you and I are the only persons who have paid attention to the order I presume it is a false alarm, and we can return to our respective occupations." He shut the door and stumbled up the stairway; Smith returned to his quarters and had a laugh with Dyer over the figure made by the commanding general as he came to receive the reports of his staff.[12]

Another day, Smith was ordered to go out on a reconnaissance to a certain creek on the road to Big Bethel. The Twentieth New York Volunteers were his escort. After they passed Hampton, the regiment took up its formation for a movement into the enemy's country with skirmishers and flankers making a most auspicious appearance. When the creek was reached and no sign of an enemy discovered, the order to return was given. In a minute, Smith was without an escort. The entire regiment had scattered to pillage, and every house and farmyard was ransacked. Smith did his best to stop the plundering, but there were too many groups for him to do much. He later remembered one soldier staggering along under a feather bed and a rocking chair. Smith passed one farm where four or five soldiers were trying to get a very large mule away with the owner quietly watching them. Baldy spoke to him about his efforts and the farmer replied, "If they can get the mule away, they are welcome to him." When Smith left, the fight was still going on, and he learned later that the mule was the victor. Smith reported the action of the regiment, but he feared the commanding general saw no malfeasance in the business.[13]

William Farrar Smith made one more reconnaissance with the New York Zouaves under Lieutenant Colonel Gouverneur K. Warren, whom Smith believed afterwards was one of the best and most distinguished Union generals of the war. On this occasion, they saw no enemy and rested upon reaching Newport News, and then marched back in an orderly manner. The exposure to the hot sun brought back the old troubles in Smith's head that he first suffered during a bout of malaria before the war, and the doctor ordered him out of the field and into the mountain air. Smith went to Brattleboro in Vermont to try the water cure. On July 18, he was recommended for transfer from the staff of General Butler to that of Major General Irwin McDowell. But Smith's poor health kept him in Vermont through the battle of First Bull Run.[14]

The Third Vermont Volunteers were in camp at St. Johnsbury, Vermont, when Governor Fairbanks offered Smith the command of the regiment on July 19, 1861. The secretary of war had, to this time, refused to allow regular army officers to accept higher commissions in volunteer regiments. Smith went to St. Johnsbury and talked with the governor about this matter. The governor asked Smith to take the regiment to Washington and expressed the hope that the Vermont influence would be strong enough to get Smith permission to take the colonelcy. On arriving in Washington during the last week in July, Smith was informed that the secretary of war had approved his commission. The final approval was aided by General Winfield Scott, who had before this shown a distinct interest in the Vermont troops and who specifically requested that Captain Smith command the Third Vermont. Smith was commissioned a colonel on July 23, to date from April 27, making him the ranking officer of Vermont troops. His appointment was well received by his new regiment.[15]

As a regimental commander, Baldy carefully observed the sergeants and found those who were attentive to their duties. When any vacancies occurred, he took the best sergeants and made them officers. Smith made one orderly sergeant a captain, and he made others lieutenants. Those promoted had always performed their duties very efficiently and were the best officers in the regiment. This created a great deal of bad feeling among some of the officers as subordinates were promoted to positions higher than those of their commanding officers. But Smith believed that if a man did not have the capacity or desire to learn his duties, he certainly had no business complaining when those below him were promoted. Baldy submitted his choices for promotion to the governor of Vermont, and he sent them their commissions. The governor always carried out Smith's wishes in every respect.[16]

Smith's duties would soon expand. Major General George McClellan had been appointed commander of the Division of the Potomac to defend the nation's capital and reorganize the army in the East after the Federal defeat at First Bull Run. On August 1, McClellan, who had been a friend of Baldy's during their time at West Point, ordered the commander of the Third Vermont Volunteers to take command of all troops at the Chain Bridge in Washington, D.C. The position was an important one, for it guarded not only the bridge but the reservoir that supplied Washington with water. On August 4, McClellan reorganized the Division of the Potomac and gave Smith the command of a brigade consisting of his Third Vermont along with the Second Vermont, Sixth Maine, Thirty-Third New York, Co. H, United States Cavalry, and Captain Thaddeus P. Mott's battery.[17]

Camp life in Smith's brigade went according to a schedule presented in his first general order. Reveille was at 5:00 a.m., followed by policing the separate company camps at 5:10, and an hour of company skirmish drills starting at 5:45. After a 7:00 breakfast, any sick men were marched to the surgeon's tent. At 8:30, each company presented men, equipped with knapsacks, haversacks, canteens, and twenty rounds of ammunition, for guard duty to the assistant adjutant general. From 9:00 to 12:00, the brigade had target practice. There was roll call for dinner at noon followed by company drill at 2:00 and another policing of the company camps at 4:00. At 5:00, there was battalion drill. There was then company inspection of the men's arms and tents followed by retreat parade at sunset. Tattoo was at 9:30 and taps at 9:45 when all lights were extinguished except for tents of the company officers and orderly sergeants. The men did not have drills on Saturday, when they were expected to wash their clothes. On Sundays, except in case of an attack or other military need, the men's work was suspended, and they were permitted to rest as much as possible and attend divine services after the customary Sunday morning inspection.[18]

Smith's officers had some special responsibilities. The company officers were responsible for roll calls. The officer of the picket guard was in charge of the daily guard. All these officers reported to the field officer of the day, who was also responsible for the camp policing, general supervision of the company drill, instruction of company officers, and direct supervision of the battalion drills. The colonels of the regiments and commanders of detached companies were to report to Smith the numbers and types of drills held each day and the efficiency and advancement of the men. The importance of drill was impressed on the men by having strict regulations about sick call, limiting passes to three men per company except on public business, and signing passes only on Saturday. Anyone found outside the camp without a pass, except for getting water, would be arrested by the provost marshal.[19]

Smith, remembering the violations of private property under General Butler, directed that all men found trespassing upon private property would be immediately arrested. Smith was faced with a violation of this order in late August when men in the Sixth Maine under Captain Benjamin F. Harris committed gross excesses in a private home and seized horses in the fields. Smith recommended that the guilty soldiers, who were arrested, be dismissed. Concerned about the safety of his men, Smith reported that Harris had permitted his men on their return trip to camp to straggle in every direction. The soldiers were thus exposed to being cut to pieces by a few determined enemies. Because of this, Smith recommended Harris' dismissal as well.[20]

Another area of military discipline that caused particular concern for the brigade commander was the laxity of the picket guard. In August, McClellan urged Smith to be very watchful against an attack at night. Smith was to caution his pickets to be on the alert, keeping out patrols well towards the Great Falls and watching in the direction of the Louisville Road as well as on the river. His men were to be prepared to repel an attack. Nevertheless, despite Baldy's attempts to keep an alert guard, the officers and men continued to ignore Smith's direction. Since the pickets were constantly being found asleep on their posts, Smith arranged a plan with one of McClellan's aides to try and break the habit, for it endangered the safety of the brigade and communications over the Chain Bridge.[21]

Smith planned to take the first perfectly incontestable case of a picket reported asleep on post and have charges drawn under the articles of war whereby the picket would be tried by a general court martial. After the conviction, the judge-advocate would press for the extreme punishment under the law and have the convicted picket sentenced to be shot. Then on the day before the execution, the general-in-chief would recommend mercy for him since the soldier was the first case and send a pardon to Smith the night before the execution. The idea of the pardon would be kept secret among the staff officer, McClellan, and Smith in order not to rob the conviction of its effect.[22]

In early September, Private William Scott of Smith's old regiment was convicted of sleeping on his post. Smith's plan was faithfully carried out. Every arrangement was carefully made to execute the sentence, and every person in his brigade, except Smith, was ignorant of the proposed pardon. The night before Scott was to be shot was dark and stormy, and the road exceedingly bad. As the night passed without any order from headquarters, Baldy became very anxious. He finally wrote a letter to McClellan's aide Major Seth Williams that the execution was scheduled at 9:00 a.m., and he had not received the expected pardon. Williams wrote back to change the scheduled time to 11:00 and promised that the order would reach Smith before that hour. The pardon reached the worried brigade commander in good time. Scott had in the meantime made all his preparations for death. Instead of the order of execution, the pardon was read to Smith's brigade, on parade to witness the execution. This incident would have gone unnoticed except that nineteenth-century historians, like L.E. Chittenden in his *Recollections of President Lincoln*, asserted that a timely visit by the president to Smith's camp saved Scott's life. In fact, Smith's plan never included the president, nor did Lincoln participate in this ruse to make the pickets more alert.[23]

William Farrar Smith's added responsibilities as a brigade commander were appreciated by McClellan, and on August 13, Smith was appointed brigadier general of volunteers. Before the middle of August, Smith's pickets were sent across the Potomac River at the Chain Bridge. On September 3, McClellan was informed that the enemy had appeared in force opposite the Chain Bridge and towards Great Falls and were about to advance along the whole line. McClellan rode to Smith's headquarters at the Chain Bridge. He was determined to move his brigade across the river during the night and to entrench a position on the Virginia side as the surest method of saving the bridge.

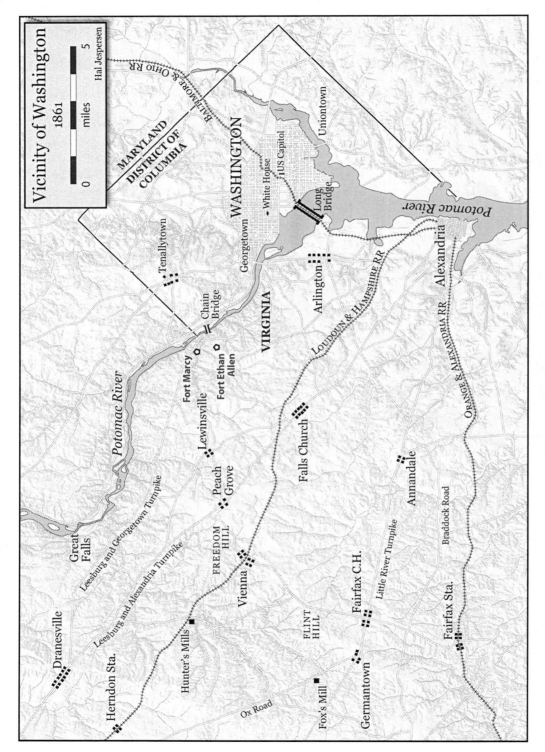

Vicinity of Washington, 1861.

Early in the night, Smith crossed his brigade and at once commenced the construction of Forts Marcy and Ethan Allen. He encamped his brigade at Camp Advance.[24]

On September 11, Baldy organized an expedition to make a reconnaissance of Lewinsville, five miles from camp. Lieutenant Orlando M. Poe of the Topographical Engineers was ordered to make a report and sketch of the village. Smith ordered an escort of 1,800 men under the command of Colonel Isaac Stevens of the Seventy-Ninth New York State Militia to accompany Poe. Stevens' force included his own troops and companies from the First United States Chasseurs, Second and Third Vermont, Nineteenth Indiana, some cavalry, and Captain Charles Griffin's battery. The expedition left Smith's headquarters at 7:30 a.m. with instructions to cover and protect a reconnaissance of the village of Lewinsville and vicinity. It was to determine all the facts that would be required for its permanent occupation and defense. Stevens' expedition proceeded quietly, steadily throwing out skirmishers in advance, exploring the ground on both flanks to the distance of a mile, and entering the village at 10:00 a.m.[25]

There were four roads that converged in Lewinsville. The expedition came to the village from the eastern road. The reconnaissance went on entirely uninterrupted. All possible information possible was gained as to the position of the enemy. The reconnaissance was completed about 2:15 p.m., and the order was given to form a column for a return to Camp Advance.[26]

The withdrawal immediately became difficult. Considerable delay occurred in collecting the skirmishers on the western road and in the woods between that road and the southern road. Soon, Confederate Colonel J.E.B. Stuart opened infantry fire from the western road and woods. This endangered the Union rear and left. By this juncture, nearly all the skirmishers had returned, and all the commands were formed. Captain Griffin was ordered to move his battery to protect the Union rear from the severe and accurate enemy artillery fire from the south. The expedition withdrew from the village in perfect order, though exposed to heavy artillery fire.[27]

After a half hour of unanswered fire from Stuart's infantry and artillery, Griffin's battery arrived and, after an hour of firing, silenced the Confederates. Smith had heard the firing from camp and proceeded to take command, giving orders to have all available forces follow him, including Captain Mott's battery. On arriving on the field, Smith placed Mott's battery in position. Mott directed fire towards the smoke from the enemy's battery and towards the direction of Griffin's shell fire. As soon as Stuart's battery ceased firing, Mott directed his attack on woods occupied by Confederate cavalry, causing the cavalry's evacuation with a number of riderless horses. Smith ordered Mott to Griffin's former position. Mott then fired on withdrawing Confederate infantry on the western road—this caused some confusion in the Confederate ranks. Griffin's battery moved down the road toward camp but was soon placed in a second position to repel Confederate infantry movements on the rear of the Union withdrawal. Colonel Smith sent the Seventh-Ninth New York State Militia out on the return trip, on the Union right, to protect the flank. The Confederates advanced no further. The expedition returned safely from its successful reconnaissance, but not without loss. Two soldiers were killed, thirteen were wounded, and three were reported missing.[28]

On September 25, at 9:00 a.m., Smith led another reconnaissance to Lewinsville to collect forage. His force included 5,100 infantrymen, 16 pieces of artillery, and 150 cavalrymen. Smith placed artillery with infantry support on the hills and knolls along his route to protect his rear. He also threw out skirmishers to protect his flanks. At this time, there were no signs of the Confederates, with the exception of a few cavalry scouts. Smith ordered the quartermaster to load his ninety wagons—this was accomplished by 3:00 p.m.—and directed them well on their way back to camp. Smith then sent orders to draw in the skirmishers, and at 4:00 p.m., as they were moving in, word came that the enemy were advancing over the hills from the southern road. At 4:30 p.m., the Confederates placed two guns about 2,500 yards from the Federal right and opened fire on Mott's battery. Mott's and Griffin's batteries at once replied. After the Federals fired about thirty rounds, the Confederates withdrew. At 5:30 p.m., Smith's force began to return to camp and arrived in perfect order by 7:00 p.m.[29]

On September 27, 1861, Smith ordered one thousand axe men to cut down the timber between Fort Ethan Allan and Mary Hall's House. Also, that day, with his wife visiting him at camp, Smith obtained a seven-day leave of absence. Nonetheless, Smith remained long enough to follow McClellan's orders to direct his command on September 28 to march to Fall's Church in connection with other advances and help to determine that the hills near Washington had been evacuated. The following day Baldy discovered the orders to advance had not been communicated to one of the lead regiments and tried to address the problem. Unfortunately, the movement began late in the evening, and the result showed the hazards of night attacks. These troops were mistaken for enemy troops three times by other Federal units. Commanders finally ended the firing but not before at least six soldiers were killed, and several others were wounded. Though some blamed Smith for not coordinating with other commanders, the fault fell mostly to McClellan for hastily ordering the men without proper time to plan. Despite this incident, McClellan favored Smith for higher command. On October 3, General McClellan gave him command of a division. McClellan praised his new division commander: "He possessed great personal courage & a wonderfully quick eye for ground & for handling troops."[30]

William Farrar Smith's longest command—that of division commander in the Army of the Potomac—was about to begin. Smith's tenure as regimental commander and brigade commander was rather brief. His leadership showed his characteristics of careful planning and preparation. His insistence on comprehensive drilling and fair but firm discipline would be hallmarks of his commands. Smith and his men's preparation would continue in his new role as a division commander. Such work would be essential for the challenges ahead.

CHAPTER III

Smith Readies His Division

Drills, Reconnaissances, and Army Politics

The autumn and winter months of 1861 found the general preparing his troops for the next spring's offensive against the Confederates. Smith's new command comprised three brigades. He was assigned Brigadier General Winfield Scott Hancock's brigade that included the Fifth Wisconsin, the Forty-Third New York, and the Forty-Seventh and Forty-Ninth Pennsylvania. In addition, Smith initiated formation of the Second Brigade. As the Vermont troops came in the autumn, Smith suggested to McClellan that they be allotted to him to form a single brigade. McClellan agreed, and Smith had the Second and Third Vermont from his old brigade joined with the Fourth, Fifth, and Sixth Vermont regiments to form the Vermont Brigade. Smith correctly supposed that the quota of Vermont troops would not amount to more than one brigade and hoped that the Vermont troops would make their own record. Smith considered carefully his choice for the command of his fellow Vermonters. On October 22, 1861, he selected Brigadier General William T.H. Brooks, who had served longer than Smith and whom Smith had known for some years, for the post. Smith felt Brooks was an excellent soldier and Brooks' father was a Vermonter, which seemed to give him a bond with the brigade. The men under him got used to his severe discipline and became very fond of him. The Third Brigade was composed of the Thirty-Third, Forty-Ninth, and Seventy-Seventh New York and the Sixth Maine. The Third Brigade was commanded by three brigadier generals during the fall and winter. The first was Isaac I. Stevens, who led the expedition to Lewinsville in September. His transfer led to the appointment in November of John M. Brannan, whom Smith had helped save the Key West lighthouses. Brannan was transferred to Key West, and in February 1862, the command was given to John W. Davidson, a West Point classmate and friend of Smith.[1]

Smith carried his idea of the importance of drill into his division command. The troops in the division drilled four times daily and paraded under arms half an hour after daybreak. The deep mud in January and February brought the suspension of battalion and brigade drills, though picket duty continued with one regiment of each brigade taking turns performing picket and fatigue duty on the forts near the camp. The general did not give special favors to his officers. If an officer was not on guard or excused, he was ordered to appear with his men on parade at reveille roll call.[2]

Baldy's officers were of various talents and backgrounds. Many tried their best to learn their duties; others were men of intelligence who were excellent officers. Some, however, were men who, the moment they got their shoulder straps on, thought they knew it all. They "trusted to God," and did not study anything or try to do their duty.

But as a general rule, the officers in his division were competent. Officers were examined, and ineffective ones were removed and replaced.[3]

By the end of 1861, the division was in a fair state of discipline. Its health, however, was one of the worst in the army. In mid–November 2,000 were on sick report, most of them from the Vermont Brigade. A medical report of December 12, 1861, showed about twenty-five percent excused from duty due to sickness. Between three-fourths and nine-tenths of these had probably never been out of the state, and division doctors felt the Vermonters were going through acclimation. But Smith believed that a more accurate reason for the illness was that between July and September his men were encamped on the banks of the Potomac where "very many of the men had intermittent, remittent and typhoid fevers as well as typhoid pneumonia and diarrhea."[4] When they left the region for the new camp at Camp Griffin, Langley, Virginia, on October 9, the men were placed in a much healthier environment. Smith ordered half his division vaccinated. In mid–November, he also permitted the picket reserves to have fires, and sentries were relieved every four hours.[5] Nevertheless, in February 1862, while the sickness of the Vermont Brigade had abated, the report was still large.[6]

A partial cause for the poor health was the inadequate supply of fuel. Brannan's men were prevented from cutting their own wood and, even if they had done so, they would have had to carry it themselves because of the lack of teams. On December 23, the brigade stole rails to cook their meals and prevent themselves from freezing. Brannan informed Hancock of the theft but warned the temporary division commander of the danger to his men's health from the lack of fuel.[7]

Smith also had problems with supplies during the fall and winter. In the Vermont Brigade, the lack of proper clothing became more serious as winter approached. On October 21, Smith informed Governor Fairbanks by telegraph that the men of the Second and Third Vermont regiments needed 850 coats, 1,500 pairs of pantaloons, and 100 tents. By the beginning of November, there was a temporary improvement in the condition of the Second Vermont regarding clothing and equipment. The Third Vermont had to wait until the middle of November to receive the needed coats.[8]

Despite poor health and inadequate supplies, units from the division were occupied with foraging, frequent reconnaissances of the area near Camp Griffin, and occasional skirmishes with the enemy. On October 14, Smith sent out a party of fifty, which seized eighteen head of cattle, and on November 21, his foragers returned with seventy wagon loads of oats, hay, and corn.[9]

With the division commander constantly anxious to determine the location of the enemy near the camp, reconnaissance work occupied much more time than foraging. During October and November, Smith ordered several reconnaissances to Freedom Hill, Vienna, Flint Hill, and Peacock Hill. These were intended to cover the work of the topographical engineers who were mapping the region and to observe any enemy movements in the area. Most of these reconnaissances were unopposed by the enemy. Sometimes, however, Confederate pickets or cavalrymen fired on the Federals, but these skirmishes caused little loss on either side.[10]

On November 26, Baldy was temporarily relieved of command because of illness. The poor health of the division had finally affected its commander. Ill with typhoid fever, Smith travelled to his home in New York City, and the division command fell to Hancock. During December, Hancock continued sending out reconnaissances to monitor the whereabouts of the enemy. On December 30, Smith returned to his command.[11]

Earlier that day, Smith was in Washington giving testimony before the Joint Committee on the Conduct of the War. He discussed issues relating to the division, including the poor health of his men and the general competency of his officers. On the subject of the small arms that his men used, he felt the Springfields were the best rifles. He went on to say that the Enfields were "exceedingly rough and tear the men's hands to pieces when they are going through the manual. No bayonet, as a general thing, will go on any rifle, except the one it is intended for. But in the case of the Springfield rifles, any one bayonet will fit them all." He also suggested that the army could save money by reducing the number of paymasters.[12]

The committee members then turned to his role during the Ball's Bluff Affair, a fiasco that had resulted in the loss of nearly 1,000 Federal troops. This minor battle's losses were due to poor planning and communications among the Federal commanders and had led to the Joint Committee's formation to investigate the mishap. In reality, Smith had not participated in that engagement, but he was in the general vicinity. Two months prior to the hearings, on October 19, Brigadier General George McCall had gone on a reconnaissance to Dranesville about the time of the incident at Ball's Bluff. Smith's division was ordered to be a supporting distance of McCall. Brigadier General Frederick W. Lander had testified that Smith was within supporting distance while McCall had reported that he could have gotten support easier from reinforcements at Centreville. Smith testified that he was with his division four to seven miles from camp covering the Alexandria and Leesburg Turnpike. He supposed his division was between six and seven miles from Dranesville and sufficiently near McCall to support him.[13]

Two days after Smith returned to camp, there was a joyous break from the monotony of camp life. Hancock's brigade celebrated New Year's Day 1862 with a day-long festival. The celebration included several contests with cash prizes. Men of the different regiments competed. Soldiers of the Fifth Wisconsin won the first two contests: a foot race of one thousand yards and a race called "jumping three jumps." A former sailor from the Sixth Maine won the third event: climbing a greased pole. The evening ended with the brigade trying to capture a soaped pig. The pig still eluded the entire brigade at sunset.[14]

During February 1862, Smith ordered two expeditions against the Confederates. On February 6, he requested permission from McClellan to test the Confederate pickets at Flint Hill and Hunter's Mill simultaneously to ascertain their actual strength. McClellan approved the move but cautioned Baldy not to engage a force larger than his own.[15] The next morning at 4:00, the Fifth Pennsylvania cavalry proceeded to Freedom Hill where the regiment divided. Two companies under Smith's assistant-adjutant general Captain Leonard D.H. Currie proceeded on the road through Vienna towards Flint Hill for the purpose of driving the enemy's pickets. Currie's squadron divided on approaching Flint Hill in an attempt to get in the rear of the enemy. The Confederates discovered this move and immediately fled to Germantown. Captain Jacob P. Wilson's squadron then moved to Hunter's Mill and discovered a portion of the enemy's reserve secreted in Mrs. Peck's House. Wilson's company charged the house. When the assault came within fifty yards, the enemy opened a brisk fire from the house and nearby woods. Notwithstanding this attack, Currie's men broke through the doors and windows, killing one man and capturing four prisoners. Currie's other company, under Captain John O'Farrell, found another portion of the Confederate reserve in a nearby log cabin. This cabin was attacked, and the Federals captured six prisoners but suffered one fatality.[16]

Meanwhile, Major Joseph L. Moss, who had command of three companies, proceeded directly from Freedom Hill to Hunter's Mill. Here, Moss's squadron succeeded in driving back the enemy's pickets some two or three miles. From Flint Hill, Moss started to Fairfax Court House. His command came across ten or fifteen Confederate pickets and pursued them to within one mile of Germantown, wounding two and capturing three of the enemy together with a valuable four-horse team. Moss entered Fairfax Court House after reconnoitering to the right and left of the village. The squadron stayed a half hour. The expedition had swept the enemy pickets from Fairfax Courthouse to Hunter's Mill, having been within three fourths of a mile of Germantown and taken thirteen prisoners and a provision wagon while suffering only one killed and one wounded.[17]

The Fifth Pennsylvania Cavalry under Colonel Max Friedman made another expedition on February 22, 1862. The regiment left camp at 3:30 in the morning and proceeded with the Forty-Third New York as far as Vienna. The Forty-Third was posted there, and the Fifth proceeded to Flint Hill. On arriving there, the command captured two pickets. Friedman left one squadron at Flint Hill to cover his rear and keep his communications with headquarters open and proceeded to Fox's Mill. At Fox's Mill, learning from an African American man the location of a small Confederate force, the command proceeded double-quick and captured five Confederates and two citizens. They next moved to Hawkhurst's Mill and to Hunter's Mill but found no Confederates. At Hunter's Mill, Friedman met Colonel Hiram Burnham's Sixth Maine, which covered the Fifth Pennsylvania's return to camp.[18]

During the winter, the Senate Committee of Military Affairs delayed its confirmation of Smith's appointment as a brigadier general. One possible reason for this delay was Smith's removal of Colonel Abner Knowles from the command of the Sixth Maine. Hancock, while he was temporary division commander, had found Knowles unable to discipline and drill his men. Smith held a board of examination which showed Knowles deficient. Smith forced Knowles' resignation in January. The rapid improvement of the Sixth under its new commander, Colonel Hiram Burnham, furnished the best evidence against Knowles. Nevertheless, Knowles sought revenge by persuading Maine Senator William Fessenden and Massachusetts Senator Henry Wilson, who chaired the Committee of Military Affairs, to block Smith's confirmation. Smith or his counsel was constantly called before Wilson's committee to answer seemingly hundreds of little charges, all of which were entirely false or of no possible importance. The charges were finally terminated.[19]

On February 18, Brooks wrote his father that another possible reason for Senate opposition to Baldy's confirmation was that someone through the Vermont Brigade contacted the Vermont senators to influence them against Smith. Brooks did not know if the nomination had been acted on, but there was trouble with it, and he doubted that it would get through the Senate. Five days later, Brigadier General George G. Meade confirmed this talk of Senate opposition to the confirmation of Smith. He stated, "I don't think they will succeed in rejecting him, but they have fought so hard that his friends on two occasions have thought it advisable to postpone taking a vote." As historian Stephen Sears wrote: "Politics, domestic as well as army, had ever to be in the thoughts of the part of the Potomac army's generals."[20]

While Baldy waited for the Senate to take action on his rank confirmation, he and other division commanders turned their attention to the strategic questions for the coming campaign. On March 7, McClellan called them together to determine the line of operations against the Confederates. Before the generals was the question of how best to approach the Confederate capital, Richmond, Virginia, in the coming spring Federal offensive. President Lincoln and Secretary of War Edwin Stanton favored a plan that stressed protection for Washington and included a campaign overland in Virginia to capture Richmond, beginning with the seizure of Manassas Junction. McClellan believed that the use of the overland course compelled the Federals to fight the Confederates on ground of the enemy's choosing. The numerous rivers between Washington and Richmond would enable the Confederates to take up positions that favored their defenses. Instead, McClellan asked his generals if they supported his plan to move the army to Annapolis, thence down the Chesapeake Bay and up the Rappahannock, landing at Urbanna and advancing on Richmond from there. Smith joined seven other generals in favor of McClellan's campaign plan.[21]

Another war council was held to consider a number of strategic and tactical issues. It considered a possible alternative to the Urbanna route. The first proposition queried, "Is it, or not, advisable as a preliminary to offensive operations that the base of the Army of the Potomac be changed from this one, it now has in front of the capitol to another one further south, in the lower Chesapeake, the army to move by water to its new position?" This proposition was approved by Generals Smith, Henry M. Naglee, Louis Blenker, McCall, Franklin, Fitz John Porter, Erasmus D. Keyes, and Andrew Porter. Generals J.G. Barnard, Samuel P. Heintzelman, Irwin McDowell, and Edwin V. Sumner opposed it.[22]

An amendment to hold the right bank of the Potomac as far down as Dumfries and Warrenton Road was rejected. Smith voted with the majority. Another proposition asked, "Is it desirable before changing the base of operations of the Army of the Potomac to the shore of the lower Chesapeake that the batteries on that river should be first taken by the Navy?" This was rejected. Smith voted with the minority who favored the proposition. He was joined by Blenker, Keyes, McDowell, and F.J. Porter.[23]

There was a discussion about the timing of the proposed movement. Smith said that he would wait until the season was so far advanced that they could depend upon not being cut off from their supplies by the state of the roads. If there were no prospect of transportation at a very early day, then Smith suggested movement via the Occoquan River. He thought the third week in March was the earliest date the roads would be passable. He would wait until about a week after that for transportation. Smith also considered the clearing of the Potomac as a preferable, but not necessary, prerequisite to a change of base.[24]

On March 8, President Lincoln and Secretary Stanton reconvened the twelve division commanders without the army commander present or having notified him of the meeting's content. Lincoln announced that he accepted McClellan's Urbana Campaign Plan as the majority of the commanders had decided. The president qualified his acceptance by permitting an advanced guard of 50,000 men to sail from Annapolis for Urbana with another 50,000 to follow only on condition that the Confederate batteries on the Potomac were destroyed or abandoned and the capital's defenses were secured. Lincoln then announced that he had decided to reorganize the twelve divisions into five corps and place five senior generals in command of them. McDowell, Sumner, Heintzelman, and Keyes would command First through Fourth Corps of the field army. Major General Nathaniel Banks would be given the corps that would remain behind as part of the capital defenses.[25]

Major General George B. McClellan and his division commanders. From left to right: William F. Smith, William B. Franklin, Samuel P. Heintzelman, Andrew Porter, Irwin McDowell, George B. McClellan, George A. McCall, Don Carlos Buell, Louis Blenker, Silas Casey, and Fitz John Porter (Mollus Collection, United States Army Heritage and Education Center, Carlisle, PA).

Also, during the winter, Secretary Stanton called some of McClellan's division commanders, including Smith, to Washington, desiring their support for the reorganization of the army into four field corps. While some of the division commanders supported delay in the reorganization to let the fighting determine the best generals, Stanton wanted only a categorical answer. The generals all agreed to reorganization. Smith felt the selections of Sumner, Keyes, and Heintzelman gave the corps mediocre commanders. McDowell was pushed forward by favoritism but was better than the others. Smith later asserted,

> The worst enemy of McClellan could not have handicapped him more severely than by giving to him three old officers of moderate talents, utterly without experience in the handling of large commands and naturally hostile to a young man who had risen to supreme command with a bound, while they had been toiling up through long years of service to be regimental commanders, or lower, and had learned all they knew of their profession by the rule of thumb as it were, and never studied the higher branches of the art of war.[26]

Smith believed that McClellan was also hurt by the jealousy of many Republican party leaders and Stanton, whom McClellan thought would help him. Treasury Secretary Salmon P. Chase had offered to ally with McClellan, but, being turned down, also became an enemy of the army commander. Lincoln was also at fault for appointing generals who were hostile to McClellan. Three of the four corps commanders had voted against McClellan's upcoming Peninsula Campaign plan. As for Smith's view of McClellan at the outset of the war, Smith recalled that he "was intimate with McClellan and thought he was <u>the</u> man who would bring us out of the war successful which was the thing I most wished for."[27] McClellan provided the nation a great service by not pushing the army into battle before it was drilled and disciplined, or before a well-organized artillery was ready to take its share of labor in a battle.[28]

The report that Confederate General Joseph E. Johnston had fallen back from the line he had occupied during the winter caused the army to move in the direction of Centreville. The Confederate withdrawal made the approach to Richmond by the Urbanna route impractical. Smith's division was posted at Flint Hill on March 10. While there, a conference of McClellan's generals was fixed at Fairfax Court House. It again took up the subject of a forward and aggressive campaign. McClellan proposed to alter his plan of operations to disembark the army at Fort Monroe. His generals unanimously supported their commander. All believed that a direct march toward Richmond meant crossing too many rivers. Instead, establishing the base on the Peninsula at Old Point Comfort would avoid this concern and provide a splendid harbor for naval and commercial vessels. Two navigable rivers, the James and the York, led into the hostile region. They provided two lines of transit for supplies and were capable of being defended by the navy. A road paralleled both rivers, and the climate was mild. It seemed an ideal country for an aggressive campaign, especially considering Federal superiority on land and sea. Lincoln approved McClellan's plan but qualified it to ensure protection of Washington.[29]

On March 13, Smith's division became the Second Division of the Fourth Corps, under Brigadier General E.D. Keyes. McClellan reviewed the division on that day and "found it in admirable condition and spirits."[30] Two days later, the division moved to Cloud's Mill, four miles northwest of Alexandria. On March 22, Smith ordered his division to move the next day. The division embarked on the twenty-third and left Alexandria by 5:00 in the afternoon. They arrived at Fort Monroe on March 25, 1862.[31]

Ever the task master, Smith, during the winter of 1861–62, had seen to it that his troops were properly trained and competently led. He had done his best against his men's chief enemy, camp sickness. The winter reconnaissances gave some of his men experience in skirmishing and this helped ready them for the more serious combat ahead. Initially, however, the general had found that politics were a greater nuisance than the Confederates. The Lincoln administration's actions against McClellan, and the Senate's efforts against Smith, set an unfortunate pattern of political involvement in the high command that would last for the rest of the war.

CHAPTER IV

Tactical Insight Frustrated

Smith's Division Moves Up the Peninsula

While W.F. Smith's men would fight well on the peninsula in the coming months, their commander would have his insightful advice for improving tactics during battle rejected by his superiors. Twice, Baldy would urge troop maneuvers and assaults that would have led to greater victories, but each time his superiors opposed his suggestions.

Upon arrival to the peninsula in March, Smith's men temporarily camped at Hampton, Virginia. The camp was on open ground, and the troops were soon annoyed by a small Confederate tugboat, which fired its single mounted heavy gun at the Union soldiers. Without doing any material damage, the boat kept the camp demoralized by a "damnable iteration" day and night.[1] Smith's field pieces could not reach the tug. Smith urged Commodore Louis M. Goldsborough, who commanded the Federal Fleet, to send a small, fast vessel to drive the tug away, but Goldsborough declined to act. On March 27, 1862, Smith's division went out on a reconnaissance of Watt's Creek. The division crossed the mouth of the creek but found no enemy batteries. The troops returned to camp on the morning of the twenty-eighth.[2]

Smith's command began its movement up the Peninsula on April 4. Smith sent his troops towards Young's Mill, with one brigade pushed forward to the road from Big Bethel to Warwick. After crossing Watt's Creek, his skirmishers frequently encountered Confederate pickets. Having proceeded about two miles, the country opened, and Young's Mill appeared visible about a thousand yards in advance of the woods. After reconnoitering the enemy position and being satisfied that there were no heavy guns, Baldy immediately deployed three regiments of the Second (Vermont) Brigade and kept the other two brigades in reserve. With his advance, the enemy retired from their works.[3]

On entering the works, which appeared well constructed, Smith found them deserted, but fires were still burning with rations half-cooked. He deployed his command, sending the Second Brigade pickets forward to guard the front toward Warwick Courthouse, the First (Hancock's) Brigade pickets to the right toward Big Bethel, and the Third (Davidson's) Brigade pickets to the left to Deep Creek. On the morning of the fifth, the division proceeded in the direction of Williamsburg with the Seventh Maine deployed as skirmishers to protect the front, the Second Brigade watching the road to Deep Creek, the Third Brigade in the center, and the First Brigade watching the right. Rain began about 7:00 a.m. and continued pouring in torrents, rendering the roads nearly impassable.[4]

On arriving at Warwick Courthouse, Smith pushed the Third Brigade across the stream with Captain Charles Wheeler's battery while he collected the remainder of the division in the open field on the opposite side of the creek. After resting for forty-five minutes, the troops proceeded, but the crude roads slowed progress. After two miles, the Lee's Mill forts came into sight. Smith deployed Davidson's brigade out of sight along the edge of the woods, with orders to hold the front. Davidson formed his regiments rapidly in line under fire of the enemy's shell and canister. Wheeler's battery tried to reply to the enemy's fire. The Confederate fire from forts on the Federal right forced Smith, however, to withdraw the battery out of action and place two guns to command the road out of sight. He then directed Hancock's brigade to cover the right flank with the Fifth Wisconsin covering another road to the right of Lee's Mill. Smith brought the Second Brigade up in reserve about halfway through the woods. These positions were held until April 7.[5]

On the night of April 5, the division camped in the swamp without tents, and many soldiers were without food. Some men built wooden platforms to elevate themselves from the water. Smith bivouacked near the line of battle, making his bed at the foot of a pine tree with nothing but his overcoat for shelter. He made it a habit of sleeping at the very front.[6]

On April 6, Smith ordered Hancock to send two regiments on a reconnaissance from the division camp at Warwick Courthouse to the enemy defenses on Warwick Creek. If a suitable place could be found for an assault, Hancock was to send word to Smith, who would bring the other two brigades to reinforce him. Smith did not tell Keyes because he believed that Keyes avoided responsibility. Smith only told Keyes of his plan until after the reconnaissance was in progress. Keyes, however, limited the action to only a reconnaissance by showing Smith a circular he had just received that prohibited any offensive operations until the line had been thoroughly examined by the engineers. Smith informed Hancock of the change. While the circular had come from McClellan, it was actually instigated by Keyes. The Fourth Corps commander was afraid of being repulsed in an attack and used unreliable sources to report to McClellan that the Confederates were in great strength in his front.[7]

Hancock's men had found the enemy in possession of the whole length of the creek. His skirmishers met the enemy's pickets at every point on the Federal side of the river and drove them to it, and to several places across from it. In each case, Confederate earthworks were discovered, and all, with one exception, had artillery in them. By damming the creek at different points, the Confederates had made the stream unfordable. The banks of the stream on the Confederate side appeared generally higher than those on the Federal side. But in one case, at some chimneys in an open field, the ground on the Union side was higher than the Confederate battery opposite it. This battery had only one gun, but there was evidence that another, having two additional guns, existed behind this one and was sheltered by the woods. Smith believed, nevertheless, that the Federal position at Burnt Chimneys gave his men the ability to break the Confederate Yorktown line across the creek. Smith mentioned his plans and actions afterwards to McClellan, who consoled Smith by saying, "Had you moved and won, it would have made you a major-general."[8]

On the evening of April 7, Smith moved the First and Second Brigades, together with the batteries, to the vicinity of the Yorktown Road, which extended from Warwick Courthouse to the Four Corners. The Second Brigade was on the right, thrown forward on the crossroads guarding the road to Lee's Mill. The Third Brigade was placed on the left of the division, while the First Brigade was placed in the center covering the ground between the other two brigades. On the ninth, the Sixth Maine, assisted by engineer officer Lieutenant Cyrus B. Comstock, made a reconnaissance of the one-gun battery first observed by the Hancock reconnaissance three days earlier. There was a brisk skirmish with the enemy in which one Union man was killed and at least ten of the enemy were killed or wounded.[9]

The result of the various reconnaissances, made under the immediate direction of Smith, led to the belief that the weakest point of the enemy's line near Lee's Mill was at a place called Dam No. 1 covered by a one-gun battery. It was decided to push a strong reconnaissance across Warwick Creek to silence the enemy's fire and ascertain the actual strength of the position. On April 15, McClellan ordered Smith to advance the next morning to stop the work being carried on by the enemy near and in the rear of the one-gun battery. He suggested that the directed fire of sharpshooters placed at the edge of the stream and four to six guns positioned at intervals in front of the enemy earthworks would stop the activities of the Confederate working parties. If the enemy were driven away, Smith was to cautiously advance a few skirmishers across the dam to penetrate the woods and ascertain whether there was a place for a foothold. While the chief object of the movement was to force the enemy to discontinue its work in strengthening its batteries, silence its fire, and gain control of Dam No. 1, an additional objective was to "take advantage after that of any opportunity that may offer itself to push the advantage."[10]

When Smith began his operations at Lee's Mill on April 16, he was directed by McClellan to be prepared to support the reconnoitering party with a real attack. Smith had been anxious for some time to test the enemy lines with an assault by part or all of his division, but he had been blocked in his efforts by Keyes, who failed to see any proper place for a general assault. Now, Smith finally had his chance, if the opportunity occurred, to break the Confederate lines.[11]

In accordance with McClellan's instructions, Smith proceeded to reconnoiter the one-gun battery and the works in its vicinity. Smith posted Captain Mott's battery on the right of the road leading from Yorktown to Lee's Mill. He sent the Fourth Vermont to the right through some pines, with instructions to open fire if they saw working parties, and the Third Vermont to the left with the same instructions. The remaining three regiments of Brooks' brigade were held in reserve. Hancock's brigade was instructed to hold the road from the Four Corners to Lee's Mill, posting two batteries in the vicinity of Mrs. Curtis's House. Davidson's brigade was placed, with one battery, at the Four Corners.[12]

On the infantry opening fire, the enemy replied with shell. Smith directed Mott to open fire with his battery. Mott's range was about 1,100 yards and his fire was very accurate. The enemy replied with shrapnel and shell, which burst all around. One shell exploded against the wheel of one of the guns, killing three men and wounding more. Smith was next to the battery at the time but never flinched. He stood watching the effect of the Federal fire upon the enemy's fort as cool and collected as though he were reviewing the division. Not until the six guns had succeeded in silencing the Confederate guns after about an hour's brisk firing on their works did Smith move to the rear. Before he left, he ascertained from personal observation that the gun in the angle of the upper work had been replaced by a wooden gun, and that scarcely anyone was visible above the parapet.[13]

About noon, McClellan arrived on the field. Deeming Smith's position as important, he ordered Smith to prepare to put the whole division into this position. Smith directed Hancock's brigade to move up in support and replaced that brigade's vacated position with Davidson's brigade. The rest of the Vermont Brigade was pushed forward into the woods on the flanks. While Smith, McClellan, and Keyes were discussing the operations, Lieutenant E.M. Noyes (of Brooks' staff) reported to the generals. Noyes had made a daring reconnaissance by crossing the stream below the dam and got within twenty-five yards of the enemy's work. He found the stream to be about waist deep. Wagons were also seen about this time in the rear of the works, as if removing stores. Smith obtained permission to place as many guns as he could on the crest of the opening, about five hundred paces from the Confederate advanced works. Under cover of these guns, skirmishers would cross the creek below and at the dam to ascertain if the works had been sufficiently denuded to enable a column to affect a new lodgment.

At about 3:00 p.m., Smith got eighteen guns under Captain Romeyn B. Ayres in position about five hundred yards from the works. Smith opened fire, and for some time, the enemy responded emphatically. He stayed at Ayres' side during the entire engagement and remained under fire, although his staff frequently urged him not to expose himself. At length their fire slackened. He ordered four companies of the Third Vermont to cross the creek and test the strength of the enemy. With slight opposition, these companies crossed the creek and gained possession of both the rifle pits in front of the enemy's right and of an earthwork three hundred yards in rear of the pits. Moreover, about half a dozen of the men actually penetrated the work itself, driving out quite a number of the enemy by means of lusty yells alone. (Most of the Vermonters' ammunition had gotten wet and was therefore useless when they crossed the stream.) Unfortunately, instead of giving the agreed upon signal of waving a white flag to show possession of the works, a messenger was sent back who failed to reach either Brooks or Smith. Smith's ability to read the situation was also impaired by the effects of two serious falls from his horse during the engagement. These left him partially dazed for the remainder of the fight. Consequently, at the time, he did not realize the advantage his Vermonters had obtained. The ammunition failing, and with no reinforcements reaching them, these companies were ordered back to the Federal side of the stream. They had held the enemy's rifle pits for about forty minutes.[14]

As soon as the practicability of crossing the stream was demonstrated, a section of artillery was ordered to the right to enfilade the rifle pits covering the enemy's right. At 5:00 p.m., under artillery fire, Smith ordered another authorized reconnaissance. Three companies of the Fourth Vermont moved along the abatis in front of the water toward the end of the dam with the view of crossing on the dam. The Sixth Vermont was ordered to act in concert with this movement by throwing four companies across the stream below the dam. As the artillery opened, the three companies of the Fourth advanced toward the end of the dam, and the four companies of the Sixth dashed into and across the stream. These movements caused the enemy to display its strength and reinforcements by opening a terrific fire of musketry from their rifle pits. On seeing this, Smith sent an aide to order the movement of the Fourth suspended just as they reached the end of the dam. The commander of the Sixth, seeing that the intense cross-fire caused heavy casualties among his men, and that the concerted action had been suspended, gave orders to withdraw. Smith met Hancock near sunset in the batteries of artillery and told Hancock that the division had accomplished everything that he desired during the

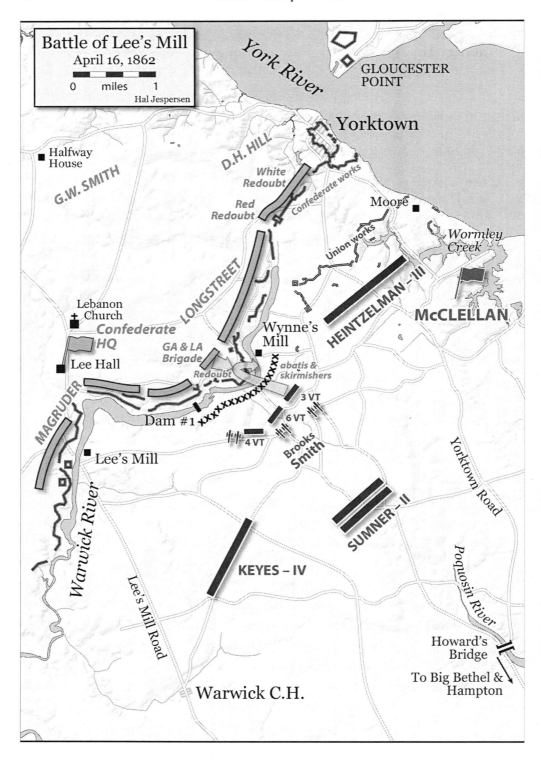

Battle of Lee's Mill, April 16, 1862.

day. Moreover, Smith later reported that his men had been gallant under fire and steady and ready to obey orders throughout the engagement.[15]

The army commander was initially pleased with Smith's operations at Lee's Mill. During the battle, he wired Mrs. Smith that Baldy was well and that her husband had most gallantly and skillfully gained a great military advantage. The commander wrote to Stanton again praising Smith for his silencing of the one-gun battery and urging Smith's immediate confirmation by the Senate as brigadier-general of volunteers. Stanton replied, "Good for the first lick! Hurrah for Smith and the one-gun battery!"[16] He also told McClellan that he requested Smith's confirmation. McClellan believed all the chief objects of the operation were fully and handsomely accomplished. The dense forest came up to the very edge of the stream on the enemy's side, effectually concealing everything from view and completely covering the Confederate infantry. McClellan supported Smith's orders to cross the skirmishers to ascertain the real state of affairs on the enemy's side, since McClellan believed there was no other way of obtaining the information. The loss sustained in accomplishing this was regretted but was considered small in comparison with the importance of the object in view.[17]

During the night, Smith ordered three strong breastworks thrown up: one on the right for four guns, within three hundred yards of the enemy; one on the left, with eight embrasures; and one in the center, for four guns, each within five hundred yards' range. Smith, concerned for his wounded Vermonters, asked McClellan after the battle if a flag of truce could be sent so that medical assistance could be rendered to wounded Vermonters lying on the Confederate side of the river. A flag of truce was not approved until the afternoon of April 18, and then to bury the dead. The position occupied by Smith enabled the Federals to prevent the enemy from working on its entrenchments and from renewing their artillery fire. The Confederates tried to disrupt this situation by two early morning attacks on Smith's division on April 18. Their attempts to carry his guns were thoroughly repulsed each time; some prisoners were captured.[18]

Smith attempted to locate the enemy in his front. The next day, he ordered Davidson's brigade out on a reconnaissance of the front to ascertain if the enemy had any force or rifle pits on the Federal side of the creek. If so, he was to drive the enemy over the stream. Davidson's brigade pushed to about four hundred yards from the creek without finding any significant enemy force or pits. The sounds of the enemy working could be heard, but Davidson decided not to challenge them because the ground was thoroughly protected by their artillery. Four days later, there was another sharp skirmish between Smith's men and the enemy—the result was a similar repulse of the Confederates.[19]

Smith's actions at Lee's Mill had been sustained by his army commander. Smith had hoped that the operation would have offered him the opportunity to commit his division to a grand assault at the weakest point of the Confederate line. He believed this would have broken the line and caused a general Confederate withdrawal. He was not permitted to expand the operation because of McClellan's orders that prohibited inducing a general engagement. After the war, Smith faulted himself for engaging so many soldiers during this operation. But, having made the engagement and having gained a foothold, he believed he should have committed his entire force to press his advantage to score the victory. One Confederate general and postwar writer also agreed with Smith's assessment that a stronger attack would have been successful. Edward Porter Alexander states, "Had the assault been made with a larger force, a lodgment could probably have been made."[20] Comte de Paris Louis Philippe and John C. Ropes both believed the greater enterprise Smith had hoped for "would have been rewarded by a striking success."[21]

But Smith was not alone with second thoughts about the Lee's Mill action at the time. Brooks wrote his father on April 22 that "the affair had no great object and no great effect. We were ordered down to stop the enemy in his works, that he had commenced in our front. This was soon accomplished but we got engaged a little beyond this, in something we did not exactly finish."[22] The only satisfaction Brooks derived from the action was the knowledge that his men acted coolly in all circumstances and could be relied upon for heavy fighting. Keyes also believed that Smith's use of the Vermont regiments in an attempt to break enemy lines and cross them through the creek had a disastrous result. Even McClellan had written home on April 18, before he knew all the details of the operations, that he considered most of the loss of nearly two hundred soldiers as "uselessly incurred."[23]

The failure of the assaults raised questions in the minds of some congressmen. Republican Congressman Justin Morrill of Vermont sought information regarding the cause of the heavy casualties incurred by his fellow Vermonters. A respected gentleman from New York, H.L. Suydam, told Morrill that he had seen and spoken with Smith during the action and believed Smith was drunk. Suydam also claimed that Baldy had fallen off his horse twice during the battle. On April 22, Morrill offered a resolution requesting the President remove any army officer who was habitually intoxicated. No officer's name was included in the resolution, but it pointed to Smith by alluding to the commander of the Lee's Mill operation.[24]

The newspapers reported Morrill's charges and almost at once recognized them as referring to Smith. However, the newspapers almost in one voice pronounced Morrill's charges against Smith unfounded.[25] The major Republican papers, the *New York Times* and *New York Tribune*, supported the character and skill of Smith. On April 23, 1862, the *Tribune* correspondent defended the Lee's Mill efforts to silence the enemy fire and gain knowledge of the enemy works. He wrote that the objects were "accomplished with eminent success."[26] The next day, the correspondent cited the protracted conference of Smith with his superiors to support his claim of the unlikelihood of Smith's drunkenness. To even further illustrate Smith's good behavior, the correspondent published a letter of Smith to his family dated April 17. The letter read, in part, "I had a severe fall from my horse going at a very fast gait and was stunned and jarred so that I am still lame. A second fall she gave me, while Ayres was playing on the works with 18 pieces of artillery. Without any warning, she reared with me, and the girth breaking. Of course, I went down."[27] The correspondent finally cited a letter from the general's aide in which he wrote, "Everybody behaved splendidly, except the General's horse."[28]

On April 25 and 26, the *Times* correspondents recounted that several officers and friends of Smith visited Morrill to tell the congressman that Smith had not been the slightest degree intoxicated during the engagement at Lee's Mill. On April 27, the *Tribune* correspondent gave an eyewitness account of the battle to show Smith's skill and bravery. While Mott's battery was under fire, causing the loss of seven men, Smith had shared the battery's danger and had tempered "by cool words the impetuosity of the artillerists, and by his good judgment contributing not a little to the work of silencing the enemy's battery."[29] Smith, except when he conferred with Keyes and McClellan from 10:30 a.m. to 3:00 p.m., was in advance of his batteries at "so close a range that musket balls fell in showers and where every man was in peril." The correspondent corroborated

Smith's account of the falls from his horse. The first fall was caused by the horse tripping over uneven ground. The correspondent saw Smith almost the whole day and stated the charge of intoxication was "entirely groundless." On May 2, the *Times* called on Morrill to retract his charge in the face of the baselessness of his story.[30]

While the Democratic newspapers also condemned Morrill's charges as slanderous, they saw the charges as a means of political persecution of Smith, one of McClellan's friends. On April 24, the *Philadelphia Daily Evening Bulletin* defended Smith by stating, "A brilliant military career and a spotless private character are first attacked in the great legislative assembly of the nation, and that on no better authority than camp-gossip, or the fiction of political tricksters…. The attacks on General William F. Smith come from the same class of politicians that have been attacking General McClellan." The *Burlington, Vermont Sentinel* asserted that Smith was assailed by abolitionists because "he was democrat and bitterly hostile to the emancipation schemes of the abolition wing of the republican party," for which they "seem determined to fight him to the bitter end."[31]

The newspapers were not alone in their condemnation of Morrill's charges. On April 24, McClellan wrote to Smith, promising to defend him against the accusations. The following day, McClellan wrote to Lincoln that the allegations against Smith were untrue. McClellan had been with Smith most of the time from noon to 5:00 p.m. During that time, Smith was severely injured twice by his horse: the first time when the horse ran into a quicksand hole and threw Smith and the second time when the girth broke. McClellan saw Smith just before and after the first fall and noted nothing that indicated Smith was intoxicated. He hoped Lincoln would clear up the matter involving a man whom he described as "one of the best commanders I have in this army." The next day, McClellan wrote Baldy's wife reassuring her that the charges were entirely erroneous and that he had written Lincoln to clear her husband of all related allegations.[32]

On April 26, two other generals wrote Smith sustaining his innocence. Keyes wrote his Second Division commander that the charges were entirely groundless. He had met with Smith during the battle for forty-five minutes and had found him entirely sober. Brooks wrote to Smith stating that he was with him during the battle and collaborated Smith's account of the horse accidents. Brooks had been under Smith since October and knew him never to be drunk.[33] On April 28, a court of inquiry was held at Smith's request to investigate Morrill's charge. The *Times* correspondent found the feeling pervading the army on this subject to be one of intense indignation. From the testimony of a great number of officers, there was not the slightest doubt that the whole story was "a most wanton and outrageous slander." Captain Ayres, General Davidson, as well as two or three of Smith's aides who were with him at the time, testified on the general's behalf.[34]

Morrill, faced with a growing storm of criticism because of his charges, sought information to justify his claims. H.L. Suydam wrote Morrill on April 23 recounting his charges that "General Smith was too much under the influence of liquor to command a devoted band of volunteers." C.H. Chapman wrote Morrill that Major Oscar S. Tuttle of the Sixth Vermont told his brother that Smith was a notorious drunk and had been drunk all winter at Camp Griffin. Samuel Thompson, a drum major in the Fourth Vermont, and Erastus Tarbell, a private in the Third Vermont, also stated in letters that Smith had been drunk at Camp Griffin. Nonetheless, despite his efforts, Morrill had no evidence that Smith was drunk at Lee's Mill except for Suydam's testimony. This paled in significance to the dozens of eyewitnesses and participants of the battle who maintained Smith had been sober and courageous during the battle.[35]

Morrill received three letters rejecting his claims. Lieutenant Colonel L.A. Grant of the Fifth Vermont wrote that the charge was entirely false, stating, "There is no doubt of its falsity and great injustice is being done Genl. Smith."[36] James McKean wrote to Morrill that Smith's assistant adjutant general, Captain Currie, told him the charges were without foundation. Finally, on April 30, Smith wrote Morrill a blistering letter charging Morrill with slander: "It is now my turn to speak, and here, face to face with a brave foe, I turn back to you, an assassin, and you *must* prove your charge against me, or make your retraction as public as the libel."[37]

Morrill renewed the matter of Smith's drunkenness in the House of Representatives on May 2. He began by explaining that he proposed his resolution based on the testimony of Suydam, for whom Republican Congressman Jacob Chamberlain of New York had vouched. Morrill then submitted Suydam's letter of April 23 and Smith's letter of April 30 to the congressman. Morrill stated that while he acted properly in making the resolution, he felt to do justice to the case he would put forward a testimonial submitted by all the regimental commanders, four lieutenant colonels, and three majors of the Vermont Brigade that flatly contradicted Suydam's letter. The testimonial stated that the charge that Smith was drunk at Lee's Mill was unequivocally false, that the information that the charge was "based upon was given by some person or persons who were actuated by a willfully malicious and unworthy motive to defame the service of the United States," and that Smith justly deserved the confirmation of his appointment as brigadier-general of volunteers. The Vermont Brigade officers concluded their memorial by stating that it had been written without Smith's knowledge and with deep confidence in their division commander. After submitting this, Morrill said he had no further comment. Democratic Congressman Charles Biddle of Pennsylvania stated that he had been told by one of McClellan's aides that he observed Smith during the battle and that the charge of drunkenness was utterly unfounded. Biddle deeply regretted the injustice done to Smith. Morrill defended himself by saying that he made no charge against Smith but simply submitted evidence pro and con in the case. Biddle stated that he interpreted this as an entire retraction of the charge.[38]

Democratic Congressmen Daniel Voorhees of Indiana and William Richardson of Illinois supported Biddle's rejection of Morrill's charges. Voorhees had conferred at length with Colonel Thomas M. Key, McClellan's judge advocate, and stated that Key had been with Smith during the battle and found him sober throughout. Key observed that Smith's falls came from his unruly horse. Key emphatically repelled the charge made by Morrill. Voorhees hoped that such "injurious and unfounded accusations" would not be repeated in the House. Richardson commented "that our armies would do better and gain more and greater victories if the 'riot act' could be read, and both Houses of Congress dispersed to their homes at the very earliest possible day."[39]

The matter was finally put before the Senate Committee of Military Affairs. On May 6, Senators Jacob M. Howard of Michigan, Milton S. Latham of California, Henry M. Rice of Minnesota, and James W. Nesmith of Oregon travelled to Yorktown to investigate the charges against Smith. After their investigation, they were entirely satisfied that the imputations were without the slightest foundation. In their report of May 13, 1862, Howard, speaking for the committee, stated that all the witnesses concurred in the opinion that Smith was among the first officers of his rank, always ready and able to perform promptly any duty assigned him. The Committee fully and unequivocally acquitted "all officers and all others engaged in the taking of Yorktown from the charge, as the evidence before them was highly in favor of the gallantry and meritorious conduct of all engaged in reducing that strongly fortified place."[40]

While faced with Morrill's charges about Lee's Mill, Smith remained active in command of his division. On April 25 and 26, his artillery under Ayres destroyed a parapet of sandbags the enemy had erected on their works to screen their sharpshooters. The sharpshooters remained a serious problem. They effectively continued to cut down Smith's pickets in front of Hancock's and Davidson's brigades. The Federal pickets were stationed in open woods, while the Confederates were covered by a heavy undergrowth thirty or forty paces away. Smith concluded that an expedition to clear the area of sharpshooters was needed. At 6:00 in the morning on April 29, Smith ordered Hancock to advance three regiments of his brigade and one of Davidson's to cover a strong working party in felling trees. They were clearing out the undergrowth for a considerable distance in front of the division picket line and making defenses of logs for the pickets. While a portion of his force covered the pioneers in their work, Hancock advanced the Sixth Maine toward the creek. The enemy's pickets and scouts were soon driven back. The Sixth pushed up to the creek on their right and within one hundred yards of the stream on their left. Between their left and the stream, the Confederates had thrown up a breastwork of logs. Hancock examined the position and found that the work was thoroughly covered by the Confederate works on the other side of the river. He decided not to assault this breastwork unless he could also attack the works on the opposite side of the river. His orders did not include such a major operation. Smith sent word, upon Hancock's inquiry, that the assault on the breastwork should not be made.[41]

Hancock held his position at about forty paces in front of the Confederate breastwork for an hour. The Confederates then rose up with the intent of charging Hancock's skirmishers. At this moment, a deadly and well-directed volley from Hancock's skirmishers caused the enemy to subside with evident loss. By 2:00 in the afternoon, the pioneer work was substantially completed along the whole front of Davidson's and Hancock's brigades. Hancock ordered the troops slowly withdrawn with the skirmishers of the Sixth Maine bringing up the rear.[42]

In late April, Smith's division also faced the serious challenge of the rapid increase in sickness. Remittent fever, diarrhea, and dysentery were the predominant illnesses. Hancock's brigade was encamped in low, wet ground, and the heavy rains kept much of camp under water. In addition, medicines and appliances to comfort the sick were slow in arriving. Hard work and exposure also took their toll on the men. Davidson, having been disabled by the strain, was granted a leave by Keyes. Smith took direct command of Davidson's brigade on April 28 and transferred temporary command to Hancock on May 2. Keyes reported the poor health of Smith's division to the army commander.[43]

Soon after daylight, on the morning of May 4, Hancock rode up to Smith, bringing two escaped slaves who informed Smith that the works in front of the division had been evacuated. At about 5:30 a.m., Lieutenant George A. Custer and Captain Theodore Read, Brooks' adjutant, crossed the dam and took possession of the works. The Fifth Vermont being near at hand, Smith ordered it forward at once to occupy the works.[44]

Work was immediately commenced on the dam to make it passable for artillery and cavalry. At about 7:00 a.m., Smith ordered a cavalry squadron pushed across the dam to reconnoiter. Shortly thereafter, Captain William P. Chambliss, commander the squadron, reported that he had come up against the rear guard of the enemy, which consisted of a large force of cavalry and a force of infantry. Chambliss was ordered to retire, as Smith was then in no condition to support him. This information was telegraphed to McClellan and Keyes. About 8:00 a.m., Smith's artillery began to cross the dam. Smith immediately ordered a battery and Hancock's brigade forward to support the cavalry. After 11:30 a.m., Smith made two reconnaissances, one to ascertain if he could turn the head of Skiff Creek, and the other to find a practicable route to the Yorktown Road since the road directly in front of Smith was impassable. Both of these reconnaissances were successful.[45]

Between 2:00 and 3:00 in the afternoon, Brigadier General Edwin Sumner, Keyes' immediate superior, came up and ordered the division forward on the Yorktown and Williamsburg Road. The order to advance upon the enemy lines was given at 6:30 p.m. Hancock's brigade, preceded by its skirmishers, led in line of battle and Brooks' brigade followed in double column. Smith took personal command of the two right regiments; Hancock took command of the two on the left. Before the first line got deeply into the woods, Smith took the responsibility of halting the third line and ordered it to remain in support of the artillery and as a reserve for the other troops. Finding it impossible to cross through the woods in front, Smith endeavored to find Sumner to get authority to halt the troops. Failing in that, he sent an aide to Hancock to order a halt.[46]

About 8:00 p.m., while endeavoring to get the troops of the right wing into order, Smith heard from Hancock. The Second Brigade commander had taken responsibility for halting the left wing upon finding that it was impossible to get through the woods and keep his formation because of the loss of daylight and the very dense and tangled undergrowth. The right wing was immediately ordered to bivouac in the open field where it then found itself.[47]

The next day would begin the first significant engagement of McClellan's peninsula campaign, the battle of Williamsburg. The main Federal assault was led by Brigadier General Joseph Hooker's division on the Union left against the Confederate Fort Magruder. Smith's division was placed on the Union right, away from this effort. Unfortunately, the success of Hooker's attack was limited because Smith's efforts to boldly strike the enemy in their left flank was frustrated by his superiors.[48]

At daylight, on May 5, it was raining hard. General Sumner ordered Smith to fall back to the edge of the woods to allow the troops to get their knapsacks and rations. Smith then proceeded to post the command in its new position, and while doing so learned that the enemy's works extended to the right as far as could be seen. Smith ordered Captain Charles Stewart to make a reconnaissance to the right of Fort Magruder, but he found no suitable point of attack.[49]

Stewart informed Baldy, however, that an African American man had told him that there was a road about three miles away which crossed a dam on the right and led to Williamsburg. Smith ordered Stewart to take an escort and investigate the accuracy of this report. A little after 10:00 in the morning, Captain Currie returned to Smith from Stewart and reported that a redoubt had been found apparently unoccupied, commanding a dam over which it was practicable for artillery to cross. This report was immediately given to Sumner, who insisted on seeing Stewart. Stewart confirmed his previous report. Smith received permission to order a brigade forward to the opposite side of the creek to take the enemy's work that commanded the dam. Hancock was immediately detached for that purpose. Based upon the information of Stewart's reconnaissance, Smith pointed out to Sumner that with capturing the redoubts and using the good road into Williamsburg that had been found behind the fort, his division could shake the enemy out of its position and perhaps succeed in cutting off its retreat. But Sumner opposed Smith's use of his other two brigades in this flanking movement. Nevertheless, Smith subsequently authorized Hancock to advance further if he thought any advantage could be obtained without endangering his command and to request reinforcements from Smith if he needed them. Smith believed that if Hancock won such an important advantage, the corps commanders present would change the point of attack to the extreme Confederate left.[50]

Hancock accordingly detailed three regiments from his brigade and two from Davidson's brigade, which was under his temporary command, and a six-gun battery under Lieutenant Andrew Cowan. Hancock proceeded to his objective. The dam at this work was about seventy-five yards in length, the breast of it forming the roadway across the creek. Hancock crossed the dam and placed his artillery, at short range, on the crest of the hill in front of the enemy's fort. He pushed his skirmishers up the right and left sides of the road; these were followed by a column of assault which entered the fort. Finding the fort unoccupied and being in possession of it, Hancock left a garrison of three companies from the Thirty-Third New York to protect his rear. At noon, Hancock sent a message to Keyes and Smith that the position at Cub Creek Dam had been occupied and asked Smith to send a brigade of infantry to secure his rear from assault from the woods on his right and left.[51]

General Smith replied that he would immediately send four regiments of infantry and a battery of artillery. Hancock accordingly advanced and quietly took possession of the next redoubt. Feeling that his rear and right flank would be protected by the reinforcements, Hancock determined to advance his line sufficiently beyond the redoubt to drive the enemy out of the two nearest works in his front and to make a diversion in favor of Hooker's command, which was engaged with the Confederates directly in front of Fort Magruder. Captain Charles C. Wheeler's battery of four guns having joined Hancock at this time, the artillery was advanced about six hundred yards in front of the redoubt. The infantry was then all ordered to lie down, while the battery was directed to open fire upon the Confederate-occupied redoubts in front preparatory to an assault, when the expected reinforcements arrived.[52]

At this time, the enemy lined the parapets of the two redoubts with infantry and delivered their fire; they immediately directed artillery upon Hancock's men. Hancock's batteries replied with precision and threw shells into both redoubts. This shelling, combined with the fire of his skirmishers, finally drove the Confederates out of their works. The advanced Federal skirmishers killed many of the enemy as they emerged from the gorges on the right side of the works. There was now no apparent obstacle to prevent Hancock from taking possession of these redoubts once reinforcements arrived. At this juncture, Hancock received word from Sumner that he must fall back to his first position. Knowing Smith's disposition to strengthen him and to make a movement in his direction, Hancock sent a message through Lieutenant Cyrus R. Crane to Smith that reinforcements were needed.[53]

During Hancock's maneuvers, Smith and the rest of his division were held in reserve by Sumner. The only action this portion of the division saw came about noon. Four pieces of Captain Mott's battery were ordered into position in front of the Vermont Brigade, more to annoy and distract the enemy than to accomplish any permanent good. The objective apparently was attained. After Hancock's first requested reinforcements from Smith, Baldy was ordered to detach a brigade from the division to support Hooker.

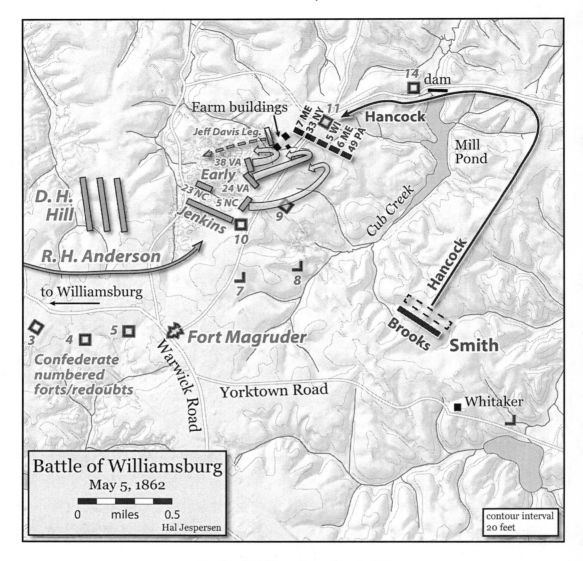

Battle of Williamsburg, May 5, 1862.

General Brooks' brigade was selected for this purpose, but Smith went back to contest the breaking up of his command and to ask permission to go with the two remaining brigades of the division to reinforce Hancock. Permission was granted, and the remainder of the division was being drawn out on the road when Smith received orders not to proceed, but to place his troops in a position to resist an attack on the ground then occupied. This was done, but later in the day, Smith again urged that he might be allowed to proceed to support Hancock. He felt this would be the quickest way of terminating the attack upon the left. Knowing what was occurring on the Federal left and feeling that the army was being defeated without reason, Smith sent two aides to McClellan. They conveyed Smith's belief that if McClellan did not wish his army to be beaten by the enemy's rear guard, he had better come and take command.[54]

Crane now presented Smith with Hancock's second request for reinforcements.

Smith told Crane to tell Hancock, "I have wanted and have tried to re-enforce him, but that General Sumner has positively forbidden to allow any re-enforcements to be sent to him until more troops come up from the rear." Crane gave Hancock the message at about 3:30 p.m.[55]

Hancock then sent Lieutenant Francis U. Farquhar to Sumner to describe his brigade's position and to show the disadvantage of falling back. He did state that he would obey the order to fall back if no answer should arrive after a reasonable time had elapsed. In order to furnish all the assistance possible, Hancock's battery threw percussion shells into Fort Magruder and caissons passing into the fort. This annoyed the enemy so much that they finally brought out one or two pieces of artillery, but after an artillery duel, the Confederate guns ceased fire. Affairs remained in this position, and Farquhar had not returned by 4:20 p.m. Hancock addressed a written communication to Smith stating that he would wait a reasonable time to get an answer from Sumner before falling back.[56]

Smith met Farquhar and sent him to Sumner with a renewed request to reinforce Hancock. Permission was again granted, and again the troops were ordered to advance down the road to reinforce Hancock. General Brooks, in command of the Vermont Brigade, led the reinforcements. He got as far as the Cub Dam when Sumner ordered the reinforcements to return to their former position to resist an attack. Brooks swore vigorously at being sent back from the right—where they were most wanted—to the center where they were not needed at all, but he had to obey this order. Smith, exasperated by Sumner's lack of tactical acumen, replied to Hancock's 4:20 dispatch that "in regard to falling back or occupying the position you could exercise your discretion, and act without reference to reinforcements."[57] Smith also sent a still more pressing dispatch to McClellan to come, for he supposed then that his orders and promises of reinforcements would cause Hancock to be captured, in which case Smith would be tried for disobedience of orders.[58]

Not having received reinforcements, Hancock decided to withdraw at 5:10 p.m. As he was giving orders to fall back and occupy the crest on which the redoubt was situated, Hancock observed that the Confederates were placing infantry into the redoubts on his front and that his skirmishers were firing on them. Hancock immediately dispatched another staff officer to Smith to notify him of the state of affairs. The Southern forces persisted in their attempts to form their lines in preparation to charge his artillery. Hancock ordered some shells be thrown into the enemy, and then directed the artillery to retire rapidly, piece by piece, to his second line. Seeing Confederate Brigadier General Jubal Early's brigade break through the woods in front of the right flank of his advance line, Hancock ordered the two regiments on the left of the battery to fall back in line of battle to the crest on the left of the redoubt.[59]

The Sixth Maine and Forty-Ninth Pennsylvania, which were on the left of the battery, retreated steadily until they came to the crest forming a perfect line. The Fifth Wisconsin, which was on the right of the battery, then commenced retiring in the direction of the redoubt, disputing the ground inch by inch and being assisted somewhat by the artillery from the crest. Hancock secured his right flank with the Seventh Maine and Thirty-Third New York and some artillery. Having sufficient infantry to line the whole crest, Hancock ordered the artillery back to a third position on the plain between himself and the dam. He then threw two companies in the woods on the left to give him notice of the approach of the enemy from that direction. By the time Hancock had protected his flanks and lined his men behind the crest in line of battle, the advance of Early's two lead regiments, the Twenty-Fourth Virginia and the Fifth North Carolina, were under the crest and within thirty paces of his command. Hancock ordered a forward movement to the crest. The whole line advanced cheering, and on arriving there, delivered two volleys. The order was then given to charge down the slope, and with reiterated cheers, the whole command advanced in line of battle. A few of the Confederates were bayoneted; the remainder then broke and fled. Lacking protection in his rear and expecting an assault from that quarter at any moment, Hancock ordered a halt at the foot of the slope and delivered a terrible fire along the whole line, expending from fifteen to twenty rounds. The plunging fire from the redoubt, the direct fire from the right, and the oblique fire from the left were so destructive that apparently no Confederate who had advanced within five hundred yards of the Federal line left the ground unhurt. The Confederates were completely routed and dispersed. Early's brigade lost 508 men in its failed assault; Hancock's loss was only 100 soldiers.[60]

The second line of Confederates, yet in position on the front, seemed to halt paralyzed. When this advance moved, Hancock, having sent for a section of artillery, directed a few shells to be thrown at them, causing them to disappear. Now, late in the evening and no reinforcements in sight, Hancock could not, with prudence, pursue the retreating enemy. He held his position, believing it to be the best ground should the enemy renew the contest. For six hundred yards in front of the line, the whole field was strewn with the enemy's dead and wounded.[61]

About 5:00 p.m., shortly before the Confederate attack, McClellan arrived on the field where Smith was positioned. McClellan overruled Sumner's decision against further movements and permitted Smith to reinforce Hancock. Smith's aide, Captain Currie, overtook the rear guard of Brooks' brigade on its return trip and convinced the Third Vermont to march to aid Hancock, who was at that time under the Confederate attack. Baldy rode ahead to meet with Hancock, but by the time he arrived, the enemy was repulsed. Smith announced that he was bringing up strong reinforcements. The Third Vermont arrived presently. Hancock posted these men on the right and rear. Brigadier General H.M. Naglee's brigade, under Smith's direction, then arrived and was followed by two regiments of Davidson's brigade, all of which Hancock posted, by Smith's orders, to meet any contingency. That night the troops bivouacked in the rain on the ground they had so handsomely won.[62]

Smith commended Hancock for his victory. Baldy's report noted Hancock's brilliant plan of battle and the coolness of its execution as well as his swift action of moving from the defense to the offense. While Smith praised Hancock for the flanking action, he considered Sumner's refusal to allow him to use his entire division to bring a clear-cut victory on the Confederate left as "a beastly exhibition of stupidity and ignorance."[63] As at Warwick River, orders from superior officers had kept Smith from fully using the apparent advantages that his insight had revealed but which Keyes or Sumner failed to see. Instead, they approved only mere reconnaissances or limited actions which could bring only limited results. Smith did not blame his army commander for Williamsburg. Both McClellan and Smith realized that had McClellan arrived on the field at 1:00 and approved Smith's plan for using his and Brigadier General Darius Couch's divisions to attack the Confederate left, the effect of such a movement would have been to cut off the retreat of the greater part of the troops engaged against Hooker. McClellan also endorsed Smith's view of Sumner. He wrote his wife that Sumner was a "greater fool than I had supposed."[64] He found "our troops in wrong positions, on the wrong side of the woods—no system of cooperation, no orders given—roads blocked up."[65]

Smith's command moved up the Peninsula and on May 11, 1862, rested near New Kent Courthouse; on the twelfth it marched to the Pamunkey River at Cumberland Landing. The command stayed at White House from the thirteenth to nineteenth and then moved to the left bank of the Chickahominy near New Bridge, ten miles northeast of Richmond. While there, the division was transferred from Keyes' corps to the new provisional Sixth Corps under Major General William B. Franklin.[66]

The change of commanders was significant for Smith. Baldy now had a commander who had been an old friend from their Lighthouse Service days and whose ability he deeply respected. During the time that Smith served under Franklin, they had the same headquarters, the same tent, and had common mess; there was never the slightest disagreement between them as to plans or details. They generally saw things the same way, and when they did not, Franklin was the senior officer, and in that way the matter was settled. Regarding his tenure under Franklin, Smith wrote to his daughter after the war, "Under such a man service was a pleasure and I thought of his reputation, in everything I did, as much as my own." Franklin also remembered his relationship with Smith as harmonious. He wrote to Baldy, "I recollect no occasions when we disagreed, or had any discussions of orders that I thought it proper to give, and to which you demurred." After the war, Franklin would also identify Baldy as one of his two "most intimate comrades in the service."[67]

About noon on May 23, Smith ordered Davidson to move his brigade and Wheeler's battery up to Mechanicsville and occupy that point to protect the rear of Brigadier

Brigadier General William F. Smith (seated, second from left) and staff and Captain Romeyn B. Ayres (seated, far left) at the Gaines' House (G.H. Houghton, Civil War Photograph Album, no. 47. Vermont Historical Society).

(From left) Brigadier Generals Winfield S. Hancock, William F. Smith, and John Newton (G.H. Houghton, Civil War Photograph Album, no. 46. Vermont Historical Society).

General George Stoneman's advance, which was to operate on the Virginia Central Railroad. Davidson moved his brigade and artillery across the stream, but with night coming on and knowing nothing of the approaches to the village or of the enemy occupying the place, Davidson determined to postpone further operations until the next morning. On advancing his pickets six hundred yards, they were fired upon by those of the enemy. At daybreak, Davidson attacked the village. The enemy opened with artillery and infantry fire. The enemy infantry was protected by houses, barns, trees, and hedges. Davidson advanced his battery of four pieces a section at a time. Finding it difficult to silence the enemy's guns with four pieces, Davidson sent back to Stoneman for a section of horse artillery. As soon as it arrived, Davidson pushed forward his whole line of skirmishers and his pieces to within between three hundred and four hundred yards of the village. Concentrating his fire, Davidson silenced the enemy pieces and drove the Confederates out of the houses. As soon as this was accomplished, the Seventy-Seventh New York was thrown into the village upon the heels of the retreating enemy, who in their flight left behind some of their knapsacks and the flag of the Eighth Georgia.[68]

After occupying the village, Davidson drove the Confederate skirmishers across the bridge over the Chickahominy on the Dispatch Road to Richmond and cut the nearest bay across the river. After the skirmish, the brigade encamped near the Hogan House on the Chickahominy and picketed the many-coursed swampy stream. On May 26, the brigade moved down the river five miles to Gaines' Farm and encamped there until June 5. The men were employed in doing picket duty and building corduroy roads and bridges.[69]

Meanwhile, McClellan's army was divided by the Chickahominy River. General

Joseph E. Johnston took advantage of this and attacked the Fourth Corps at Seven Pines on May 31. The next day, the Vermont Brigade was ordered to cross the river at New Bridge to assist in the successful Federal counterattack. High water in the river, however, interfered with the construction of the pontoon bridge. The brigade waited on the bank until 10:00 a.m., when they were ordered to return. The Sixth Vermont stayed to guard the bridge.[70]

On June 5, the return of Davidson's brigade reunited the division. It then crossed the river and moved up on the right bank to a hill near Golding's House about a mile north of Fair Oaks and half a mile south of the river. Facing a large increase of advancing enemy pickets in his front, Smith took every precaution to be ready for any emergency. Over two regiments were daily under arms from 3:30 a.m. until a half hour after broad daylight. Breastworks were constructed. The men worked on the night of the eighth at the redoubt so that it was in working order by the ninth. Smith's rifle pits and two epaulements for guns were completed on the ninth. Unfortunately, sickness caused by lack of sleep reduced the number placed under arms to one regiment per brigade. Wet clothes and the malaria from the swamps also increased illness among the men. Hundreds fell because of fevers, diarrhea, and scurvy.[71]

Smith was concerned about his men and their condition. He tried to eliminate any unnecessary alarm to or assignment for his men. When there was a minor reconnaissance in his front and he was ordered to offer reinforcements, Baldy requested in the future that he be given advance warning as to such needs. The order had led to a large portion of his command being exposed to inclement weather. He wanted to be able to judge the number and need for men in the future. One night, he asked his new corps commander to order the firing in his front to cease. Smith claimed, "The firing itself is utterly useless and only serves to excite the nerves and disturb the rest of the men of my division."[72] When on another occasion the army commander ordered Smith to furnish an additional force of 250 men, Smith requested the extra assignment be rescinded. He pointed out that six hundred of his men were on fatigue duty daily and that he had a party on the New Bridge. With picket guard and other duties, this meant nearly an entire brigade was daily at such work. Smith reported that his men had hardly any rest and that the additional duty would be "pretty severe on them."[73]

Smith was also concerned about the apparent apathy of the army commander in fraternizing with enemy pickets. Early in the Peninsula Campaign, Smith had given orders prohibiting conversations between his pickets and the enemy pickets. Without his knowledge, the pickets of Brigadier General Fitz John Porter had been permitted to meet with the enemy pickets to trade northern newspapers for southern ones. Smith gave orders to his pickets to fire upon both parties until McClellan explained the situation to Smith. Smith argued that Northern papers probably provided the Confederates with better information than the Richmond papers gave to the Federals. Moreover, Smith's main objection was that from the points where the pickets of both sides met to talk, the positions of all his troops and guns were plainly visible and the Confederates, in going out and coming back, took great pains to look at them.[74]

The Peninsula Campaign thus far had been one of both pride and frustration. Smith had proudly watched his men perform well on their advances. But Smith twice had seen opportunities won and lost—at Warwick River and again at Williamsburg. The problem of politics in the army also continued to bedevil him. But these difficulties would soon seem minor in comparison to what General Lee had in store for McClellan's army.

CHAPTER V

Shielding the Retreat

Smith's Division from the Seven Days to Harrison's Landing

By June 25, 1862, McClellan's army was before the Richmond defenses, but the army commander still felt the time was not right to make a major attack. He believed that General Lee's force numbered twice his own force. In fact, Lee's force counted some 101,000 troops while McClellan's force came to 105,800. McClellan also received reports that Major General Thomas J. "Stonewall" Jackson was about to strike his right and rear. Moreover, McClellan's forces were still divided with Porter's Fifth Corps all alone north of the Chickahominy River. McClellan could not remove the Fifth Corps to the south side of the river yet. The administration had still not revoked its order to the army commander to keep his right wing extended to the northeast of Richmond to link up with the left of McDowell's force, which was expected to move southward toward Richmond to reinforce McClellan's army. Consequently, the initiative passed to Lee, who took advantage of Porter's isolated position to strike the Union forces on the north side of the river. On June 26, the Confederate attack at Mechanicsville opened the Seven Days Battles.[1]

On the evening after the first day of battle, McClellan passed by the Sixth Corps headquarters on the way to Porter's corps. Generals Franklin and William F. Smith urged him to withdraw all the troops from the north bank of the Chickahominy, destroy the bridges, and leave the tired troops to watch the river while the forces south of the river attacked in force. Such a Union offensive could beat Lee's army there and capture Richmond before Lee could make the long detour by Mechanicsville and defend the Confederate capital. McClellan considered the generals' advice but ultimately rejected it. He was still convinced that he faced "great odds."[2]

Smith's major service in the campaign was to act as a rear guard to protect McClellan's change of base to Harrison's Landing. Smith's division also was responsible for thwarting several Confederate attempts to capture his position. On June 26, Smith's division held the extreme right of the line at Golding's Farm, picketing the wood behind Garnett's House. During the night, the division built a redoubt on the crest of the wheat field in its front. By daylight of the next morning, the redoubt was completed. The Confederates made no attempt to interrupt the work. Also, during the night of the twenty-sixth, Smith detailed a heavy working party, supported by a portion of the Second Brigade, to construct an epaulement for a large portion of the reserve artillery on Garnett Hill, in front of Smith's lines at Golding's. The labor proceeded quietly through the night, and by morning the men were sufficiently well covered to continue the work during the day.[3]

About 8:00 on the morning of the twenty-seventh, the Second Brigade support was relieved by the entire First Brigade. Six batteries were brought forward to Golding's Plain to prepare for an advance. The Confederate columns were soon seen forming on the Nine-Mile Road and behind Garnett's House. Smith began making dispositions to encounter the Confederates but was ordered to do nothing that would bring on a general engagement. To defend his division's constructed works, Smith ordered Hancock to fall back a few hundred yards into the woods on the left bank of the little creek behind him, keeping a strong picket in the rifle-pits. Artillery was placed in position on the high ground on the right bank of the creek to cover Hancock's left flank.[4]

Considerable maneuvering with the Confederate infantry occurred but no advance was made. About 10:30, the Confederates opened some three or four batteries from the crest of the hill near Garnett's. Smith's guns replied briskly, and after an hour the enemy fire slackened and ceased. Threatening demonstrations continued during the day. At about 6:30, artillery again opened a heavy fire on one of Smith's batteries, which replied and soon silenced the enemy fire. Meanwhile, Smith used his heavy guns against the Confederate columns attacking Porter's left flank at Gaines' Mill. The long range (two- and one-half miles) guns prevented great accuracy, but the Confederates were forced into the cover of the woods out of Smith's view. Serious loss was suffered at least by Brigadier General Roger A. Pryor's brigade of Longstreet's division. Porter later thanked Smith for his "splendid" artillery fire at Gaines' House.[5] Moreover, Brigadier General Daniel Butterfield reported that "too much credit cannot be given to the artillery practice of General Smith's command across the Chickahominy upon the overpowering masses of the enemy thrown on his left. The fire of Smith's artillery was deadly and precise and materially assisted in silencing an enemy battery planted in an orchard near Gaines' House about noon."[6]

Late in the evening, after sundown, the Confederate infantry from Garnett's House commenced an assault on Hancock's brigade. They forced back the Federal pickets rapidly and advanced to a little crest in the wheat field separating the two forces, about forty yards distant from Hancock's line. At this point, the Confederates fired. Hancock's men spiritedly replied and held their position. The Confederates, taking advantage of the crest, were partially sheltered from the Federal fire. The severe fire convinced them not to advance beyond the crest. The contest of musketry continued until long after dark, when the Confederates retired. A near exhaustion of cartridges and the danger of the lines becoming confused in the dark prevented Hancock's advance.[7]

During the action, the Second Brigade supported and assisted the First Brigade. Brooks took charge of the right of the Federal line, which included the Fourth Vermont. Brooks brought up the Second, Fifth, and Sixth Vermont to support Hancock and attempted to strike the enemy behind their left flank. The Confederates withdrew, however, before Brooks' men were in position to make this flanking movement. Davidson's brigade had been ordered to reinforce Porter, but the order was countermanded. The brigade only suffered from the Confederate artillery fire during the day. Despite Smith's assistance, Porter's force suffered a costly defeat at Gaines' Mill on June 27 and would convince McClellan to begin a retreat of the army to the James River.[8]

On the morning of the twenty-eighth, in order to protect the troops from the enemy artillery fire from Gaines' Hill, the division changed its lines. As the division withdrew to the edge of the wood, enclosing Golding's Farm, the Confederate artillery opened from Gaines' Hill, Garrett Hill, and the river valley above the Federals. The movement was so far advanced that little damage was done. Mott's battery, the only one that could be brought to bear, opened, apparently with good effect. After forty-five minutes under artillery fire, Smith received a notice that two enemy brigades were moving down upon his front. He directed Davidson to dispose his force accordingly. His troops were formed under artillery fire. When that ceased, the Seventh and Eighth Georgia regiments attacked, but they never got farther than a simple epaulement that the division had previously abandoned. The Thirty-Third New York and the Forty-Ninth Pennsylvania musketry, along with the great precision of Mott's battery's shrapnel fire, severely repulsed this assault. Smith was under severe fire, giving his orders in his usual unruffled manner and personally supervising the artillery. Several Confederates were captured, and their acknowledged loss was 150 men. The Confederates sent over a flag of truce so that they might bury their dead, and Captain Ayres discovered in going out to meet them that they had sixty pieces of artillery already in position and all ranged upon the small strip of woods where the division lay closely packed. By keeping the flag of truce out until dark, he tricked the enemy into holding their fire during the day.[9]

That evening, McClellan ordered the Federals holding the lines in front of Richmond to pull back to a new position in front of Savage's Station. They would form the rearguard to cover the White Oak Swamp crossings. As part of this movement, at daylight on the morning of the twenty-ninth, Smith's division moved to the Trent House and formed in line of battle to cover the retreat of the wagon train and prevent the enemy's use of the bridges in Smith's front. Later, the division fell back slowly to a position Franklin assigned Smith between the river and Savage's Station. Finding his flanks unprotected at this position, Smith was permitted to fall back to Savage's Station. After a couple of hours' delay there, McClellan ordered Smith to take his division to White Oak Swamp. After marching two miles, Franklin ordered Smith to return because Sumner's Second Corps was engaged with the enemy and needed its flanks protected. Smith returned and divided his command. He placed Hancock's brigade in the woods on Sumner's right to repel an anticipated attack and to hold the Richmond and York River Railroad, but the brigade was not engaged. Brooks' brigade was placed in the woods on Sumner's left. The Third Brigade was held in reserve.[10]

General Brooks soon faced the enemy and fought them until after dark. Brooks placed the Fifth Vermont on the right and Sixth Vermont on the left. The Second Vermont supported the Fifth, and the Third Vermont supported the Sixth. In this manner, the brigade entered the woods that bound the plain to the left and south of the station. All the regiments advanced together but found it difficult to keep their lines dressed in the woods or to hold their direction. The Fifth Vermont was the most intensely engaged. The regiment advanced through the woods on the right of the Williamsburg Road into an open field. Seeing some Confederates in a deep gorge two hundred yards away, the regiment at double-quick speed bayonet-charged the Confederates. When the Vermonters came within forty or fifty yards of the gorge, the Confederate force broke and retreated. The regiment's position was mainly in the open field, the left partially protected by a few scattered trees, and the center and right by a few trees and a slight swell of the ground in front. The enemy opened upon the regiment with two volleys of musketry and continued a galling fire until after dark. A battery further down the road poured grape and canister into the Fifth with deadly effect. Two companies directed their fire mainly upon the battery, which helped to silence it. During the engagement, a cross-fire was also opened upon the Federals from the edge of the woods to the left. Two or three of the left

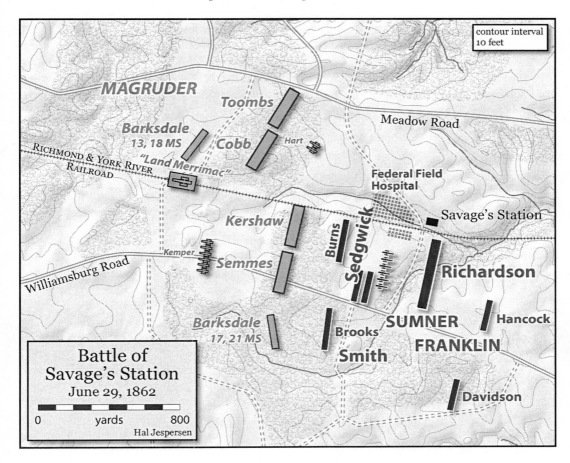

Battle of Savage's Station, June 29, 1862.

companies changed their front so that they would partially face the woods and thereby escape an enfilading fire. The enemy's fire ceased shortly after dark, and the Fifth was left in undisputed possession of the position assumed.[11]

The experience of the other three regiments of the Vermont Brigade was less severe. Each suffered from the fire of the enemy artillery and infantry, which was often hidden by thick woods. But in each case, the regiments returned the fire and held their positions until the brigade was ordered to withdraw.[12]

Hearing Brooks' heavy fire, Smith took two regiments of the Third Brigade to his support, but Brooks had driven off the enemy before Smith reached his position. On Smith's march towards Brooks, Smith put the Forty-Ninth New York in front. The route lay through an open wood where the Forty-Ninth maintained a strong alignment. As Smith's force reached a point under musket fire, Smith turned to look after the other regiment, the Twentieth New York, and saw it was in terrible confusion. Turning back, Smith directed the colonel to halt and form the regiment. The men seemed incapable of getting into line. Smith then directed the first sergeant to step to the front, call the roll, and order the men to fall in as their names were called. That did not accomplish the purpose, and Smith returned to the colonel and said, "I see what is the matter,—take your regiment back to the reserve." Before Smith had overtaken the Forty-Ninth, the fight was over.[13]

About 10:00 at night, after the arrangements were made for leaving the wounded, the division left for the White Oak Swamp. As Smith drew out his command, he passed the Twentieth New York and was "very cordially hissed" for his negative view of them. Smith took no notice of the occurrence. The division reached the White Oak Swamp about half an hour after daylight on June 30. Smith waited at the bridge until all his men had crossed. He then placed his command in position to cover the retreat of the trains and established his headquarters. Smith had not slept the preceding five nights, but still felt he could not sleep. After the defensive arrangements were made, he decided to try a cold bath in an outbuilding next to his headquarters.[14]

The plain on which the division was placed was about fifty feet above the stream but was commanded by a bluff on the other side. Smith ordered a brigade, not in his division but assigned to him, to ensure that the bluff was not occupied by the enemy. The brigade commander reported to Smith that dispositions were made that notice would be given at once of an enemy approach. Smith placed a battery overlooking the bridge crossing. After the Union forces had crossed, the bridge was destroyed at 10:00 in the morning. With these dispositions made, Smith finally got to his cold bath. Despite Smith's attempts to protect his position, Jackson used the inequalities of the ground on the north side of the swamp to approach within easy artillery range without being discovered. Jackson quietly brought forward seven field batteries to the brow of the hill. The guns were hidden by the underbrush, and their presence was not discovered by Smith's command.[15]

About noon, just as Smith was putting on clean underclothes, Jackson opened fire upon the plain and all exposed portions of Smith's division. Smith finished his dressing in what he hoped was dignified haste and called for his horse. His groom, frightened by the cannonade, had mounted the horse and sought seclusion in the woods. Smith noticed that the Twentieth New York, which had the day before demonstrated such inability to get into line, showed surprising ability in dissolving their formation and seeking cover. About four hundred were corralled by Smith's staff, and the remaining six hundred returned when the army was on the James River. The other regiments threw themselves flat on the ground. Smith's artillery only fired four shots in reply and then hastily abandoned its position. Wheeler's battery, with insufficient men to man the guns, was ordered to the rear of the field. Mott's battery fell into confusion and soon became useless. Ultimately, this battery left the field broken up and in disorder with many of its horses scattered. One of Mott's guns was left behind. Only Ayres' battery maintained the unequal fight until it was ordered to move to the right and rear. By moving the guns, Baldy was able to conceal his artillery by a thick and intervening wood. Eighteen Federal guns then commenced a rapid and generally accurate fire for the rest of the day.[16]

Smith moved to a less exposed position and devoted himself to restoring order. Through the officers' active exertions to rally and form the troops, order was restored, and the whole division was ordered back a short distance. The men took up a position at the edge of a strip of woods that commanded the open field and the roadway to the bridge crossing. At this position, Ayres set up his guns to prevent the passage of the enemy across the plain. Smith rode along his lines exhorting his men to coolness; his own composure restored confidence to them.[17]

The Confederates continued firing the entire day but made no serious attempt to cross White Oak Swamp. Colonel Thomas T. Munford's Confederate cavalry and some skirmishers crossed, but the division fire soon caused the cavalry to retire. Some of the

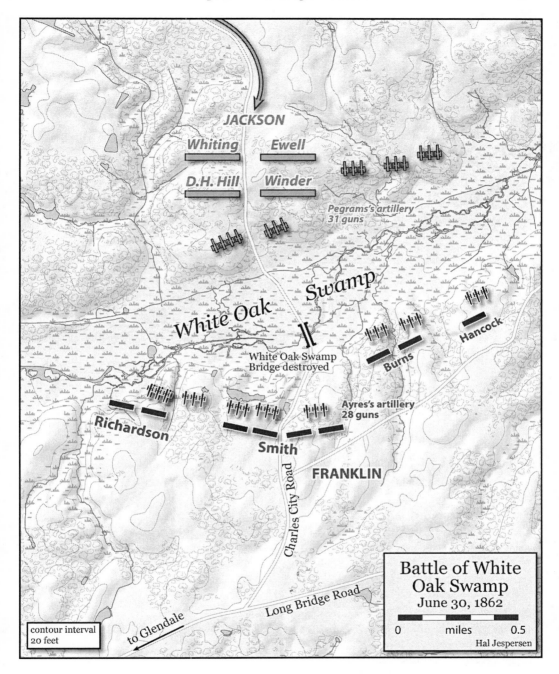

Battle of White Oak Swamp, June 30, 1862.

skirmishers did remain on the south side of the swamp during the day. Jackson had
reportedly been eager to push forward, but the destruction of the bridge and the strong
position of Smith's division prevented his advance until the next morning. Fortunately,
Smith's division did not face Jackson alone. Franklin had Brigadier General Israel B.
Richardson's division of the Second Corps placed on Smith's left and had additional

The Rearguard at White Oak Swamp—showing General W.F. Smith's division. General Smith is on horseback in the center directing the defense. Brigadier General W.T.H. Brooks is in the rear on horseback, right of center, immediately right of the United States and regimental flags (The Miriam and Ira D. Wallach Division of Art, Prints and Photographs: Picture Collection, New York Public Library).

brigades in reserve if Jackson crossed in earnest. Nonetheless, it was the firm front that Smith had established on the afternoon of the June 30, 1862, which deterred Jackson. Largely in consequence of this, the mass of the Army of the Potomac was able to reach Malvern Hill without serious delay or disaster.[18]

During the afternoon of the thirtieth, Smith rode a short distance to the rear on the road designated as his route of retreat and found the way blocked with wagons. Fearing the inability of his division to withdraw over the assigned path, he sent out his best staff officer, Captain Preston C.F. West, who found a clear road leading by Charles City. Knowing that a small escort would be ample protection for the supply train, Smith started the train on its way. By 10:00 at night, the wagons had all disappeared, and Smith's tired soldiers were again called upon to commence a night march—this time for Turkey Creek—which they reached about 5:00 in the morning on July 1. Hancock's brigade led the way, and Davidson's brigade served as the rear guard of the division. Franklin later recalled that finding this unused road on which his corps retired made the concentration of troops at Malvern Hill possible and was due to "the fertile brain of General Smith, who ordered the exploration."[19]

While moving down this road, Smith came upon an abandoned sutler's wagon. Franklin and Smith, who had been separated from their mess kits for three days, seized the contents of the wagon, which consisted of brandy and cigars. They subsisted on these, with the occasional addition of raw pork and hardtack begged from a passing soldier. On coming into possession of this jetsam, the two generals started an old West Point song with the refrain, "Hurrah, hurrah! Cigars and cognac." When Smith was a small boy, he had been mustered out of a church singing school for want of ability, and since Franklin equally lacked musical ability, the singing must have caused amusement among the troops. But the generals had their own fun out of the performance.[20]

As Smith rode along the road, the pain from exhaustion was unrelenting. He was constantly falling asleep in the saddle. After a minute or two, he would lose his balance and wake up, but that interval of time was enough to give him horrible nightmares of seemingly interminable lengths. In the morning, the excitement of posting his division and the expectation of an imminent battle jolted him awake.[21]

After two hours of rest on the morning of July 1, the command was again turned out to form a line of battle toward the right of the Federal position near Turkey Creek. This line, a mile long at the front, was in a favorable position facing the enemy. During the day, the battle of Malvern Hill was fought, but Smith's division was not engaged. Smith, however, did suffer one casualty. A captain in the Seventh Maine raided the division headquarters' kitchen and took Smith's kettle dinner. The officers of the Seventh bent their knees around the savory mess as if it had been an altar, and each, putting his hand in the dish, soon got his share of the bacon, cabbage, and delicious Virginia beans.[22]

The division remained in line of battle until 11:00 at night. At this hour, they drew out near the road and waited there until after sunrise for artillery and other troops to pass. Davidson was assigned the delicate duty of holding the ground until the rest of the division had crossed the two narrow bridges over Turkey Creek. He was then directed to retire his own brigade and destroy the bridges. Davidson successfully performed these tasks.[23]

Shortly thereafter, McClellan ordered the division to start for Harrison's Bar. Hancock's brigade once again led the division. The men, already suffering from deep-seated fatigue, were subjected to a drenching storm that soon made the roads excessively muddy and subsequently difficult to traverse. The stronger men could hardly drag one foot after another, and the weaker fell out by the hundreds, some to die of exhaustion, and others to join the long caravan of stragglers. Many of the men were demoralized by the sickening feeling of defeat and retreat and the expectation of rear attack. Nevertheless, Smith was perfectly calm and collected. When Hancock's brigade surgeon arrived with a hurried and important message, Smith received it with a quiet, pleasant bow of inquiry. He prepared his answer, gave his orders, and resumed his other duties. Smith was a little excited only once that awful day. Because of the critical situation, it became necessary to abandon some of the transportation. Smith rode along the line of his own transportation, clearing the road of the wagons so that the rear guard of infantry and artillery might pass. He once or twice ordered a teamster out of the road. The man did not obey. With no time to arrest him, Smith grappled the wagon driver by the neck and for half a minute kept him "in that peculiar state of gyration which a hungry soldier often communicates to the body of a rebel rooster about midnight."[24] Smith had no more trouble with that teamster.[25]

To show that he was still with his men physically and spiritually, Smith rode to the head of his column and waited for his division to pass. After repeating this, he took a short cut to find a camping place for the division. On reaching the vicinity of Harrison's Landing, Smith came to a steep path which led down to a valley. The clay soil and the heavy rain made walking precarious. The descent was so steep that he dismounted to lead his horse down. Smith had no sooner touched the crest of the ridge when his feet went out from under him. The bridle was pulled out of his hand and he plowed a hollow track clear to the bottom, the excess of mud falling over his legs in cataracts.

On reaching the bottom, Smith looked up and saw his dejected horse with head down. Smith could not get back to him and was in a quandary when a soldier appeared and led Smith's horse to him. Carrying several extra pounds of mud, Smith rode off. He finally reached Harrison's Landing only to find that stakes and flags already designated the campground of each brigade in the army. The division reached camp about noon on July 2.[26]

During the afternoon, Smith took time to look over Harrison Landing, which was a large plain of bottom land below Evelington Heights. The plain and the roads from the landing were within easy artillery range from the bluffs. The bluffs covered with guns would make egress almost impossible and could trap the army on the plain. Smith went to army headquarters, but found only the army adjutant-general, Seth Williams. Smith told Williams about his anxiety over encamping the men under unprotected heights. By this time, Smith's sleeplessness had made him unusually excitable. Williams tried to calm the irritated Smith. Smith left him saying, "If that bluff is occupied in the morning, this army will be captured, handcuffed, and sooner than be a prisoner, I will go down the James on a log."[27] Smith left headquarters and found a vacant tent. Using a saddle for a pillow, he lay on the ground at about 3:00 in the afternoon and slept without waking until 8:00 the next morning. His men bivouacked for the night in the mud, exposed to the severity of the weather. Many were without food, fires, and dry clothing.[28]

The next morning, Smith was awakened by the sound of enemy artillery. He feared catastrophe was upon his division but soon received orders to take his division and drive away the Confederate cavalry from the plateau. Brigadier General J.E.B. Stuart had placed howitzers on Evelington Heights. The Federals moved on Stuart's left and forced Captain John Pelham's battery to take a new position a half mile to the rear. Federal batteries east of Herring Creek began to press Pelham. Without reinforcements nearby, Stuart withdrew. Smith, after occupying the heights, selected a position and ordered his men to entrench. He advised Franklin to come up with the other division of the corps. Smith also sent Davidson's brigade on a reconnaissance of the enemy position. The brigade cut off some of the Confederate force and returned with six guns and some prisoners. The success of this little skirmish had an electrifying effect on the sagging morale of the men.[29]

The next day, before Brigadier General Henry Slocum's division arrived, Stonewall Jackson came along and felt Smith's entire line. But since Smith was so well covered, Jackson made no assault. Federal reinforcements put Smith's division beyond danger. Thus, the fire of Stuart's battery made the Federals appreciate the position which Smith mentioned to Williams, and consequently saved the army from Jackson, who could have trapped the Federals if he had occupied the bluffs. For his service in the Peninsula Campaign, Smith was recommended for brevets of major, lieutenant colonel, and colonel in the regular army. The recommendations came from Franklin and McClellan.[30]

Smith's division remained in camp at Harrison's Landing for six weeks. While there, sickness in the army became widespread, affecting almost everyone. Due to the intense labor, heat, insects, and impure drinking water, hundreds died of disease. Over sixty percent of some regiments were on the sick list. Leaves of absence were given freely, and thousands availed themselves of the opportunity of visiting home. Baldy was among those who left temporarily on sick leave. He received a twenty-day leave and left for his home in New York City on July 18. Sickness from the malarious district of the Chickahominy may not have been the only reason, however, for his departure. General

Franklin wrote to his wife, "The sun was too much for him, but I think the young wife had as much to do with his desire to get away as anything else."[31]

Smith also believed he could leave the field since no Federal movements were probable and since a Confederate attack was not likely with the navy on the Federal flanks. But more importantly, while Smith was pleased by the announcement on July 10 that the Senate finally confirmed his appointment as brigadier general of volunteers, he had grown greatly disheartened by the performance of the army commander. Smith believed there was no question that the Peninsula Campaign proposed by General McClellan was a wise one. Had he carried it out vigorously instead of reaching out for General McDowell's expected arrival from the north, it would have been at least as good as when he first proposed it and would have probably saved the army from the necessity of a change of base from a false line. Smith considered the Seven Days Battles as directed by nothing except accident. When Baldy reached Harrison's Landing, he wrote his wife "saying I had arrived safely but that General McClellan was not the man to lead our armies to victory." He intended to go to Washington to ask for duty elsewhere. McClellan realized Smith's coolness to him. McClellan wrote his wife that he thought Smith would not return, saying that Smith "had not seen the decency to bid goodbye after all I have done for him! Such is gratitude—I no longer expect such a feeling. I don't care to have him come back."[32]

While on leave, Smith was promoted to major general of volunteers. He also inquired about transferring from the Army of the Potomac. He was told that his commission as major general was issued with the supposition that he was with the Army, and the Secretary of War expected him to remain. Smith decided to stay because he had a corps commander in whom he had unbounded confidence and a division ready for any work that they might be asked to do; those things were too important to give up in order to try his luck in another field. Smith returned to his division camp in early August, even though, according to General Franklin, he still was "looking not well."[33]

Meanwhile, McClellan at Harrison's Landing had been waging a losing battle to convince Washington to keep his army on the Peninsula. McClellan begged for reinforcements to renew the campaign. Major General John Pope, commanding the newly formed Army of Virginia in front of Washington, urged the administration to withdraw the Army of the Potomac back to Washington and remove McClellan from command. The new general-in-chief, Henry Halleck, visited McClellan in late July to talk over the situation. McClellan promised to renew the attack with 20,000 reinforcements. Halleck told the army commander that they would be sent. A few days later, however, Pope, Stanton, and Chase convinced Lincoln to remove the army from the James. They wished to unite the Federal armies in the East under Pope and follow an overland strategy in Virginia. McClellan could not persuade Lincoln that he had established a superior position from which to assault Richmond and that the withdrawal of the army and a subsequent overland campaign would be disastrous.[34]

For Smith, the Seven Days Battles had shown once again that soldiers often fought better than their generals led. His division had helped shield McClellan's change of base and won recognition from the army and corps commanders. The fighting, however, had caused Smith to doubt McClellan's ability to defeat the enemy. The Army of the Potomac's move northward would again provide evidence of Smith's abilities as a division commander. It would also increase his frustrations over having his tactical insights ignored by his superiors.

CHAPTER VI

Smith in the Maryland Campaign

*Hard Fighting, Insights Frustrated Again,
and McClellan's Departure*

By the end of August, the Army of the Potomac had abandoned the peninsula. On August 16, 1862, Smith's division evacuated Harrison's Landing. It marched via Charles City Courthouse, Williamsburg, Big Bethel, and Hampton, and arrived at Fortress Monroe on August 22. The progress of the Sixth Corps as part of the general withdrawal was apparently slow. McClellan wrote his wife, criticizing the slowness of Franklin and Smith's troops and stating that Franklin and Smith "have so little energy."[1] McClellan believed Franklin's continuing illness caused his lack of efficiency. McClellan added, "I presume I ought also to make a great deal of allowance for Smith also on the same account—so we will try to be as charitable as we can under all their circumstances."[2] The division embarked upon transports on the twenty-third and arrived at Alexandria the next day. The division remained in camp near Fairfax Seminary until August 27, when it was ordered to Centreville to support Major General John Pope's Army of Virginia. It marched six miles and encamped at Annandale. On August 29, the division, with the rest of the Sixth Corps, moved towards Centreville but bivouacked six miles from Alexandria. The next day the division resumed the march and arrived at dusk at Centreville, where the defeated forces of Pope were met in full retreat from General Lee's victory at the Battle of Second Bull Run. The division remained in the works at Centreville until the night of August 31, when it moved out to Fairfax Courthouse, and thence, on the following day, to Fairfax Seminary, where it remained until September 6.[3]

The Federal defeat at Second Bull Run led directly to recriminations among the Union high command about who was to blame. Historians find enough fault among the major figures. Pope had failed to use his numeric advantage in the first day's attacks effectively and then left his flank exposed to General Longstreet's crushing attack on the second day. McClellan was also open to criticism for failing to bring available reinforcements to Pope's aid. Ultimately Pope and the administration blamed Fitz John Porter for not attacking Jackson's flank as Pope ordered. Accordingly, Porter was court-martialed later in the year, a verdict not reversed until 1886, when Confederate documents proved Porter could not have attacked because General Longstreet's forces blocked him.[4]

Smith remained behind at Fairfax Courthouse on the day after the battle of Chantilly. There, Smith saw Porter and Pope apparently discussing future movements and seemingly on the very best of terms. Afterwards, when Smith read Pope's charges against Porter, he could only conclude that the charges were the outcome of some conferences which took place later at the War Department. Smith believed it was impossible that Pope could have thought, at Fairfax Courthouse, that Porter had positively disobeyed orders. Smith returned to his men and met McClellan at Franklin's headquarters in Alexandria. The army commander gave Franklin and Smith an account of his visit to Washington and his reception by Lincoln, Stanton, and Halleck. It would seem that they were all greatly demoralized. Stanton threw his arms around McClellan and called him his dear friend. Halleck called on McClellan to save the country.[5]

In the wake of his victory at the Second Bull Run, General Lee decided to move northward. He hoped that this campaign would win Maryland for the Confederacy, earn diplomatic recognition from Britain and France, and even force the Union to sue for peace. On September 4, Lee's army crossed the Potomac and three days later concentrated at Frederick, Maryland. Lee intended to move west of South Mountain to open a supply line into the Shenandoah Valley. He would first have to capture the Union garrison at Harper's Ferry before proceeding to his next objective of cutting the Pennsylvania Railroad at Harrisburg. On September 9, Jackson's corps and portions of the Longstreet's corps were ordered to capture the garrison.[6]

Meanwhile, McClellan ordered his army northward to locate the Confederates. As part of this general advance, the Sixth Corps was moved to Darnestown on September 6, then through Dawsonville and Barnesville en route to Buckeystown, covering the road from the mouth of the Monocacy to Rockville. The march was briefly interrupted on September 11 when Baldy's division brushed with Confederate cavalry three miles south of Urbana. No Federal soldiers were lost, and General Franklin wrote his wife, "The thing was gallantly done, and the responsibility was as great as though a battle had been fought."[7] The Sixth Corps arrived at Buckeystown on September 13. On the same day, in Frederick, a Union soldier discovered a copy of Lee's orders, lost by a careless Southern officer. The orders gave McClellan a clear picture of the whereabouts of Lee's army, divided in five parts. Upon finding Lee's orders, McClellan decided to capture the passes in South Mountain in an effort to surprise Lee's scattered army.[8]

McClellan ordered Franklin to move his corps from Buckeystown through Jefferson to Crampton Pass in South Mountain, which was just beyond Burkittsville. Carrying the Pass would furnish the means of reaching the Confederate flank and place the corps on the most practical route for the relief of Harper's Ferry. At 4:00 in the afternoon on the thirteenth, Smith's division was in Jefferson. Smith reported that Harper's Ferry was under attack from forces on the north side of the Potomac and requested permission to attack the Confederate in the rear. Franklin moved forward to Burkittsville. Just beyond this village, the Confederates were protecting Crampton Pass.[9]

The carrying of Crampton's Pass by Franklin was executed rapidly and decisively on September 14. The corps passed through the town, under heavy artillery fire from the crest of the mountain on the left. Slocum's division was formed on the right of the road leading through the gap while Brooks' brigade and the Third Brigade under the command of Colonel William H. Irwin were formed on the left. Franklin sent Slocum's division forward, and it soon became actively engaged with the enemy. Smith sent Brooks' brigade forward upon the left of the road to dislodge the Confederates from the woods upon Slocum's flank and support Slocum's main attack on the right.[10]

Brooks found the enemy in position behind a stone wall at right angles with the road. As soon as the nature of the ground and the exact position of the wall could be determined, the Fourth and Second Vermont were deployed while the other three regiments were held in reserve on the edge of the town. The Vermonters advanced against the wall and immediately carried it. Some fifteen or twenty Confederates were captured. The Fourth and Second Vermont then pushed up the rocky side of the mountain by climbing the ledges and struggling through the bushes until they reached the crest. Here, the Fourth was sent to the left to attack a battery firing from the summit. The Second continued over the crest and down the opposite side of the mountain. It reached the base as Slocum's division scattered the enemy. Six officers and 115 men of the Sixteenth Virginia, cut off by the promptness of the movement, surrendered themselves and their battle flag to the Fourth. The Fourth did not reach the battery, however, before it limbered up and escaped by a wood road leading down the mountain. The other Vermont regiments followed the movement by the main road.[11]

The brigade bivouacked at the point where Slocum's division ceased the pursuit and, on throwing out pickets, found an abandoned twelve-pound howitzer with horses. Supported by Brooks' movement, Slocum's division cleared the pass, forcing the Confederates down the mountain in great confusion. After the gap was cleared, Irwin's brigade came up without opposition. While Slocum's division was primarily responsible for the success, Slocum reported that Brooks' advance "did much toward the accomplishment of the work assigned to the corps and rendered our victory more complete than it would otherwise have been."[12]

On the morning of September 15, Smith's division was sent into Pleasant Valley, west of South Mountain, to begin the movement toward Harper's Ferry. Franklin and Smith examined the Confederate position and concluded it would be suicidal to attack it. The whole breadth of Pleasant Valley was occupied, and batteries swept the only approaches to the enemy position. The two generals estimated that the Confederate force equaled their own and that the enemy position was too strong for the corps to carry. The Confederate force was actually less than a quarter of the Sixth Corps, and the two Federal generals' overestimation left Confederate Major General Lafayette McLaws' hastily formed line unassailed. Most significantly, their decision sealed the fate of the Federal garrison at Harper's Ferry. Historian Mark Snell in his definitive biography of Franklin sees this decision at Pleasant Valley as the Sixth Corps commander's greatest failure in the war. As Baldy agreed with his friend's action and never criticized it later, he shared in this failure.[13]

When the Confederates began to retreat, Smith pursued them with the Third Brigade and a battery. The battery fired a few shots into the retreating cavalry. The Confederates withdrew too quickly through the valley, however, for Smith to have any significant effect on the enemy. In fact, the gap between the two forces were so large, the Confederates were unaware they were even being followed. Smith also sent the Sixth Maine to obtain possession of the pass two miles south of Crampton's Pass. After a sharp skirmish, the Sixth captured the pass and four prisoners. A section of light artillery was placed at this position, which severely shelled the enemy in the valley and scattered their cavalry in all directions. The regiment returned to the division at nightfall. The next day, McClellan ordered Franklin's corps to join the rest of the army east of Sharpsburg. The corps left their encampment in the rear of Rohrersville, in Pleasant Valley, at 5:30 in the morning on September 17.[14]

As the Sixth Corps began to march to rejoin the rest of the army, the battle of Antietam was commencing. In the previous few days, McClellan had failed to attack Lee's divided troops, allowing the Confederate commander time to concentrate his forces. After learning of Jackson's victory at Harper's Ferry, Lee decided against retreating into Virginia. Instead, he chose to stand and fight McClellan's army near Sharpsburg, Maryland. Lee's forces would still be significantly less than McClellan's. He had less than 35,000 men until A.P. Hill's men arrived in the afternoon. McClellan's effective troops numbered about 75,000. By day's end, Lee's numbers would rise to 55,000, but McClellan's would also expand to just under 90,000 men. Unfortunately, the Union Army commander would not effectively use his significant numerical advantage. He began the attacks on the Confederate left at dawn, with Major General Joseph Hooker's First Corps. It was followed by Major General Joseph Mansfield's Twelfth Corps. After these attacks were stopped, in mid-morning Major General Edwin Sumner's Second Corps attacked, but it was stopped after some initial gains. These attacks failed because McClellan order them in a seriatim fashion rather than making them simultaneously.[15]

As the fighting expanded in the center of the battlefield, about 10:00 a.m., Baldy's division arrived on the field leading the column of the Sixth Corps and was directed to General Sumner, commanding the Union right. Expecting an attack, Sumner ordered Smith to form his division closed in mass, facing to the northeast. Just as the leading brigade, the First, had been placed, Lieutenant Colonel Joseph Taylor, Sumner's Adjutant-General, came galloping up to Smith and said, "The enemy's skirmishers are advancing from the front, and if you don't get some troops out there immediately, our artillery will be captured."[16] Without referring the matter to Sumner, Smith directed Hancock to deploy his force under Taylor's guidance. Hancock's brigade drove away the Confederate skirmishers, who had advanced close to the batteries. Hancock detached some companies to occupy buildings and fences in front of his position. The Confederates moved up two batteries and opened fire on Hancock's position. Despite severe enemy artillery fire, Hancock's skirmishers and artillery silenced the Confederate batteries and forced their withdrawal after losing several limbers. The First Brigade assisted in saving two batteries and held its position during the remainder of the action, sometimes under very heavy artillery fire.[17]

The next brigade to arrive was Smith's Third Brigade under Irwin. Smith formed up the brigade and ordered it forward to meet the approaching enemy. The brigade, animated by the words and examples of Smith and its own officers, dashed at the enemy and was soon hotly engaged with them. The Confederates could not endure the brigade charge and broke in confusion. The brigade drove the Confederates to the little church at the edge of the woods, but at this point, a severe flank fire from the woods on the right threw the Thirty-Third and Seventy-Seventh New York slightly into confusion. Smith, riding along the line and discovering the advanced and unprotected position of the two regiments, sent an aide to order them to retire. They closed up, faced by the rear rank, and discharged a close and scorching fire, driving back and scattering the enemy. Some of the men were then ordered to lie down behind the crest of a slope, facing the woods and open ground to its right. The rest of the brigade were ordered to face to their proper front and form behind a crest nearly at right angles to the other.[18]

With Irwin being heavily engaged, Smith sent for Brooks' brigade to support Irwin. Smith intended to place Brooks on Irwin's left in front of the Hagerstown Turnpike. In this position, Brooks' right could also take advantage of the crest which shielded Irwin's brigade. Without Smith's knowledge or consent, however, Sumner ordered Brooks' brigade to reinforce Brigadier General William H. French's division, which had nearly expended its ammunition. On reaching French's right, Brooks found that the enemy had been checked and repelled. The brigade then occupied a position on French's right,

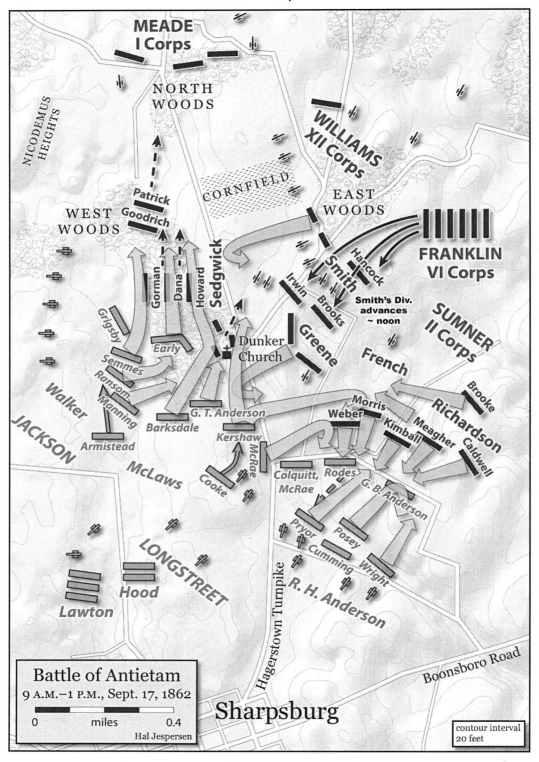

Battle of Antietam, September 17, 1862.

which situated it on Irwin's left. Brooks stayed there for the remainder of the day and night, frequently coming under enemy artillery fire. Smith later complained in his report about this detachment of Brooks' brigade. He wrote, "It is not the first or second time during a battle that my command has been dispersed by orders from an officer superior in rank to the general commanding this corps, and I must assert that I have never know any good to arise from such a method of fighting a battle and think the contrary rule should be adopted of keeping commands intact."[19]

By this time, Franklin joined Smith, and Baldy reported his movements and position to him. After talking matters over, the two generals agreed that they could make an assault on the Confederate left without repeating the tactical blunders made in previous assaults. They determined to have the Sixth Corps mount an attack in the area of the West Woods; their target would be the high ground of Nicodemus Hill, to the left and rear of the Confederate position. Franklin went to Sumner and presented this plan, but Sumner disapproved it since the repulse of the Sixth Corps would imperil the safety of the army.[20]

Convinced that Franklin had been correct in his idea of attacking the Confederate left, Smith sent an aide to McClellan to ask him to come to his part of the field. On his arrival, McClellan, who had learned of Smith's movements through his aides, thanked Baldy in person for his valuable services. Smith had thoroughly examined the topography of the locality and found a hill that apparently commanded the Confederate left. He told McClellan, "If you will allow me to take that hill with my division, I will drive out the enemy's left flank in short order."[21] McClellan told Smith that the Union right would make no further aggressive movements. The army commander could neither bring himself to overrule Sumner nor personally lead a renewed offensive. Smith realized that the opportunity to crush the Confederate left was lost. He was sustained by a Confederate participant, Lieutenant General Stephen D. Lee, who cited Sumner's refusal to continue the Federal assault as a main reason for saving the Confederate left flank. Later historians sustained Franklin's and Smith's position on renewal of the attack. As J.C. Ropes states, "Franklin's proposed attack on the rebel left, upon troops exhausted by several hours hard fighting, whose losses had been enormous, who had moreover been driven, in some cases in disorder, from their original positions, was conformable to all the rules of war, and, it could hardly have failed of complete success."[22] Kenneth Williams also agreed that if McClellan had adopted Franklin's and Smith's advice, "the result would have been the practical annihilation of Lee's army."[23]

Smith understood that McClellan intended to have Major General Ambrose Burnside attack the Confederate right. If Burnside succeeded in turning the flank, Lee would be separated from his line of retreat and from reinforcements coming from Harper's Ferry. But to accomplish this goal, Burnside should have attacked much earlier. Smith believed that McClellan should have removed Burnside after he permitted Confederate sharpshooters to resist Federal advances for five hours and then delayed the final attack for three hours. Had McClellan given a "fighting general" the command of the Union left, McClellan's plan could have brought the desired result.[24]

Meanwhile, a Confederate battery advanced and opened a severe fire along Irwin's flank and through the line of the Twentieth New York. Sharpshooters opened from the woods on the right and from the extreme left. The artillery and infantry fire from the Confederates was rapid and accurate. In a short time, Irwin's loss was very heavy. About 4:30 in the afternoon, Smith moved a battery consisting of three rifled guns to reinforce

Irwin. The fire from these cannons forced the withdrawal of the enemy massing on the left.[25]

Sharpshooters reopened their fire on Irwin's left; this endangered the newly placed battery. About 5:00, Irwin, without prior approval of his division commander, ordered the Seventh Maine forward to dislodge these sharpshooters. The regiment soon drove the Confederates back. The Confederates then opened fire on the regiment from the front and left flank. The Seventh fixed bayonets and rushed forward in line with a cheer, advancing nearly a quarter of a mile at the double-quick. The Confederates, however, regrouped and soon attempted to flank this attack and cut off the Seventh Maine's line of retreat. Having disposed of most of their cartridges, the Seventh retreated, sending the enemy another volley as they attempted to follow. This drove the enemy back. The regiment, closing up on the colors, marched back in good order to their former position on the left of the Third Brigade.[26]

The Third Brigade with the rest of Smith's division held its position for the rest of the day and night. The battle was not continued the next day. Both Franklin and his Second Division commander supported renewal of the attack on the Confederate left, but Franklin was the only corps commander that wished to recommence the attack. Leading historians also agree with Franklin's and Smith's view that the attack should have been renewed on the eighteenth. Historian Stephen Sears pointed out that with more reinforcements and a stronger position, McClellan's prospect for victory on September 18 was greater than the day before.[27]

Franklin informed McClellan at 10:00 on the morning of September 18, 1862, that the enemy was moving a battery of his right and asked for attack orders, setting Nicodemus Hill as the target. But McClellan did not respond until 5:45 in the evening and then only to give orders for the next morning. These orders finally allowed Franklin to send a brigade to take possession of the heights on the right of the woods. The entire corps was permitted to support this move. He was to make dispositions to hold that position. But at 4:30 the next morning, Franklin was ordered to ready his troops to move in any direction if the enemy appeared to be retiring. By then, Lee had escaped over the Potomac. Later in the morning, Smith went forward and found where the enemy's left flank had been and saw the hill that he had asked McClellan for permission to capture; taking that hill would have enabled the Federals to flank the Confederates.[28]

The fight at Sharpsburg was "the bloodiest single day of the war." Called the Battle of Antietam, it was, nevertheless, strategically significant in turning back Lee's first invasion of the North. The battle's success also had another importance. Back in July of 1862, Lincoln had decided to abandon his hands-off policy on slavery and to issue a proclamation freeing the slaves in the seceded states. He purposely delayed the proclamation until the Union forces had won a major victory on the field. With the strategic victory at Antietam, Lincoln issued the preliminary Emancipation Proclamation on September 22. It stated that all slaves in the states in rebellion would be emancipated on January 1, 1863. Slaves in Union-held territory or Union slave states would be exempt. It was now apparent that the war for the Union had also become a war to end slavery.[29]

During the week after Antietam, McClellan came to the Sixth Corps and asked Franklin what kind of a corps commander Smith would make. "None better," responded Franklin. McClellan was seeking a new commander for the Twelfth Corps to replace Major General Joseph Mansfield, who had been mortally wounded during the battle. The relationship between the army commander and Smith had been strained since the

Peninsula Campaign because Smith had been critical of the change of base and position first taken up at Harrison's Landing. Because of this, Smith suspected that McClellan avoided giving him a corps command. Major General Henry Slocum was appointed to the Twelfth Corps, but he outranked Smith. When the First Corps command became vacant, it was given to Major General John F. Reynolds. Smith believed that Reynolds was the finest choice for promotion. And if selection were based on merit, Reynolds should have been chosen before Slocum. Therefore, when this did not happen, Smith saw that neither seniority nor merit guaranteed promotion, and believed that, in his own case, his criticisms prevented his promotion.[30]

Nevertheless, McClellan showed he still had confidence in Smith and respected his views. One morning shortly after the announcement of the preliminary emancipation proclamation, Smith was called to army headquarters near Sharpsburg. Smith found McClellan in the company of several other generals. McClellan passed to Smith a letter that the army commander had written and asked Smith for an opinion. It was a letter to the president taking issue with him on the Emancipation Proclamation.[31]

Back during the Peninsula Campaign, McClellan had shown Smith a letter also critical of the administration's direction of the war. In this previous letter, McClellan advocated a conciliatory approach to the Southern people and stated the Federal armies' purpose in the South was merely to execute the laws and protect property. Smith asked McClellan, "General, do you not see that looks like treason, and that it will ruin you and all of us?"[32] Smith convinced McClellan to destroy that letter. Now, Smith read this second letter carefully and said to McClellan in a low voice, "General, that letter forwarded would utterly ruin you,—the army would not support you, nor would the country support you, and without reference to the constitutionality of the Proclamation in a civil sense, it was in the opinion of most military men, I thought, necessary as a war measure."[33] Smith could not imagine "a more suicidal thing" than writing this letter and urged McClellan to burn it.[34] He had McClellan's best interest in mind but possibly overreacted to McClellan's letter. The Army commander had expressed similar feelings to the president when Lincoln visited the camp in early October. Nonetheless, Smith was correct that such a letter would certainly aid McClellan's enemies in Washington. The letter was never sent. While McClellan continued to doubt the wisdom of the proclamation, he decided not to challenge the document. On the contrary, he issued a general order on October 7, 1862, to discourage any criticism of official government policies.[35]

Smith's division remained at Sharpsburg until September 22, when it moved to Bakersville where it was encamped from September 23 to October 11. On October 3, Lincoln, McClellan, Franklin, and Smith reviewed the Sixth Corps. While at Bakersville, Smith became increasingly concerned about the condition of his men. On September 30, he ordered his brigade commanders and his chief of artillery to investigate the condition of their regiments and batteries. The commanders were to determine the ability of their men to take the field again and to consider the need for reorganization, recruiting, clothing, and camp equipage.[36]

Smith reported the results of this investigation to Franklin on October 6, 1862. He asked for a thorough reorganization of his division before taking the field again. He gave three reasons for his request. First, the officers and men were debilitated from the labors, hard marches, privations, exposures, and excitements which they had experienced since last April; a campaign before resting and refitting would lose the services of several experienced men, whose places could not be filled except after months of drill and experience. Second, the transportation allowance was so insufficient that even officers had been unable to take a proper amount of clothing with them. Many of the men were ragged, filthy, covered with vermin, and barefooted. They had not been allowed to take sufficient cooking utensils to prepare properly cooked food. The result was an increase in the number of sick soldiers—a situation which would only worsen if the march continued. Third, absenteeism in Smith's division was so large that he requested that all absentees be ordered to report and should be allowed time to arrive before another movement. Absentees totaled 153 officers and 5,080 men while those assigned only numbered 1,315 officers and 6,221 men. Smith hypothesized that many of the absentees were deserters, that some had been discharged on surgeon's certificates without proper information given to his command, and that not a few would never be fit again for duty. Moreover, the 775 men of the 137th Pennsylvania, though present for duty, were totally undrilled and undisciplined and had officers unable to teach the manual of arms. Since this regiment was enlisted for only nine months, Smith suggested that it was not worth the labor and time to train the men and recommended that it garrison some fort. Smith did not have sufficient men to serve two-thirds of his batteries, and his artillery horses were thin and weak enough to require rest and shelter.[37]

He then offered two serious recommendations. First, he requested that his command be restored to its proper proportions by filling up the old regiments rather than by adding new ones. Since he had the organization in his old regiments for fourteen thousand men, no further expense would be necessary for the payment of new officers. More importantly, recruits became useful much sooner by integrating them into old units with men who knew their duties. Second, Smith recommended that sick men in the future not be separated from their regiments without the colonels having full information.[38]

On October 23, McClellan wrote Franklin regarding Smith's request for the reorganization of his division. Since the date of Smith's request, seventeen days had elapsed. Within that time, McClellan asserted that care and attention must have produced some improvements. He was reluctant to believe that such a distinguished division would be considered less efficient than the other divisions in the army or that it could not be relied on for future service in the campaign. Thus, Smith's investigation was for naught and his recommendations ignored.[39]

Smith's requests for remaining in place had been ignored before McClellan's decision. On October 11, the division moved to Hagerstown. From there the Vermont Brigade was transported by railroad to Chambersburg and the Third brigade to the Maryland/Pennsylvania line. Both brigades searched for the enemy, but the Confederate cavalry was gone. Brooks' brigade served then as provost guard at Hagerstown and the Third Brigade, now under Brigadier General Francis L. Vinton, simply encamped one mile away. On October 29, Smith's division was ordered to a point on the road from Boonsboro to Williamsport about two miles from Williamsport to support Williamsport or either of the other divisions of the Sixth Corps. The next day, the Vermont Brigade was ordered to remain in camp to support Williamsport while the other two brigades followed the rest of the corps via Boonsboro and Berlin to New Baltimore, Virginia, where the division arrived on November 9, 1862. The Vermont Brigade was to leave the camp on November 1, and endeavor to overtake the corps.[40]

By the time Smith's division had reached New Baltimore, the army had a new commander. McClellan had been replaced by Major General Ambrose Burnside. Smith devotedly supported McClellan until after the Peninsula Campaign where Smith was to write during the post war years, "we took shelter from a retreating army."[41] In a memoir written after the war, Smith declared that McClellan had four major defects as army commander. First, despite a number of good commanders to choose from, McClellan had picked some poor subordinates, such as Charles P. Stone and Burnside. Also, he was too reluctant to overrule subordinates who were his friends since he believed they were all competent. Second, he was too cautious in his planning. Smith pointed to McClellan's reluctance to push Hancock's forces on April 6 and the Vermont Brigade at Lee's Mill, and his sanction of Sumner's halt of the Federal assaults on the Confederate left at Antietam as examples. Baldy believed that, particularly at Antietam, McClellan, having Lee's plans, should have pushed everything and "made an end of the war at Antietam."[42] Third, McClellan did not quickly form expedients. His inability to deal with the withdrawal of McDowell's corps from his Peninsula Campaign strategy showed this. Fourth, while McClellan was extremely knowledgeable of the intricacies of military science and theories, he failed to put it to good use. Nevertheless, Smith conceded, "I think with all his weaknesses, McClellan was very badly treated and knew more about war than anyone who came after him."[43]

Smith thought even less of the new army commander, Burnside, who Smith felt had bungled the Union attack on the Confederate right at Antietam. Baldy did benefit from Burnside's reorganization of the army on November 14. The army was divided into three grand divisions, consisting of two corps each. Franklin was promoted to commander of the Left Grand Division and Smith replaced him as Sixth Corps commander.[44]

As a division commander, Smith had shown both the ability to lead several larger subordinate commands as well as the potential for higher command. In addition, his personal bravery was exhibited. Despite his subordinate role, Smith's leadership was crucial in the Seven Days Battles in Virginia. He played an important part in skillfully holding the Confederates at Golden Farm, Savage's Station, and White Oak Swamp. His tactical insight was shown at Williamsburg and Antietam. In both cases, Smith urged flanking movements against the enemy that could have given the Union greater tactical success. There is little doubt that Baldy's superiors' refusal to take his advice lost important opportunities for surer Federal victories. Smith was also personally courageous in directing and encouraging his men during the battles of Lee's Mill and White Oak Swamp. Smith was undoubtedly pleased by his promotion to corps commander, but this, like so many of his accomplishments, would be bittersweet.

CHAPTER VII

Smith's Corps Command During the Fredericksburg Campaign

The Trials of a Democratic General

In November 1862, Smith's accomplishments in the Peninsula and Maryland Campaigns were rewarded by his advancement to the command of the Sixth Corps, comprising three divisions. The First was commanded by Smith's former Vermont Brigade commander, W.T.H. Brooks; Brigadier General Albion P. Howe replaced Smith as Second Division commander, and Brigadier General John Newton commanded the Third.[1]

Smith, despite his critical view of McClellan, later wrote that it was "an outrage upon the country, and the Army" to relieve McClellan after he had taken the army into Virginia. Smith substantiated his view by pointing out that McClellan had placed the army in an excellent military situation in the face of the enemy. Yet, at the outset of his command, Burnside surrendered this position. When Burnside was given command of the army, he had 152,000 men concentrated in the vicinity of Warrenton. Had he sent 25,000 to hold Warrenton and another 25,000 to cover his rear, he still would have had over 100,000 men. The Federal force would have been larger but for the unjustified fears of the administration, which held back over 76,000 men to guard the capital. Nonetheless, at the same time, Lee's two corps were greatly separated. Lieutenant General Thomas J. "Stonewall" Jackson's corps was at Front Royal while Lieutenant General James Longstreet's corps of 38,000 men was eighty-seven miles away at Culpeper Court House. This meant that Longstreet was alone to face a Federal force thrice his size. The new Union army commander had a clear opportunity to defeat half of Lee's army while the other half was not within supporting distance. Apparently, at the time, however, Burnside (as well as Baldy Smith) did not know where Lee's forces were. Consequently, Burnside, with his new Sixth Corps commander's support, decided to withdraw from Longstreet's front and proceed southeastward to Fredericksburg.[2]

Burnside, with Lincoln's approval, began the movement to Fredericksburg on November 15. Two days later, the army reached the Rappahannock. Burnside's swift action surprised General Lee, who had lost track of his enemy for several days. The Army of the Potomac continued its march, keeping on the left bank of the river. During the march, the Sixth Corps suffered many hardships. They marched during inclement weather on poor roads, sometimes without their daily rations. By November 19, the entire army had arrived across the river from Fredericksburg at Falmouth. But the army was unable to cross the river because General-in-Chief Henry Halleck failed to send the pontoon materials to bridge the river as planned. The materials did not arrive until the end of the month. Nonetheless, Halleck directed the army commander to continue the campaign. He was reported to have told Burnside to fight the battle even if he faced defeat.[3]

On December 3, Burnside called a conference of his Grand Division and corps commanders. The new army commander had divided his six corps into three grand divisions. The Right Grand Division was commanded by Major General Edwin Sumner, the Center Grand Division was commanded by Major General Joseph Hooker, and the Left Grand Division was commanded by Major General William Franklin. As a result, Baldy became the commander of the Sixth Corps. Burnside began the conference by stating that within a few days, he proposed to cross the river to offer battle to Lee, and, that after a close study of his engineers reports, he had chosen Skinker's Neck as the point of crossing. Skinker's Neck was about twelve miles below Fredericksburg and offered all the necessary military features for a crossing. Sumner and Franklin supported the crossing while Hooker opposed the plan, believing that Lee's army could repulse the Federal attempt to cross the river. Responding to Hooker's opposition, Smith stated, "If you will put the Sixth Corps in the lead, I will stake my reputation that I will cross and hold the head of the peninsula formed by the river at Skinker's Neck."[4] Burnside closed the conference stating that his plans were final and that his generals were to await orders to move.[5]

On December 5, the Sixth Corps was ordered out and given instructions to find a new camp. They moved in a severe rainstorm that soon changed to snow with a biting wind. After the First Division found a new place about a mile from Belle Plain, the bad state of the roads delayed their baggage trains until late in the night. When the trains did arrive, the ground was too wet for the soldiers to sleep upon. The next day the Second Division continued its march and encamped a few miles from the First Division. But the baggage trains did not arrive until the following morning. The men huddled under their shelter tents with two inches of snow for bedding while tentless officers crouched around campfires in the woods. As one of Baldy's officers wrote in his diary, "Oh how cold!" Smith could be proud of his corps, in light of these trials, tribulations, and hardships. A morning report of December 10 showed that the camps were thoroughly policed, the officers and guards attentive, and the arms and equipment in very good order.[6]

Burnside's plan to cross at Skinker's Neck soon had to be dropped when the Confederate forces concentrated in that vicinity. Three or four days after the Grand Division and corps commanders' conference, Smith was at Burnside's headquarters, and the commanding general invited Smith to take a ride with him. Riding along on the hills near the river, Burnside pointed out some fine positions for artillery and said, "My reserve artillery has as yet had no chance to show its value, and I am going to make the crossing here at the town and below, under cover of the guns of the reserve artillery."[7] Smith commented, "You can cross here without great difficulty for this bank dominates the other," but calling attention to the range of hills on the other side a mile or more back from the river, he warned, "when your army is across your troubles will begin."[8] "Oh!" said Burnside, "I know where Lee's forces are, and I expect to surprise him. I expect to cross and occupy the hills before Lee can bring anything serious to meet me." Smith then said, "If you are sure of that, there is no more to be said on the subject."[9] Yet Burnside's delays ultimately allowed Lee to concentrate his 74,000 men along the hills south and west of the town. Despite the Union army's larger force of 113,000 men, the terrain and Confederate defenses clearly favored the defenders.[10]

On the afternoon of December 10, 1862, Franklin received an order to have the head of his command at a designated point on the river, about one and a half miles below Fredericksburg, at daylight on the morning of the eleventh. He would then begin his crossing over two bridges, which would be found ready. Smith was ordered to take the advance. When Smith arrived at the crossing, he found that the completion of the pontoon bridges had been delayed by enemy sharpshooter fire from the other side of the river. Two batteries placed on the bank opened with canister and shell fire and forced the Confederates to disappear; the work was resumed. The bridges were completed about one o'clock in the afternoon, but Smith did not receive orders to begin the crossing until four o'clock.[11]

Smith then ordered Brigadier General Charles Devens' Second Brigade of the Third Division to begin the movement using both bridges. As soon as the skirmishers, under Colonel Frank Wheaton, Second Rhode Island, were ready to cross, Smith opened a heavy artillery fire on the houses on the plateau near the crossing to drive out any enemy holding them. This fire was maintained until his skirmishers reached the plateau. The Second Rhode Island met with opposition from five companies of Confederate skirmishers but succeeded in driving the Confederates back without difficulty. After Devens' brigade crossed, the remainder of the Third Division and the First Division followed. The troops were rapidly moving across when Burnside ordered Franklin to send no more troops than were necessary to hold the bridges. Smith recalled all his troops except Devens' brigade, which was left to keep the bridgehead. Devens threw out a line of pickets to the left and front and held the position during the night. Smith believed that Burnside's order was given because the bridges opposite Fredericksburg had not been finished. Nevertheless, owing to the lateness of the hour, Baldy did not have enough time to deploy his command and take any defensive position. Thus, he was glad to have the light of the next day for that purpose.[12]

Smith realized that all chance of surprise was now over. If the Federals persisted in crossing, they must fight for the hills south of the river. Burnside had proposed a surprise, but by ordering the army to the riverbank forty-eight hours before the attack, he had given Lee sufficient time to concentrate on the Federals and to fortify his positions on the hills. Burnside had persisted in crossing the river after all hope of a surprise had faded away, and now the Federals would have to fight under great disadvantage. There was, however, a very fine opportunity for turning what had been done into a feint and crossing the main army at Skinker's Neck. This might have resulted in the desired surprise and certainly would have placed the Federals in a better position. But this was not done.[13]

On the morning of December 12, the Sixth Corps recommenced passage of the river. The corps was ordered to align itself parallel to the old Richmond Road, with two divisions in front and one in reserve. The road ran parallel to the river and was approximately one-half mile southwest of the river and five or six hundred yards northeast of the range of hills occupied by the Stonewall Jackson's corps. The Sixth Corps' left would be protected by the First Corps, and its right would be protected by Deep Run, a tributary of the Rappahannock River. Brooks' First Division crossed and took position in front of Devens, relieving his skirmishers. Howe's Second Division was then ordered across and formed in line of battle on the left of General Brooks. Newton's Third Division was then crossed and formed in columns in reserve. As soon as the crossing was completed and the lines formed, Smith pushed the command forward. Brooks held the

Richmond Road and Deep Run with one line in front of the run, and Howe occupied the crest of a hill (over which ran the Richmond Road) with his right at a sharp turn of Deep Run. Part of Newton's division served as a connection with Reynolds' First Corps, which was formed on Smith's left. These movements were all accomplished under the cover of fog. When the fog lifted, Smith's lines became visible to the enemy occupying the hills in front. The troops of the Left Grand Division were as well protected as the topography would allow, and there was nothing to be done but maintain the skirmish line—which was more than a mile from the river and engaged nearly all the time—and to submit quietly to the feeble and erratic enemy artillery fire.[14]

After Reynolds had placed his corps on the left of Smith's, the two corps commanders met with the Left Grand Division commander to look over the situation. The three generals were on the most intimate social and official terms and had often discussed questions of general interest to the command. After looking at the maps, they unanimously agreed that the only reasonable plan was to put the forty thousand men of the Left Grand Division into columns of assault that night and, the next morning at daylight, rush the Confederate right flank at Prospect Hill and turn it just south of Reynolds' left. They would use the early morning fog to screen the assault from enemy artillery. As Smith covered the bridges, it was necessary that the Third Corps, then waiting behind the bridges on the left bank of the Rappahannock, relieve the Sixth Corps at dark to give sufficient time to place the forty thousand men into position. The three generals also wanted the men to get some rest in their places before the attack was made. The generals believed that Lee, being on the exterior, had longer lines than their own, which left him without enough force on his right to resist Franklin's assault. The three generals figured the demonstration on Lee's left would prevent a shift of any of his force from that flank. Besides this, they believed that the countryside was sufficiently open to permit them to turn the hills, which terminated to the right of the Richmond Road in front of Reynolds' corps.[15]

About five o'clock in the evening, Burnside met the three generals and was given their plan. Burnside did not explicitly state that the plan would be adopted, yet Franklin, Reynolds, and Smith discerned as much from the interview. As the army commander rode off, Franklin followed him and impressed upon him the necessity of placing the Third Corps under Franklin's command. Burnside told Franklin that he would receive his orders in two or three hours. Under the supposition that the orders would soon arrive, Franklin gave Reynolds and Smith orders to do all the preliminary work possible; that being done, the two corps commanders returned to Franklin's headquarters to await the arrival of Burnside's messenger. The three generals waited all night long. Franklin sent two messengers to Burnside to beg him to send the orders. About 3:00 a.m., Reynolds said he had a hard day's work ahead and must get some sleep. He did ask, however, to be sent for if he was needed. Franklin and Smith were too anxious about upcoming events to sleep and sat waiting until about 7:30 a.m. when Brigadier General James Hardie brought Burnside's order.[16]

Hardie, like Franklin and Smith, had long anticipated Burnside's orders. He went to the army commander's tent twice in the early morning only to find the order not ready. Instead, Hardie found Burnside hastily writing orders. Not wanting to detain Hardie any longer, Burnside gave him a pencil copy of Franklin's order to take to the Left Grand Division commander. Burnside assured Hardie that this was a duplicate, and that the full order would be sent by telegraph. Hardie left about 6:00 a.m. and, after a very difficult ride, arrived at Franklin's headquarters around 7:15 a.m. The telegraphed orders from Burnside had not arrived and Hardie's copy was the first order Franklin saw.[17]

Burnside's order stated, "Keep your command in position for a rapid movement down the Old Richmond road; and you will send out at once a division at least, to pass below Smithfield, to seize, if possible, the heights near Captain Hamilton's, on this side of the Massaponax, taking care to keep it well supported and its line of retreat open."[18] This vague and confusing order convinced the three generals that the army commander had rejected their plan of an attack in force on the left. First, by delaying the order until after sunrise, Burnside had made it impossible for Smith to move his corps into columns of assault or for Brigadier General George Stoneman's Third Corps to cross the river to protect the bridges. Second, by ordering an assault by only a well-supported division, Burnside appeared to reject the scope and force of the attack that Franklin and Smith had advocated. Moreover, Smith believed the wording of the order showed Burnside still relied on effecting a surprise. His order called on Franklin to "seize" the heights, which implied occupying an unguarded position. If he meant to capture a strongly defended position, the order should have been to "carry" the heights. Finally, the reference to moving down the Richmond Road indicated that the bulk of Franklin's command presumably was to cut Lee's retreat off once the Confederates vacated their lines.[19]

Despite Burnside's order showing little resemblance to the plan of the three generals, in fact, Burnside had largely adopted the idea of making the primary attack on the Federal left. His orders, however, were so vague and confusing that none of the Left Grand Division leaders understood the army commander's intention. Moreover, Brigadier General James Hardie, who delivered the orders and had gone over them with Burnside, did not convey his superior's intentions with Franklin. Given the order and the lateness of the hour, Franklin moved to act upon it as quickly as possible.[20]

Franklin, Reynolds, and Smith agreed that the order meant to send a well-supported division in an armed reconnaissance of the enemy's lines. Smith later commented on such a limited order, "Nothing more imbecile could be imagined."[21] Franklin chose Reynolds' corps for the assault since his troops were closest to the point ordered for the assault, and Smith's corps was still needed to protect the bridges. Reynolds ordered his largest division under Major General George G. Meade toward the point indicated in the order. Brigadier General John Gibbon was ordered to advance his division on Meade's right to support the attack. When Confederate cavalry and artillery endangered Meade's left, Reynolds sent Brigadier General Abner Doubleday's division to drive the enemy away.[22]

Smith's Corps would play a more limited role. It would protect the First Corps' right flank, and its artillery joined Reynolds' batteries to support the First Corps' assault, but the Sixth Corps largely stayed on the defensive. Smith maintained his line from the previous day with Brooks' Division and Howe's Division on each side of Deep Run in his front and Newton's Division in reserve. The Sixth Corps' primary role was to continue to protect the bridges while the First Corps was engaged. Bridge protection was particularly important because of Burnside's order "to keep the line of retreat open." The Confederates subjected Smith's corps to severe artillery fire. The Sixth Corps' skirmishers hotly engaged the enemy and finally silenced the Confederate fire. Throughout the morning, Smith did not want to advance his skirmishers too far as his lines were divided by Deep Run, and he wanted to maintain communications between his two front divisions.[23]

As Meade moved for the attack, Franklin ordered two divisions of the Third Corps to cross on the bridges and support Reynolds. Meade's division, striking at a gap in the Confederate front lines, carried the woods, crossed the Richmond Fredericksburg and Potomac Railroad tracks, and gained the crest of the hill, capturing two flags and about 200 prisoners. Gibbon's division also crossed the railroad and pushed the enemy back into the woods, but the density of the woods caused the connection between the two divisions to be lost. The limitation of the attack, because of Burnside's order, however, undermined the permanent success of the mission. Confederate reinforcements soon overpowered Meade and Gibbon and repulsed the Federals. Two divisions of the Third Corps came up to support Reynolds' attack, but they arrived only in time to relieve Meade's and Gibbon's divisions after their withdrawal and repulse the Confederate counterattack. During the afternoon, Newton's division was moved to support the First Corps after Reynolds' engagement and acted as the reserve for the Left Grand Division during the battle.[24]

Baldy's corps made only one infantry assault during the battle. About 3:00 p.m., Brooks attempted to extend the picket line on the left of the railroad and gain better control of Deep Run. He ordered Colonel Alfred T.A. Torbert's brigade, supported by one or two regiments, to move the line forward. The line and its supports advanced with a spirited bayonet attack and drove the 16th North Carolina beyond the road about six hundred yards in advance of Brooks' position. With the object being attained and not wanting to bring on a general engagement, Smith ordered the supports for the picket line to return to their first position. As the supports fell back, Confederate Brigadier General Evander M. Law's brigade counterattacked, causing Torbert's lead regiments to rapidly retreat. Two North Carolina regiments of Law's brigade then attempted to drive back Howe's division skirmish line. As the Confederates approached, they soon found themselves confronting Howe's line in front, Colonel Henry Whiting's Vermont Brigade on their left flank, and Brigadier General Daniel Sickles' division, led by Brigadier General Joseph Carr's brigade, on their right flank. The flanking fire from Sickles' and Whiting's soldiers and the artillery and infantry fire from Howe's line caused the North Carolinians to first reel, stagger, and finally break and retreat. Besides this repulse, the Confederates engaged in three separate artillery attacks on Howe's lines during the day. In each of these skirmishes, Howe's artillery drove the enemy from the field.[25]

The battle was the first for the Sixth Corps' bounty men. These soldiers had been paid a bounty to enlist and had come to the corps just a few days before the battle. Smith placed the bounty men in the front to save the veterans for heavy work. As the wounded bounty men were carried back through the ranks of the old soldiers, the latter would cry out, "Take good care of those men; they have cost the Government a great deal of money." During the afternoon, Smith heard some musket fire in his front and went to ascertain the cause. While riding along behind a regiment lying with their faces to the ground, a round shot struck the knapsack of a soldier. It was cut open, sending a cloud of underclothes into the air, and high above them floated a scattered pack of cards. The soldier, hearing the shouts of laughter, turned over to see what had happened. When he saw the mishap that had befallen him, he made a feeble effort to join in the laughter.[26]

Earlier in the afternoon, Burnside sent modified orders to Franklin to make a vigorous attack with his whole force. Unlike his orders that morning, the army commander's orders this time clearly showed his intention for the Left Grand Division to make a full attack. When the orders arrived about 2:25 p.m., the First and Third Corps were

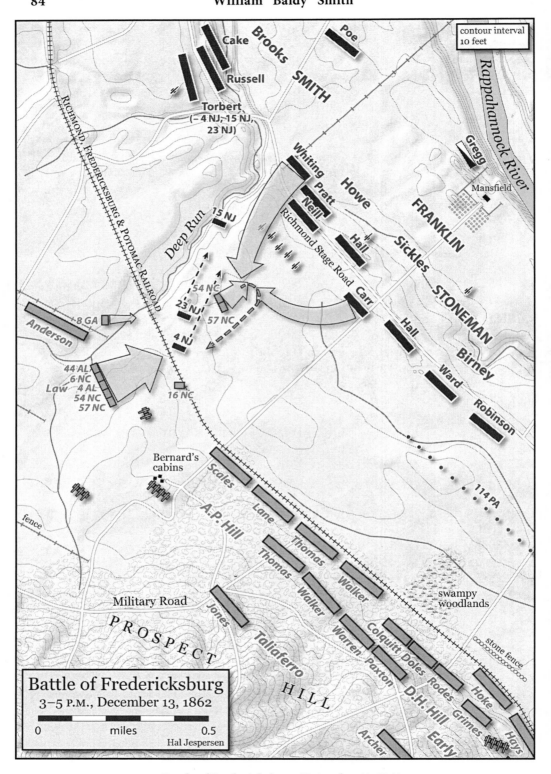

Battle of Fredericksburg, December 13, 1862.

already fully engaged; Franklin believed it was impossible to make any modifications of his troop placement. Had Franklin attacked with the Sixth Corps, the only troops in position, any disaster to the corps would have severely endangered his whole command. Franklin also believed the strength of the enemy and lateness of the day further justified not sending in Smith's corps. Moreover, Smith believed that since his corps covered the bridges during the battle, he could not possibly leave this position unless first relieved by at least two divisions. Evidently, both Franklin and Smith believed Brigadier General William W. Burns' division of the Ninth Corps, which came to help guard the bridges in the late afternoon, was insufficient protection for the only means of retreat for the nine divisions on the left.[27]

While the Left Grand Division was engaged, the Right Grand Division, which had previously occupied Fredericksburg, repeatedly assaulted Marye's Heights south of the town. The Confederate artillery and infantry occupied a strongly entrenched position behind a stone wall and severely repulsed every attack. Unable to break the Confederate lines, the Federals withdrew to the town in the evening.

The Left Grand Division held its position during the night, with the men sleeping on their arms. Soon after daylight on the fourteenth, the Confederates opened upon the Federal lines, but in twenty minutes, the Sixth Corps' batteries compelled the enemy in its front to retire. This was the last appearance of the enemy's artillery in front of the corps while it was on the south side of the river. The skirmish line during the day continued to be active, and at night the men again rested on their arms.[28]

On December 15, Newton relieved Howe's much exposed troops. About 6:00 p.m., Franklin ordered Smith to supervise the withdrawal of the Left Grand Division across the river. The move began shortly thereafter. The Sixth Corps was ordered to cross after the other troops, and everything was done quietly and expeditiously. The artillery was placed on the north bank while Captain R.B. Ayres positioned sufficient guns to form the line at the bridge head. Devens' and Torbert's brigades formed the line to cover the troops, and the pickets were ordered in only after the line was nearly formed. The recrossing during the night was done without loss and without interference from the enemy. By 4:00 a.m. the troops were all across, and everything was ready for the bridges to be removed.[29]

After the battle, Smith had four interviews with Burnside. The first was on the night of the fourteenth. According to Smith, Burnside told him of his grief over the great losses. Smith made some remark about the fate of soldiers and changed the subject. Burnside also said that he did not personally lead the Ninth Corps that day because the generals on the right made such references to the demoralization of their commands that he feared to make the attempt. Smith told Burnside that he "would promise to take the Sixth Corps against the enemy, and that there was no demoralization among the officers of that corps that would stop them."[30] After the army had recrossed the river, Smith saw him again, and Burnside told Smith that he had it in his mind to relieve Sumner from command, place Hooker in arrest, and give Franklin the command of the army.[31]

At Burnside's and Smith's third meeting, Reynolds was present. Burnside said that the men on the left did not fight well enough. To this Reynolds and Smith replied that the list of killed and wounded proved the contrary. Burnside then said, "I did not mean that; I meant there were not muskets enough fired," adding, "I made a mistake in my order to Franklin; I should have directed him to carry the hill at Hamilton's at all hazards."[32] At the fourth interview, Burnside said that the mistake was that Franklin did not get the order early enough on the morning of the attack, but Smith told him that the order should have arrived before midnight and directed the Federal left to make the grand attack that Franklin, Reynolds, and Smith had recommended to Burnside on the twelfth.[33]

The disaster at Fredericksburg was followed by attempts to determine the cause of the defeat. The Joint Committee on the Conduct of the War came to the Army of Potomac Headquarters to question leading figures. On December 19, Burnside and Franklin provided their testimony. Both argued that the failure of the attack was due to "the great strength of the [Confederate] position, and the accumulation of the enemy's force there." Both claimed that the delay in the arrival of the pontoon bridges gave the enemy sufficient time to prepare for the Federal attack. As Franklin said, "Had the bridges arrived when the army did, the army would have driven an enemy of 500 or 1,000 men from the heights and been in occupation of the heights that they were obliged to attack." Nevertheless, on the same day, Burnside wrote a letter to Halleck where he held himself fully accountable for the Fredericksburg defeat.[34]

To Franklin and Smith, Fredericksburg was not only a costly tactical blunder but a major strategic mistake. In answer to questions from the Joint Committee, Franklin had testified that in future operations, a new strategy was needed. The army should move against the Confederate capital from its south side by way of the James River. On December 20, Franklin and Smith wrote to Lincoln making a similar suggestion to abandon the overland strategy to take Richmond. They wrote that the plan of campaign already commenced would not be successful for two main reasons. First, the present line of communication was in danger of interruption. The distance from Fredericksburg to Richmond was sixty-one miles. It would be necessary to keep up the lines of communications from Aquia Creek Landing to Richmond. The heavy use of troops to protect the road or a rebuilt railroad from the landing would alert the enemy to the line and expose communications to Confederate attacks. This would constantly oblige the army to shift additional men to protect the lines. If a wagon train was used as the source of supplies, the trains would be so enormous that a great deal of strength of the army would be required to guard them. The troops would be so separated by the trains, and the roads so blocked by them, that the advance and rear of the army could not be within supporting distance of each other.[35]

Second, on the overland route, the enemy were able at many points to strongly post themselves and repulse Federal attacks. The total strength of the Union army was possibly insufficient to drive the Confederates away, and even were they driven away, the result would not be decisive. Confederate losses in their strong positions would be comparatively slight, while the Federals' would be enormous.[36]

Franklin and Smith then suggested to the president their plan to bring victory in the East. They first set down three prerequisites for any successful campaign. First, all the troops available in the East would need to be massed. Second, they should approach as near to Richmond as possible without an engagement. Third, the line of communication should be absolutely free from danger of interruption. The two generals then asserted that a campaign on the James River would fulfill these three prerequisites better than any other campaign. They gave three reasons. First, on the James River, the army from both north and south could be concentrated more rapidly than they could be at any other point. Second, the army could be brought to points within twenty miles of Richmond without the risk of an engagement. Third, communication by the James River could be kept up by the assistance of the navy without the slightest danger of interruption.[37]

Franklin and Smith followed this suggestion with some details about their proposed James River campaign. They hypothesized that by concentrating the troops in the East, they would be able to raise 250,000 men. The men available for the movement included the Army of the Potomac, troops in Florida and the Carolinas, regiments in process of organization, those who were on extra duty and furlough, deserters, and stragglers. One hundred and fifty thousand of these men would be landed on the north side of the river while one hundred thousand more would be placed on the south back, both groups as close to Richmond as possible. All soldiers were to carry three days' provisions on their persons, one hundred rounds of ammunition, and light baggage. Every third day, a corps or grand division would be provisioned from the river. The two armies marching up the banks might meet the enemy on or near the river. By means of pontoons—kept afloat and towed so as to be reached at any point—one army could in a few hours cross to assist the other. If the enemy declined to fight on the river, the army on the south bank, or a portion of it, would take possession of the railroads running south from Richmond, while the remainder would proceed to the investment or attack upon Richmond. Whether the investment of Richmond led to the destruction or capture of the Confederate army, or not, it certainly would lead to the capture of the capital, and the war would be on a better footing than it was then.[38]

Two days later, Lincoln replied to Franklin's and Smith's letter. The difficulties that the generals pointed out pertaining to the Fredericksburg line were "obvious and palpable." But Lincoln reminded the generals, "If you go to James River, a large part of the army must remain on or near the Fredericksburg line, to protect Washington." Lincoln also reminded Franklin that the Left Grand Division commander had supported the withdrawal of the army last July.[39]

Franklin replied for himself and Smith on December 26.[40] Both generals supposed that Washington and Harper's Ferry would be garrisoned sufficiently, and that the Potomac would be impassable except by bridges. Franklin had supported the army's withdrawal back in July because of its debilitated and unhealthy condition. He also feared the prospect of remaining in an unhealthy region during the hot summer months of August and September. At present, the army's health was good, and the cooler spring months for an offensive were ahead.[41]

Franklin's and Smith's action of sending these letters may have opened them up to the possible charge of insubordination. Sending their critique of the current strategy directly to the president certainly was outside the chain of command, for Franklin and Smith did not seek Burnside's permission to send the letters. Perhaps they did not consult the army commander because they believed the overland strategy was forced upon him and so he was not responsible for the current approach. Also, neither general believed the letters were aimed at their army commander. Both Franklin and Smith feared that if Burnside were removed, Hooker would succeed him, making matters worse both for the army and themselves. Their advice focused entirely on the Eastern Theater strategy that was determined in Washington. Now considering the third consecutive failure of an overland strategy with the debacles of the First Bull Run and Second Bull Run and now with the tragic defeat at Fredericksburg, the two generals believed it their duty to offer a reasonable alternative to this strategy. Franklin acknowledged, and presumably Baldy may have recognized, given the political atmosphere that they had observed, that such an action could end their careers. But the seriousness of the current situation was too great not to attempt to change a course that they sincerely believed "could not be possibly successful."[42]

While Smith was trying to convince the Chief Executive to abandon the over-land strategy, his men were dealing with more basic problems of camp life. The greater part of the men's energy was absorbed in procuring fuel and keeping the fires burning. On December 22, a newspaper reported from the Third Division, "Our troops are not dispirited in the least by our late reverse. They laugh, joke and perform their duties with the same earnestness as if they were fresh from victorious fields, and I am sure they would fight as well tomorrow as they did on the 13th of December."[43] But, the First Brigade, Second Division morning reports of late December show a far grimmer picture. The basic duty of policing the camp had been entirely disregarded. Large quantities of leaves and rubbish were scattered about the company streets and mess tents. A dead animal that was on a road near one of the camps lay unburied. Guard duty was entirely neglected and "so far as accomplishing any object for which Guards are detailed, or that of maintaining the discipline and instruction of the troops, it might as well be dispensed with entirely."[44] The sentinels did not receive the proper instructions and were not required to carry out those which were given. An officer of the day and officer of the guard did not visit, much less frequent their posts.[45]

This situation had improved by the end of the month. The sentinels were alert, and officers of the day did their assignments. The hospitals were in satisfactory condition, and most of the policing was being done. But one captain of the day reported "the horrid state of clothing of the brigade—especially in the way of pants and shoes." He found "many sentinels with one half of their feet entirely on the ground and in one instance 2 privates [sic] pants were so [horrid] as to be indecent and in every instance requisitions had been made for a long time."[46]

In January 1863, the men established permanent camps and built comfortable quarters for the winter. Smith and his men expected to be settled in until the spring. On January 16, Smith unexpectedly received orders from Burnside to ready his corps to march the next morning. They were to take three days' cooked rations and have the supply train loaded with hard bread and small commissary stores. Each man was to carry sixty rounds of ammunition. Smith had had no hint of this general movement. The order was not preceded by a formal conference with the Grand Division commanders, so the campaign they were to inaugurate had not been explained.[47]

Burnside intended to move the army up the Rappahannock, cross the river, and flank the Confederates above Fredericksburg. Meanwhile, the Sixth Corps exhibited a great deal of feeling against their army commander. Back on December 30, without Smith's knowledge of their intentions, two of Baldy's generals had gone to Washington to express their dissatisfaction with Burnside. General Newton, the Third Division commander, had already done so to Franklin and promised to talk to influential persons in Washington when he was on leave. Newton and one of his brigade commanders, John Cochrane, gained an interview with Lincoln. Cochrane believed that Newton, Franklin, and Smith considered the crossing of the river below the present Federal position at that time to be infeasible and urged the president to investigate Burnside's planned campaign. Newton endorsed Cochrane's statement but also privately believed that the army had lost the spirit needed to fight the campaign because it had no confidence in Burnside. Newton kept his anti–Burnside feelings to himself but told the president that the army was dispirited and urged Lincoln to investigate the problem.[48]

Burnside delayed the movement until January 20. He had sensed the resentment of the generals of the Left Grand Division. On the day of the movement, he told Henry

Raymond of the *New York Times* that Franklin, Smith, and others "seemed to think that any movement at this time was predestined to failure."[49] Burnside considered removing these generals because of their opposition, but in view of the difficulty of replacing them at such a late hour, he finally decided to order them back to their commands.[50]

With the campaign ahead, Smith endeavored to suppress this anti–Burnside sentiment because it was weakening discipline. Also, Smith believed that a change in the command of the army would worsen its situation. He therefore called the general officers of the Sixth Corps together and declared to them that whatever opinions they might individually entertain of the commanding general, or of the orders under which they were about to move, the Sixth Corps would be expected to do its duty and preserve its high reputation for efficiency. This was warmly agreed to by the generals present.[51]

The evening before the movement, Franklin told Smith, "Your corps led off in the last campaign, but Reynolds was pretty severely handled, and you must lead off again."[52] The head of Smith's command was again at the appointed place at the proper time, and he went to examine the ground over which they were to operate. The crossing for Franklin's grand division was to be at a point just above Bank's Ford. Smith found that this crossing was in a bend of the river concave to the Federal movement. This was tactically unsound. Smith was naturally indignant at so plain a blunder that would unnecessarily endanger his men. He met the Army's chief engineer, Lieutenant Cyrus B. Comstock, whom Smith supposed responsible for the selection of the crossing place, and expressed his views in terms more concise than diplomatic. Comstock listened quietly to Smith's remarks and then told Baldy that Burnside had himself selected the crossing and would listen to no suggestion with reference to any other place. With that, Smith returned to his headquarters.[53]

At nine o'clock on the morning of the January 20, Smith's corps, in the advance, moved from their position five miles below Falmouth. The corps marched seven or eight miles. The weather was fair and the roads dry and hard. That night around 10:00, a northeast storm set in with high wind and a deluge of rain. The next day the storm and army continued. Smith put a whole regiment at the drag ropes of a wagon loaded with pontoons, and they could not move it an inch. Smith wrote Franklin, "It is not possible to get these boats into the rivers so that we can make a fight today, and the enemy will have all night to concentrate against us."[54] Not a single boat arrived at the crossing point. The pontoons spread along the route for two miles, blocking the roads and preventing any of the artillery from being placed in position. The corps' march only progressed two or three miles.[55]

The next day, the storm continued, and the order to march was countermanded. The men built huge fires and dried themselves as well as they could. With the roads nearly impassable and the fords not reached, the campaign was abandoned. The next day at daybreak, the Sixth Corps marched back to its camp. Generally, the men marched back with more animation and vigor than could have been expected after their exposure to the storm. A number of them, however, joined the stragglers who filled the roads and fields. These squads of soldiers suffered from want of food and care and from fevers and colds. This abortive campaign also brought destruction to hundreds of horses, wagons, and artillery carriages.[56]

During the day on which the movement was abandoned, Franklin and Smith were invited to lunch with Burnside. The army commander's friends from Rhode Island had sent him a galantine of turkey, and he decided to share it with two of his generals.

During the lunch, Smith noticed that Burnside's actions were very peculiar. At times, he was silent and moody, and then he would break out and talk rapidly about matters. In one of his talkative moments, he said to Franklin and Smith, "In a day or two you will hear of something that will surprise you." He did not offer any explanation, and the two generals asked for none. Two more times he uttered the same remark, and the two generals left without learning the cause of the surprise. They did not have long to wait.[57]

Despite the role of the weather in bringing an end to the movement, Burnside blamed the disloyalty of his generals for the failure of the Mud Campaign. On the day that he abandoned the campaign, January 23, Burnside wrote General Orders No. 8, subject to Lincoln's approval, dismissing some of his generals from the army and removing others from their commands. Baldy's Sixth Corps was particularly cited. The commanders of the First Division, Third Division, and First Brigade, Third Division were to be dismissed because Brooks had spoken against the policies of the government, and Newton and Cochrane had gone to Washington to criticize Burnside's plans. Brooks, in a letter to his father on February 17, denied that he had spoken against the policy of the government or had used language tending to create insubordination. Nevertheless, Brooks' 1862 letters to his father show the First Division commander's strong anti-administration sentiment. During the Peninsula campaign, Brooks believed Lincoln and Stanton were devoid of any generalship. He commented on Jackson's threat to Washington, "If he will only capture the executive and congress there might be some aleviation [sic] of the disgrace."[58] In October, he condemned the Emancipation Proclamation as "military despotism."[59] While the charges against Newton and Cochrane were more valid, both testified before the Committee on the Conduct of the War on February 9 that their discussions in Washington did not interfere with Burnside's plans. Cochrane claimed that he had simply urged presidential inquiry into Burnside's campaign.[60]

While dismissing three of Smith's generals, Burnside's order also removed Smith from command of the Sixth Corps and Franklin from command of the Left Grand Division. The only reason given for this was that these two generals could not be of any "further service to this army."[61] Smith wrote to Burnside after the order was published to determine the cause of his removal. Burnside did not answer for two years. Finally, in 1865, Burnside wrote to Smith that he dismissed some generals who could not give earnest support to an overland campaign and had openly expressed to officers and formally to authorities in Washington that such a campaign would be unsuccessful. Burnside considered Smith one of these generals. But, Burnside added, "It may be proper to say that after reflection and consultation, I decided to take your name from the list, as I believed that not withstanding your committal against the campaign, you would give your cooperation, and had I been allowed to issue General Order No. 8 your name would not have appeared in it."[62]

Lincoln met with Burnside on the night of January 23 and refused to endorse the order. Instead, Burnside was relieved of command. Believing he had few other options, the president decided to appoint Joseph Hooker to become the new army commander on January 25. Political factors played an important role in Hooker's selection. Lincoln understood that Hooker had popular support, particularly within his own party. Hooker had the support of the influential Committee on the Conduct of the War and Treasury Secretary Salmon P. Chase. With the same order that appointed Hooker to succeed Burnside, Lincoln also relieved Franklin of command. Union officer and postwar historian the Comte de Paris commented on Franklin's relief years later in his multivolume work on the Civil War. He attributed Lincoln's action to Franklin's faithfulness to McClellan that created too many enemies in Washington. As one newspaper reported on the promotion of Hooker and the removals of Burnside, Sumner, and Franklin: "It is probable the recent conference at Washington between the President, the War Department and Republican Senators and Representatives, has precipitated these changes. The radicals now have entire possession of the Army of the Potomac."[63]

Franklin's removal left Smith in temporary command of the Left Grand Division. The *New York Times* believed the removal of Franklin was justified if the reports were true that his devotion to McClellan made it impossible to serve any other army commander. Referring to the new Left Grand Division commander, the paper said, "Though a bosom friend of Gen. Franklin—always camping near, and constantly with him—he has showed an antipathy for Gen. McClellan only equaled by Franklin's admiration."[64] The *Times* overestimated Smith's dislike for McClellan but not his affection for Franklin. Smith's tenure in the Army of the Potomac, nevertheless, soon came to an end. On February 4, Smith was relieved of command of the Sixth Corps and transferred to take command of the Ninth Corps, which was to be detached from the Army of the Potomac and sent to Fort Monroe. As soon as he learned of the order, Smith wrote to the Adjutant General to inquire about the reason for his transfer. Baldy wrote that he felt complimented by his assignment to the Ninth Corps but regretted leaving the Army of the Potomac with which he had been so long associated. His request for the cause of his transfer, however, was not answered.[65]

General Meade, a friend of both Smith and Franklin, thought the cause of Smith's relief was "his affiliation with Franklin, and the fear that he would not co-operate with Hooker."[66] Smith confirmed Meade's view. Smith believed, "Hooker caused me to be promptly relieved from duty with the army, which was proper for I had far less confidence in him than in Burnside."[67] Hooker still supported Smith's transfer because it "will conduce to the good feeling and efficiency of this army, and, perhaps to that of the Ninth Corps."[68]

Baldy, in his farewell address to the Sixth Corps, stated, "Your soldierly qualities makes [sic] it a high honor to command you, and long months of association with you makes me regret the separation." To his old division, he recounted the past. He urged the Second Division not to forget their valor and success on the Peninsula and at Antietam, where they faced an advancing enemy and "drove them back in confusion and saved the right wing at The Antietam."[69]

On the day of Smith's departure, a large number of officers assembled at his headquarters about noon to bid their late commander farewell. Nearly two hours were spent in mutual leave-takings with the general standing in his tent and grasping each officer by the hand as they filed past him. When he came to take his departure, nearly two hundred mounted officers, in full dress with sash and gauntlets, escorted him. Smith was reported to be universally loved by the officers and men of his command.[70]

Perhaps one of his staff best summed up Smith's relationships with his men and superiors. Major Thomas W. Hyde, the Sixth Corps acting inspector general, recalled:

"Baldy" Smith was a kind man to his subordinates, and had the soul of a great soldier in him. He was at times a perfect Ishmaelite to his superior officers, as they found out to their cost. I have seen him handle his division in a way that Napoleon would have loved and yet sometimes, when the pall of superior authority fell over him, he was a dreadful kicker. He wrecked the chance of a greater name in these ways. Still, he was so kind to me when he commanded forty thousand men—to me, still a boy with all a boy's freshness and belief in everybody—that he ranks yet in my mind among the greatest commanders of the war.[71]

Unbeknownst to Smith, his command of the Ninth Corps was to be temporary. While Hooker did recommend Smith's relief from duty in his command, he urged Halleck to give the permanent command of the Ninth Corps to Smith. On the day Smith was transferred, Halleck wrote Hooker that Burnside was the permanent commander of the Ninth Corps, and Smith's tenure could only be temporary.[72]

Smith began the ordered movement of the Ninth Corps to Fort Monroe on February 6. The Third Division struck tents on the Rappahannock River, near Falmouth, and proceeded by train to Aquia Creek and thence by transports to Fort Monroe, where it arrived on February 10. It then proceeded to Newport News. The Second Division struck tents on February 9 and followed the same route as the Third Division. It arrived at Newport News on February 11. The First Division left its camp on the Rappahannock on February 10 and joined the other two divisions at Newport News. Smith was ordered to report to Major General John Dix, who was to use the corps as he needed it but was required to keep the corps together as much as possible.[73]

Smith determined to make the corps a model in efficiency and condition and prepare it for whatever service was in store for it. During the time the corps was in Newport News, much attention was given to regimental, brigade, and division drills. About five hours each day were devoted to these exercises, and they were of great value in perfecting the discipline and adding to the efficiency of the corps. The men did not find the drills irksome and became very proud of their efficiency. Better conditions also improved morale. The men were immensely relieved to leave the mud and filth of Falmouth. Quarters at Newport News had bunks and fireplaces. The weather was delightful, and the men had plenty of soft bread. Smith also tried to improve morale by urging Dix to give permission to increase the number of furloughs for the corps.[74] In the latter part of February, Generals Dix and Smith reviewed the corps.

Smith's tenure with the Ninth was brief. Only twelve days after Smith's transfer, Halleck wrote to Burnside, "If [it is] agreeable to you to resume the command in North Carolina and of the Ninth Army Corps, please come to Washington." Burnside replied on February 17 that he would leave for Washington at once. Burnside assumed command of the Ninth Corps a month later.[75]

Smith lost not only his Ninth Corps command, but also his qualifications to be a corps commander. On March 4, Congress adjourned without confirming Smith's commission as major general of volunteers. He reverted to the rank of Brigadier General, and since permanent corps commands required major general rank, Smith could not serve as head of a corps. On March 8, he turned his temporary command over to Brigadier General Orlando B. Willcox.[76]

The next day, Smith visited Lincoln and asked that the period of his service as a major general be considered a leave from his office as a Brigadier General of Volunteers, so that he could again take his place in the regular army. He also wanted to have a leave of absence of as long as the service would admit. The following day Smith wrote to Lincoln:

> I am so certain that somebody has made false & slanderous accusations against me to you that I deem it due to my own reputation to appeal to your well known sense of justice to let me know the nature of the charges against me, and to say to you that if I cannot refute to your entire satisfaction any reports affecting my zeal in the war, my character, or my capacity so far as it has been tried I am willing to have it optional with yourself to accept my resignation or dismiss me from the service.[77]

Lincoln decided neither to give Smith a new command nor dismiss him. After Smith formally lost the command, he received orders to proceed to New York and await orders. On March 19, while at home in New York City, he received thirty days' leave of absence. Baldy could take small consolation in his recent promotion to Major of Engineers in the regular army.[78]

The reasons for the Senate's failure to confirm Smith as a major general of volunteers can only be suggested. It was highly unlikely that Smith's military performance would have caused anyone to hesitate in his confirmation. He had won brevets for his work on the Peninsula and had been critical to the Federal success at Antietam. He was not seriously engaged at Fredericksburg, but this was not his fault. One possible reason was that no vacancies existed at the corps command level in the East that would have necessitated his promotion to major general. Even had there been an opening, Hooker's and Burnside's opposition would have been sufficient to block Smith's appointment. Nevertheless, Smith's military service justified his confirmation if immediate practical need did not.[79]

The more probable reason for Smith's demotion was that Smith fell victim of a campaign by some administration and congressional Republicans to purge the army of friends of McClellan, the leading Democratic general. Smith had a long association with McClellan and his Democratic general-friends, F.J. Porter and W.B. Franklin. Smith's relations with McClellan had cooled since the beginning of the war, but Baldy believed McClellan was clearly superior to Burnside and Hooker as an army commander. Smith was a dear friend of Porter since they were classmates at West Point. Smith was totally devoted to Franklin. The Republicans eliminated Porter and Franklin from high commands. Porter was unjustly court-martialed for Pope's defeat at Second Bull Run and was dismissed from the army. The Committee on the Conduct of the War was in the midst of planning to make Franklin the scapegoat for the Federal disaster at Fredericksburg. In addition, Smith had been an opponent of the administration's overland campaign and was a strong advocate of the peninsula strategy, long identified with McClellan. Smith blamed the War Department for Porter's court-martial and defended Franklin against the charges that he was the cause of the Fredericksburg defeat. Finally, Smith's contempt for Hooker, the current Republican favorite, added an important reason to press for Smith's demotion. The Senate thus found an easy means to reduce the authority of one of the more troublesome of McClellan's general-friends.[80]

The Republican efforts to purge the army of Democratic generals was central to the motives of the Joint Committee of the Conduct of the War when they resumed hearings in Washington in February and March. The earlier testimony given in December about logistical blunders originating in Washington and challenges faced by commanders on the field had embarrassed the Republicans. They now changed the direction of the questions to find a Democratic general to blame for the disaster, and Franklin became their scapegoat. Burnside, probably seeing an opportunity to shift responsibility to others, changed his story and now blamed Franklin and Hooker for the entire disaster. In regard to Franklin's role, Burnside claimed that his order to send "one division at least" meant "two or three small divisions, or one large one." In fact, Franklin had done this with engaging the entire First Corps. Nonetheless, Burnside testified that Franklin's failure to commit his entire command to battle caused the defeat. Burnside devoted even more criticism to Hooker for his lack of cooperation in contributing to the attack on the Confederate left. In his testimony, Franklin correctly pointed out that he was not initially ordered to commit his entire command. Burnside's orders on the day of the battle, his letter to Halleck on December 19, 1862, and his December testimony, proved that the army commander's initial orders indicated an expectation to take Captain Hamilton's Crossing and the heights above Fredericksburg with two well supported divisions and then attack with the whole command all along the line. Franklin believed that Burnside's order in the afternoon to attack with his whole command was actually a request to attack if he could, and Franklin told Burnside it was too late in the day and impossible without severely endangering his entire command. Franklin also testified that shortly after the battle, knowing what had occurred on the left, Burnside had made no criticism of Franklin's performance. Both Franklin and Reynolds testified that the reserve divisions were needed to protect the bridges as Burnside's order had directed.[81]

The committee, uninterested in determining the true cause for the defeat at Fredericksburg, blocked Smith's attempts to help Franklin. Smith wrote an affidavit that entirely supported Franklin's testimony. It included Burnside's rejection of Franklin's and Smith's plan to make the main attack on the left. Smith also recounted his post-battle interviews with Burnside that showed that the army commander believed Franklin should succeed him in command of the army. But Smith's affidavit was ignored, and suggestions that he testify before the committee were rejected. Given the Joint Committee's primary goal, they determined to ignore Halleck's serious logistical failures, Burnside's vague orders, and Hooker's failures, and in their final report, blamed Franklin, helping to justify the administration's removal of Franklin from his command and making a Democratic general the scapegoat for the Fredericksburg disaster.[82]

The committee's injustices, however, were not overlooked by postwar historians and writers. Smith, determined to clear Franklin's record, slightly revised his original affidavit and had it published in *Battles and Leaders*. *New York Times* war correspondent and historian William Swinton understood Burnside's feeble attempt to put the blame on Franklin. He wrote, "Judging by the orders in which General Burnside's original intent and will are revealed, rather than by the inspirations of afterthought, it is manifest that, if he designed to make the main attack from the left, he at least made no provisions for giving effect to this intention."[83] The Comte de Paris also denied that Franklin's failure to make the general attack was his fault. It was the Comte de Paris' position that Franklin could not have been expected to go beyond the literal execution of his orders because Burnside never made his feelings clear, and the orders were "vague or contradictory."[84] Citing Smith's article, John C. Ropes supported Franklin's view that Burnside's order was to take a division "well supported" and capture the heights on the Confederate left and right. Ropes called a plan based on such an underestimation of the enemy "a wild and absurd plan of battle."[85] Ropes believed "That the object ordered to be attained was of such limited scope was the fault of Burnside alone."[86] Burnside's modification of his original orders in the afternoon was "received too late to admit of the necessary dispositions being made for the employment of the troops in any other way than that in which they were at the time occupied."[87] Swinton and Ropes agreed that the plan of Franklin, Smith, and Reynolds for the main attack on the left was the best possible strategy for the Federals, but both doubted if any plan could have succeeded against such a strong Confederate position.[88]

Modern historians have widened the critique of the Fredericksburg campaign. They point out that President Lincoln's push for a successful campaign despite the General-in-Chief's failure to adequately support the significant logistical needs of the campaign endangered its success from the outset. Despite the loss of surprise and the concentration of Lee's army, Burnside believed his superiors in Washington gave him no alternative but to attack. Burnside's confusing orders in the morning and his failure to convey his overall strategy to his two front line Grand Division commanders kept his strategic intentions hidden from them. But historians also criticize Franklin for not taking more initiative on the field to take advantage of Meade's breakthrough regardless of his view of Burnside's orders. They are also critical of his failure to follow Burnside's afternoon orders, particularly as the army commander relied on Franklin to make the main Federal attack.[89]

Finally, one other factor helped to explain the failure on the field. Franklin's biographer, Mark Snell, notes that the recent reorganization of the Army of the Potomac with its Grand Division structure placed commanders in new positions where they were unfamiliar with each other's approaches. The communication problems on the day of the battle reflected this unfamiliarity. Had Franklin had a better understanding of Burnside's intentions, he may have put into action the plan they had discussed the night before. Had Burnside known better Franklin's methodical tactical approach, his orders would have been more explicit and detailed. Similarly, had Reynolds known better of Franklin's approach to allow his subordinates wide tactical discretion, he may have taken a greater role on the field and supported Meade's breakthrough. In short, these commanders had not had the time prior to the battle to train and work together in their new positions, so under the stress of combat, they failed to reach their full potential.[90]

The War Department, in particular, pushed the Republican policy to eliminate McClellan's influence in the army. Smith later wrote, "Stanton was so hostile to McClellan that he persecuted every person whom he thought was a friend of McClellan."[91] Stanton grew particularly hostile to Franklin and Smith after their letter to Lincoln suggesting he abort the overland campaign. Stanton apparently believed Smith's demotion to Brigadier General was insufficient punishment for his association with McClellan. After being on leave a month, Smith wrote to the adjutant general on April 20, 1863, noting that his leave of absence had expired and requested orders. But Baldy did not receive a reply to his inquiry. Convinced that his war service had merited commendation rather than punishment, Smith became annoyed by the administration's failure to restore him to a field command.[92]

Some prominent citizens of New York City went to Washington to ask Stanton whether it was not wise to use all willing hands and to put Smith into the field. Stanton said he would at once order Smith to duty and asked where he would like to be sent. To this inquiry, Smith wrote Stanton that he had no preference except that he did not wish to be sent to the Department of the Gulf, because the heat there gave him severe headaches and would subsequently make him unfit for duty. In a few days, on May 25, 1863, Smith received orders to report to Major General Nathaniel P. Banks in New Orleans. Smith promptly got a certificate from two medical doctors in New York stating that his condition had a "tendency to congestion of the brain during the last several years when in a hot climate and from his present state of health, think that it would be exceedingly unwise to send him to a warm or malarious climate on a tour of service, at any time from May to October inclusive."[93] The certificate blocked Smith's order to New Orleans.[94]

The attempt of Stanton to send Baldy to the Gulf forced Smith to conclude that he was under a ban from which he could not escape. He considered leaving the army altogether and starting out afresh in civil life. At least in a civilian occupation, Smith wrote, "my enemies would be of my own making and would have behind them no despotic power."[95]

Smith's corps commands, particularly his supportive work at Fredericksburg, had not tested his tactical ability. Serving under an unsuccessful army chief—General Burnside—Baldy did his best and kept his command fit for future operations. As Sixth Corps commander, he addressed both tactical and strategic failure by questioning Burnside's plan of operations and the overland route. Smith's challenge to the plans of his superiors and his ties to other Democratic generals led to his departure from the Army of the Potomac. Apparently, Smith's demotion in rank and command was not sufficient punishment. Secretary of War Stanton had Smith thinking of resignation. Fortunately, the coming Gettysburg campaign gave Baldy an opportunity to resume some service, although political difficulties would continue to bedevil William Farrar Smith's wartime activities.

CHAPTER VIII

Smith's Command
in the Gettysburg Campaign

Ancillary Military Efforts
and Continued Political Trials

Just when Smith was seriously considering resigning from military service, the erstwhile corps commander found that Major General Darius Couch had been given the new command of the Department of the Susquehanna. Couch, disgusted by serving under two incompetent army commanders, obtained relief from his Second Corps command in the Army of the Potomac, and Lincoln gave him the newly formed department in eastern Pennsylvania. Smith considered Couch an excellent commander and "the soul of honor and justice."[1] As soon as Smith learned of Couch's new command, Smith wrote to him and told him that if he could aid Couch, to apply for him. Couch complied with Smith's request, and Baldy was ordered to report to Couch for temporary duty on June 17, 1863. But Smith had not heard the last of Secretary of War Stanton.[2]

Since Smith's departure from the Army of the Potomac, the Federal position in the East had declined. As Smith had feared, Hooker proved as incapable of commanding the army as Burnside. In May, General Lee had humiliated Hooker at the Battle of Chancellorsville. In early June, Lee moved northward to begin his second invasion of the North. To resist this campaign, the Army of the Potomac moved between Lee and the Federal capital, and the Department of the Susquehanna attempted to strengthen local defenses.[3]

Smith's first duty under Couch was to inspect the defenses of the Susquehanna on June 20 and make such dispositions as were necessary for the river's defense. Five days later, Smith was placed in command of all troops on the south side of the Susquehanna in the vicinity of Harrisburg. He had command of the First Division of the Department. These troops were composed of several brigades of Pennsylvania militia and New York National Guardsmen. From June 26 to June 30, Smith was busily engaged in strengthening the defenses at Bridgeport, opposite the city of Harrisburg, and at Marysville. He was to protect the bridges of the Northern Central and Pennsylvania Railroads.[4]

Strengthening the defenses around Pennsylvania's capital included several different tasks. The rock cut of the Northern Central Railroad below Fort Washington near Bridgeport was barricaded. Rifle pits were constructed on the top of the cut, in several positions occupied by the troops down the river, and in front of the small work on the hill opposite Harrisburg. The narrow pass of the Northern Central Railroad and the common road at the end of North Mountain on the river, one mile below the end of the

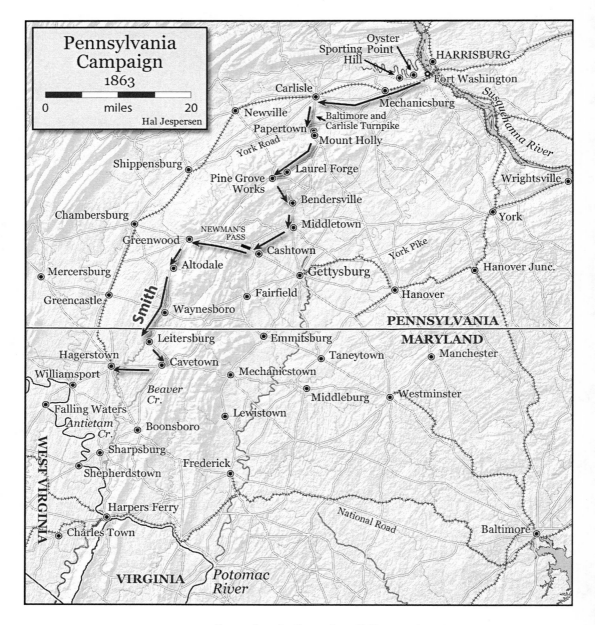

Pennsylvania Campaign, 1863.

Pennsylvania Railroad bridge, were filled by small works of rock, earth, and sandbags. In addition, three works were constructed on the hill opposite Harrisburg. The engine house of the Cumberland Valley Railroad was pierced for musketry, and its doors were barricaded with cross-ties and sandbags, forming embrasures for two pieces commanding the railroad.[5]

By June 28, Smith had done nearly all he could do. He sent Brigadier General Charles Yates' brigade to secure the Pennsylvania and Northern Central Railroad bridges from attack by way of Sterretts Gap or other passes in North Mountain.

Nevertheless, he admitted to Couch that his forces were weak above and below the bridges, and he requested two more regiments. Couch could only send him one. Smith had combustible materials placed at the west end of the Public Bridge so that, if necessary, the bridge could be destroyed at a moment's notice. Confederate Lieutenant General Richard Ewell sent a cavalry brigade towards Sporting Hill with the intention to determine whether an infantry force could capture Harrisburg. The brigade under Confederate Brigadier General Albert Jenkins with a section of artillery came to Smith's picket line near Oyster Point, an intersection of two roads leading from Carlisle about three miles from Fort Washington. The Confederates drove in his cavalry pickets but failed in moving the infantry pickets.[6]

On June 29, Smith sent the regular cavalry on the Carlisle Road. There it engaged and drove in enemy pickets but was obliged to retire under enemy artillery fire. The next day, learning that the Confederate infantry had left Carlisle, Couch and Smith determined to march all the available force to try and get into a position to assist the Federal pursuit of Lee's army. Smith's force totaled around 3,000 men. Lee had decided to concentrate his divided forces at Cashtown, while the Army of the Potomac, under its new commander Major General George Meade, advanced northward from Maryland. Smith ordered the cavalry forward and found a portion of enemy at Sporting Hill. Brigadier General John Ewen's Twenty-Second and Thirty-Seventh regiments, New York National Guard, went forward to support the cavalry. A section of Captain Henry D. Landis' battery was immediately ordered up. Some of Jenkins' force was found in position and attacked about 4:00 p.m. The attack stopped the enemy infantry fire, but the Confederates countered with artillery fire. The Federal artillery arrived on the ground about 5:00 p.m. and soon silenced the enemy fire. The enemy retired, and Ewen returned to camp.[7]

Ewen's command was ordered forward to occupy Carlisle but did not march until the next morning. His command had had no food since breakfast and lacked enough rations and blankets. A considerable portion of the command had also been working in the trenches during the preceding night. Owing to the delay in procuring and preparing rations, it was daylight before a meal could be obtained; immediately after breakfast, Ewen marched for Carlisle. The troops were refreshed by the inhabitants of the small villages along the march, who stood at their doors with offerings of food. Colonel William Brisbane, commanding the Pennsylvania Brigade, was ordered to move on Carlisle by the mud road at daylight but, owing to a want of transportation, did not move until about 9 a.m. The remainder of Smith's command under Brigadier General Joseph F. Knipe was directed to march as far as practicable and encamp and then move at an early hour the next morning.[8]

Smith visited headquarters to receive instructions and make arrangements for recrossing the river and for supplies and transportation. After arrangements were completed, Smith ordered the force immediately under his command to move toward Carlisle. The Eleventh New York Artillery refused to march, alleging that as artillery troops, they would not move as infantry. Smith referred the matter to Couch. This delayed Smith's start until 3:30 p.m. Finally, leaving orders with Knipe to carry out Couch's instructions regarding the refractory regiment, Smith left to join the advance. Hearing rumors of a large cavalry force in the vicinity, Smith sent out scouts on the crossroads. He then moved forward, entering Carlisle at sunset with the New York brigade in the lead. Smith pushed on the road toward Mount Holly in an effort to occupy the gorge in the South Mountains that night.[9]

Ewen had passed through the town and marched on the Baltimore Turnpike for about a mile and a half when Smith, going forward to examine Ewen's position, received word from his scouts that a large cavalry force of the enemy was in the immediate vicinity on the York Road. Smith decided to concentrate his command in Carlisle and face the Confederate force. He ordered the leading brigade to return to the town and hurried back to post the Pennsylvania militia, which was at the time passing through the town. As Smith returned, he passed many stragglers from his command. They filled the road for several miles. These new soldiers were unaccustomed to the exhausting effects of a long march. Before Smith entered the village, enemy guns had opened on his force.[10]

Confederate Major General J.E.B. Stuart had ordered Brigadier General Fitzhugh Lee to Carlisle to seek rations and find a portion of the enemy. With a force of 3,300 cavalrymen and seven guns, Lee had approached the town from the direction of Mechanicsburg. He did not know that Smith's forces occupied the place. Shots were exchanged with Smith's pickets. Several shells were fired over the town, and one or two went up Railroad Street into the square. Landis' battery, posted in the square, replied with three shots.[11]

Under these circumstances, Smith determined to content himself with simply holding the town until morning. On returning to Carlisle, the regiments were subdivided into detachments to guard the several approaches to the town. The Pennsylvania regiments were posted in the northerly portion; the Thirty-Seventh Regiment, with one field piece, guarded the central portion under the immediate command of Smith; and the Twenty-Second Regiment, with the one remaining field piece, protected the southerly portion of the town under Ewen's command. Skirmishers were also thrown out. Before Smith could get a line of skirmishers out, Fitzhugh Lee sent a summons to the town to either surrender or send out the women and children. Smith answered that the women and children would be notified to leave. In less than half an hour, Lee sent another message warning that if the town was not surrendered, it would be burned. Smith replied that one answer had already been given. He received two deputations: one of the town's men urging him to surrender, and one of ladies begging him to fight it out. He then sent a volunteer aide, Mr. Ward, to communicate with Knipe and ordered him to march at 3:00 a.m. Knipe was to report the position of affairs to Couch. Smith took as much territory in the town as he could cover and posted the troops to make a good defense. The artillery covered the streets, and the infantry units were placed in the streets and the houses on the lines of approach. In the meantime, the enemy opened a battery on the town. Smith's artillery did not reply as he deemed the fire too inaccurate and wished to save his ammunition. The 134 shots fired by the Confederates damaged several houses, wounded men, and killed one horse.[12]

About eleven o'clock that night, Smith sent another aide, Captain James Dougherty, to order Knipe to move immediately. Dougherty was captured and his orderly wounded. About midnight, a third and last summons came to surrender, to which Smith responded that the message had been twice answered before. Dougherty was sent in with this third flag of truce, principally to give the impression that Lee's force was very large and could easily destroy the town. During the night, a delegation of ladies called on Smith, asking where they could go to be sheltered from the shells that were coming into the town. Smith told them he thought the cellars to be the safest place for them. The women replied, "But they are full of your soldiers."[13] Stuart's forces set fire to the boardyard, gasworks, government barracks, and principal arsenal buildings situated about half a mile east from the town, all of which were consumed. They were too far away for Smith to protect.[14]

About one o'clock in the morning, the firing virtually ceased. Soon reports came in that the enemy was moving off on a country road that intersected the turnpike about two and a half miles from Carlisle. By daylight, there was nothing to oppose Smith's force. The casualties were twelve wounded, one fatally.[15]

The ladies of Carlisle seemed to think Smith had protected their homes, but he realized that had his troops not occupied Carlisle, the Confederates probably would not have disturbed the town or burnt the barracks. These ladies, however, remembered Baldy for his defense of their town. On November 5, 1863, as a testimonial of their gratitude for his defense of the town against the enemy on July 1, the ladies presented Smith with a beautiful silver pitcher. In a letter of thanks, Smith stated that he hoped the war would not reach Carlisle again. A very old lady also wished to do something in recognition of the defense. She painted a cabinet picture of Smith from a photograph and sent it to his family. It was a good likeness in every respect but the hair, which was profuse and red![16]

Smith placed his command near the burnt government barracks on July 2. His men waited all the next day for provisions. On the two previous days, supply trains had been prevented from arriving because the road was occupied by the enemy. Supplies arrived by railroad during the evening. The supplies that Smith could draw from the citizens were extremely limited, though they tried their best to aid his troops. Also, on July 3, Knipe's command joined Smith at Carlisle.[17]

While Smith was having his division supplied, he received orders from Couch for his movement southward. Couch wrote to Baldy that Halleck was anxious for him to send a force by rapid marches to operate on Lee's flank, if possible near Cashtown, in order to make a diversion in favor of Meade's army. Couch felt Smith's movement would serve that purpose.[18]

While Smith was at Carlisle, the advance of the Army of the Potomac under General Reynolds encountered a Confederate division at Gettysburg. The two army commanders raced their forces to concentrate there on July 1. Lee's forces pushed the Federals southward through Gettysburg, but the Federals under General Hancock maintained a strong position on Cemetery Ridge. Two more days of heavy fighting occurred before Lee decided to give up the campaign and return south.[19]

Smith agreed to make a diversion in Meade's favor, but realized that his command suffered under two major handicaps. First, supplies were difficult to gather from the countryside, and provision trains were insufficient and unreliable. The men suffered from a lack of food, clothing, shoes, and tents. Second, Smith's troops, only recently mustered to meet the present emergency, were insufficiently trained and lacked proper discipline. Many of the men could not even sustain long marches. The adjutant general wrote Stanton that Smith's New York artillerists were "perfectly worthless and will have to be sent back."[20] Couch warned Meade that while Smith should have nearly 10,000 men, "one half are very worthless, and 2,000 cavalry, with a battery, can capture the whole party in an open country.... Smith will endeavor to get in their [the Confederates] rear, but you must not expect that his raw militia will kill a great many."[21] Overcoming these handicaps, Smith was able to straighten out these problems and fulfill Couch's orders.[22]

At 6:00 a.m. on July 4, Smith's three brigades, commanded by Brisbane, Ewen, and Knipe, and two batteries commanded by Landis and Captain E. Spencer Miller, left Carlisle and moved six and a half miles on the Papertown Road to Mount Holly. At Mount Holly, Smith was detained for two hours by the arrival of Confederates under a flag of truce. They were escorting 2,000 paroled prisoners captured by the Army of Northern Virginia at Gettysburg on July 1. Wishing to prevent the enemy from getting information about his strength, Smith was forced to accept the prisoners and turn the Confederate escort back. The Thirty-Seventh New York Militia was left at Mount Holly to watch the Carlisle and Baltimore Turnpike, and the command moved toward Pine Grove Furnace. A most furious rainstorm set in at 1:00 p.m. It raised the creeks, carried away bridges, and made the roads very difficult for the artillery and trains. Ewen's command was left at Laurel Forge to cover the entrance to the narrow valley and watch a road leading over the mountain to Bendersville. The remainder of the force concentrated at Pine Grove, whence the Eighth New York Militia was sent out to hold the pass from Pine Grove to Bendersville. Despite the inexperience of the men and the heavy rains, Baldy was able to have his advance units march the seventeen miles from Carlisle to Pine Grove in the mountains by 6:00 in the evening, a "very creditable performance."[23]

The next day, Smith ordered Knipe's command to hold the crossroads from Mount Holly to Cashtown and Pine Grove to Bendersville, while Ewen crossed the mountain to the Mount Holly and Cashtown Road, holding the pass in his rear and being within a mile of Knipe. Brisbane's Pennsylvania Brigade was to hold a byroad from Pine Grove to Cashtown. Captain William H. Boyd, First New York Cavalry, joined Smith at Pine Grove. Smith directed Boyd to pass by Bendersville, in the direction of Cashtown, and to try and ascertain the movements and position of the enemy. Boyd fell upon the enemy and captured eight wagons and a number of prisoners. During the day, a small train with much needed provisions came up; the troops had found it impossible to gather enough food from the countryside. On July 6, Smith marched his brigades by three different roads, concentrating at Newman's Pass behind Cashtown. He was, however, too late to intercept the trains that had gone by that route. That evening, he wrote Couch that he would move the next day toward the next gap south, and so on up the Cumberland Valley, holding the gaps and keeping well in the mountains, where he could make a good fight.[24]

Before daylight the next morning, Meade momentarily stopped Smith's movement in the Cumberland Valley by ordering Smith to march to Gettysburg. Meade wished to use Smith's force to cover his advance, protect the hospitals and public property, and supervise hospitals for Confederate wounded. Smith advised Meade of the importance of the Cumberland Valley but said he would leave in the morning. Before Smith began his move to Gettysburg, Meade countermanded his order and told Smith to continue his pursuit of the enemy. Nevertheless, Meade remained concerned that Smith's raw militia forces would be no match for Lee's army without the Army of the Potomac being within supporting distance. Smith's command then marched to Altodale. Smith's trains had failed to overtake him, and an officer was sent to Chambersburg to procure supplies. A small supply being procured, troops reached Waynesborough on July 8, where Smith found Brigadier General Thomas H. Neill with a brigade of infantry and cavalry. Neill's brigade had been in Smith's original division, and Baldy was delighted to have some of his old men with him as he went through the Cumberland Valley. For the next two days, Smith waited at Waynesborough for rations to come up and for instructions from Meade.[25]

Smith's feelings towards the Army of the Potomac were still strained. He asked Couch, "If you send an order for this command to report to Meade, will you at the same time order me to return to you, leaving Knipe in command? You can appreciate how unpleasant it would be for me to serve under existing circumstances with the Army of the Potomac."[26] Couch was agreeable, but Smith's militia division did not join Meade's army. While Smith did not want to serve in the Army himself, he wrote the following to Meade's adjunct general, Seth Williams:

> My command is an incoherent mass, and, if it is to join the Army of the Potomac, I would suggest that the brigades, five in number, be attached to old divisions, and thus disperse the greenness. They cannot be maneuvered, and as a command it is quite helpless, excepting in the duty I have kept them on in the mountains. I have here about 4,000 men, and I suppose 2,000 have straggled away since I left Carlisle.[27]

Smith concluded, "I am utterly Powerless, without aid and in the short time allotted, to infuse any discipline into these troops." Meade undoubtedly agreed with Smith's assessment of his raw recruits and for that reason declined to have the men join the Army of the Potomac. The army commander had no intention of using Smith's command in combat.[28]

Not all Smith's units proved ineffective. The following day, one of his units, the Twentieth Pennsylvania Cavalry, was directed to search for Confederate stragglers. A detachment of forty troopers captured fifty Confederate prisoners and three wagons between Greencastle and Hagerstown.[29]

On July 10, Meade ordered Smith to occupy the enemy to the best advantage and be ready to join the Army of the Potomac or General Couch, as circumstances might require. A reconnaissance by Neill's cavalry found the enemy in force on the right bank of the Antietam. Smith's and Neill's infantry supported this movement, which pushed the Confederate cavalry back a mile and across the Antietam. Another desperately needed supply train arrived in the evening. Nonetheless, Smith continued to complain about the want of provisions and the impossibility of bringing up the supply trains with sufficient celerity. Every effort was made to supply the command with rations from the people, but the Confederates had cleaned out the region.[30]

On July 11, Colonel Brisbane's brigade, supported by the Sixty-first Pennsylvania of Neill's brigade, made a reconnaissance to Marsh Mill, which was about four miles from camp. The enemy had occupied the mill on the previous day. Brisbane's force destroyed twenty-four barrels of flour, which had been ground for Lee's army, and all the grain in the mill. The party returned about dark. Smith's two New York militia brigades moved at dusk to Leitersburg and encamped there for the night. These two brigades left Leitersburg at 6:00 the next morning and reached Cavetown at noon on July 12. That night, Smith ordered Brisbane to remain at Waynesborough to guard Smith's communications. After posting his troops at Cavetown, Smith reported in person to Meade and recommended that his command be distributed among the old divisions of the Army of the Potomac. Under the supposition that this was to be done, Smith ordered Brisbane to Hagerstown and moved with the rest of the command to the Boonsboro Turnpike, near Beaver Creek on July 13. Meade declined to divide the militia, as the stint of its soldiers was nearly up. He had offered to attach the division to one of his corps, but Smith advised against this—evidently because the greenness of the troops would not be diluted.[31]

On July 15, Smith received orders from Couch and Meade to send the New York militia home, via Frederick, and the necessary orders were given. Halleck blocked these orders for two days until he was overruled by Stanton, who had been urged by Governor Horatio Seymour that the rioting in New York City necessitated the return of the New York regiments. The Pennsylvania militia were concentrated at Hagerstown, under Brisbane, who was appointed military governor with instructions to watch the fords at Williamsport and Falling Waters.[32]

As soon as Smith had given the necessary orders to the New York National Guard troops, he started for Chambersburg, which he reached about 1:00 a.m. He disturbed Couch, who received him sitting on the edge of his bed in one white garment. With the invasion over, Smith desired to return to his home in New York City to see if he could be of service in restoring order. Smith asked to be relieved or simply be given authority to visit New York. Couch told Smith that he could not relieve Smith and that Stanton had directed him to place Smith under arrest for losing a gun during the campaign, sending the New York National Guard out of the department without authority, and accepting paroled prisoners in violation of standing orders.[33]

Smith explained each incident to Couch. The battery brought into the campaign by Captain Miller lacked limbers, and the deficiency was eked out by fore-wheels of farm wagons. In crossing a creek on the way to Pine Grove, an axle-tree was broken and the gun had to be left where it was stranded. Both Meade and Couch had permitted the National Guard to leave the department. Halleck had objected to this, but Stanton was finally the one who ordered the National Guard to New York City only a day after Smith had done so. Couch had approved of Smith's accepting the paroled prisoners. Seeing the charges as unjustified, Couch telegraphed Stanton that he was certain there was some mistake and that he would not act on the order until it was repeated. The order was not repeated. The Secretary of War's latest attempt to malign Smith convinced the general that Stanton's personal hostility had lost none its intensity since Smith had left the Army of the Potomac and was based on nothing more than that which had cost Porter and Franklin their commands.[34]

Lincoln also was eager to censure Smith. In an unsent letter to Meade, he expressed exasperation at Lee's escape into Virginia. The president, utterly ignorant of the situation Smith found himself in with raw recruits, insufficient provisions, and bad roads, condemned Baldy for his slow progress to Hagerstown and for his inability to catch Lee's army.[35]

Even with the handicaps of Smith's command, and Stanton's feeble attempts to punish Smith, Baldy's department commander and generals in the Army of the Potomac appreciated his work. Couch wrote to Smith, "I should like to have you with me if there is to be any fighting done by us, but my opinion is that General Meade should give you a corps. In that case, I would feel that it was all right, and that it was for the best."[36] Couch also told Smith that his move by Pine Grove "was the very best thing you could have done."[37] Meade did not give Smith a corps command, but in a special order thanked Smith and his troops "for their zeal and promptitude, which, amid no little privation, have marked their efforts to render this army all the assistance in their power."[38] Meade also called attention in his report to Smith's earnest attempts at cooperation. Meade's chief engineer, Major General Gouverneur K. Warren, wrote to Smith, "We are all much pleased with the way you behaved at the Harrisburg bridge and Carlisle. It was a great help to us."[39]

Nevertheless, Smith's First Division was now dispersed, and Smith was essentially without a command. Couch urged Smith to remain at Hagerstown for the present and watch the river. He would send Smith all the troops necessary for that purpose. Smith also was ordered by Meade to send enough force to Williamsport to prevent any communications between the wounded prisoners of war there and the Confederates in Virginia.[40]

The situation for Smith at Hagerstown grew increasingly difficult. On July 20, Couch placed Smith in command of all troops in Maryland from Harper's Ferry to Hancock. Unfortunately, this put some of Major General Robert C. Schenck's Middle Department troops under Smith's command, including Brigadier General Henry H. Lockwood, who was Smith's senior. Halleck tried to put all the commands under Meade, but this did not improve the situation. On July 23, Smith wrote Couch that he had been trying to do his duty in a credible manner, but obstacles had been placed at every step and asked to be relieved from "this embarrassing position ... my present position is simply insupportable, because I cannot give a single order that I am certain I have the power to force the execution of."[41] Also, as Lee had fallen back, the militia were getting mutinous. Smith urged recalling the troops or placing the area under Couch's department; he hoped for the latter. Couch replied that Schenck would settle the matter with his troops. If the troops were mutinous, Smith was ordered to fall back to Greencastle.[42]

Smith replied to Couch that a regiment in Colonel Emlen Franklin's brigade refused to go on picket, and that the command was generally dissatisfied with detention there. Since Franklin did not have a regiment that would force the refractory one to its duty, Smith offered him other regiments to enforce obedience. Smith told Couch, "I think there is no danger of trouble so long as the men are left quietly to do as they please about picket duty, but Colonel Franklin's fear is that they may decline, some of them, to go on picket, and then comes the danger of trouble. If I give any order, I shall certainly use my utmost force to carry the order out."[43] Despite the problems, Smith believed there was value in having troops watch and defend the fords, being ready to concentrate if a crossing was attempted. Smith felt this guard should be permanent, no matter where the theater of operations was, and should be placed under Couch's department instead of the Middle Department. The problem of the mutinous soldiers ended by late July because Franklin's brigade's term of service expired, and the men were mustered out of service.[44]

During August 1863, Smith's duties consisted of watching the river and supervising a hospital for Confederate wounded prisoners with a command of 400 men. While doing this, he became involved in a disagreement with Postmaster General Montgomery Blair. Blair asked Smith to return the house he took as his headquarters to the owners, Mr. and Mrs. William Hamilton. Blair's wife was a good friend of Mrs. Hamilton. While Blair admitted that Hamilton favored secession, Hamilton had not done anything "more disloyal than Democrats generally."[45] Besides, Mrs. Hamilton owned the house. Smith wrote that he would vacate the house and make compensation for any damages as soon as Hamilton was willing to pledge allegiance to the United States. Smith also commented that he was not aware of any alliance between disloyalty and Democracy. Blair tried to circumvent Smith's requirement by producing a letter from Hamilton's father-in-law attesting to Hamilton's taking the oath. Blair also did not mean to charge Democrats with disloyalty. Smith insisted on Hamilton taking the oath again to be sure, stating, "I have taken the oath several times, since the war began, and have felt it no hardship."[46] Smith was conscious of the appearance to the public, especially Union people, of a known Southern sympathizer taking the oath to get back his house. If the

Postmaster General insisted, Smith would return the house, but he required a note from Blair attesting to Hamilton's loyalty to protect Baldy from the charge of vacillation.[47]

In his final letter to Blair, Smith made a revealing comment about his politics. He stated, "I am with no party that does not insist upon a rigorous and intelligent prosecution of the war, till the Gov't is entirely successful, and the cause of the trouble is eradicated. That may be as far from the Democratic Creed, as I think it is from that of the Republicans."[48]

Smith was increasingly frustrated at serving in such an unimportant capacity. While he had great esteem for Couch, he desperately wanted to be promoted to major general. Still, he feared that if he made any stir, the War Department would treat him like W.B. Franklin, who had been sent to serve under Banks in Louisiana. Finally, on August 23, he requested a transfer to "duties which will at least seem more important than those I am at present performing."[49] Three days later, he was relieved from duty and ordered to report to the Adjutant General in Washington.[50]

Despite his accomplishments and insights as the commander of two corps and as a division commander under Couch, Smith was a victim of a hostile war secretary's policy against General McClellan's friends. Stanton and other Republican leaders became a major obstacle to Smith's advancement and just influence in the army. Only a major achievement on Smith's part and strong support by a very influential general would allow Baldy to return to higher command.

CHAPTER IX

Smith Secures the Army
in Chattanooga

An Engineer of Victory

Relieved of his unimportant duty in Maryland, Smith travelled to Washington for new orders. He hoped to be given a division command so that he could distinguish himself enough to be re-promoted to major general of volunteers. He realized that he faced stern opposition from the administration and Congress. On September 5, 1863, he was given orders to report to Major General William S. Rosecrans, commander of the Army of the Cumberland. When Baldy arrived at Chattanooga on September 30, Rosecrans told Smith he wanted to make him chief engineer of the army. This was not an attractive offer, since Smith knew staff officers were rarely promoted to major general, but he reluctantly accepted because of the precarious position of the army and the need to strengthen the defenses of Chattanooga. He was appointed chief engineer on October 3.[1]

In the wake of the Federal defeat at Chickamauga, the Army of the Cumberland had fallen back to Chattanooga on September 21. Confederate General Braxton Bragg did not vigorously follow up his victory but positioned his army on Missionary Ridge and Lookout Mountain. Bragg believed he could capture Chattanooga, and possibly the Army of the Cumberland, by a partial siege of the city. Bragg held Rosecrans at "his mercy and his destruction was only a question of time."[2] When the Confederates occupied Lookout Mountain and Valley on September 24, the Federals' direct communication with Bridgeport was cut. Their supply line had to be redirected to much longer and more difficult routes by Jasper and over Walden's Ridge, north of Chattanooga. The direct line was only twenty-seven miles long while the longer routes were as long as seventy miles. This led Rosecrans to try to restore the short line of communications along the Tennessee River while improving the long routes by Jasper.[3]

Rosecrans initially planned to recover the command of the river from Chattanooga to Bridgeport as soon as Major General Joseph Hooker's reinforcements arrived. Hooker, with the Eleventh and Twelfth Corps, had been sent west to help Rosecrans. Rosecrans intended to have Hooker's force come up Lookout Valley to Wauhatchie. As soon as Hooker had secured mountain passes and cut off Bragg's army from the valley, Rosecrans intended to then throw a pontoon bridge across the Tennessee River below the mouth of Lookout Creek to connect with Hooker's force. Supplies then could be brought upriver from Bridgeport, landed at Kelley's Ferry, and hauled across Lookout Valley to the pontoon bridge near Lookout Creek. The army commander ordered four steamboats to be constructed in Chattanooga and a fifth built at Bridgeport. Rosecrans

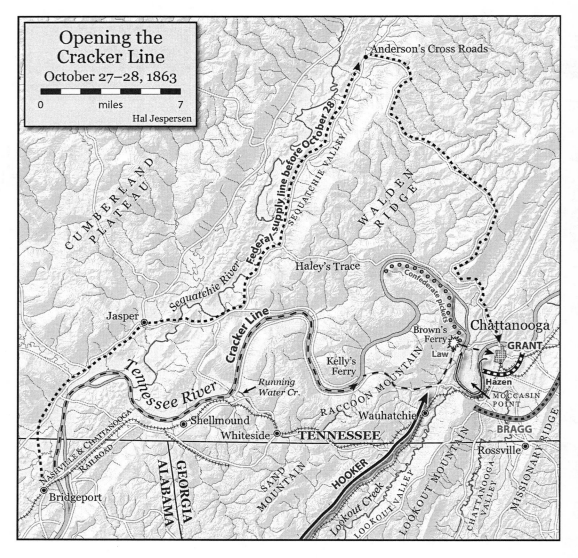

Opening the Cracker Line, October 27–28, 1863. From David A. Powell, *The Battle Above the Clouds: Lifting the Siege of Chattanooga and the Battle of Lookout Mountain* **(El Dorado Hills, CA: Savas Beatie, 2017), 16. Reproduced with permission of the author.**

also directed his engineers to appropriate two old sawmills in the city to begin cutting planks for the pontoons. He then would occupy and fortify Lookout Valley opposite the passage at the northern end of Lookout Mountain. This movement would completely cover the road in the Valley from there to Bridgeport and give the Federals practical possession of the Valley and the river. To assist in taking the Valley and in holding it, Hooker was advised to concentrate troops at Bridgeport and move into the Valley as soon as he received enough supplies to sustain a twelve-mile march.[4]

Unfortunately for his army, Rosecrans' plan to restore the short line of communications was blocked by Confederate initiatives. On September 30, Major General Joseph Wheeler's Cavalry Corps crossed the Tennessee River north of Chattanooga. Two days later, they attacked a lightly defended Federal, eight hundred mule-team wagon train. The supplies were seized or destroyed, resulting in serious losses in food and ammunition reserves for the army. It also brought a swift end to Rosecrans' short line plan. On October 4, he had to redirect most of Hooker's Twelfth Corps to protect the railroad from Wartrace to Bridgeport from Wheeler's raid. Rosecrans ordered the remainder of Hooker's force to concentrate between Stevenson and Bridgeport and await further instructions.[5]

On October 9, Rosecrans sent a division to Anderson's Crossroads to protect the wagon trains there. The next day, Hooker was directed to build a corduroy road from Bridgeport to Battle Creek. Despite Rosecrans' work, he lost the shortest route on the north side of the river on October 11. Longstreet ordered sharpshooters to the south bank of the river and effectively closed Haley's Trace. Rosecrans sent 250 sharpshooters to repulse the enemy, but this proved ineffective. The loss of Haley's Trace left the Federals with two even longer routes from Bridgeport to Chattanooga. The Anderson Road was fifty-five miles long, and the Poe Road ran for seventy-one miles. Both had to overcome a rise of nearly 1,400 feet at Walden's Ridge.[6]

In the face of these reversals, Rosecrans tried to improve some of the remaining routes. For instance, on October 14, Rosecrans ordered Hooker to construct a twelve-mile railroad from Bridgeport to Battle Creek. But serious doubts existed about the army's ability to survive at Chattanooga while the longer routes were being completed. Quartermaster General Montgomery Meigs, who had come to Chattanooga to evaluate the army's conditions, reported on October 16, "It will require much work and more time than I fear can be spared."[7] Moreover, Meigs warned Stanton that at least six miles of the longer routes would become almost impassable when the rains came. Assistant Secretary of War Dana wrote on October 18, "It does not seem possible to hold out here another week without a new avenue of supplies."[8]

Restoring the short line in the near future seemed equally unlikely. On October 16, Rosecrans told Dana that possession of the river at least as far up as the head of Williams Island was "a sine qua non to the holding of Chattanooga, but that it is impossible for him to make any movement toward gaining such possession until Hooker's troops are concentrated and transportation gets up."[9] Hooker's troops were scattered along the line of the railroad and could not be concentrated before October 21. If the Confederates did not interfere sooner, the movement upon Raccoon Mountain and Lookout Valley would be attempted. The very next day, Rosecrans changed his orders. If the Confederates attempted to cross the river, Hooker was ordered to move his command up Lookout Valley. He was to make preliminary preparations to move promptly and effectually. The Twelfth Corps was to be placed as far down as possible to protect exposed positions of the railroad. Otherwise, Hooker was to wait for Major General William T. Sherman's force to come before making a complete concentration of his force and moving into the Valley. Sherman would not arrive for four weeks.[10]

The condition of the army in Chattanooga continued to deteriorate because of the decrease in supplies. After October 2, only two-thirds rations were issued, and corps commanders were given the option to issue only half rations. By October 16, Dana and Rosecrans admitted the situation looked threatening. Dana reported, "Nothing can prevent the retreat of the army from this place within a fortnight, and with a vast loss of public property and possibly of life, except the opening of the river." Rosecrans seemed to agree with Dana. He wrote, "The rains have raised the river and interrupted our pontoon bridges. The roads are very heavy. Our future is not bright…. This army, with its back to barren mountains, roads narrow and difficult, while the enemy has the rail-road and the corn in his rear, is at much disadvantage." Two days later, he reported, "Roads horrid. Forage and animals failing."[11]

Rosecrans' inability to execute a specific plan to regain the short line was a major reason for the army's worsening problem. On October 12, Dana reported:

> Our animals starved and the men with starvation before them, and the enemy bound to make desperate efforts to dislodge us. In the midst of this the commanding general devotes that part of the time which is not employed in pleasant gossip to the composition of a long report to prove that the Government is to blame for his failure…. I have never seen a man possessing talent with less administrative power, less clearness and steadiness in difficulty, and greater practical incapacity than General Rosecrans.

Rosecrans had "no strength of will and no concentration of purpose." Four days later, Dana's opinion of Rosecrans did not improve. Dana stated:

> Rosecrans seems to be insensible to the impending danger and dawdles with trifles in a man-ner which can scarcely be imagined…. With plenty of zealous and energetic officers ready to do whatever can be done, all this precious time is lost because our dazed and mazy com-mander can not perceive the catastrophe that is close upon us nor fix his mind upon the means of preventing it. I never saw anything which seemed so lamentable and hopeless.[12]

During this time, Smith served as chief engineer and watched his army's condi-tion decline. When Smith first came to Chattanooga, he roomed with Rosecrans, who offered his hospitality until Smith found permanent quarters. During that time, Smith was engaged in surveying the army and the lines. Smith told Rosecrans that the army would receive insufficient supplies if they had to travel over the longer routes above the river, and that a shorter line of communications was needed. Especially after the autumn rains began, the mountain roads above the river often became nearly impassable. Rose-crans replied that his commissary was receiving supplies in large excess of his require-ments. They also differed on the best approach to restore the short line. Smith disagreed with Rosecrans' view that General Hooker must occupy Lookout Valley and seize the passes of Lookout Mountain before a bridge could be thrown across the Tennessee River from Moccasin Point. Baldy insisted that movements from Bridgeport and Chattanooga must be done in unison. He believed that Hooker's solitary movement would be blocked either through Bragg's superior forces attacking Hooker or by the Confederates closing the passes to Raccoon Mountain. An attempt to lay the bridge first would alert Bragg to the movement and would likely lead to the Confederates seizing the passes in Raccoon Mountain and blocking Hooker's movement towards Chattanooga.[13]

As chief engineer, Smith started his duties by beginning the construction of boats for bridges and laying out the lines of fortifications. At the time of Smith's arrival at Chattanooga, there were two trestle bridges over the river, but the rising water carried one away, and the other was soon taken down to save the material. Work was immedi-ately begun on boats and on preparation for the construction of a pontoon bridge. The latter was finished on October 6. Smith established a flying ferry just above the pontoon bridge.[14] The ferry was capable of taking a wagon and team but was only used by small parties desirous of crossing when the main bridge's traffic was moving in the oppo-site direction. Smith attended to various engineering duties, principally superintending work on the fortifications. Smith intended to make a system of fortifications that would be able to stand a siege with a small garrison and thus diminish the number of men required to hold the position at Chattanooga.[15]

Assistant War Secretary Dana was impressed with the new chief engineer. He wrote that Smith "infuses much energy and judgment into that branch of operations."[16] But on October 14, Dana claimed that there were natural and logistical limitations to Smith's efforts. The river had risen ten inches, causing the trestle bridge to be taken up and leaving only the new pontoon bridge to connect Chattanooga with the north side. For some unknown reason, the work tools for the fortifications had not arrived. This delay cut Smith's work force by ninety percent, allowing only one thousand men to work at a time.[17]

Despite his work, Smith was aware of the worsening situation. He became convinced that it was impossible to collect provisions, ammunition, and forage sufficient to maintain the garrison for the fortifications. Moreover, he believed that by October 14, by reason of the loss of animals and want of rations, the army had lost its mobility. It could no longer prevent a flank march by Bragg or retreat without utter disorganization. During all this time, Smith did not confer with Rosecrans on regaining control of any part of the old routes by river and road to Bridgeport. As a result, while Smith was aware that Rosecrans had planned to have Hooker attempt a recovery of the short line at some undetermined date, Smith was unaware of Rosecrans' ideas about a cooperative movement with the force at Chattanooga. Despite his friendly feelings toward his army commander, Smith agreed with Dana that Rosecrans "has no administrative talent, and so we have been going to the bad ever since I came here."[18]

In superintending the fortifications, Smith rode daily on the hills surrounding Chattanooga. From them he looked down upon the face of Raccoon Mountain. In carefully studying the situation of the army and trying to determine some means by which it could be relieved, Smith became convinced that if the Federals could seize the northern end of Raccoon Mountain and hold the mountain passes, the army would restore its control of the river down as far as Williams Island. Then, by using the north side of that island or the adjacent shore of the river, the army might establish a depot for supplies sheltered from artillery fire and from any infantry attack. Thinking that this idea was practical, Smith went to his army commander on the afternoon of October 18. He told Rosecrans that he planned to make a reconnaissance the following day to see if the army could make a foothold on Raccoon Mountain that would regain the river down to that point. Rosecrans said, "That is a very good idea, and I will go down with you."[19]

The next morning at eight o'clock, the two generals set out on their reconnaissance. Shortly after crossing the Tennessee River, they passed an army hospital. Rosecrans stopped to visit his wounded men. Smith stayed outside and reminded Rosecrans of the long day's work ahead of them. Smith had waited a half hour when Assistant War Secretary Dana came along on his way to Bridgeport. Not wanting to waste any more time, Smith accompanied Dana for a short distance. After separating, Smith went down toward the riverbank and began his examination near the lower end of Williams Island but could not find a position secure enough to resist a strong attacking force. Smith then abandoned all idea of carrying out the plan and started back for headquarters.[20]

Not long after leaving the riverbank, Smith saw a Federal battery in front and to his right. As Smith knew of no battery in that place, he turned his horse and went into it. He asked the captain why the battery was there. The captain replied, "To defend the crossing here at Brown's Ferry." The battery was on one of two high banks. Between the banks, a road led to the river. On the opposite side of the river was a range of steep hills, about 100 to 150 feet in height. Directly opposite the Federal battery was a gorge between the hills with a good road leading down to the river. These two roads could be joined by a boat and thus together constituted Brown's Ferry. The topographical features of the locality attracted Smith's attention, and upon further discussion with the captain, he found that they had an agreement with the picket on the other side that persons going down the river should not be fired upon. Smith sat down on the bank of the river for two hours, within a thousand feet of a rebel picket who thought him some soldier not on duty. Smith examined the enemy-held hills opposite and the gorge between the hills as far as he could see them. He considered the possibility of men scrambling up the hills. Baldy estimated the distance and position of the reserve of pickets and the supporting force near it guarding that portion of the Valley.[21]

Smith believed that if those hills could be taken by surprise, and a bridge built across, several benefits would result. The Army of the Cumberland would be within three miles of Lookout Mountain. The movement would regain Kelley's Ferry Road, seriously interrupt the communications of the enemy up Lookout Valley and down to the river on Raccoon Mountain, and prevent Bragg's men from defending the Raccoon Mountain passes by forcing them to expose their flanks to the Federals. Smith believed Raccoon Mountain was lightly defended. If this was true and the troops in the hills near Brown's Ferry were surprised and captured, the movement would be a success. Smith realized the expedition was based partly on "audacity and luck," but he believed the desperate Federal situation required a reasonable risk to restore the short line.[22] Besides, Smith thought the chances for success were "more than probable."[23]

Smith hypothesized that if a force should leave Bridgeport for Lookout Valley on the same day that the Federals in Chattanooga seized the heights, they could be assured that it would not be stopped by Confederate forces. When the force from Bridgeport reached Lookout Valley, the whole army would be practically united to defend the Valley and the short line of communication by road and river. Because of darkness, Smith concluded his examination and returned to headquarters.[24]

On arriving at headquarters, Smith found that Major General George H. Thomas had replaced Rosecrans as commander of the Department of the Cumberland. The next morning, Smith reported to Thomas and offered to step down as chief engineer if the new department commander had someone else he would prefer for the post. Smith admitted to Thomas that he had reluctantly accepted the position when Rosecrans had appointed him. Thomas replied that he desired no change and directed Smith to put down a second bridge at Chattanooga.[25]

Smith then told Thomas that while he had enough boats for a second bridge, he would rather use them elsewhere. Smith explained to Thomas what he had found via the reconnaissance of Brown's Ferry. Baldy then proposed to Thomas his plan to seize Brown's Ferry as part of a cooperative movement with Hooker's force to retake the short line. Smith believed that movements from Bridgeport and Chattanooga must be done at the same time; this would prevent the Confederates from focusing on a single movement. Thomas considered Smith's plan to take Brown's Ferry and after a few hours called Smith back. Thomas conferred with other officers, and they felt the plan was militarily unsound and would cause the loss of two of his best brigades. These unnamed officers accused Smith of wanting the notoriety associated with a big slaughter. Smith convinced the department commander that the plan was sound and that he believed that any officer, who through ignorance or ambition, had needlessly caused the death of a soldier, was guilty of murder. Thomas then approved Smith's plan; Baldy at once started to prepare for the movement at Brown's Ferry.[26]

On October 23, Thomas sent Hooker orders to concentrate the Eleventh Crops and one division of the Twelfth at Bridgeport. Thomas also informed Hooker that a force from Chattanooga would cooperate with him by establishing a bridge across the river at Brown's Ferry and seizing Raccoon Mountain; this movement would give Hooker an open road to Chattanooga when his forces were ordered into Lookout Valley. That night, Major General Ulysses S. Grant, commander of the newly formed Military Division of the Mississippi, arrived at Chattanooga and took personal command of operations there. Smith was optimistic about the new military division commander. Dana told Smith that Grant thought highly of Baldy and had said that Franklin and Smith were the ablest officers in the army. Dana also told Smith that Grant would rely upon his knowledge and judgment regarding the army's situation at Chattanooga. Smith believed that he now had more influence on the campaign than he did when he was with the Sixth Corps in the East.[27]

The next day, Smith showed Grant and Thomas the position at Brown's Ferry, and the two commanders accepted the importance of the position and Smith's plan to capture it as part of the cooperative movement to open the river. But Grant also determined that the strength of the Brown's Ferry movement alone could be sufficient to prevent the Confederates from blocking Hooker from joining up with Smith. Grant believed that the immediate capture of Brown's Ferry and the hills flanking it would enable him to place enough Federals in the valley to enable Hooker to link up with Smith. The Federals would be in a position to strike the right flank of any Confederate force that entered the valley. This change to Smith's original plan was important as Hooker's forces were delayed, and the Brown's Ferry movement would occur prior to Hooker's arrival.[28]

Later, on the twenty-fourth, Grant told Baldy he would appoint Smith as the chief engineer of the Military Division of the Mississippi. Smith was disappointed by this proposed promotion. He told Dana, "I am farther off than ever from a command."[29] Dana reassured Smith that Grant wanted the benefit of Smith's knowledge. The next day, Smith's desire for command was temporarily satisfied. Grant gave Smith command of the Brown's Ferry operation. Grant wrote:

> Smith had been so instrumental in preparing for the move which I was now about to make; and so clear in his judgment about the manner of making it, that I deemed it but just to him that he should have command of the troops detailed to execute the design, although he was then acting as a staff-officer, and was not in command of troops.[30]

Smith's grasp of the strategic importance of Brown's Ferry was equaled by his tactical genius in planning the movement. Smith was directed to make all the necessary arrangements for the expedition to affect the lodgment. Two brigades and three batteries of artillery would be necessary. Baldy carefully and wisely choose the two brigade commanders to lead the expedition. Fellow Vermonter Brigadier General William Hazen was a proven fighter who had shown his tough leadership both at Stones River and Chickamauga. Equal to Hazen was the other brigade commander, Brigadier General John Turchin, who also showed his leadership at Chickamauga. The three batteries of artillery would be commanded by Major John Mendenhall, one of the most reliable artillery officers in the Army of the Cumberland. Meanwhile, Smith arranged for fifty

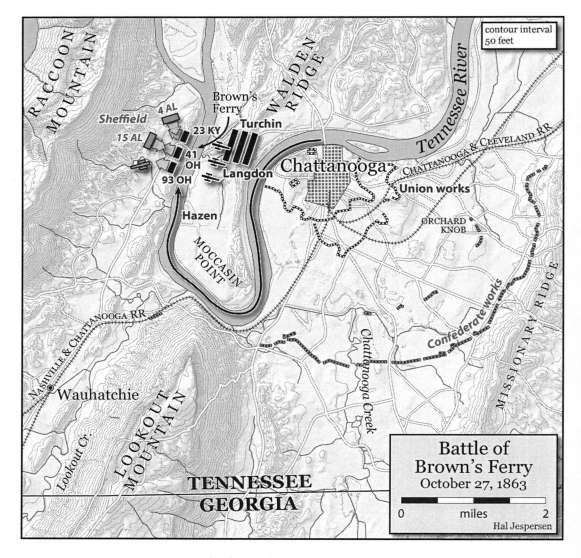

Battle of Brown's Ferry, October 27, 1863.

pontoons, capable of carrying a crew and twenty armed men each, and two flatboats, able to carry forty men and seventy-five men, to be prepared.[31]

Fifteen hundred men, under Hazen, were to embark in the boats. Under the cover of darkness, they would travel down the river about nine miles, seven of which would be under the fire of enemy pickets. Smith believed it was better to take this risk than attempt to launch the boats near the ferry. Although the enemy pickets might see Smith's boats, they would not know where the landing was to take place; therefore, the Confederates could not concentrate with certainty against the assault. The remainders of Hazen's brigade and Turchin's brigade under Smith's immediate command were to march across Moccasin Point and encamp out of sight in the woods near the ferry. There, they would be prepared to move down, cover the landing of the boats, and embark as soon as the boats had landed the river force and crossed to the north side. The artillery was also to be placed in the woods during the night and go into position as soon as the boats had begun to land. In case of disaster, the artillery would also cover the retirement of the troops. The equipage for the pontoon bridge was to be moved down to the river as soon as the troops were across. Axes were to be issued to the troops for cutting abatis for defense as soon as the ridge was gained. Hazen's brigade was to take the gorge and the hills to the left, while Turchin's brigade was to extend from the gorge down the river.[32]

At 6:30 p.m. on October 26, 1863, Turchin's brigade and the part of Hazen's brigade under Smith's immediate command moved from Chattanooga, crossed the Tennessee, and bivouacked in the woods near Brown's Ferry. Because of the hard work of the Michigan Mechanics and Engineers, the boats and oars were ready that night. At midnight, the portion of Hazen's brigade that was ordered to descend the river in pontoons was awakened. Under the superintendence of Colonel Thomas R. Stanley, it marched to the landing and quietly embarked. At 3:00 a.m., the fifty-two boat flotilla moved noiselessly out. Hazen desired to reach the point of landing slightly before daylight and soon learned that the current would enable him to do so without using oars. After moving three miles, the pontoons came under the guns of the enemy's pickets, but keeping close to the opposite shore, they were not discovered. The Confederate pickets posted near Lookout Creek did spot the boats, but after some conversation among themselves, the pickets concluded that the boats were only adrift. The moon was obscured by clouds, and a slight fog benefited the expedition, but it was the perfect order and stillness that prevented discovery.[33]

Stanley had divided the boats into two fleets, one to be landed at Brown's Ferry and the other at a gap above it. Stanley directed the landing of the latter group. These boats easily landed without alarming the enemy. The men disembarked quickly, soon gained the top of the bank, and surprised the enemy pickets. The assault at Brown's Ferry was not as smoothly accomplished. About 5:00 a.m., when the first boat was within ten feet of the landing, the pickets discovered the movement and fired a volley harmlessly over the heads of the men. The disembarkation was effected rapidly and in perfect order. Each party performed correctly the part assigned to it with so little loss of time that the crest was soon occupied. Hazen sent his skirmish line out and ordered entrenchments started before Confederate reinforcements arrived to drive the Federals back. Colonel William Oates and his six reserve companies of the Fifteenth Alabama came up boldly along what amounted to almost the entire front. They were particularly strong along the road and gained the hill to the right of it. The advanced Federal regiment, the Twenty-Third Kentucky, fell back while returning the enemy's fire. The Federal force on the road was in danger, but at this moment, Federal reinforcements came up. As planned, the empty pontoons were rapidly sent to Brown's Ferry Landing where Smith waited with Turchin's brigade and part of Hazen's brigade. Smith also requested a third brigade to be brought up to be held in reserve. Thomas approved this request and sent Brigadier General Walter C. Whitaker's brigade. The remainder of Hazen's brigade was swiftly ferried across the river and these reinforcements, soon to be followed by Turchin's brigade, countered the Confederate attack on the road leading from Brown's Ferry. After a gallant but short engagement, the outnumbered and outflanked Confederate defenders were driven away. The Confederates moved all their troops out of the Valley and toward Lookout Mountain. Turchin's command took position on the hills to the right, and Hazen's united command took those to the left of the road by 8:00 a.m.[34]

As soon as the skirmishers were thrown out from each command, the soldiers were set to work felling an abatis, and in two hours the command was sufficiently protected to withstand any probable attack. As soon as all of Hazen's and Turchin's brigades were across, the Federals began to construct a bridge across the river at Brown's Ferry. Despite an hour-long enemy bombardment, the Brown's Ferry bridge was completed at 4:30 p.m. under the skillful superintendence of Captain P.V. Fox, First Michigan Engineers, and Captain George W. Dresser, Fourth Artillery. While the engineers were laying the bridge, the accuracy of the Confederate artillery made work uncomfortable, if not difficult. To encourage the men not to mind the fire and to keep them working, Smith went upon the bridge to share his troops' danger. Finally, their fire proving ineffectual, the Confederates withdrew. The next day, the two coats and vest worn by Baldy were found to have been cut clean through just under the collar on the back of the neck by a shell fragment which, had it cut an inch deeper, would have killed him. The Federal artillery placed in position was not used, but credit was due to Mendenhall for his prompt placing of his guns. Whitaker's brigade arrived at Brown's Ferry around 10:30 a.m. and served as a reserve for Smith's command for the rest of the day.[35]

Six Confederates were taken prisoner, and six Confederates were buried by Smith's command. Twenty beeves, six pontoons, a barge, and about 2,000 bushels of corn fell into Federal possession. Smith's loss totaled only six killed and thirty-two wounded or missing.[36]

At daylight on October 27, as part of the plan Smith and Thomas had matured and Grant had approved, Hooker's command, consisting of the Eleventh Corps and a division of the Twelfth Corps, moved by the direct road from Bridgeport by way of Whiteside and entered Lookout Valley at Wauhatchie. By the afternoon of the twenty-eighth, Hooker's column had joined Smith's forces at Raccoon Mountain. By 8:00 p.m., Grant would report to Halleck that the cooperative movement "has proven eminently successful," and "The question of supplies may now be regarded as settled."[37]

To assure that Grant was correct, the disposition of Hooker's troops needed to anticipate a Confederate response to these Federal successes. Smith and Hazen discovered, however, that Hooker made no such arrangement. Hazen went to Hooker and urged him to consolidate his forces on the eastern slope of Raccoon Mountain, but Hooker dismissed the advice. Smith then reported the matter to Thomas's chief of staff, Brigadier General Joseph J. Reynolds. Baldy urged him to have General Thomas to send troops to reinforce the area in anticipation of an enemy attack. Unfortunately, Reynolds neglected to pass on the message.[38]

The next night, the Confederates attacked the one division of the Twelfth Corps at Wauhatchie, seeking to crush the isolated division before the Eleventh Corps could reinforce it from three miles away. The Confederates inflicted heavy losses on Hooker's poorly disposed forces. The Confederates were finally repulsed after the Eleventh Corps arrived. Longstreet, who had been in charge of holding the short line from the Federals, decided any further challenge would be "impracticable."[39] The only route by which his troops could reach the Federals was a difficult mountain road that was not usable for artillery and was entirely exposed to the Federal batteries on the other side of the river. While the Federals' position was connected by an easy and short route, Confederate artillery would have to travel fifty miles.[40]

The praise for Smith's expedition was almost immediate. Dana wrote Stanton on October 28, 1863: "Everything [is] perfectly successful. The river is now open, and a short and good road in our possession along the south shore.... The great success, however, is General Smith's operation at the mouth of Lookout Valley. Its brilliancy cannot be exaggerated."[41] Thomas published an order on November 1 thanking Smith and his command

> for the skill and cool gallantry displayed in securing a permanent lodgment on the south side of the river at Brown's Ferry, and in putting in position the pontoon bridge, on the night of the 26th instant. The successful execution of this duty was attended with the most important results in obtaining a safe and easy communication with Bridgeport and shortening our line of supplies.[42]

Smith hoped that his actions might warrant a promotion. He wrote his wife on October 31, "I think General Grant and General Thomas are going to ask for my promotion but then I want to get back my old date or else the pill will be as bitter as ever."[43] Grant was certainly impressed by Smith's accomplishments. On November 12, he expanded the scope of Baldy's role by appointing him chief engineer of the Military Division of the Mississippi. On the same day, Grant sent a request to Secretary Stanton, recommending that Smith be placed first on the list for promotion to the rank of major-general. Grant stated, "He is possessed of one of the clearest military heads in the army; is very practical and industrious. No man in the service is better qualified than he for our largest commands."[44] Thomas seconded Grant's request for Smith's promotion

> for the industry and energy displayed by him from the time of his first reporting for duty at these headquarters; in organizing the engineer department, and for his skillful execution of the movements at Brown's Ferry, Tenn., on the night of October 26, 1863, in surprising the enemy and throwing a pontoon bridge across the Tennessee at that point—a vitally important service necessary to the opening of communication between Bridgeport and Chattanooga.[45]

The authorities in Washington, however, failed to act on the recommendations of Grant and Thomas.[46]

Despite this inaction, at Chattanooga, Smith, who had so often been frustrated in the East, had finally proven himself an engineer of victory. Serving under an appreciative commander, he had helped secure the army and reopen its supply lines. His engineering for victory on a logistical level, as well as on a tactical and strategic levels, was to continue. With Grant's success in the coming battle of Chattanooga, William Farrar Smith would finally earn his promotion and a trip east.

CHAPTER X

Smith's Continued Success at Chattanooga

And His Triumphant Return East

With the Brown's Ferry expedition over, Smith's command remained at Brown's Ferry cutting timber, digging entrenchments, and building roads. Smith took special care to protect the bridges at Brown's Ferry and Chattanooga. He placed an officer and twenty-three men on the Chattanooga bridge to watch for driftwood and be ready with pike poles to put it through between the boats or break its force. An officer of the day was to check every six hours to report any neglect of duty on the part of the guard. Smith was also assigned several duties to improve the Federal position along the short line. He was placed in charge of securing the lines in Lookout Valley and working on the defenses in front of Chattanooga. He also directed work on the roads from Brown's Ferry to Chattanooga. He ordered Lieutenant George Burroughs to construct a tête de pont opposite Bridgeport to cover the bridges. A defensive line was to be laid out to secure the "Moor's Spring Pass." Slashing timber, building blockhouses, and digging rifle pits were methods to be used if needed. Works were to be constructed at "Gordon Coal Bed" to hold that pass. Smith ordered Captain William E. Merrill to proceed to McMinnville and lay out works to cover the different roads. Smith ordered Hazen's brigade to move into the gorge in Lookout Valley while keeping a small picket force at the hills at Brown's Ferry. If Hooker were attacked, however, Hazen was to return to his former line to hold the tête de pont there.[1]

On November 4, 1863, Longstreet received orders to move against Burnside's force at Knoxville. On receipt of this intelligence, Smith, considering that the Federals had sufficient space to make maneuvers in their front and that the enemy's line was near enough to the Federals for a sudden dash and surprise, suggested to Grant and Thomas to advance Thomas's picket lines and draw out the Army of the Cumberland to threaten the seizure of the northwest extremity of Missionary Ridge. There was a possibility that a demonstration might cause Bragg to recall the troops then starting for East Tennessee. Smith realized that the Federal move would have to be limited in scope because of the Army of the Cumberland's still weakened state. But Grant decided to order Thomas to attack Missionary Ridge for the purpose of threatening Bragg's communications at Cleveland. This meant not only a battle for Missionary Ridge, but an aggressive campaign thirty miles beyond. As the order significantly differed from what Smith recommended, he did not consider it a result of his suggestion.[2]

On the seventh, Smith rode along the front with the military division commander. While riding, Grant told Smith of his order to Thomas. Smith asked Grant if Thomas had informed him about his plans to implement the order. Grant replied that "when he had confidence enough in a man to leave him in command of an army, he had confidence enough to leave the plans to him." The assertion did not coincide with Smith's ideas of what a great captain would do, but Smith felt propriety would not allow him to say anything further. On reaching his headquarters, Smith found a note from Thomas to go to his office.[3]

Upon arrival at Thomas's office, Smith found the major general very much disturbed. Thomas said, "You must get that order for an advance countermanded; I shall lose my army."[4] Smith explained that the order was not a result of his proposal, but he suggested they ride up the river on the west side and make a reconnaissance to determine the soundness of the order. The two generals, accompanied by the chief of artillery, Brigadier General John Brannan, went to a point opposite the mouth of the South Chickamauga and climbed up a steep hill overlooking the country from the river to Missionary Ridge. They saw that Bragg's line extended too far north for Thomas to hope to outflank the Confederates without jeopardizing the safety of his own lines. During the reconnaissance, Smith studied the ground carefully and realized that it offered an opportunity for Sherman to turn the Confederate right flank, which was the one to attack, for the purpose of separating Bragg both from his troops in East Tennessee and from his own natural line of retreat. Upon the generals' return, Smith told Grant that it was impossible for Thomas to attack the extremity of Missionary Ridge with the force he then had and that everything must wait for Sherman. Grant at once countermanded the order.[5]

While the reconnaissance probably saved Thomas's force from a severe repulse, it was also the prime cause for the subsequent Federal plan of battle at Chattanooga. Smith reported to Grant the character of the country, how far Bragg's lines extended on Missionary Ridge, which was occupied by Bragg, and the probability of outflanking Bragg and capturing the northern end of the ridge. Sherman arrived on November 15, and the next day, examined the same ground with Smith. Smith explained to Sherman his role in the coming battle. He was to get to the northern end of Missionary Ridge before Bragg could concentrate a force sufficient to resist him. Sherman agreed to this plan of battle, and orders to this effect were issued on November 18.[6]

With Grant's approval, Baldy devised the complete plan of battle. Smith's plan was as follows: On crossing the river at Bridgeport, Sherman's leading division was to take the road to Trenton and threaten a crossing at Lookout Mountain at Johnson's Crook. It was hoped that this would convince Bragg that the actual attack was on his left and cause him to withdraw troops from his right, the true Federal objective. The remaining divisions of Sherman's army were to go to selected camps near the place of crossing opposite the mouth of South Chickamauga Creek. One brigade was to go to the North Chickamauga, where 150 pontoons were awaiting them. The brigade would descend the river and secure the landing on the left bank of the Tennessee. One division of Thomas's force was assigned to Sherman. As soon as Sherman's army was across the river, Sherman was to march for the northern end of Missionary Ridge. Arriving there, his advance was to turn to the right.[7]

Meanwhile, Thomas's four divisions, starting from Chattanooga, were to go obliquely to the front and left and unite with Sherman's right, making a continuous line of battle. The intended effect was to ensure that the instant Bragg's flank was turned and his line reached, he could not present a front against the attack, and thus would be rolled up and pushed off to his left, away from his supply line to Ringgold and over the old field of Chickamauga. Hooker, with Brigadier General John W. Geary's division of the Twelfth Corps and two brigades of the Fourth Corps, was to hold Lookout Valley and threaten the pass into Chattanooga. Major General Oliver O. Howard's corps was to be held in reserve and was to go to Sherman or to be used by Thomas, as circumstances dictated.[8]

To facilitate the move, Smith directed his engineer troops to make several preparations. First, the works at Chattanooga were put in a strong defensible condition to enable a comparatively small force to hold that place and thus bring every available man into the field. By November 21, the works were made impregnable. Second, material had to be collected for two bridges and put in convenient positions for use. One bridge train in the Department of the Cumberland was scattered from Bridgeport to Chattanooga. This was collected in the vicinity of Brown's Ferry by November 17. The two sawmills in Smith's charge ran night and day, and materials were prepared for a bridge to assist Sherman's river crossing at the mouth of the South Chickamauga. As the river measured only 1,296 feet in width where the bridge would be placed and the river current was gentle, no trouble was anticipated in the mechanical part of the operation. The Chickamauga also required bridging at its mouth to afford facilities for the occupation of the north bank. This stream was about 180 feet wide.[9]

Smith was also responsible for providing boats to cross Sherman's lead brigade. The North Chickamauga, a stream emptying into the Tennessee on the right bank about eight miles above Chattanooga, was selected for the launching site. The boats were taken to the creek on byroads through the woods and not exposed to the view of the Confederates at any point along the distance. Smith determined to put the boats in the water there, loaded with soldiers, and float them down to the point of crossing. Such an operation would be quicker and quieter than one that launched the boats at the place of passage. By the night of November 20, 116 boats, furnished with oars and crews, were in the creek; the creek was cleared of snags to its mouth, and all the citizens in the vicinity were put under strict guard to prevent the information getting to the enemy. Colonel Daniel McCook assisted Smith by selecting the roads, clearing the creek, furnishing the crews for the boats, and keeping the citizens under guard.[10]

The rest of the bridge material and about twenty-five boats were parked behind a ridge of hills within 400 yards of the place of crossing and were entirely concealed from the enemy. During this time, Smith was faced with number of engineering problems caused by the rains and driftwood. Despite all of Smith's efforts to protect the river bridges from driftwood, on November 20, the pontoon bridge at Chattanooga was carried away, and its material lost. The next night, the flying ferry at Chattanooga was disabled, and the pontoon bridge at Brown's Ferry was so injured that it was not fully repaired until November 24. This left only the steamer *Dunbar* at Chattanooga and a horse ferryboat at Brown's Ferry for communications. On the twenty-third, however, the flying ferry was repaired and in operation. Fortunately, the troops had been placed in position before the bridges were lost.[11]

At midnight on November 24, the boats, with the designated brigade, left the North Chickamauga and landed quietly on the left bank of the Tennessee, both above and below the mouth of the South Chickamauga; the business of ferrying over troops then began. Soon after the boats had landed their first load, Smith deployed Colonel George Buell's Pioneer Brigade on the right bank to vigorously begin work to clear the ground on the shore, level it where necessary for the passage of troops to the boats, and prepare a steamboat landing. Smith also assisted the passage by having Brigadier General James H. Wilson bring up the *Dunbar*. The steamboat crossed about 5,000 infantry men and one battery of artillery. At daylight, 8,000 troops were across the river and in line of battle.[12]

Smith had hoped to build two pontoon bridges across the river, but the rise in the Tennessee had increased its width and left Smith with only enough boats to build one bridge. The bridge was begun about 5:00 a.m. on November 24. The work on the bridge across the river was done from both ends. Also, Captain Fox's Michigan Engineers began the bridge across the South Chickamauga. The work proceeded with great vigor under Smith's personal direction. At 12:20 p.m., the two bridges were completed. The bridge over the river was nearly 1,400 feet in length. That same afternoon, two pontoon bridges were thrown across the Chattanooga Creek to connect the center and right of Thomas's command. On the twenty-fifth, an additional bridge was rapidly constructed across the Citico Creek at its mouth, and an unused bridge was thrown across the river at Chattanooga.[13]

A week earlier, the battle around Chattanooga had begun as planned. Sherman's advance division moved on Lookout Mountain on November 18. Bragg, deceived by this feint, moved a division to reinforce his left flank. But when Sherman's division moved to Wauhatchie on the twenty-first, the Confederates realized the true nature of the Federal move. The next day, Bragg began sending troops to his right.[14]

On November 23, Grant changed Smith's plan of battle. Hearing reports that Bragg was falling back, Grant ordered Thomas's force, reinforced by Howard's corps, to determine the truth of such reports by pushing back the enemy pickets and making them reveal their lines. After some fighting, Thomas established his lines parallel to and within about a mile of the base of Missionary Ridge. Thomas's advance led his command too far away from Sherman's right to make the contemplated junction and resulting oblique order of battle. Sherman would have to turn Bragg's flank without Thomas's support. Moreover, Thomas's action further alerted Bragg to his right flank. Bragg sent a division and brigade to his right.[15]

At 1:00 p.m. on the twenty-fourth, Sherman moved his three divisions, supported by a brigade from Howard's corps and a division from Thomas's command, towards the Confederate's right flank. After moving two and a quarter mile from the river without loss, Sherman found a deep valley separated his position on a ridge of hills from Missionary Ridge. All the prior Federal reconnaissances had not detected this valley. Finding this unexpected break in the hills at 3:30 p.m., Sherman halted for the night and fortified his position. Sherman's failure to move any further on the twenty-fourth gave Bragg critical time to strengthen and fortify his lightly defended right flank. On the twenty-fourth, Major General Patrick R. Cleburne's division was moved to the right flank. The next morning, three additional Confederate brigades arrived on the right to reinforce Cleburne's command.[16]

On November 25, Sherman, with three times the strength of the Confederate right flank, made two major mistakes that allowed the Confederates to hold their position. First, Sherman's move to flank Bragg's right, which the original plan directed, was never executed. Moreover, the weakest point of Cleburne's line at the apex of the ridge was not exploited after the Federals had concentrated their morning attack there. Instead, Sherman ordered his afternoon attacks against the western side of Tunnel Hill, immediately in his front. This was the strongest position on the Confederate right. Second, Sherman's assaults were uncoordinated or were carried out one behind the other. Sherman was not able to take advantage of his potentially overpowering numbers. These attacks were eventually repulsed, and Sherman returned to the lines of November 24. Fortunately for the Federals, their victory was not dependent on Sherman.[17]

Early on the morning of the twenty-fourth, Hooker was in Lookout Valley holding the Federal right. Thomas was ordered to make a demonstration on Lookout Mountain as early as possible after daybreak. If possible, the demonstration could be developed into a full assault. Hooker, with three divisions, moved to take Lookout Mountain. The mountain was defended only by one division, but the Confederates used the natural obstacles to give a severe fight. Hooker's troops, however, extending beyond the enemy on both flanks, constantly forced them back. By noon, his troops had rounded the slope of the mountain and were facing east. By late afternoon, the Confederates stabilized their position, and Hooker entrenched for the night. During the early morning hours of the twenty-fifth, the Confederates withdrew all their forces to defend Missionary Ridge. Soon after 10:00 a.m., Hooker moved down the slope into Chattanooga Valley and on toward Missionary Ridge via the Rossville Gap. By 3:00 p.m., he carried the pass and began to sweep along the ridge with a brigade supported by a division in the valley on either flank.[18]

While Hooker was moving on Missionary Ridge, Grant grew concerned about Sherman's inability to push forward. He ordered Thomas's four divisions to advance and carry the rifle pits and ridge in front of them. Thomas's line of battle, nearly three miles in length, swept over the open plain and captured the pits. Thomas's divisions then ascended the steep ridge and pressed the Confederates to the top. The Confederate defenders had been placed at a serious disadvantage by their own engineers who had misplaced their final line of trenches at the top of the ridge, thus allowing the Federal attackers to use the terrain between them as a shield. The Confederates should have placed their trenches at the military crest—a geographic line a little lower down on the slope from where they could see and fire upon the oncoming Federals. At the same time, Hooker rapidly drove in Bragg's left flank. Hearing the firing on their left coming increasingly closer, the troops opposing Thomas's charge became demoralized and retreated. Hooker's troops finally formed a junction with Thomas's extreme right division and caught many prisoners between them. Thomas's extreme left division moved to aid Sherman but was checked until dark. This allowed the greater part of Bragg's force, which had been massed on the right, to escape.[19]

While the battle of Chattanooga was a great Federal victory, the final method of capturing Missionary Ridge and pushing the Confederates back caused at least one general to criticize the final battle plan. Smith, along with other generals, had watched the battle from Orchard Knob and believed the original plan would have resulted in a greater success. The plan that Smith developed would have resulted in flanking Bragg on his right and separating him from his lines of supply and communications, which could have led not only to winning the Confederate position, but possibly destroying Bragg's army. Instead, the final battle plan, while it captured the Confederate position, allowed Bragg to retreat on his line of communication. Smith later criticized Grant for moving Thomas on November 23, thus forcing Sherman to attack the Confederate right alone. Smith blamed Sherman for not capturing the weakly defended Confederate right on the twenty-fourth and criticized the force and direction of his attack on the twenty-fifth.

Smith credited the final success of the battle to Thomas, who ordered Hooker's attack on Lookout Mountain and his move on Missionary Ridge. Thomas's command, in conjunction with Hooker, turned the Confederate left and pushed them south.[20]

While Smith was later critical of the actions of those above him, his superiors praised the chief engineer for his contribution to the battle. Sherman, in his report, cited the work done to transport his men across the river. He wrote:

> I will bear my willing testimony to the completeness of this whole business. All the officers charged with the work were present and manifested a skill which I cannot praise too highly. I have never beheld any work done so quietly, so well, and I doubt if the history of war can show a bridge of that extent (viz., 1,350 feet) laid down so noiselessly and well in so short a time. I attribute it to the genius and intelligence of General William F. Smith.[21]

Grant credited Smith with the "most excellent system of fortifications which defend Chattanooga" and with the personal reconnaissances that led to plans for securing the short line and footing on Missionary Ridge.[22] On November 30, Grant wrote to the president stating that he had sent an earlier letter to Stanton recommending Baldy for promotion. In his note to Lincoln, Grant wrote, "Recent events have entirely satisfied me of his great capabilities and merits, and I hasten to renew the recommendation and urge it."[23] Grant asked that Smith's name be placed first on the promotion list of all those he previously recommended.[24]

After the battle, Smith concentrated on his duties as chief engineer of the Military Division of the Mississippi. Smith kept the Topographical Bureau busy with requests for reports and maps regarding the area and engineering equipment. Among the reports he received was one on the conditions of the Tennessee River at Muscle Shoals, Alabama. Smith was interested in finding out when the river was passable at this location. Colonel Buell's Pioneer Brigade was ordered to complete a bridge across West Chickamauga Creek. Another bridge was constructed across the South Chickamauga near Shallow Ford. Smith ordered the Thirteenth Michigan to the South Chickamauga to commence cutting timber and rafting it to the sawmills. The commander, Major Willard G. Eaton, was to examine Mission Mills to see if it was a sawmill and report its capacity. Major Henry S. Dean's Twenty-Second Michigan assisted the Michigan Engineers in constructing a wagon road and bridge between Chattanooga and Lookout Mountain. On December 14, Smith proceeded to New York City on business connected with his department. The next day, Smith urged Grant to inspect the railroad to Bridgeport because of its poor condition. He wrote that repairs and improved administration were urgently needed, stating, "Very many cars have run off the track and upset, and no attempt seems to have been made to get them back into service, and I think everything and everybody connected with the road need overhauling."[25] While in New York, Smith was authorized to purchase photographic apparatus, a lithographic press, and other materials for his department.[26]

Smith did not return to Chattanooga until after New Year's Day, 1864. On January 2, the Brown's Ferry bridge was ordered to be dismantled. The pontoons were anchored to the banks of Lookout Creek near its mouth. A boom was constructed above and below the boats to prevent damage from drift. The bridge at the mouth of the South Chickamauga was also taken apart and the material used where it was needed. Smith also ordered the collection of the boats that had scattered along the river during the last two weeks.[27]

While serving as chief engineer, Smith discussed with Grant the best strategy to bring the war to a victorious conclusion. Grant had grown to respect Smith's strategic acumen and urged him to express his views in writing to Dana, who could use his influence to affect Stanton's policy. Accordingly, on January 15, 1864, Smith wrote to Dana of his plans for the coming campaign. Halleck had proposed to send Sherman's entire force west of the Mississippi to cooperate with Banks' campaign against the Confederates in the Trans-Mississippi area. To do that effectually would delay the campaign against Atlanta for another season. Smith considered Atlanta to be the center of the Confederacy. When Atlanta was taken and the army that defended it beaten, the major enemy force would be destroyed; the force west of the Mississippi would be entirely cut off and compelled to surrender without a battle. Placing the Western armies west of the Mississippi would enable the Confederates to concentrate their forces and enter the free states either by crushing the Army of the Potomac or avoiding it by going through Kentucky.[28]

The first step against Atlanta was to get Longstreet out of Tennessee, which could be accomplished in three ways. First, a winter campaign could force him out. Second, Longstreet could be forced out by a movement of the Army of the Potomac in North Carolina that threatened Raleigh and Wilmington and entirely separated the Army of Northern Virginia from the Army of Tennessee. Third, the movement of a heavy column threatening Atlanta could force the Confederates to bring Longstreet to the aid of General J.E. Johnston, who had succeeded Bragg. The first possibility, if men could be supplied in East Tennessee, was the quickest and best course if energy could be infused into the Department of the Ohio. Once East Tennessee was cleared, the entire line to Chattanooga should be held and a six months' supply of provisions accumulated at the latter place, so that if the railroad were cut, it would be a matter of small consequence. The line of operations on Atlanta should then be selected, and all the available force of the three western departments put on it. Advancing through Mississippi offered the advantage of covering the lower Tennessee, but the Alabama River was the best line of communication, and Mobile, when taken, would provide a fine base.[29]

To make this movement to Atlanta at all practical, Smith thought an effort should be made to occupy North Carolina, leaving Virginia isolated and breaking up the lines of communication between Atlanta and Richmond. Smith believed that Virginia by itself could not support an army for a month. Wilmington might also be readily closed. He concluded, "Let us keep steadily in view the vital points in this business & not be drawn away from there by others which would be very well to have but which will come by possession of the first."[30]

On January 18, Lieutenant Colonel Cyrus Comstock and Smith submitted a memorandum to Grant suggesting that 60,000 men be landed at Norfolk, Virginia, or New Bern, North Carolina, to operate against the railroads south of Richmond and ultimately against Raleigh and Wilmington. Grant adopted their view. The next day, Grant wrote to Generals Halleck and George Thomas and stated his wishes to abandon all previous routes of attack toward Richmond, instead sending a force of 60,000 men into North Carolina to threaten the enemy's interior lines.[31]

Smith's strategic insight and tactical and logistical successes probably positively influenced the view of the administration. In late December 1863, Dana had discussed with Stanton and Halleck the coming campaign. All agreed that East Tennessee had to be cleared of the Confederates but felt the Army of the Potomac could not accomplish this with Meade as commander. Smith and Sherman were mentioned as possible successors. Both Stanton and Halleck believed Smith "would be the best person to try." They still had doubts about his disposition and personal character, but Dana removed these doubts. Grant favored Smith for command of the Army of the Potomac, and Lincoln, Stanton, and Halleck agreed.[32]

Grant continued to push for Smith's promotion to major general of volunteers dated back to his first appointment. This would not only rectify the actions of the Senate in March 1863 but would also allow Smith to take high command in the West or the East because the date of his first appointment would enable him to out rank almost all the field commanders. In a letter to Halleck on January 13, Grant renewed his request for Smith's appointment so that he could be given command of the Department of the Ohio. Grant added that if Smith were given a higher command, the Military Division commander would favor either Major General James B. McPherson or Major General John M. Schofield for the Department of the Ohio position. Halleck replied that Smith's appointment would be made as soon as there was a vacancy. Stanton also told Assistant Secretary of War John Tucker that the only reason that Smith was not promoted was the lack of a vacancy. He hoped the Senate would create the vacancy and assured Tucker that Smith was first on the list. Stanton committed his department to that action. He had hoped Smith would be promoted so he could be sent to take command of the Department of the Ohio. Evidently, by the end of January, Stanton felt that Smith was needed more to command the troops at Knoxville than the Army of the Potomac. In his conversation with Tucker, Stanton stressed Smith's abilities and the importance of the command of the Department of the Ohio. When the Senate refused to create the vacancy for Smith, the department command was given to Schofield.[33]

Despite Grant's efforts, Smith believed that the war would end before he got his second star back. Baldy still had enemies in the army. Hooker wrote to Stanton on February 25 blaming Smith for reports in the *New York Tribune* that criticized Hooker's advance at the battle of Ringgold. Hooker explained that he appointed Smith to the Ninth Corps "as I recognized in him the evil genius of Franklin, Brooks, and Newton.... As for Smith, he has had an ascendancy over Grant, who is simple-minded, but it will not be likely to be long-lived."[34] Hooker evidently saw Smith as an obstacle to his resuming command of the Army of the Potomac. He was working actively to get Meade removed and to succeed him.[35]

Nevertheless, many of the generals in the Army of the Potomac looked forward to Smith's appointment. Major Charles Mundee wrote to Smith, "I saw and spoke to a number of Major and Brigadier Generals, and all express the same feeling, that of gratification;—especially Generals Sedgwick and Newton."[36] O.E. Babcock wrote to Smith on February 9 that he hoped the rumors about Baldy's appointment as Army of the Potomac commander were true. Grant told him that he expected the same. From Washington, Brigadier General James Harrison Wilson, a former West Point student and close friend of Smith, wrote Baldy about the on-going push to have him made commander of the Army of the Potomac. On February 10, Wilson wrote, "The War Department and no doubt, General Halleck, are for you, but <u>Mr. Lincoln</u> is <u>slow to move</u>."[37] Four days later, Wilson wrote, "The authorities will neither remove Meade nor <u>move</u> him."[38] Meade, Stanton, and Lincoln tried to shift the responsibility for the Virginia Campaign to one another. Wilson and Dana supported Grant's promotion to lieutenant general and general-in-chief of all the Federal armies. Then, he could put forward whom he chose, direct all armies in unison, and place these armies where they were most needed. Wilson was assured that Lincoln and Stanton would gladly leave the control of the armies to Grant. On February 27, Wilson wrote that he and Dana believed Grant's promotion would ensure that Smith would be given his deserved command. Wilson feared that some enemy of Smith had influenced Lincoln, but he was unable to discover who that person was.[39]

On March 10, Baldy talked with Colonel John Rawlins, Grant's chief of staff. Rawlins told Smith that the day before, the secretary of war had urged Grant to replace Meade. Grant had asked about bringing one of his generals from the Western Theater to assume the command of the Army of the Potomac. Grant suggested Major General James McPherson, but Stanton insisted the army be commanded by a man who had served with it. The secretary advised Grant to select Smith "who is well known there and has the confidence of all." Smith doubted, however, that Grant would make any change in the army command.[40]

The controversy over Smith's appointment to major general and command of the Army of the Potomac entered the newspapers in early March. On March 5, the *Boston Daily Evening Transcript* reported that Major General Daniel E. Sickles' testimony before Congress about the battle of Gettysburg would necessitate Meade's resignation from the army command. In that case, Hooker or Smith would be likely successors. Grant was said to recommend Smith. By March 12, the *Transcript* was joined by the *New York Times* and *Tribune* in reporting that Smith would fill the vacancy created by Grant's promotion to lieutenant general and that Baldy would be given the command of the Army of the Potomac. It was believed that Grant wanted his generals to be able not only to obey orders but be familiar with his thinking. The *New York Herald*, in an editorial critical of the Republican influence in the army, condemned the Republicans' criticism of Grant. It stated, "And now Grant comes forward, as if to put his power to the test at once, with that very bad boy, Baldy Smith, and is likely to carry him through also."[41] Smith, was cited as "a chronic admirer of McClellan whom the radicals have therefore hated and harried through the war."[42] The *Herald* praised Smith's anticipated appointment as major general as "progress."[43]

On March 15, Lincoln nominated Smith to fill the major generalcy of volunteers vacated by Grant's promotion to lieutenant general. The next day, Brigadier General Hugh J. Kilpatrick was cited as a source of reports that Smith would succeed Meade as army commander. If Smith had any chance of becoming army commander, he would have to be promoted major general of volunteers as of the date of his first appointment. On March 18, 1864, the Senate, in executive session, decided to return the nomination to Lincoln. They declined to confirm Smith's nomination to major general as of July 1862 because doing so would cause him to outrank a large number of "meritorious officers."[44] On March 23, the president sent Smith's name back to the Senate, proposing that Smith's commission date from his confirmation. Smith's commission as major general of volunteers, dating March 1864, was confirmed the same day without referring it back to the Senate Committee of Military Affairs. There was still some doubt if Meade was to be retained as army commander, but Smith's recent-dated commission made him ineligible to be Meade's successor. On March 24, the *Times* mentioned that Smith was to fill a chief of staff type position under Grant. But this proved to be false. On March 31, Major General Smith was assigned to duty under Major General Benjamin Butler, commander of the Department of Virginia and North Carolina. It would be over a month before Smith would receive the long-awaited appointment to a high command.[45]

Essentially, there was only one reason—albeit significant in nature—that kept Smith from becoming commander of the Army of the Potomac. Smith addressed this matter in a letter to Wilson on March 16. Smith had a conversation with Grant about the coming campaign but feared "if I say anything more to him it may pass from official to officious and that is what I wish to avoid a tendency towards." Smith had supposed Grant still endorsed his North Carolina campaign, but now found that "Meade's statements and Halleck's wisdom had rather befogged him. With ample means to make his important movement wherever he pleased, and at the same time leave Washington and the free states safe, he had determined to take the line of operations on which he found the Army of the Potomac and work on that." Smith then expressed to Wilson his criticisms of the overland route. First, there existed the problem of communications. It was impossible to protect the Orange and Alexandria Railroad without draining the fighting force in front. There was the unnecessary need of changing the base, and the delicacy of such movements. The James River could not be assured as a line of communications unless the entire south bank from Suffolk was absolutely controlled.[46]

Second, the overland plan did not realistically consider how to defeat Lee's army. Smith believed there was no hope of forcing Lee into a battle until he wished to fight, and there was nothing worth the risk before Lee got to Richmond. At Richmond, he could easily cover his line of communication with the South and stand an indefinite siege with Grant's army holding only the north bank of the James. The army could not hold both banks on the present line. The army could not cross the James above Richmond and ignore Lee's force unless it cut loose from the Federal base. Such a change of base would fail to protect the capital, which was the main concern of the overland proponents. During the change, the Federals would risk being beaten in front and being crushed in the rear. Finally, placing an army before Richmond and besieging it without cutting all its supply lines would allow Lee to retreat quietly with his army intact and his line well covered.[47]

Smith then turned to his North Carolina campaign plan. If the siege of Richmond could be avoided, and the army placed both on the enemy's lines and near the Federal base, Lee would be forced to come and fight the Federals on their own ground or starve and disband his army. Smith felt that the vicinity of Weldon was such a place and that the Federals could get there by secrecy and celerity. Smith figured that there were enough men for the campaign and to keep Washington and the line of the Potomac perfectly safe from invasion until the North Carolina force "could smash things generally and then do what was necessary to get Lee's army between the upper and the [nether] millstones." He felt also that the western army must also move and make a demonstration so serious as to prevent any desperate efforts to reinforce Lee.[48]

Smith's views were altogether different from the overland plan that Grant had adopted. While Grant was in Chattanooga, he had endorsed and highly respected Smith's strategic plans. But on February 17, 1864, Halleck wrote to Grant on the latter's endorsement of the North Carolina plan. Halleck opposed any plan that did not keep the main Federal force in the East between Washington and Lee's army. He objected to committing any significant force to either a Peninsula or North Carolina campaign. While Halleck did not directly endorse the overland strategy, his opposition to any alternative left little doubt about his views. Although Grant's decision on the coming campaign needed only Lincoln's approval, Halleck's opinion was important. After going to Washington and conferring with Lincoln, Stanton, Meade, and Butler, Grant decided to abandon the North Carolina plan and adopt the overland strategy.[49]

The influence of Brigadier General John Rawlins was also important in changing

Grant's strategic views. Rawlins helped convince Grant that the better and safer line of operations was overland against Lee's army wherever it might be encountered, and not through the innovative movements proposed by Smith. As Rawlins wrote to his wife, "the General does not mean to scatter his army, and have it whipped in detail ... it has been in my constant, firm advocacy of massing large forces against small ones, in other words, of always having the advantage of numbers on our side. Such is the General's notion of battles."[50]

Grant's determination to follow the overland route led him to keep Meade as army commander. Since Meade supported the overland strategy and had regained the confidence of the administration, Grant felt it was better to retain Meade than give the command to Smith, who strongly opposed his adopted campaign.[51] Grant was also impressed by Meade's willingness to step down if the lieutenant general wanted someone else to lead the Army of the Potomac. Meade's retention as army commander directly led to Smith's failure to be commissioned major general of volunteers back to the date of his first appointment. The Senate needed to block such a commission because it would have enabled Smith to outrank most of the generals in the East, including General Meade.[52]

Back in October, Smith had come to Chattanooga and been appointed chief engineer. Normally, as a staff officer, he would not have been noticed again. But, his conception and execution of the Brown's Ferry movement secured his army and brought him prominence with Grant and Thomas. Smith's insight in planning the original move at Chattanooga and his success in bringing Sherman into the battle made Grant aware of his chief engineer's strategic, tactical, and logistical skill. Grant, grateful for Smith's work, tried hard to get Smith the higher command—a command worthy of Smith's abilities, talents, and dedication. But, Smith's knowledge of the Eastern theater directly conflicted with the administration's strategic plans. Grant's support for Smith did win Baldy his long-sought after promotion and confirmation as major general. But Grant, unwilling to challenge his president's views and try an innovative and probably victorious strategy, decided on a plan that unintentionally resulted in a war of attrition. Grant now had to rely on his superior numbers. Smith was assigned to Butler's department for unspecified duty. He was about to face what would be his last and most controversial tenure as a corps commander.[53]

CHAPTER XI

Smith in the Bermuda Hundred Campaign

A Critic of Defeat

Smith was appointed to unspecified duty under Major General Benjamin F. Butler, commanding the Department of Virginia and North Carolina headquartered at Fort Monroe. Grant assured Smith that he would be assigned a large command in the coming campaign. Nevertheless, Smith was disappointed because his promotion to major general was dated March 1864. This left him junior to many of his former juniors in the East and without the army command he had expected. Moreover, he believed that the Army of the Potomac was once again attempting a costly and ineffectual campaign. While Baldy would avoid much of this campaign by being involved in operations on the James River, he would soon become anxious about his department commander's plan.[1]

Before Baldy could engage in his new assignment, he and his wife had to deal with a personal tragedy. Their firstborn infant son, Frank, namesake and godson of Baldy's close friend, General Franklin, had recently died. The sadness over this loss was evident to those around them. Lieutenant Colonel Cyrus Comstock and Brigadier General John Rawlins both commented on the tragedy and the impact on the Smiths. It would cast a shadow on Baldy and his wife throughout the spring and summer as Baldy engaged in three major battles while his wife dealt with the grief and consequential depression.[2]

On April 1, 1864, Butler disclosed to Smith his plan for the upcoming campaign. He intended to move up the James, land at Bermuda Hundred, and advance on Richmond from the south. Smith strongly disagreed with this approach. He believed that Petersburg's importance as the hub for Confederate transportation and supply, and its apparent small defending force, made the "Cockade City" the far better objective for Butler's campaign. But having only reported to Butler two or three hours earlier, Smith did not object. In the interests of good relations with his new commander, he merely said, "Before adopting that plan I think you will require information from the river which the flag of truce boat can get for you."[3]

The next morning, Grant met with Butler, who called for Smith. The latter expected Butler to present his plan at this meeting. In such a discussion, Smith felt obligated to reveal his opposition to Grant, but he did not wish to antagonize Butler. Baldy decided to use the excuse of needing to attend to other duties and did not attend the conference; he did not suppose Grant would settle the question of a campaign in a matter of two hours. Unbeknownst to Baldy, however, Grant and Butler had discussed the campaign on the previous day. After Grant left, Butler told Smith that Grant had approved his plan and had written out his instructions. Grant would operate overland in Virginia, his objective being Lee's army. Butler was to collect all troops not needed for garrison duty and operate on the south side of the James River with Richmond as his objective. Approximately 23,000 men in Butler's department were to be placed under Smith. This force would be joined by Major General Quincy Gillmore's command of 10,000 coming from South Carolina. Butler's entire command would be called the Army of the James. Butler was first to move on City Point, entrench, and concentrate his field army there. Directions were not given at that time for further movements. If Lee was forced back on Richmond, Grant hoped to unite the Army of the Potomac with the Army of the James. Consequently, it was critical for Butler to stay close to the south bank of the James as he advanced. Butler was left in charge of all minor details of the advance. In this role, Butler intended to adapt Grant's instructions to his plan. Instead of concentrating his army at City Point, Butler decided to secure that position with only a small force and land the remainder at Bermuda Hundred. After establishing a base there, Butler would begin the advance along the south bank of the James.[4]

Grant later said that, on April 2, he had pointed out to Butler "the apparent importance of getting possession of Petersburg."[5] Butler, however, never derived this from his orders or conversation with Grant. During April, Grant never explicitly designated Petersburg as an objective. Butler's objective was to approach Richmond, cooperate with the Army of the Potomac, and hold close to the south bank of the James during his advance. Butler concluded that Grant's order meant an advance directly towards Richmond along the south side of the James. During the conversation of April 2, Grant told Butler that if he could hold the Richmond and Petersburg Railroad cut for ten days and secure the proposed bases at Bermuda Hundred and City Point, Grant might join him there. However, if Lee's army was forced into the entrenchments around Richmond, Grant might instead meet Butler on the James above Richmond. Then, the Armies of the Potomac and the James would unite to invest Richmond with the navy holding the James. The conversation seemed to reinforce Butler's interpretation.[6]

Long after the war, in his *From Chattanooga to Petersburg* (1893), Smith asserted, "No one can doubt that General Grant made a very grave mistake in not directing General Butler to capture Petersburg at once."[7] At the time, Smith was greatly disappointed because he believed Grant's instructions and conversations with Butler ignored the great value of Petersburg. Smith's only hope of capturing Petersburg was to convince Butler to use his discretion to capture the city.[8]

Despite Grant's instructions and Butler's desire to land at Bermuda Hundred, Smith still believed Butler's natural line for an offensive movement should be toward Petersburg with the Appomattox River on his right flank. Capturing and holding that great railroad center would throttle the Confederacy and force Lee back from Grant's front. It would provide an excellent base for the Army of the James to attack Richmond. If Petersburg were captured and not held longer than necessary to destroy the railroads and bridges, the damage probably still would be great enough to cause Lee to fall back. With the Federals at Petersburg, the Union base at City Point would be well covered, and if necessary, a retreat would be easily accomplished. From City Point, the navy could perfectly protect the flanks of Butler's army. As a base it offered advantages for offensive movements and great security against a large force. Bermuda Hundred could also be a secure base, but the narrow neck of the peninsula on which it was located would enable the Confederates to resist Butler's advance.[9]

Faced with taking part in a questionable campaign, Smith returned to his proposal for a campaign in North Carolina. Smith discussed his views with Butler, who voiced no objections. Baldy even wanted to call the army the "Army of the Cape Fear River." Smith told Butler of Grant's former support of the campaign, so Butler sent Smith to Grant to determine if he still planned a campaign in North Carolina. After meeting with Smith, Grant wrote to Butler that no campaign other than the one on the James River was intended for Butler's department.[10]

On April 19, Butler placed Smith in command of the troops and camps of instruction at Yorktown and Gloucester Point. While overseeing these camps, Smith was faced with the problems of the freedmen. Smith asked Butler to send his best Black regiment to guard the contraband camps in the vicinity as the white soldiers had been committing all sorts of depredations, and as he continued, "I want to get some of them shot for it when caught in the act."[11]

By the end of April, Smith was still not reconciled to Butler or his plans. Smith believed that Butler's inefficiency was due in part to his spending so much time with simple administrative duties and ignoring his responsibilities in the field. Smith urged one of Grant's aides, Lieutenant-Colonel O.E. Babcock, to get Grant to send Butler a staff officer to perform the administrative duties of the department so that Butler could concentrate on the army in the field. Babcock wrote to Smith that Grant wanted Butler to have his own way with all minutiae. Grant thought that Butler's generals could render Butler "all necessary aid to execute the details" in the field.[12] Baldy wrote his wife, "I don't like General Butler and there is no use trying to."[13] Smith hoped that Butler would be ordered to New York before the move began. Smith thought the army command and the coming campaign were terrible responsibilities to leave in the hands of a man who had "never set a squadron in the field. The whole thing (the campaign) is against my opinion and I wash my hands of it; though I am willing to acknowledge it will be a brilliant thing if it succeeds."[14] Smith also wrote his close friend General Franklin with a similar viewpoint. He stated:

> I am here in an anomalous position under Butler with a campaign, or movement rather, before us which I dread as being full of unnecessary risks, & of the kind that may produce the most terrible disaster. I came near having what I should most have preferred a large column to move on the southside of the James but that has been reduced to a force that can't do much good & may be swallowed up & is under Butler & is to move in the worst possible way.[15]

In his letter to Franklin, Smith also assessed his own decline in influence and position. He told Franklin of his promotion: "The War Dept. did all it could to get back my old date but the trouble was in the Senate." Smith also wrote of his lack of success to advance to high command: "I came near being assigned to the Dept. of the Ohio & I came nearer going to the command of the A of P which I lost through Grant who had first recommended me. The Pres't & Sec'y had determined on it & thought Grant would certainly do it & relieve them from the responsibility." Smith noted that his influence was gone and that he was unable to dissuade Grant from his poor opinion of Franklin. Baldy believed Banks and Halleck were responsible for affecting Grant in this respect.[16]

Smith then turned to his evaluation of the Army of the Potomac. He felt that the campaign might be a success, but "blunders sometimes turn out that way & I fear the old A of P is again doomed to receive a flogging at Lee's hands." Smith's bitterness over his loss of status was also directed against fellow generals in the East. He wrote, "Meade is as malignant as he is jealous & weak as he is either & Hancock & Warren are his right bowers now. Burnside still sports on the wave of popularity & is one of those men who will never get killed in battle. Grant knows what he is but has not the nerve to put him where he belongs. Hancock is both ambitious [sic] & deceitful & now lives by Meade."[17]

On April 30, by Butler's directions, Smith ordered a brigade in Brigadier General Alfred Terry's command to land at West Point to give the Confederates the impression that it was the starting place for the Federal offensive. The navy would ferry the troops, cover the landing, and protect the flanks of the force while in position. The position would be entrenched, and the wharves rebuilt. Colonel Guy Henry's brigade landed at West Point and began building a good dock. Smith sent word to Henry that as soon as he felt his position secured, he could make a reconnaissance of his vicinity.[18]

Butler received his final orders on April 30. On the evening of May 4, he was to move his forces as far up the James as possible by daylight, and then push on with the greatest energy for the campaign objective. On May 2, Smith was formally assigned the command of the newly formed Eighteenth Army Corps. Smith's division commanders initially were respected friends. W.T.H. Brooks rejoined Smith as his First Division commander, and Brigadier General Isaac Wistar was Smith's Second Division commander. But, before the campaign began, Brigadier General Godfrey Weitzel, an old associate of Butler's, replaced Wistar, who was reduced to a brigade commander in the Second Division.[19]

During the night of May 4, Gillmore's Tenth Corps and the Eighteenth Corps were all embarked on transports in the York River, and on the early morning of May 5, moved up the James. The convoy of various navy vessels was a motley array. Coasters, river steamers, ferryboats, tugs, screw and side-wheel steamers, sloops, schooners, barges, and canal-boats raced or crawled up the river toward the designated landing. To ensure the safety of the movement, Generals Smith and Gillmore led the advance with the army gunboats. They captured Confederate signal stations along the way. Brigadier General Edward Hinks' Black Division, nominally attached to the Eighteenth Corps, landed at Wilson's wharf, Fort Powhatan, and in late afternoon, at City Point. The rest of the Eighteenth Corps and the Tenth Corps landed at Bermuda Hundred. The Eighteenth and Tenth Corps each numbered nearly eighteen thousand infantry and artillery soldiers. There was no opposition to the landings.[20]

By 9:00 a.m., on May 6, the two corps were in position on the line, from Walthall's Landing on the Appomattox across to the James, and began entrenching. The line was about three miles long. This was the narrowest part of the peninsula formed by the James and Appomattox rivers, and the line was well chosen to defend a great entrenched camp and base of supplies. As a base for offensive operations, however, it was inadequate. The Richmond and Petersburg Turnpike was about two miles from the center of the line, and from there to Petersburg was about seven miles. Two unfordable streams, Swift Creek and the Appomattox, intervened. Richmond, the objective of the army, was covered by the works at Drewry's Bluff, a little over four miles from the lines. Even if these works were carried, they would be extremely difficult to hold because they were open in the rear.[21]

Smith assessed his position as one between two fortresses with wet ditches. Whichever way the army moved, it was weakened by the loss of two paralyzed forces: one holding the line of entrenchment and one necessarily posted to protect the army from the works behind it. Smith believed that Butler could follow Grant's instructions of April 2 and concentrate his force at City Point. From City Point, Butler's natural route for any effective purpose would be via Petersburg, a position of more value than Drewry's Bluff and more easily held, with a base perfectly covered. Smith believed Petersburg would surely have fallen on the sixth or seventh of May.[22]

While the entrenching continued, at 4:00 p.m. on May 6, Smith sent Brigadier General Charles Heckman's brigade of 2,700 from Weitzel's division toward Port Walthall Junction to cut the Richmond and Petersburg Railroad. Simultaneously, General Gillmore was to make a corresponding advance. Gillmore, however, did not comply with the plan because of what he deemed "good and sufficient reasons."[23] Heckman approached the Confederates, who positioned themselves behind a fence. After taking measures to protect his flanks, Heckman advanced. Meeting sterner resistance than he expected and not desiring to bring on a general engagement for such a limited objective, he decided to advance no further. He engaged the enemy for a time with infantry and artillery fire. He then collected his wounded and returned in good order back to Federal lines. The attack failed for three reasons. First, Gillmore failed to carry out Smith's suggestion to make a corresponding move on the right. Butler had ordered Gillmore to make the move, but the Tenth Corps commander failed to act. Second, the Confederates arrived first at Port Walthall Junction, giving them a naturally strong position made stronger by the railroad embankment. Third, Heckman, in determining not to advance further, overestimated the size of the enemy. He believed the two regiments of South Carolinians were "at least two brigades" when in fact they numbered only six hundred men.[24]

Smith tried to correct the failure of May 6 by planning an attack for the next morning. He told Butler that it was of vital importance that the road should be cut, both for troop morale and the campaign objective. He suggested a detail of one brigade from each division in the entire command would be sufficient to make both a feint and real attack. Proportionately drawing the detail from both corps would also prevent creating weak points in the lines across the neck. He thought a strong feint should be made at the same place that Heckman had attempted to cut the road and the real attack made elsewhere closer to Richmond.[25]

Butler agreed with Smith's suggestions and ordered one brigade of each of Gillmore's three divisions and Smith's two divisions to report to Baldy. Smith was to assign a division commander to direct the expedition. He gave the command to Brooks. Brooks was to take Gillmore's three brigades and Brigadier General Hiram Burnham's brigade of his own division to make the real attack. Heckman would make the feint in the same place as on the sixth.[26]

On the morning of the seventh, Brooks' force left camp and took the Bermuda Hundred road to Port Walthall Junction. He had not proceeded far before coming upon a small enemy force at the opposite end of a causeway leading through a marsh. The Eighth Connecticut Volunteers were thrown out as skirmishers and were supported by the balance of Burnham's brigade. The ground was difficult to operate in, with dense undergrowth and fallen timber in every direction. Colonel Harris Plaisted's brigade was thrown to the right. It proceeded down a ravine under perfect cover, soon crossed the pike, and reached the railroad, which it began to cut. Colonel William Barton's brigade proceeded to the railroad to the left of Plaisted but soon faced the stern opposition of a large enemy force. Colonel Jeremiah Drake's and Burnham's brigades supported the other two brigades, and the enemy soon disappeared from their front. Work continued on cutting the road. However, orders were misunderstood, and Plaisted's brigade was withdrawn before its work was completed. Nevertheless, between 300 and 500 yards of road were destroyed, together with a trestle bridge, the telegraph line on the railroad, and two telegraph lines on the turnpike. A large steam saw-mill belonging to Confederate authorities was also destroyed.[27]

Heckman advanced without opposition to the place he had occupied on the sixth and found the enemy in their former position. The enemy opened with artillery. By moving one regiment to the right, Heckman's force escaped the enemy's fire. Heckman's artillery replied and succeeded in blowing up a caisson, silencing the Confederate guns. Heckman was ordered to attack the Confederate right as Brooks attacked in front, but finding the enemy a serious threat to his left flank, he did not advance, instead continuing his artillery fire. After Brooks sent word that his object was accomplished and that he was retiring, Heckman's brigade retired to camp as well.[28]

Butler wished to continue the destruction begun on the seventh. On May 8, Butler ordered Smith and Gillmore to take their entire corps, excepting those necessary for the defense of the line of entrenchments, and attack the Richmond and Petersburg Railroad the next morning. Smith's and Gillmore's single purpose was to destroy as much of the railroad as possible. On the morning of May 9, Gillmore moved out to Chester Junction, gained his objective without opposition, and began destroying the railroad.[29]

Smith sent his two divisions to cut the railroad and push the Confederates back to their works on the right bank of Swift Creek, three miles from Petersburg. Brigadier General Gilman Marston's and Burnham's brigades of Brooks' division led the advance. Brooks was followed by Wistar's and Heckman's brigades of Weitzel's division. Before the corps struck the railroad, it was reported to Smith that a Confederate force was positioned at Port Walthall Junction. With the object of continuing on to Petersburg, Smith asked Butler and Gillmore to send reinforcements southward to crush this enemy force. Butler, while not confirming Smith's goal, did send Gillmore with part of his force to support Smith. The railroad was finally taken, for the expected enemy opposition did not materialize. After Weitzel crossed the railroad, Brooks advanced to it and then marched along it in the direction of Petersburg. Weitzel, leaving the destruction of the railroad to a brigade of the Tenth Corps, moved south on the Richmond and Petersburg turnpike. Smith's men were now facing due south with Brooks' command on the left and Weitzel's force on the right. About a mile beyond Walthall Junction, a country road crossed the railroad, running obliquely toward the turnpike. Marston's brigade took this road and connected with Weitzel's division on the turnpike. Burnham's brigade continued to follow the railroad.[30]

Brooks' force did not meet significant opposition until reaching Swift Creek. Weitzel's command met stiffer resistance. At Tinsberry Creek, the Confederates were found in position with artillery and infantry. Weitzel deployed Heckman's brigade, its center resting on the pike, and moved it forward. Wistar's brigade was held in reserve. The enemy fire becoming heavier, Weitzel moved Wistar in line on Heckman's right. At the time that Marston's brigade connected with Weitzel, the Confederates charged Heckman. Heckman repulsed the attack and pursued the Confederates. The Confederates were driven back well beyond Arrowfield Church. They then opened artillery fire from a field work, commanding the road on the south side of Swift Creek. Weitzel's artillery was unable to silence this fire and forced to retire. Smith allowed Weitzel to use his discretion in deciding whether he should continue the attack. Convinced that pushing the small remaining enemy force across the creek to occupy the north bank would be too costly, Weitzel suspended the attack. He pushed forward a strong line of pickets and bivouacked for the night. Two brigades of the Tenth Corps assisted Weitzel. One took a position on the right of Wistar, and the other acted as a reserve for the division.[31]

Burnham's brigade of Brooks' division also engaged the Confederates at Swift Creek. The brigade dislodged the Confederates from the north side of the creek and pushed them back from behind trees, houses, and fences on the other side. The brigade held the field and was posted near the north bank of the creek. The enemy assailed the lines at various points twice during the night, but each assault was repulsed, and the Confederates were driven back across the creek.[32]

By the day's end, the Army of the James was positioned on the north side of Swift Creek. It found that the creek was not fordable. The stream was very narrow with steep banks; no crossing was possible except via the bridges, both of which were guarded by enemy artillery and infantry. The railroad bridge, being only covered with ties, was nearly impassable in the face of opposition. Nevertheless, that evening, Butler told his corps commanders that on the following day, they were to advance beyond Swift Creek and destroy the bridges on the Appomattox River. General Hinks, who had made a reconnaissance to within four miles of Petersburg on May 9, was ordered to move on Petersburg along the south side of the Appomattox. Butler hoped that Hinks could carry the city while the Confederates were busy defending the creek. He was expected, at least, to create a diversion.[33]

After Butler left, the two corps commanders discussed the operations for the next day. Several hours had already been spent in ineffectual efforts to find a place that offered a fair prospect of forcing a passage of Swift Creek. This led Gillmore and Smith to write to Butler and suggest an alternative plan of operations. They suggested that after destroying the road between them and Chester Station, the army cross the Appomattox on a pontoon bridge, which could be quickly constructed across the river below Smith's headquarters, and cut all the roads thta came into Petersburg on that side. Such a bridge could be readily constructed in one night, and all the work of cutting the roads, and per-haps capturing the city, could be accomplished in one day. The corps commanders pre-dicted this would not involve heavy losses. If the army stayed before Swift Creek and was successful the next day, the roads coming into Petersburg on the south side of the Appo-mattox would still remain intact, with the river between the army and the roads. Even then, Butler would be forced to adopt the two generals' alternative plan.[34]

Butler wrote to his two corps commanders, rejecting their well-intentioned advice and charging them with "infirmity of purpose."[35] He received three dispatches from the secretary of war that erroneously reported that Lee's army had fallen back and was in full retreat for Richmond with Grant in pursuit. Grant was marching with his whole army to form a junction with Butler. The dispatches convinced Butler that he should move directly toward Richmond. Butler believed his destruction of the railroad, in con-nection with Brigadier General August V. Kautz's cavalry raid on the Weldon Road, sufficiently severed communications between Richmond and the South. Any further destruction would be done closer to Richmond, on the south side of the James, in con-formity with the plan established by Grant and Butler. Therefore, Butler ordered his two corps commanders to withdraw their forces from Swift Creek as early as possible. Prior to the retirement, the corps commanders were to destroy the railroad bridge and complete a thorough destruction of the railroad. Hinks' African American division was ordered to oversee the work at Fort Powhatan instead of moving to Petersburg.[36]

Smith's reply to Butler's note was "dignified and conciliatory as well as explanatory."[37] He wrote the army commander that since he had never before been accused of infirmity of purpose, he would not take the charge as one seriously affecting his military reputation. His letter with Gillmore was not a protest, but merely a suggestion, "having a tendency to save waste of life to a certain extent, and to more effectually cut the enemy's communications, than any infantry force on this side the river could do."[38] General Weitzel also supported their plan. Smith admitted the alternative plan would have the appearance of a repulse and lose time if Swift Creek could be successfully passed. But the alternative was simply proposed for Butler's consideration.[39]

On May 10, Butler's army continued to destroy the Richmond and Petersburg Railroad. Brigadier General John Martindale's brigade of Brooks' division destroyed over a mile of track by itself. After destroying seven miles of track, the two corps withdrew from their advanced position at Swift Creek and returned to their entrenchments at Bermuda Hundred. The withdrawal made Butler's accomplishments temporary. Beginning that night, Confederate General P.G.T. Beauregard was able to move his force along the turnpike to strengthen the defenses at Richmond.[40]

Butler's latest campaign led Smith to form decided opinions about two issues. First, the ability of the Confederates in Petersburg to flank Butler's movement, and the creeks and ravines between Bermuda Hundred and Richmond, made the region impractical for an offensive with the force that Butler commanded. Second, Butler must actually direct the army in the field in order to make it effective. Smith had tried his best to dissuade Butler from the campaign, although he intended to do his best with the plans before him. But he did write to Butler urging him to take an active role as army commander. For instance, Smith stressed that the withdrawal must be made in accordance with some well-regulated plan published by army headquarters and not according to the separate wishes and interests of the corps commanders. Smith urged having a plan, in part, to clarify Butler's intentions. But, after being harshly rebuked for his simple suggestions for crossing the Appomattox, Smith may have concluded that he needed written orders in the coming campaign to protect himself from further charges of "infirmity of purpose." Consequently, Butler's fault-finding dampened Smith's initiative in the campaign. In a separate letter, Gillmore agreed that Butler must be more involved. He wrote, "Further orders from you, regulating the movement of the corps, seems necessary."[41]

Butler believed that he could simply give his corps commanders his campaign plan and stay at his base, expecting everything to go smoothly. He failed to appreciate his duty to direct the army in the field and settle all questions between the corps commanders and above the corps level. He did not take the field but allowed each corps to work independently without higher command. This became problematic for Butler's army. While Gillmore and Smith were good friends, they found it extremely difficult to work with one another because they often approached the campaign differently. Butler needed to convey his plans better and have his corps commanders implement them. When he was called to settle matters between the corps commanders, however, he mistook it for personal hostility between Gillmore and Smith.[42]

Butler's misunderstanding was illustrated in a small matter of relieving a tired brigade in Smith's corps. On May 10, Smith wrote to Butler that on the previous night, his request to Gillmore for relief of Heckman's brigade had been denied. Smith also needed reinforcements for Brooks to maintain his position in the face of Confederate attacks and for protection for his lines leading to the rear. He had made requests to Gillmore and one of his division commanders, Brigadier General John Turner, but they did not comply. He asked Butler, "in accordance with the usages of military service" that Heckman's brigade be relieved by other troops.[43] The letter was not intended to criticize Gillmore or Turner, who Smith understood had their own troops' needs to satisfy. Smith only intended to get Heckman's men some relief and more importantly, impress upon Butler the need for him to settle questions involving both corps. Butler did eventually send a brigade of the Tenth Corps to relieve Smith's forces, but only as part of the general withdrawal. Moreover, he only intervened to stop what he believed was a lack of cooperation between Gillmore and Smith. He still failed to recognize that such intervention was part of his duties as an army commander. Thus, Butler became more involved in the coming campaign only because he erroneously believed the two corps commanders desired each other to fail.[44]

On the night of May 11, Butler issued instructions to his corps commanders for the movement to begin at daybreak. The two white divisions of the Eighteenth Corps, reinforced by a division of the Tenth Corps, were to move out on the turnpike, extend their advance to the left, and initially keep their right on the river at or near Howlett's House. They were to press the enemy into their entrenchments, endeavoring to turn them on the left, if not too hotly opposed. Smith's move was also to cover Gillmore's right. Gillmore, with his other two divisions, was to check any movement made upon Smith's rear or upon the lines from the direction of Petersburg. Part of Gillmore's command would also form on the turnpike and serve as a general reserve. As soon as Smith had passed Chester Station on the railroad, Kautz was to move with his cavalry on the Danville Road, destroying as much of it as possible. Hinks' Black division was to move from City Point to opposite Point of Rocks on the right bank of the Appomattox.[45]

Shortly after daylight on the twelfth, Weitzel's division, followed by Brooks' division, moved by the Widow Howlett's House to the turnpike. Weitzel's division formed across the turnpike; Brooks was in reserve. Turner's division of the Tenth Corps, temporarily assigned to Smith, moved by Dr. Howlett's House on the James River near the mouth of Redwater Creek. His line was then deployed along the road leading to the turnpike. Weitzel began skirmishing shortly after leaving Gillmore's picket line. He drove the enemy in front of him until he reached the turnpike crossing at Redwater Creek. Here, the Confederates opened fire with two pieces of artillery from the pike but were soon driven away. Weitzel formed his line of battle across the turnpike north of Redwater Creek. Finding the enemy skirmishing along Weitzel's entire front, Smith moved Weitzel's command to the right of the turnpike. Six regiments of Brooks' command were then deployed on Weitzel's left with the remaining brigade under Marston held in reserve on Brooks' left flank. At the same time, Turner was ordered to connect with Weitzel's right after leaving a sufficient force to guard the open country between Dr. Howlett's House and the mouth of Redwater Creek. The whole line was then pressed forward as far as the nature of the ground on the left would allow. Weitzel's left brigade on the right of the turnpike and Brooks' entire line of battle found it difficult to force their way through an almost impenetrable thicket in the marshy country between Redwater Creek and Proctor's Creek. The right brigade of Weitzel and Turner's division, having more open country, succeeded in driving the enemy across Proctor's Creek.[46]

Smith made a reconnaissance on Weitzel's right during the afternoon and discovered that the enemy held the left bank of Proctor's Creek with artillery, and that the slopes were steep and heavily wooded. Finding also that his entire line did not out flank the enemy's line of skirmishers, Smith asked for infantry to extend his line. He also suggested that the reinforcements move around the head of Proctor's Creek and try to turn the enemy's works. Late in the day, three of Gillmore's brigades came up on his left, and the entire command was ordered to bivouac in that position and lie on their arms during the night. To further secure the position, Marston's brigade was ordered to form a second line behind Weitzel, whose troops were extended in one line. Turner was ordered to maintain connections with the road from Dr. Howlett's House and the right of Weitzel's line. A heavy rain during the day served to damage the roads, and the soldiers slept on their arms that night, drenched to the skin. During the night, Marston's brigade was ordered to report to Gillmore for the purpose of making a flank movement around the head of Proctor's Creek.[47]

Early on the morning of May 13, Smith and Brooks made a reconnaissance of Brooks' front. They found that the terrain was usable for infantry across Cattle Run, a branch of Proctor's Creek. They also discovered that beyond Cattle Run was a high hill which overlooked and commanded the left bank of Proctor's Creek in the vicinity of the turnpike. A brigade was advanced toward the hill, and sharpshooters were deployed to cover the passage of artillery down the turnpike so the guns could contribute to the attack. Skirmishers were then moved forward across the creek, and it was found that the enemy had retired. Smith's three divisions were brought across the creek and deployed across the turnpike at the Half-Way House. Weitzel was kept on the right of the turnpike, Brooks formed on Weitzel's left, and Turner was shifted from the extreme right to Brooks' left. The divisions were ordered to keep their connections between each other.[48]

Supported by the line of battle, the skirmishers were pushed forward until the enemy's line of defenses could be seen for over a mile. It had a strong profile with a ditch on the outside. Numerous embrasures for artillery were also filled. On the turnpike, the defenses had embrasures for two guns and were about one thousand yards in front of Smith's line. In Weitzel's front, the skirmishers had not been pushed to the opening and could not make any reconnaissance. The approaches to the works on Brooks' front required an advance over open ground of from three to seven hundred yards, all of which could be swept by the fire of the enemy's artillery.[49]

Smith and Brooks again reconnoitered the latter's front. The reconnaissance led Smith to send word to Butler that if the enemy line was held in force, it could not be carried by assault, and that Smith would not attack the line unless he received orders to do so. Since Gillmore had been entrusted with flanking the Confederate right, Smith felt, that unless ordered, he would not move until Gillmore had turned the enemy's line. He would then keep up with the Tenth Corps commander's success. Smith feared that if he moved without orders before Gillmore had succeeded and should be repulsed, Butler would at once report that Baldy had acted without orders. When Butler was confronted with Smith's request for an order, he told the staff officer who carried the request, "D—n him, he wants to put the responsibility on me, does he?"[50] Captain F.U. Farquhar replied, "General, from his remarks, I should think that was precisely what he did intend."[51]

Shortly after this, news was received that Gillmore had turned the Confederate works and held their extreme right. Smith was then ordered to remain in his position that night. After the right flank of Weitzel's line was placed on Proctor's Creek, the troops bivouacked in that position. Just before dark, Colonel George Cole's Second United States Colored Cavalry of 150 men reported to Smith and were ordered to picket from the right of his infantry picket to the James River. During the night, Brooks sent skirmishers under Burnham to feel the Confederate line, and they found a considerable force still in their front.[52]

At daylight on May 14, skirmishers were ordered forward, and the left of Turner's division soon occupied the enemy's works in their front. On Weitzel's front and on the right of Brooks, the enemy's skirmishers held with the most determined pertinacity and were only driven back some time after Brooks' left occupied the works on their front. Brooks' men cut down the exterior slope in such a way as to have a slight banquette on which a thin line could stand, protected by the original parapet. Burnham's brigade occupied the works, while Colonel Horace Sanders' brigade was advanced to the edge of the woods beyond the entrenchments and took position on Burnham's left. The enemy still held an interior line of works with a salient on high ground, completely commanding Smith's position. The enemy's flanks fell back on their left to the James River and on their right along the Richmond and Petersburg Railroad. The line of the earthworks that Gillmore had turned ran into this second line at the salient. Heavy artillery fire was opened on Smith's lines from this salient but was soon checked by Weitzel's sharpshooters. Shortly after Smith's new line was established, Gillmore moved to connect with Baldy's left. Turner's division was also reassigned to the Tenth Corps.[53]

The day was spent in reconnaissances. During one of these reconnaissances, Lieutenant Peter Michie found the weakest Confederate point at a line of rifle pits between two main works. Smith sent Michie to Butler with this information. Butler responded by ordering Smith to form an assault column to strike this point in the line the next morning. Part of Brigadier General Adelbert Ames' division of the Tenth Corps would be sent to Smith to fill the gap left by the assault troops. Gillmore would make a demonstration in connection with the assault. Smith wrote back that he would assault early the next morning but use part of Ames' reinforcements for the assaulting column to avoid delay in changing his lines. Smith planned to use a brigade each from Ames' and Weitzel's divisions and two regiments from Brooks' division for the attack. Because he had no reserves, Smith proposed to guard against a repulse by ordering Turner's division to cover the flank of the attacking column. Finding these troops no longer under his command, Baldy requested the return of Marston's brigade from the extreme Federal left. When he was informed that they could not be moved in time, he persuaded Butler to abandon the attack "for the want of disposable troops to form the column."[54]

On May 15, Smith reconnoitered the extreme right behind the cavalry picket. Smith discovered that there was over a mile of open, undulating country from Heckman's command, which held the extreme right of the line, to the James River and to Drewry's Bluff. This space offered every facility for the movement of a heavy enemy column on his right and rear. Smith also found a road which provided the shortest route back to the Federal entrenchments near the right. It was only defended by pickets. In light of this reconnaissance, he requested more troops, and three regiments were sent to his assistance. These were assigned to Heckman. Heckman placed them between the left of his brigade and the right of Wistar's brigade and extended his own troops to the right across the road with the right regiments being thrown back in echelon. In the afternoon, Smith went with Weitzel and Heckman to a farmhouse that was about a hundred yards to the front and right of Heckman's command. This farmhouse was situated on a knoll opposite the flank of the enemy bastion. At this knoll, a good view of the country on the right was obtained, and Smith ordered the farmhouse and outbuildings to be heavily occupied by the reserves of the picket guard. Weitzel sent sixty men to the buildings. Smith then informed Butler that the necessary extension of the line had drawn him out into one thin line of battle and that he had no regiments with which to repair a break in his line or to resist a flanking movement. Smith was told that Ames had three regiments at the Half-Way House and that they would act as a reserve for his line.[55]

Despite Smith's efforts, Weitzel's right was still three-quarters of a mile from the river. Only his pickets and the cavalry vedettes covered the space. Along the line, Smith's divisions were stronger. During the day, Weitzel constructed log breastworks along his entire front. He also advanced his pickets close to the enemy. Brooks' position was even better because he used the captured Confederate earthworks. Burnham's brigade occupied the works while Sanders' brigade still held a position in advance of this line. Besides these preparations, Smith wished to further strengthen his line because much of it was close to the enemy interior works and in danger of a sudden rush. He ordered captured telegraph wire to be stretched a short distance in front of Brooks' earthworks and Weitzel's breastworks and wound tightly around stumps. This was done along Smith's whole line except in front of Heckman's brigade because the wire had run out, and his line was furthest from the enemy position. During the night, the enemy made several ineffectual attempts to dislodge the force in the farmhouse. Captain Joseph B. Lawrence commanded the force at the farmhouse and reported to Heckman that the enemy was massing troops during the night near his position, but this was not reported to Weitzel or Smith.[56]

A short time before daylight on the morning of May 16, Smith found everything quiet on his lines. There was a thin film of clouds over the sky, but not so heavy as to interfere seriously with the moonlight or give any indication of a foggy morning. Smith returned to his quarters and bed at Friend's House. Shortly thereafter, he was aroused by heavy musketry and artillery fire on the right of his line. On going out, he found a fog so dense that a horseman was not visible at a distance of fifteen yards. Smith proceeded to the turnpike, where he established corps headquarters and communicated with Weitzel and Brooks. At 4:45 a.m., he sent word to Butler that his right was heavily attacked and needed reinforcements, as it was long, thin, and weak. Shortly after this, he sent word to have the artillery withdrawn, for the fog was so dense it could not be used, and it was so far advanced that it was in danger of being captured. The order did not reach some of the most exposed guns until it was too late. The orderly who took the order gave it to a sergeant of the guns at the caissons, but in carrying the order to the guns, the sergeant was killed.[57]

General Beauregard had opened the battle of Drewry's Bluff, the most significant engagement of the Bermuda Hundred Campaign. He had determined by the previous day that the Federal line's weakest point was its right flank. Using the gap between the Union right and the James River, he would attack there with the intention of turning the Federal right on itself while at the same time threatening their center and left to prevent Butler from reinforcing his right. Beauregard would use Major General Robert Ransom's force of 6,400 for the flanking attack and Major General Robert Hoke's force of 7,100 for the frontal attack. This would leave him about 4,000 in reserve. Beauregard's goal was to separate the Army of the James' effective force of 15,800 men from its base of operations and even more, crush it with this turning movement. Major General Robert Ransom's effective force of 5,000 advanced through dense fog and drove Smith's skirmishers across open ground. Ransom then sent Brigadier General Archibald Gracie's brigade to attack Heckman's brigade. Gracie struck it in the front and rear. In the front,

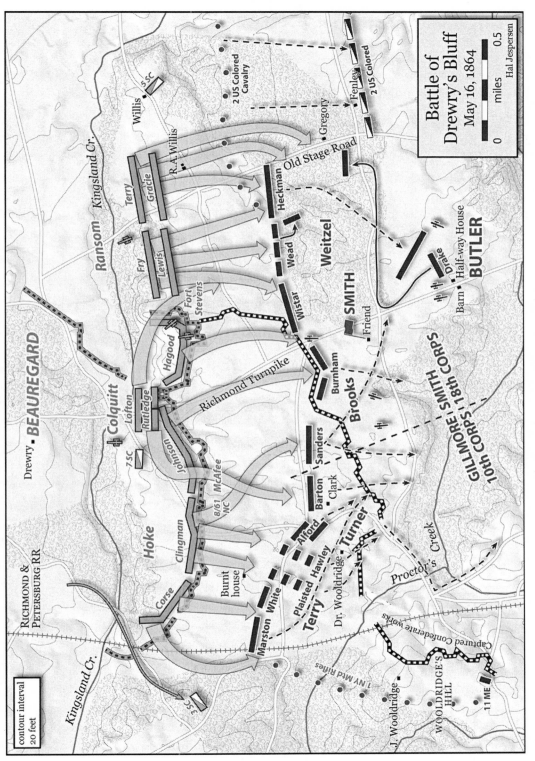

Battle of Drewry's Bluff, May 16, 1864.

the Confederates met stubborn resistance and were repulsed three times. The Confederate attack on the rear of the extreme right, however, met with unqualified success. The Confederates overwhelmed the Federals, who had no protection on their exposed flank and rear. The three regiments closest to the right were forced back in confusion and disorganization. Many Federals, including the brigade commander, were captured. The last regiment of Heckman's brigade, the Twenty-Fifth Massachusetts, was the first to check the Confederate advance on the right. It avoided similar disintegration by facing the rear and charging the Confederates. The three regiments placed on Heckman's left turned their fronts perpendicular to the line of breastworks. This arrested the Confederate advance until the regiments were ordered to fall back.[58]

After some delay, Smith learned from Weitzel that Heckman's brigade had been badly crushed. At Smith's request, Ames sent two reserve regiments from Half-Way House, the One-Hundred-and-Twelfth New York and Ninth Maine, to Smith's assistance. Smith ordered them to hold the crossroads in the rear of Heckman's right. Colonel Jeremiah C. Drake, their brigade commander, formed the two regiments on the road parallel to the turnpike and between the pike and the river. They became hotly engaged with the enemy advance but held the road and checked the enemy column, which was moving in Smith's rear. This small brigade formed Smith's right.[59]

Meanwhile, the enemy made furious assaults on Burnham and Wistar on Smith's front. On Brooks' front, each of the enemy attacks was repulsed by Burnham's brigade positioned in the former Confederate works. The brigade's line was concave so that the enemy suffered a steady, rapid, and costly crossfire. Still, without Smith's telegraph wire, the Confederate numbers would have overcome the fire. The wire caused great confusion in the attacking ranks. Brooks later told Smith that the enemy fell over the wires and were "shot like partridges."[60]

Burnham's regiments stood their ground except for the one on the extreme right. The Eighth Connecticut's commander ordered the regiment to withdraw after only feeble resistance. It fell back in confusion, but later came in behind the front line. Burnham modified the line of the next regiment on the right to protect the brigade's right flank and held on until the general withdrawal. Brooks' other brigade under Sanders was placed in a second and third line resting their right on the turnpike.[61]

Wistar's brigade was also defended by the wire strung in front of the breastworks that Weitzel had constructed. This brigade repeatedly repulsed the enemy frontal assaults. The wire again proved extremely effective. A Confederate prisoner reported the loss of 1,800 men and expressed the opinion that the wire arrangement was a "d—d rascally contrivance."[62] With the defeat of Heckman's brigade and the withdrawal of the regiments on Wistar's right, Wistar turned two of his regiments perpendicular to his front to protect his flank. In this position, Wistar repulsed three more Confederate assaults. After the last assault, the Confederates got around Wistar's right and interposed themselves between his right and headquarters. This movement was probably stopped by Drake's brigade.[63]

Starting about 6:30 a.m. on May 16, the Confederates, under Major General Robert Hoke, also attacked the Tenth Corps lines. Gillmore's left division, under Brigadier General Alfred H. Terry, repulsed the attacks. About this time, Butler ordered Gillmore to attack the Confederates, take their lines, and relieve the pressure on Smith's right. Gillmore instructed Terry and Turner, who commanded the right division, to ready their commands for the assault. Throughout the morning, Gillmore was faced with

Hoke's attacks. At the same time, faced with several reports of the Confederates turning Smith's right, Gillmore sent several regiments to Smith to strengthen his flank. Turner was also called on three times to fill the gap created by Brooks' rightward movements. The combination of Confederate assaults and Federal troop needs delayed Gillmore's attack indefinitely.[64]

The density of the fog entirely prevented Smith from reconnoitering the open country on his right. Instead, he rallied the disorganized remnants of Heckman's brigade at Half-Way House. There, he received a report from Weitzel that the enemy was moving still farther on his right. As this directly threatened Smith's communications, artillery, ammunition train, and lines, Smith immediately ordered a retirement of the whole line, instructing Brooks to inform Turner that his movements must conform to Smith's to keep up the connection between the two corps.[65]

While the line was falling back, the fog lifted so that Smith was able to observe his right. Seeing that the enemy threat on the right was not as serious as reported earlier, Smith countermanded his order to retire and ordered the line forward again. He put in the rallied troops to cover the right of the advancing line. The advance checked any further pursuit of the enemy. Unfortunately, the change in orders created some confusion in Weitzel's command. When Wistar received the order to advance, two regiments were beyond being recalled. He decided to continue the withdrawal because he only had two regiments left, and his brigade's flanks were exposed and suffering heavy artillery fire. Nevertheless, to cover the retirement, he did order his two remaining regiments, the Twenty-first Connecticut and Second New Hampshire, to return to their original positions. They reoccupied their defenses without difficulty and even managed to spike several abandoned cannons.[66]

Shortly after the advance began, Smith found Weitzel retiring due to some mistaken order. He also learned that his connection with the Tenth Corps was broken. Smith suspended the advance, believing that any forward movement would simply place his corps outside the enemy works that had been held by his men and had been assessed by Baldy to be too formidable to be carried by assault. Smith's judgment that he would be unable to retake the works was probably too hasty. In fact, about half of his command had regained their lines. Two of the three regiments that had been placed between Heckman's and Wistar's brigades regained their lines with some difficulty. Half of Wistar's brigade regained its lines. In Brooks' command, the situation was equally promising. While Brooks may not have received Smith's order to retake his lines, half of Burnham's brigade was still holding the captured enemy earthworks when Smith decided to suspend the advance. Smith may have been correct, however, in not holding the line, considering the large gap between Turner's division and Smith's left and the likelihood of a renewed Confederate attack on Smith's exposed right flank. In fact, Beauregard was in the midst of deploying Ransom's division to attack Smith's right when Smith suspected the advance. Subsequently, Beauregard called off the attack.[67]

At about 9:30 a.m., on May 16, Smith moved his entire line to the right to hold both the turnpike and the road parallel to it on its east. His new position crossed the pike near Half-way House, about three-quarters of a mile from the outer line of Confederate entrenchments. By early afternoon, the Tenth Corps connected with Smith's lines. Butler then ordered Smith to move forward to probe the enemy lines and remove the wounded. Gillmore would protect Baldy's left. Between 2:00 and 3:00 p.m. the Eighteenth Corps advanced in the direction of the point where Heckman's brigade had been attacked. Weitzel advanced four regiments of his first line in echelon. The skirmishers were advanced well but were stopped on the south side of the breastworks by a large enemy force in line of battle. After removing all the wounded that could be found, these regiments fell back to the position they had left. Brooks' command also participated in this probe, with Burnham's brigade in front. The command met no resistance, collected the skirmishers that held Friends' House and the woods to the west, and returned to their rear positions. Towards evening, by Butler's orders, the two corps returned to their Bermuda Hundred entrenchments.[68]

Smith was disappointed by the Federal reverse at Drewry's Bluff. He wrote to his wife, "I had a sharp fight today in which I lost everything I had been working two days to gain, and also lost some guns and prisoners."[69] Smith understood that Butler's ultimate strategic success was dependent on the Army of the Potomac's success. But Smith believed his army commander had made three major mistakes. First, Butler disregarded the value of Petersburg and the danger a force there presented to the army's rear. Second, Butler allowed his army to confront the strong Confederate position at Drewry's Bluff with the army's flanks exposed. Third, he underestimated the size of Beauregard's command. Smith had done his best to advance the campaign despite his misgivings. The unsoundness of the campaign's strategy and tactics undermined any chance of success.[70]

Butler was also guilty of creating a lack of confidence and trust between himself and his corps commanders. As early as May 7, angered by the slow movement of the Tenth Corps, Butler asked Senator Henry Wilson to help block Gillmore's confirmation as major general. Smith and Gillmore became weary of Butler's faultfinding and often requested written orders to avoid future reprisals. For his part, Smith never had complete confidence in Butler because of Butler's lack of military training. The Drewry's Bluff fiasco supported Smith's low opinion of his army commander.[71]

The poor relations between Butler and his subordinates and Butler's inability to do more than hold his lines at Bermuda Hundred gained the attention of the lieutenant general. Two days before the battle of Drewry's Bluff, Generals Phil Sheridan and J.H. Wilson visited Butler's command. They discussed the Bermuda Hundred Campaign with Baldy, who expressed reservations about it. About four days later, Sheridan and Wilson discussed Butler's unsuccessful campaign. They put their views in writing and sent them to Brigadier General John Rawlins and Colonel Comstock to pass on to Grant. Both urged that Butler should be relieved and his army turned over to Baldy. Sheridan and Wilson also suggested that Smith be ordered to capture Petersburg and then destroy the railroads south of Petersburg and Richmond for the purpose of cutting off supplies to Lee's army. On May 21, Grant wrote to Halleck that there was "some difficulty with the forces at City Point which prevents their effective use. The fault may be with the commander, and it may be with his subordinates."[72]

Grant continued with a criticism that he had not previously made: "General Smith, whilst a very able officer, is obstinate, and is likely to condemn whatever is not suggested by himself."[73] Grant's view may have been shaped by Smith's earlier criticism of the overland campaign in favor of the North Carolina plan. Wilson had given Smith's letter of March 16 condemning the overland plan to Rawlins to convince Grant to change his strategy. But Rawlins wrote to his wife that the letter, instead, showed to Grant "all the selfishness of [Smith's] nature."[74] Smith's recent conversations with Sheridan about Bermuda Hundred could have been equally misinterpreted by Grant. While Baldy had remarked that Butler's campaign's future was dim, he anticipated Grant's coming actions by recommending that the lieutenant general leave a sufficient force to protect Butler's lines and use the remainder to reinforce the Army of the Potomac. Nevertheless, since Smith's letter of March 16 was mistaken as selfish, so could have been his recent remarks.[75]

Grant then told Halleck that he expected Butler to occupy an enemy force nearly equal to his own. If Butler was unable to do this, Grant suggested the lines at City Point be reduced to a minimum, and the remainder ordered to him. Grant finally told Halleck to send someone to investigate Butler's department.[76]

Halleck sent Generals M.C. Meigs and J.G. Barnard to examine the army's position and find out what difficulties existed. Their first impressions were that the report of disharmony in relations to the corps commanders "may be exaggerated at least so far as General Smith is concerned." On May 24, the two generals reported more in detail. They offered two alternatives. First, they advised that an officer of military experience and knowledge be placed in command of both the Tenth and Eighteenth Corps. This would make the corps act as a unit for field operations. Then this force should assume the offensive. Second, they advised that if the first choice was not selected, then twenty-thousand soldiers should be withdrawn from the Army of the James and be used elsewhere. The two generals ascertained that Butler had great ability but not the experience and training to enable him to direct and control movements in battle.[77]

Butler evidently wished, however, to retain command in the field. He was also satisfied with the ability and aid of Smith, but not that of Gillmore. If Butler was to remain in the field, Meigs and Barnard suggested that Gillmore should be relieved. They then urged that Smith be placed in command of both corps under the supreme command of Butler. Smith could put Brooks in command of one corps and Weitzel in command of the other, unless better officers could be found. They concluded, "Success would be more certain were Smith in command untrammeled, and General Butler remanded to the administrative duties of the department in which he has shown such rare and great ability."[78]

Barnard later reported verbally to Grant. Grant asked him why Butler could not move out from his lines and push across the Richmond and Petersburg Railroad to the rear and on the south side of Richmond. Barnard replied that after events at Drewry's Bluff, Beauregard had established a strong line across the same neck of land that Butler had. Grant later reported that Butler's army, though in a position of great security, was "as completely shut off from further operations directly against Richmond, as if it had been in a bottle strongly corked."[79]

Smith also believed that Butler was bottled up. He wrote to his wife on May 23, "Both sides at work fortifying—we to stay in this hole, and the rebels to keep us in, and I think we shall both succeed." Smith was also aware of the Meigs/Barnard investigation, but neither general had yet communicated with Smith. Smith overestimated Butler's animosity towards him and figured that without anyone to contradict him, Butler would justify removing Baldy. Smith thought he would soon be mustered out and told his wife, "it will give me a chance to get away home" and "then we will have the house at Throgs Neck." The next day, Smith again wrote to his wife expressing the hope that the result of the investigation would be to send his corps to the Army of the Potomac and have someone sent to the department "to run this machine. It is now a perfectly useless command as it is, and nothing will set it right but some such change—we are in a regular muddle." If someone replaced Baldy, he would be glad, for it meant going home. On

May 25, even though Smith had visited with Meigs the previous day, he still wrote Sarah Smith, "I am waiting very anxiously to hear what is the result of the investigation by Meigs and Barnard, and what is to be done with me. I cannot tell you how I hope I shall be sent home."[80]

Without the prospect of a serious enemy attack in the days after Drewry's Bluff, Smith concentrated on several duties. First, he pushed the defensive arrangements on his front with all possible dispatch. Fatigue parties were assigned to strengthen the lines. The earthworks and redoubts were extended from the Tenth Corps lines on the right to near the Appomattox River on the left. Pickets were sent to the river itself to protect the left flank. A ravine in front of the corps was used to assist the Federal position. Strong reserve pickets were placed in front of the main works, and connections with the Tenth Corps were maintained to ensure that there were no weak points in the line. Three regiments of the Second Division and one brigade of the First Division occupied the works while the remaining soldiers were held in reserve.[81]

Second, Smith sought to maintain firm discipline in his corps. He suggested to Butler that officers who commanded fatigue parties should be held strictly responsible for the work done and the tools under their charge. He continued that when officers neglected this duty, they should be dismissed. In a general order, Smith warned that soldiers found outside their camps without proper authority from their division commander would be arrested and charged with disobedience of orders. Third, Smith had his officers survey material needs. He ordered an inspection of the men's arms and accouterments. Anyone found to have thrown these items away was to be arrested. The quartermasters were to check all transportation and order replacements and repairs.[82]

Fourth, Smith tried to maintain and improve the health of his men. The division commanders were instructed never to place their camps in low or marshy ground. During the time that the men were required to be under arms at 3:30 a.m., a ration of whiskey and quinine, or coffee if preferred, would be issued. Smith wrote Weitzel, who had given up his Second Division command to become the department's chief engineer, that he had withdrawn the working parties on May 22 because that day was Sunday, and he made it the practice not to work the men on Sundays unless absolutely necessary. Besides this, the men required rest. Smith's most important contribution to the corps' health was his formulation of a Medical Department program on May 20. This included setting the location for the medical officers and their hospital during time of battle; establishing a corps hospital for those soldiers too sick for the regimental camps but expected to recover within a month so as not to necessitate transfer to the General Hospital at Fort Monroe; sending two wagons with teams to the corps surgeon to serve as ambulances; assigning a fatigue party to serve the needs of the corps surgeons; detailing a chaplain for the corps hospital; and, finally, establishing guidelines for amputation cases.[83]

While Smith was taking care of his defense and administrative duties, he ordered several reconnaissances. He gave his reason for this in a letter to his wife on May 25: "I have been riding around to get a good idea of the country in our front, so that when the time comes for us to get out of this coop, we have been in since our escapade towards Richmond, I can get out without getting into any bad scrape."[84] On May 18, Smith sent a party down the Port Walthall Junction Road on the left of the work on Foster's Plantation. After meeting a Confederate line of skirmishers where the road forks, the party returned. Butler helped Smith's scouting by offering rewards up to $500 for valuable information. Smith sent out seven scouts, and they reported that the Confederates were working on the railroad near the Port Walthall Junction and were constructing a field work. While Smith appreciated Butler's reward system, he blocked Butler's idea of night reconnaissances. Smith told Butler that they were impractical and facilitated ambush and confusion. Also, in darkness, any Federal dead and wounded would be left on the field. He would not order one until commanded.[85]

On May 26, Smith ordered a reconnaissance in front of the Second Division to discover the location of the enemy's pickets. Colonel Arthur H. Dutton, commanding the Third Brigade, First Division, advanced his men two miles in heavy woods until they came upon the enemy skirmish line. The Confederates were found strongly entrenched and almost hidden from view by the underbrush. Dutton formed a line of battle, but as his skirmishers became engaged, he was mortally wounded. Shortly after this, Smith ordered the reconnaissance to retire, for the enemy was massing opposite the center of the entrenchments. Colonel Guy Henry replaced Dutton as Third Brigade commander.[86]

While Smith was involved in reconnaissances in his front, he was still very anxious to hear the result of the investigation by Meigs and Barnard. Actually, the investigation would have little effect on events because Grant had decided prior to receiving Barnard's and Meig's report that he needed Smith's corps to reinforce the Army of the Potomac. On May 22, Grant told Halleck to order Butler to send Smith's command to Meade's army. On May 24, Grant temporarily delayed the order, for the lieutenant general thought Lee was falling back to Richmond, and he could use Smith's force better where it was. Halleck hoped that the Eighteenth Corps would join Grant because, as Halleck stated, "I do not like these divided commands, with the enemy intervening. I would rather use them altogether under your own eye."[87] On May 25, with Lee making a determined stand between the two Annas, Grant decided to send for Smith.[88]

When Smith had returned to corps command a month earlier, he had encountered many of the same difficulties he had experienced in the East in 1862. He was again faced with an incompetent superior who failed to appreciate his tactical or strategic insight. Consequently, his troops failed to reach their potential during the Bermuda Hundred Campaign, especially at Drewry's Bluff. The general had a great deal to criticize in Butler's handling of the campaign. Unfortunately, the critic of defeat would not lack for targets when he participated in the end of the Overland Campaign.

CHAPTER XII

The Critic of Defeat in the Overland Campaign

The Battle of Cold Harbor

On the morning of May 26, 1864, Halleck wrote Butler that Grant directed him to retain only those troops necessary to hold the James River to City Point and send the rest to the north side of the Pamunkey opposite White House to join the Army of the Potomac. This column was to be placed under Smith's command. Butler complied with the order by putting 17,000 infantrymen in condition to move at once and leaving only a sufficient force to hold the lines between the James and Appomattox rivers. He combined the First and Second Divisions of the Eighteenth Corps and the Second and Third Divisions of the Tenth Corps under Smith. General Kautz's cavalry division was to replace Smith's men in the lines and Hinks' division was to form the reserve. Smith gave the necessary orders readying his divisions to move the next morning. He wrote his wife on the day's events: "To-night a telegram came from Halleck organizing a large command under me and ordering it to be ready to move by water, so that I very soon shall be away from Butler and the anxieties I have had."[1]

On May 27, Smith received orders to concentrate his new command of four divisions behind the lines in preparation for embarking at Bermuda Hundred to join the Army of the Potomac. In a conversation with Colonel John W. Shaffer, Butler's chief of staff, Smith suggested that as the transports for this movement were not expected for three or four days, the intervening time should be devoted to the capture of Petersburg. Smith felt sure that the capture of Petersburg would be of more value to Grant than 40,000 men added to his army.[2]

Shaffer went at once to Butler and came back with a message and verbal order. Butler had long objected to taking Petersburg because he insisted it conflicted with Grant's intentions of joining the two armies. One primary objective in the Drewry's Bluff campaign was to join the armies. Now, despite being under positive orders from Grant to send Smith to join the Army of the Potomac, Butler ironically approved Smith's plan to capture Petersburg. The next day, the artillery was ordered to Smith, and Hinks' division was put under Smith's command for the move on Petersburg. Being cognizant of Butler's faultfinding, Smith asked for written instructions for the expedition against Petersburg. His requested written orders were sent at 2:30 p.m. Smith gave his preparatory orders for the movement to begin soon after nightfall. Late in the afternoon, Shaffer called on Smith and asked whether he proposed to embark his men for the move to White House as fast as the transports arrived or wait until all were at Bermuda Hundred.

Smith assumed this to mean that the responsibility of the delay would be placed on him. Smith indignantly replied that if it were left to him, he should start the men as fast as the transports arrived. The order to attack Petersburg was then countermanded. About 6:30 p.m., Butler wrote Smith that though the transports were insufficient, Grant's order directed Smith's move to his assistance with the "utmost expedition and getting on."[3] Butler expressed great disappointment at being unable to send Smith's force to attack Petersburg.[4]

About a half hour later, Smith's force was on the march in two columns. Generals Brooks' and Ames' divisions moved towards the Hundreds, while the rest of the command under the direction of Brigadier General John Martindale, who succeeded Weitzel as Second Division commander, crossed the Appomattox and took the road to City Point. The night was very dark and stormy, and the mud was very deep, but the heads of the columns reached their destination in proper time and began to embark. Halleck ordered Smith to go by transport to White House. Upon reaching this point, Smith was to repair the railroad bridge there so that troops and artillery could cross it. He was also to leave a sufficient force to hold it.[5]

Smith's command at this point consisted of about 16,000 infantry, sixteen pieces of artillery, and one cavalry squadron of about one hundred men. Smith divided the troops of the Tenth Corps among his two divisions, under Brooks and Martindale, and a newly formed Third Division under the command of Brigadier General Charles Devens. Devens' division consisted of three brigades under Colonels Barton and Drake and General Ames.[6]

Though Smith was ordered to land on the north side of the Pamunkey near White House, he knew of no landing place there. He had asked permission from Washington, through General Butler, to land at West Point and march to the designated point, but this was refused. Smith, however, took the responsibility for sending Ames' brigade of 4,000 men and one battery in fast steamers to land at West Point, and march to protect his landing. Smith asked Rear Admiral Samuel P. Lee to order Naval Captain Charles Babcock to use gunboats to cover the landing of this brigade—the orders were promptly sent.[7]

By 11:00 a.m. on May 29, the embarkation was so far advanced that Smith started to overtake the head of his command. On arriving at Fort Monroe, he received a telegram from Grant that most of the Army of the Potomac had crossed the Pamunkey. Believing his proper course was to land at White House, Smith immediately gave the necessary orders. He reached the landing at White House at 11:00 a.m. on the thirtieth. The transports were unloaded as rapidly as possible, and several fast steamers were sent back to assist in towing barges and schooners and in aiding other steamers which had run aground on the shoals in the James River. During the night of May 30 and the following morning, Smith received triplicate orders to leave a garrison at White House until it was relieved by Brigadier General John J. Abercrombie's command from Port Royal. With the remainder of his command, Smith was to move directly to New Castle on the south side of the Pamunkey and there await further orders. Upon being relieved, Smith's garrison at White House was expected to follow after and join Smith.[8]

Since his wagons and ammunition and some of his troops had not yet arrived, Smith sent an aide to ask if his command should move as he then stood or wait until he could take supplies with him. Later in the day, however, upon the receipt of a letter from Grant, Smith determined not to wait for a reply to his first letter but to march at once.

He left Ames with about 3,000 men to garrison White House and marched at 3:30 p.m. with about 10,000 men and his artillery but without wagons to carry supplies or extra ammunition. About 10:00 p.m., Smith reached Bassett's House near Old Church and distributed his troops to cover the roads leading to New Castle Ferry. There was a great deal of straggling in the ranks because the men previously had little experience in heavy marching. Smith was unable to prevent this because his provost guard had not yet overtaken him. From Bassett's House, Smith sent an aide to inform Grant of his position and to ask for further orders.[9]

The next morning at daylight, Smith received an order to proceed at once to New Castle Ferry and place himself between the Fifth and Sixth Corps. Realizing time to be of great importance, Smith moved the command without allowing the men time to get their coffee. On reaching New Castle Ferry, Smith found that he was in the broad valley lands of the Pamunkey, surrounded by hills within artillery range. If these hills were occupied by the enemy, Smith's command would be forced to carry them by assault. The Fifth and Sixth Corps were not in the vicinity. Baldy sent Captain Farquhar to tell Grant that he had determined from his position that there was some mistake in the order and to ask that it be rectified. While Smith's lines were being formed, he began the construction of a bridge across the river.[10]

During these operations, Lieutenant Colonel O.E. Babcock, of Grant's staff, arrived to say that there had been a mistake in Grant's order and that Baldy should have marched to Cold Harbor instead of New Castle Ferry. Smith's command started immediately on their march towards Cold Harbor over the road they had just traveled. Fatigue and exhaustion thinned Smith's ranks during the march. While on the march, Smith received an order from Meade directing him to follow the Sixth Corps and form on its right at Cold Harbor. Smith was to join with the Sixth Corps in an attack and hold the road from Bethesda Church to Cold Harbor. The distance between the two places was about three miles, and Smith's force of less than ten thousand men would not be able to fill the space and make an attack. Unable to obey both requirements of the order, Smith decided to aid in the attack and immediately began the formation of his lines.[11]

Smith's participation in the battles at Cold Harbor was about to begin. These were to be the last significant engagements of the Overland Campaign, north of Richmond. Beginning with the battle of the Wilderness on May 5, Grant had led the 115,000 strong Army of the Potomac against the 64,000 soldiers of General Lee's Army of Northern Virginia. In a series of costly battles, Grant and Meade were unable to realize their strategic aim of interposing his army between Lee and Richmond. Now before Cold Harbor, Lee, learning of Smith's arrival, had received reinforcements from Beauregard's command to counter the new Federal reinforcements. Nevertheless, Meade directed Smith to join with the Sixth Corps in attempting to break through Lee's lines. The two corps would have a significant numeric advantage in this sector of 30,000 to 10,000 but two Union divisions would not engage: one to protect their left flank and the other trying to connect with the Fifth Corps to Smith's right. About 3:00 p.m. on June 1, the Eighteenth Corps arrived on the field. Smith reconnoitered the ground on his right and his front. On his right, where he had no support, Smith found the roads from Mechanicsville and Bethesda Church uniting in quiet, open country and determined that this junction commanded the ground in his front. Smith was obliged to give up his third line of battle to extend his line to hold this point. In his front, Smith found the Confederate lines in a wood separated from his line by cleared ground, varying in width from 300 to 1,200 yards. He formed his lines with Devens on the left, Brooks in the center, and Martindale on the right. Devens' two lines connected with Brigadier General James Rickett's division of the Sixth Corps. Brooks had two lines with a half a line in reserve. Martindale's division was formed in battalions with his columns in echelon with the right refused. While Smith's lines were being formed, Major General Horatio G. Wright, commanding the Sixth Corps, sent an aide to ask for reinforcements because the enemy was turning his left flank. Two regiments were sent to him from Martindale's division. Shortly afterwards, a message was received from Wright urging Smith to begin the attack. Smith determined to move forward, leaving Martindale to form his troops and hold the roads and the right flank.[12]

Devens placed Drake's Second Brigade in front and Barton's First Brigade in the second line. The Second Brigade's line was formed in front of an open-plowed field with two or three fences and a few small farm buildings. The field extended for about two-thirds of a mile to a woods where the Confederates had a line of shallow rifle pits. The Confederate skirmishers had advanced to the cover of the fences and buildings in the field. Devens' artillery fired on them. At about 5:30 p.m., Devens' two brigades moved forward. The Second Brigade moved across the open space towards the wood occupied by the enemy. Subjected to a very heavy fire, the brigade pushed on resolutely, driving the enemy skirmishers back to the wood. On reaching the woods, the Federals discovered that Brigadier General William Wofford's Georgia brigade of Brigadier General Joseph Kershaw's division was entrenched behind breastworks about fifty feet from the edge of the wood. Drake's brigade at once drove the enemy from the front of the wood and the pits, advanced, and gained a portion of the breastworks. Among the first to mount the parapet, Colonel Drake waved his sword, hurrahed, and danced with exultation as he saw the Confederates retreating. "There boys," he said, "see those devils run; did I not tell you you would drive them out?"[13]

However, the Confederate reinforcements soon drove the brigade back to a slight elevation fifty to seventy-five yards from the works. In this Confederate counterattack, Colonel Drake was mortally wounded. As soon as the First Brigade arrived, the two brigades pressed on, carried the breastworks in their front, and drove Wofford's brigade 100 to 200 yards beyond the works. In the assault, 250 Confederates were captured. Wofford's brigade collapsed due to Devens' frontal assault and a flanking attack by Rickett's division on Devens' left. This breakthrough was only temporary, for Kershaw shifted reserve units to close the gap. Devens was unable to hold the entire line, and the Confederates regained a portion at right angle to the line that Devens held. This gave the Confederates a means of enfilading Devens' line. Devens personally directed two attempts to regain the entire line but was repulsed both times. The Confederates continued to inflict great loss by holding part of the line.[14]

Brooks' division's attack also had limited success. Colonel Henry's Third Brigade formed the first line. General Burnham's Second Brigade was in the second line except for the Thirteenth New Hampshire, which was placed on the extreme right of the first line. General Marston's First Brigade formed the third line. At the order, the division advanced through a wooded area some 200 or 300 yards in width. On emerging from the woods, they found open ground about 100 yards wide. The first line immediately came under enemy fire from skirmishers in rifle pits in a pine grove beyond the field and from the enemy's main line to the front and right, about 200 yards away. The pits were charged and the enemy driven out into their main line. There the Confederates

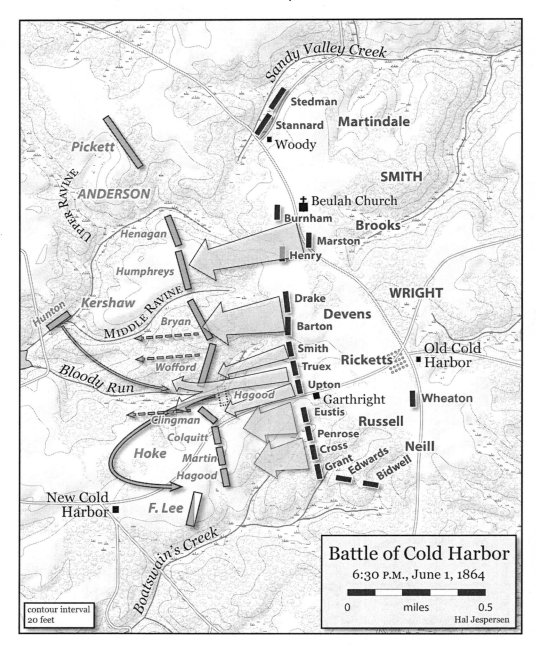

Battle of Cold Harbor, June 1, 1864.

had built strongly entrenched works. Henry determined that his men could not carry these works. He fell back and reorganized his men on the edge of the wood. This was done without serious loss except in the Thirteenth New Hampshire, which suffered the effects of severe flank fire. On Henry's right, Burnham's brigade had less success as their assault stalled in the face of intense Confederate fire. Brooks moved some of Marston's brigade to support Burnham, but the reinforcements did not alter the situation. Brooks also shifted two other regiments from Marston's brigade south to link Devens' right and Henry's brigade. Marston's soldiers captured the Confederate works in their front, but their advance put them ahead of Henry's brigade, and the enemy flank fire kept them for going any further.[15]

On the right, Martindale's division guarded Smith's flank. As Devens' and Brooks' divisions advanced, Martindale's line unfolded through a distance of 1,200 yards until it was extended in a single line of battle as far as it would reach, and a part of the distance was only covered by skirmishers. His left maintained a connection with the right of Brooks' division during the advance, but his command did not participate in the assault.[16]

The combination of Smith's advance and his need to hold the roads on his right forced his front to extend over a great distance. He had only one thin line of battle in Martindale's front and a partial second line with Brooks and Devens. About 10:00 p.m. Devens' division was reinforced by Marston's brigade, enabling Devens to extend his line to Henry's brigade. Marston found it hard to reach and hold his position on Devens' right at night because of the thick wood and intersecting ravines. The enemy made several attempts to retake the works that Devens had captured, but all efforts were repulsed. Marston's soldiers, however, suffered seriously under the enfilading fire from the works that Devens had been unable to hold and from Confederate rifle pits all along the brigade's line.[17]

While Smith was arranging his troops for the night to hold what had been gained, his aide returned from army headquarters. The aide relayed that in answer to Smith's request for ammunition, Meade had asked, "Why the hell didn't he wait for his supplies to come up before coming here?"[18] Even though Baldy was charged with want of administration for coming before fully supplied, he still believed the order he had received from Grant, and the fact that Meade knew Smith's condition when he moved, justified an earlier arrival without supplies. Smith wrote to Meade that "all the infantry ammunition I have is upon the persons of my men."[19] He requested that he be supplied immediately and a supply train be sent to White House for supplies since his forage ran out that night, and rations would be gone by the next night. At 10:30 p.m., he wrote Major General Andrew A. Humphreys, Meade's chief of staff, that his line extended from the Woody House across the Bethesda Church Road and was in the form of a very obtuse V. Smith also told Humphreys that his front line did not have a full second line and Devens' division was almost entirely out of ammunition. Smith warned that he "must leave it for the general commanding to determine as to how long I can hold this line if vigorously attacked."[20]

About 12:30 a.m., Smith received a note that Meade wrote at 10:05 p.m. Meade ordered Smith to make an attack the next morning with his whole command. This attack would be made in conjunction with an attack by the Sixth Corps. Upon receiving this order, Smith replied, "In the present condition of my line an attack by me would be simply preposterous; not only that, but an attack on the part of the enemy of any vigor would probably carry my lines more than half their length."[21] He called on Wright for about 100,000 rounds of ammunition. Southern deserters reported the enemy massing on his right for an attack early in the morning. After midnight, Humphreys and Farquhar wrote Smith that Meade was doing everything possible to get him ammunition. The order to attack was postponed until 5:00 p.m.[22]

About 7:00 a.m. on June 2, Smith received enough ammunition from Wright to fill up his boxes. During the morning, by Meade's order, Devens' division was relieved by the Second Division, Sixth Corps, and Major General David B. Birney's division of the

Second Corps was posted on Smith's right flank, where it remained throughout the day. Smith spent the day readjusting his lines and strengthening his position. He ordered Ames to send forward, as soon as possible, all wagons, supplies, and ambulances belonging to the corps. Ames was also ordered to join Smith with all the troops belonging to the corps as soon as Ames was relieved of garrison duty. Abercrombie soon arrived but delayed Ames' relief. To end this delay, Grant sent an order to push Ames forward at once. During the afternoon, Meade postponed the attack until 4:30 the following morning. Meade's plan was to have five Union corps attack the enemy in their fronts but to have each corps act for itself, independently of the others.[23]

Convinced that the Federals should make a cooperative attack, Smith sent a note to Wright asking for his plan of attack and to signify his willingness to follow the plan. Wright replied that he was going to assault the enemy in his front. Smith was thus forced to make an independent attack while maintaining his connection with the Sixth Corps. An open plain, swept by enemy fire from the front and the right, lay in front of Smith's right. On Smith's left, the open space was narrower but equally covered by enemy artillery. Near the center of his line, Smith found a ravine that could shelter his troops from the crossfire, and he determined to make his main assault through this ravine. Devens' division was placed on the right to protect that flank and hold as much of the lines as possible vacated by the troops moving forward. Smith placed two regiments on the road from Woody House to Bethesda Church to meet the extension of the Fifth Corps. Martindale's division was ordered to move down the ravine, while Brooks' division was to advance on the left, taking care to maintain the connection between Martindale and the Sixth Corps. Smith impressed upon his two division commanders the necessity of sending out a heavy line of skirmishers and flankers.[24]

Unbeknownst to Baldy, the Confederates had wisely used the pause in the fighting to physically reinforce their earthworks and align their forces in an inverted-horseshoe-shaped formation. Kershaw's division, reinforced by Major General Charles Field's division, aligned their forces so that as the Federals moved down the ravine, they would be subjected to greater fire on both flanks as well as their front. In short, the Eighteenth Corps would find themselves in a trap, enfiladed from three sides. Thick woods hide these new arrangements, preventing Smith from knowing what his soldiers would face.[25]

Brooks' and Martindale's divisions moved promptly when ordered. The enemy occupied a strong line of rifle pits in a forest in front of the First Division. At 4:30 a.m., Marston's brigade, supported by Henry's and Burnham's brigades, led the attack. Despite enemy fire on their right flank, the three brigades sprang forward with loud cheers and quickly drove the enemy from their rifle pits in front. Passing over the pits, Brooks' men emerged from the woods and found an open space. Here, the Confederates had another line of pits in front and an enclosed work on the right. The Federals moved forward, but fire from these positions was too heavy to sustain an advance. The ground was swept with canister and rifle bullets until it was literally covered with the slain. When it was apparent that further effort would only result in useless slaughter, Marston's men returned, a portion to the partial cover of an embankment from which the enemy was driven and the rest to the shelter of the woods through which they had advanced. Henry's brigade and one regiment of Burnham's brigade sustained the Federal possession of the pits and worked to strengthen them during the rest of the day. The remainder of Burnham's brigade was held in reserve and later served to maintain the division's connection with the Sixth Corps.[26]

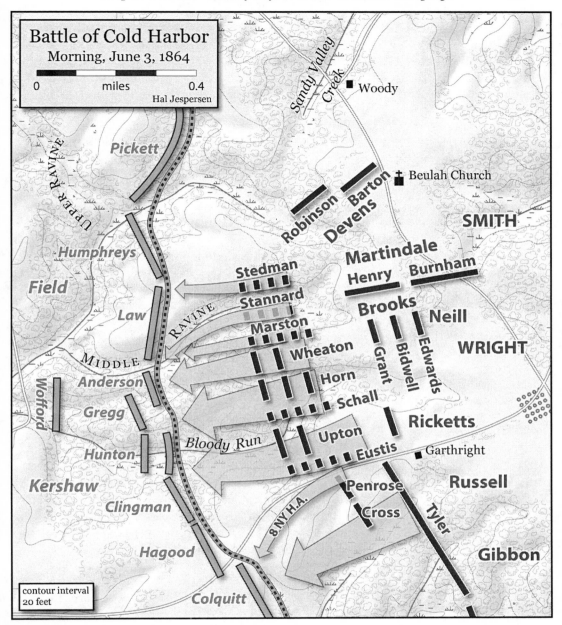

Battle of Cold Harbor, June 3, 1864.

Martindale's advance also made limited and very costly gains. His left was instructed to use the ravine near Smith's center. The ravine was skirted by woods to within seventy-five yards of the enemy's main line of entrenchments. The edge of the woods receded from the enemy's line toward Martindale's right so that his skirmishers would emerge from the woods on the right at a distance of about 250 yards. Colonel Griffin A. Stedman's Second Brigade led the attack, with Brigadier General George J. Stannard's First Brigade in support. Soon after 5:00 a.m., the assaulting column moved, with caps taken from their rifles and bayonets fixed. The enemy fell back as the assault advanced, but the column diverged from the direction of the ravine toward the opening of the woods on the right and went forward to the first line of the enemy pits. Immediately, a heavy fire of musketry, grape, and canister was poured upon the whole left flank. The intense flank fire confused the rear and pushed it constantly to the right, but, with determined bravery, the column pushed over 150 yards of level field. The head of the column reached the Confederate rifle pits, driving out the enemy skirmishers. At this moment, the enemy, from a point of their works where there had been no previous activity, opened an intense fire upon the head of the Federal column. The brigade, already decimated by the flank fire, broke upon meeting the direct fire and retired to the woods. There, they reformed and readied to repeat the attempt if ordered. Martindale then deployed three regiments of the Second Brigade to the right to protect the remainder of his column against the galling fire on his right flank. He moved the First Brigade to the left to make use the shelter of the ravine.[27]

These assaults were done under Smith's immediate supervision. It was a matter of universal surprise throughout the corps that he and his staff escaped the shower of flying balls. The corps commander did have a horse shot out from under him at the commencement of the action. Baldy, on the first sign of hesitation or panic among any of the regiments, was immediately in their midst and restored their confidence and courage. He placed Captain Joseph Denny's Provost Guard promptly to the task of controlling the corps' stragglers. During the day, Baldy met a soldier in full retreat for the rear. When Baldy stopped him, the man stated that he was going back to rally. The general advised him to go to the front and rally there, and as the demoralized soldier found his retreat cut off, he followed Smith's advice.[28]

The inability of Brooks to push over the field to capture the Confederate main works, and the costly repulse of Stedman's advanced column, led Smith to suspend the attack. After a personal inspection of Martindale's front, Smith found that he had to form a line of battle faced to the right to protect the right flank of the moving column. He determined that no further advance could be made until the Sixth Corps advanced to cover his left from the crossfire. Smith ordered Martindale to keep his column covered as much as possible and to move only when Brooks advanced. Smith then went to the front of Brooks' line to reconnoiter there. Brooks was forming his column when a heavy fire on the right began. This fire brought so severe a crossfire on Brooks that Smith at once ordered him not to move his men any further but keep them sheltered until the crossfire was over.[29]

Meanwhile, Martindale, mistaking the fighting in front of the Sixth Corps for an advance by Brooks, had determined to resume the assault. Stannard's brigade led the attack. Moving rapidly across a field under sharp artillery fire, the brigade entered an area of woods with their left resting upon the edge of a ravine. The skirmishers cautiously moved up to a location 350 yards from the enemy's works. The command was then ordered to charge over an intervening rifle pit and carry the works by storm. The enemy defenses consisted of strong rifle pits and three light field guns. These were mounted directly in the front of the Federal attackers on the far bank of a deep ravine and were situated at the convergence of an angle, the apex of which was toward the enemy. As the assaulting column moved up, Stannard lost the commanding officer of nearly every regiment in his command.[30]

The futility of the situation became evident as soon as the intervening rifle pits were cleared and as soon as Stannard's command reached a rise on the edge of the ravine. Converging musketry fire and direct artillery fire were cutting down each successive division as it rose over the knolls. It would be impossible for enough men to reach the works to produce any effect on the enemy. As no concerted action on the part of other commands was apparent, Stannard ordered the remnant of his command to retire to the rifle pits. In the engagement, Martindale's command had come within fifty yards of the enemy's main line, and the assaulting column had made three attempts to capture the works before retiring.[31]

The major assaults of June 3 at Cold Harbor lasted less than an hour. Of Baldy's three brigades that were most seriously engaged—Stedman, Stannard, and Marston—the estimated causalities numbered 1,543. Smith reported to Meade about Martindale's three repulsed assaults and the enfilading fire that prevented Brooks' advance. He had only artillery to use against this fire, and this was insufficient to silence it. Smith concluded, "My troops are very much cut up, and I have no hopes of being able to carry the works in my front unless a movement of the Sixth Corps on my left may relieve at least one of my flanks from this galling fire." At 8:00 a.m., Humphreys replied that Wright had been ordered to assault and continue his attack without reference to Smith's advance. Meade also directed Smith to continue his assault without reference to Wright's advance. Wright, however, was reportedly waiting for Smith to advance to enable him to assault.[32]

Smith then turned to survey his command to find units available for another attack. Devens' men had suffered so severely during the two previous days that they were unable to do more than defend the right flank. Of Martindale's two brigades, Stannard's brigade had lost too many soldiers to resume the assault, and Stedman's brigade was holding a line that could not be neglected. Of Brooks' three brigades, two had suffered severely from the first advance and were holding the ground gained under a terrible crossfire. The remaining brigade, under Burnham, was ordered to the front to form a column of assault in obedience to Meade's wishes. Smith reported to Meade that Martindale's division was no longer fit for attack and that only one brigade in his corps remained to make a new attack. Nonetheless, Smith had prepared this brigade to make another assault.[33]

The enemy on Smith's right, having a strong position and no force in their immediate front, could resist his advance with a severe flank fire that went through the width of his line and into the right of the Sixth Corps. Smith attempted to silence this fire with artillery but could not prevent it. At about 8:00 a.m. or shortly thereafter, Smith sent a request to Brigadier General Henry J. Hunt, army chief of artillery, for more ammunition to repel this fire. Hunt told Smith's aide that Smith's use was extravagant. Angered by this erroneous charge, Smith wrote to Meade that his advanced troops could only be protected by his artillery fire. Smith pointedly exclaimed, "It has become, therefore, somewhat of a question as to the expenditure of ammunition or muscle."[34] He insisted that all the artillery fire had been done under his orders and had not exceeded the amount necessary to cover his men. Meade replied at 10:00 a.m. that Hunt had been directed to provide Smith with all the ammunition that he required and additional batteries if he could use them. Meade urged Smith to expend as much as his judgment dictated. He informed Baldy that Major General Gouverneur K. Warren, commanding the Fifth Corps on Smith's right, was forcing the enemy back. Warren was directed to push his left forward in order to assist Smith's intended attack.[35]

Smith requested two fresh batteries of rifled guns. These would save time and the danger of sending fresh men forward with ammunition. Burnham's brigade was formed for an attack, but Smith would not order the assault until he saw a chance for success by Warren's or someone else's efforts. Wright wrote Meade that Smith's four regiments would be insufficient protection for his advance.[36]

Late in the morning Smith received a verbal order from Meade to make another attack, but he refused to obey it. Smith had carefully examined the entire front of his line and was convinced that no assault could succeed because he could not prevent the enfilading fire from the works in front of his right. Smith believed that an assault under such conditions involved a wanton waste of life. Brooks, who commanded the corps reserve, concurred with Smith's assessment. Brooks reported that a close examination of his ground showed that the attack would have been attended with the most disastrous results.[37]

About an hour after Smith had declined to obey the order to make another assault, Colonel Comstock meet Smith and told him that Grant had ordered the colonel to examine the Eighteenth Corps' lines. This visit was but the natural consequence of Smith's act, and he directed Captain Farquhar to accompany Comstock. After a reasonable lapse of time, Farquhar came back and, smiling, said, "Comstock was thoroughly satisfied and has gone back to report to General Grant."[38] Comstock wrote later in his diary that Smith's line was thought to be shaky. During the day, Major Nathaniel Michler, the acting army chief engineer, accompanied by Captain Farquhar, also examined Smith's lines. Michler reported, "Not a portion of the person could be exposed for a moment; the unerring shot of the sharpshooter warned all against rising above the hastily constructed entrenchments. All lay close to the ground, it being necessary to crawl along on hand and knees to reach the line."[39] Michler told Meade that a successful storming of the enemy position in Smith's front was impossible due to great Confederate strength and there being no suitable place in the rear to mass troops for the attack. Apparently, the army commander accepted the conclusions of these reports.[40]

Other corps were more advantageously situated for making an attack than the Eighteenth. The only attack that made any serious gains in the morning, however, was accomplished by Major General Winfield Scott Hancock's Second Corps. This corps formed the extreme left of the Federal line next to the Sixth Corps. Hancock could not hold the captured Confederate lines, however, because of a lack of reinforcements. After 11:00 a.m., on June 3, Grant visited the corps commanders to determine their opinion on another attack. Generals Hancock and Warren believed the enemy works too strong for a successful assault. Wright felt that a cooperative attack by his corps and the Second and Eighteenth Corps could gain the enemy lines. Burnside, who commanded the Ninth Corps and held the extreme Federal right, also thought gains could be made. Smith felt a lodgment was possible but was not sanguine. Faced with the general impression that the corps commanders were not hopeful of success, Grant directed Meade at 12:30 p.m. to suspend further advances for the present and strengthen what was held. At 1:30 p.m., Meade ordered his corps commanders to suspend further offensive operations for the present. The commanders were to entrench their positions and reconnoiter their lines to prepare for resuming the offensive.[41]

Smith placed his troops under cover as rapidly as possible, and his front line was strengthened. For the rest of the day, the fight was limited to the artillery and sharpshooters. General Birney's division of the Second Corps took position between the

Eighteenth and Fifth Corps and relieved some of Devens' troops around 3:00 p.m. Birney also straightened the line by advancing it and making use of an excellent ridge. Toward sunset, Smith received a request from Meade to report the condition of affairs on his front and the likelihood of renewing the attack the next day. Smith wrote Meade that he held all that he had gained and was entrenching himself as rapidly as possible. He advised against any further assaults the next day. General Wright concurred with Smith's view. During the night, General Ames' brigade arrived, having been relieved from duty at White House.[42]

The end of June brought the cessation of major Federal offensive operations at Cold Harbor. The Federal losses were staggering. From June 1 to June 10, the Army of the Potomac lost over thirteen thousand soldiers. Baldy's command lost over three thousand men, more than any other corps except the Second Corps. Of these losses, Baldy wrote, "I lost too many good men there ever to forget the battle."[43] These losses led Smith and others to evaluate the battle's logistics, tactics, and strategy.[44]

For his part in the battles, at least one modern historian pointed to Smith's contributions. Of all the corps commanders, Baldy Smith held the most promise. Unlike many of his fellow generals in the Army of the Potomac, Baldy "actively supervised troops on the field and pushed offensives with energy and spirit."[45] But Baldy's characteristic tendency to be critical of fellow generals, particularly in the case of Meade, challenged cooperation within the Union command and undoubtedly colored his assessment of the campaign afterwards. Writing long after the events, Smith found the logistics of the battle contemptible. On May 31, 1864, Grant determined to concentrate at Cold Harbor, and during the afternoon, the Sixth Corps moved for that location, about a fifteen-mile march. The Second Corps was ordered to march the same distance to form on the left of the Sixth Corps. Smith's corps, at White House, about thirteen miles from Cold Harbor, moved at 3:30 p.m. for New Castle, fifteen miles up the Pamunkey, and thence, on June 1, about twelve miles to Cold Harbor. It was placed on the Sixth Corps' right, and thus crossed the roads needed for the Sixth and Second Corps' marches. The Fifth Corps did not move at all, remaining in its position two miles to the right of the Eighteenth Corps.[46]

Smith later hypothesized that when Grant determined to concentrate near Cold Harbor, the Eighteenth Corps should have been ordered to join Sheridan's two divisions in holding captured works at Cold Harbor. These threatened the Confederate right flank. The Corps would have reached Sheridan on the night of the thirty-first, with about the same length of march it did make and would have been fresh for battle early on the morning of the first. The Sixth Corps, moving to take position on the right of the Eighteenth, would have had a shorter march than it made and should have been in position at an early hour of the same morning. The Second Corps, with a very short march, would have filled the gap between the Sixth and Fifth Corps and also have been in position for an early battle. The Ninth Corps could have marched to a proper place and served as a reserve. The army would then have presented a continuous line and an oblique order of battle, with the right wing thrown back or refused.[47]

Instead, by failing to concentrate the army against the right flank of the enemy early on the morning of June 1, the Federal forces surrendered the advantages that Sheridan had won. This failure resulted in a Federal line that left four exposed flanks in close proximity. Two of these flanks were created by the mile gap between Smith's right and Warren's left. The fire on Smith's exposed flank paralyzed his right wing and secured his defeat. Consequently, the attacks on June 1 and the murderous assaults on June 3 proved fruitless.[48]

Smith's criticism was especially directed at the order to attack on the third. Meade's plan to have the corps attack along the whole line failed to consider the benefit of the corps working together and the disadvantage of striking the Confederates' well-forti-fied works. Unless the attackers had great superiority in numbers, attacks along a whole line, where one or both flanks might be exposed, were condemned by standard military writers. The Confederates' use of trenches made the attack along the whole line even more reprehensible. The attacking force had to advance without firing. The advancing soldier provided an average target of five-and-a-half feet by two feet while the defend-ing soldier presented only a target of one-and-a-half feet by less than two feet. Smith was convinced that the defender clearly had the best chance and would be the coolest under those circumstances. He concluded that any assault over the field at Cold Harbor would be repulsed even if the attackers numbered twice the defenders and needed to attack only in the front.[49]

Smith had long opposed Grant's and Meade's overland route. Smith believed that the Virginia Campaign had brought the Army of the Potomac to the James by a series of defeats. While Smith was in Virginia, he blamed these defeats on Meade. After leaving Virginia in July 1864, Smith revised this assessment and decided that Grant was the one responsible for the series of costly losses.[50]

According to Smith's later evaluation, at the Wilderness, Grant failed in the selec-tion of the battlefield and allowed himself to be attacked before he concentrated his force. At Spotsylvania Court House, Grant allowed Lee three days to entrench and then struck the strongest part of Lee's line and was bloodily repulsed. When Confederate lines were taken on May 12, the assaults went unsupported and only succeeded because of Lee's decision not to reinforce his salient but to withdraw to an interior line. Grant's plan to push on and place his whole army between Lee and Richmond was likely to fail because Lee, with shorter lines, moved ahead of Grant and could entrench his lines close enough to Grant's to view his movements. Lee understood Grant wished to get on his right and attacked him wherever Grant presented himself. Thus, Grant's movements from Northern Virginia were predictable and allowed Lee to inflict heavy Union losses throughout the campaign. In contrast to the costly overland campaign, Smith and his close friend, General Franklin, continued to argue that the James River strategy would have saved thousands of lives and would have been more effective. Smith insisted that the effect of detaching at least 50,000 men to the Army of the James and putting a mil-itarily trained general in command would have caused Lee to leave Grant's front and enabled the Army of the Potomac to follow Lee to Richmond where he would have been eventually destroyed.[51]

Smith's view was not universally held. Wartime supporters of Grant's tactics blamed his subordinates for any tactical defeats. In his memoirs, J.H. Wilson stated that the army organization was thoroughly deficient. The staff arrangements were sadly defective and orders for movements were frequently lacking in detail and coherence, and were, therefore, executed poorly and ineffectually. Wilson and Charles Dana also blamed lack of vigor on the part of Wright and Smith for the June 3, 1864, repulse at Cold Harbor. Moreover, Wilson and Dana believed that Grant could not be blamed for the failure of that assault since it was impossible for Grant to regulate such details for so vast an army. Besides this, none of his subordinates objected to the order. Grant's supporters believed that his tactics were generally sound. Thomas Livermore believed that the Wilderness was "the turning point of the war in the East" and a substantial success because of Grant's decision to continue the march towards Richmond.[52] Wilson and Dana even believed the first assault at Cold Harbor was necessary to gain the position. Grant's advocates endorsed the overland strategy. Livermore stated the campaign inflicted on Lee the losses in men and material that were necessary to make victory possible. Wilson and Dana also defended the overland campaign since it protected Washington by keeping Grant between it and Lee and pinned Lee against Richmond.[53]

Smith was not alone, however, in his criticisms of Grant's tactics and strategy. Brigadier General Emory Upton wrote his sister on June 4 and 5, 1864, disgusted at the generalship displayed in the Virginia Campaign. Upton stated, "Our men have, in many instances, been foolishly and wantonly sacrificed. Assault after assault has been ordered upon the enemy's entrenchments, when they knew nothing about the strength or position of the enemy. Thousands of lives might have been spared by the exercise of a little skill; but, as it is, the courage of the poor men is expected to obviate all difficulties."[54] J.C. Ropes was especially critical of Grant's hopeless and aimless assaults. Ropes believed that Grant's tactics were terribly costly and failed to gain any significant advantage. The result of Grant's campaign was to reduce the army in numbers and morale out of all proportion with its adversary. William Swinton also was critical of Grant's tactic of "hammer continuously."[55] Swinton opposed the overland campaign. Since the overland campaign was unsuccessful in the destruction of Lee's army and the capture of Richmond, the result must be evaluated based on the loss inflicted on the opposing army. But the loss must also be measured in terms of the cost. Swinton concluded, "In this regard, it must be considered, the balance was very much in favor of the enemy."[56] Writing in his memoirs long after the war, Grant acknowledged this cost in regard to the battle on June 3. He wrote, "I have always regretted that the last assault on Cold Harbor was ever made.... At Cold Harbor no advantage whatever was gained to compensate for the heavy loss we sustained. Indeed, the advantages, other than those of relative losses, were on the Confederate side." William McFeely, in his modern biography of Grant, also admitted "everything had gone wrong" at Cold Harbor. Grant failed to carefully select the battlefield, and to offer artillery support for the Federal attack. The result was "carnage of fearful dimensions."[57]

On June 4, 1864, General Devens, who had performed his duty during the previous day on a stretcher, was relieved by General Ames on account of his poor health. Learning that Birney's division was being relieved, Smith reported to Humphreys that the gap between the Eighteenth and Fifth Corps would be reopened. Smith did not have any men to fill the gap and requested other troops fill the space. Warren was ordered to fill the vacancy, but, later in the day, the Ninth Corps was ordered to relieve the Fifth Corps, and Burnside was directed to connect with Smith's right. During the day, Meade paid a long visit to Smith, whose tents were pitched between the Woody House and the line of battle. Smith's tent was furnished much better than Meade's and for Meade's benefit, Baldy displayed a lunch with champagne that quite astonished everyone. Whether it was the lunch or Smith's and Brooks' company, Meade stayed there several hours, talking and smoking. At last, the generals' chat was broken up by the arrival of Burnside. Because of the Fredericksburg days, there were still poor feelings between him and Smith and Brooks. A member of Meade's staff recalled, "So they don't speak now; and we enjoyed the military icicle in great perfection!"[58] In the late afternoon, Meade ordered the Second, Sixth, and Eighteenth Corps to advance their positions by regular approaches during the night. Burnside and Smith went riding that evening, surveying the lines to determine the place and best method for connecting their corps. Burnside agreed to relieve the extreme right brigade of Ames so that Smith did not have to straddle a swamp on his right.[59]

Early in the morning on June 5, the Confederates attempted to advance their picket line under heavy musketry fire but were repelled by Smith's artillery. At daybreak, 510 soldiers of the Sixteenth and Eighteenth Georgia surrendered to the Eighteenth Corps; they were simply tired of fighting and did not want any more of it. During the day, Meade paid another visit to Smith's headquarters. During the visit, Smith asked Meade why he had ordered the repeated assaults on the third. He replied that he had developed all the campaign's movement, but the newspapers had given Grant the credit. Meade was tired of having his work ignored and decided to let Grant plan his own battles at Cold Harbor. Smith supposed that Grant simply ordered an attack 4:30 a.m. on the third and left the details to his subordinates. That night, Smith did not continue the usual artillery fire because it would interfere with work being done in his front and would keep his troops from much needed rest.[60]

On the sixth, Smith wrote to Meade that an assault was not practical from any point in his front unless batteries that would silence the enemy crossfire were first placed on the front occupied earlier by Burnside. Later in the day, Burnside assured Meade that his two divisions had secured Smith's right. Burnside also held the salient that protected Smith's right. Smith instructed Ames to ensure the connection with Burnside's left. Ames was to make proper dispositions for his command's safety and to give Burnside assistance if needed.[61]

Many wounded and dead Federals lay between the opposing lines. They had spent three days and three nights suffering without care. Some of the wounded were brought in by men who risked their lives in the act, and some were rescued by digging trenches to them. The groans of those who could not be reached grew fainter and fainter until they ceased. Grant did not request a formal flag of truce to cease hostilities to recover his dead and wounded until late on the afternoon of June 6. The request and its favorable reply arrived too late for any organized recovery of the casualties on the field that day.[62]

During the day, however, there was an informal agreement that both sides would refrain from firing for one hour to allow the collection of the dead and wounded. This truce began in front of the Eighteenth Corps by the Confederates ceasing their fire and standing upon their works and Smith's men doing likewise. Smith's men supposed there had been a cessation of hostilities at the request of Meade. But, when a Confederate officer advanced and warned that hostilities would recommence unless Stedman's brigade suspend work on a battery, the sides resumed their former positions. Between 2:00 p.m. and 3:00 p.m., Smith visited his lines and was informed by the troops of the first line that an informal agreement had been made with the enemy in their front to stop picket firing. As this was very much in accordance with his own ideas, Smith expressed a wish that this would extend all along his lines, since his men in the rear lines were suffering severely from such firing. During the night, burying parties ventured out from Smith's corps to bury the dead and got close enough to the enemy lines to hear a Confederate officer give orders not to fire on burying parties. That same night, Meade ordered Smith to push his lines forward, especially during the night, and establish batteries for his command and the connecting corps.[63]

The next day, Meade, angered by reports of the informal cessation of hostilities the day earlier, wrote Wright and Smith to find out who ordered the suspension. Neither corps commander had issued such an order, but the officers and men in the most advanced lines in front of the two corps did engage in an informal agreement with the Rebels to cease hostilities for an hour. Finally, Grant and Lee agreed on an armistice to bring in the dead. Between 6:00 p.m. and 8:00 p.m., Smith's men found and buried sixty-nine of their dead. That night, Meade ordered his corps commanders to stop pushing their lines toward the enemy and limit their operations to ensuring security.[64]

On the evening of June 8, there was a strenuous but peaceful contest between the Confederates and one of Baldy's regiments, the Thirteenth New Hampshire. The regimental band went into the trenches in the front and indulged in a "competition concert" with a band that was playing across the field in the enemy's trenches. The enemy's band rendered "Dixie," "Bonnie Blue Flag," "My Maryland," and other Southern favorites. The regimental band replied with "America," "The Star-Spangled Banner," and "Old John Brown." After the battle, Smith's men mostly kept busy in strengthening their earthworks and participating in sharpshooter and artillery contests.[65]

On June 11, Smith received orders to withdraw his command soon after dark on

Major General Smith and his staff at the battle of Cold Harbor. Left to right: Major William Russell, unknown, Captain Samuel Elder, Captain Preston C.F. West, Major General William F. Smith, Brigadier General Adelbert Ames, Lieutenant Colonel Nicolas Bowen, Captain James Fleming, and Captain L.H. Stone (Matthew Brady Photographs of Civil War–Era Personalities and Scenes [Record Group 111], National Archives).

the evening of the twelfth and move them by way of Parsley's Mill, Prospect Church, Hopewell Church, and Tunstall's Station to White House, where they would embark and proceed to Bermuda Hundred. Grant told Butler of Smith's movement. He suggested that if Butler thought it possible to seize and hold Petersburg, he should be prepared to start the expedition upon the arrival of the Eighteenth Corps. Grant did not want Butler to attack Petersburg, however, unless he believed it would be held.[66]

On the night of June 12, Smith's command began the move to White House. He withdrew shortly after dark, leaving a strong picket under the command of Colonel Henry. At daylight on the thirteenth, Smith arrived with the bulk of his command at White House. The march had been delayed by the trains and the men of the Second, Ninth, and Sixth Corps, who were all over Smith's road and in his way. He found that "with all its renown the Army of the Potomac is a straggling, disorderly set, compared to the 18th Corps, to which I never yet have had time to do justice in the matter of discipline."[67] Rawlins urged Smith to send his troops to Bermuda Hundred as fast as possible. This was the first indication to Smith there was a need for urgency; however, the reason for it was not shared. The embarkation was begun immediately, but the corps was much delayed by the lack of transportation. During the day, Colonel Henry arrived, with his command having successfully served as the rear guard of the corps and brought his men off with little molestation from the enemy.[68]

Smith departed with his men on the thirteenth, leaving General Ames behind at White House to ensure that the entire corps would soon embark. On board the steamer *Metamora* in the York River, Baldy wrote to his wife, "I am once more away from the Army of the Potomac and Meade is, I suppose as glad as I am. I once more go to Butler under the old system and that is very unpleasant but there is always an air of brains about Butler and that is far better than the smell of blood on Meade's clothes…. I am trying to make up today by sleeping for a terrible night of headache and unrest."[69]

As he steamed to Bermuda Hundred, Smith was unaware that he would soon be ordered to attack Petersburg. He had long desired to have the opportunity to capture the "Cockade City." His assault on Petersburg, however, would become his most controversial battle. His relief as Eighteenth Corps commander, less than five weeks later, however, was not based on his actions in this battle but on his continued criticisms of the Overland Campaign and the bloody repulses at Cold Harbor.[70]

CHAPTER XIII

Smith Before Petersburg

The Last Campaign

Smith's effectiveness as a corps commander at Drewry's Bluff and Cold Harbor had been limited by superiors who overlooked such elementary tactics as protecting their flanks. Smith's reconnaissances and ingenuity staved off major disaster, but he could not completely overcome Butler's inexperience or Meade's inadequacy. Because of these army commanders, the Eighteenth Corps suffered greatly during the Bermuda Hundred and Virginia Campaigns.[1]

On the morning of June 14, 1864, Smith visited Sarah Butler on his way to her husband's headquarters. He told her that he was thoroughly disgusted with what his superiors had made him do and with the general conduct of the war. Smith considered the campaign from the beginning as a desperate butchery concocted by the Federals, which cost the Confederates comparatively little. He told her that the campaign had lost seventy thousand men and would end the war for the Union if it failed. Smith recounted how the corpses of his Massachusetts men were piled high without any significant result. He placed the blame for the losses on Meade. Butler's wife felt Baldy shielded Grant from this blame. Smith was glad to resume his position under General Butler.[2]

Based on his orders from General Grant on June 11, Butler decided to order Smith to capture Petersburg. By sunset of June 14, Smith reported in person to Butler and was surprised by orders to move on Petersburg at daylight. Smith realized that it was a mistake to have kept the purpose of the movement from him until this point. He could have made better arrangements for his troop movement to Bermuda Hundred in preparation for the offensive against Petersburg. Butler assigned the Department's cavalry under General Kautz's and General Hinks' Black division to Smith's command. Baldy then began ordering deployments of his various divisions. Kautz was ordered to cross the Appomattox River at 1:00 a.m. Kautz was to proceed with as little delay as possible to threaten the line of fortifications near the Norfolk and Petersburg Railroad, and at the same time protect the left flank of the infantry.[3]

Most of Smith's infantry would have only a very brief rest after disembarking from their transports, breaking camp between 2:00 a.m. and 3:00 a.m. General Hinks' two brigades at Broadway Landing were ordered to march behind Kautz and take up a position across the Jordan Point Road as near as possible to the enemy works. General Brooks' division and two brigades of Ames' division under Colonel Louis Bell were ordered to travel along the City Point Road and form a line of battle on Hinks' right. General Martindale's division was ordered to proceed on the River Road to a point near the City Point Railroad and await orders. The transports arrived all night and, apart from Hinks' and Kautz's commands, it was impossible to determine what troops were present or would soon arrive.[4]

Information from Butler led Smith to believe that his force would encounter no line of works until they reached the main line near Jordan Hill. The Confederate entrenchments encircled the city at a distance of two miles from it and consisted of strong redans or batteries connected by infantry parapets with high profiles, all with ditches. Baldy's force would have to march six or seven miles to come up to them. But Butler reported that the Confederate line would have only a small force, and the works were described as being such that cavalry could ride over them at almost any point. Smith was also told that his right flank on the Appomattox would entirely command the enemy position near the river.[5]

Kautz's march was unavoidably delayed, which suspended the movements from Broadway until 4:00 a.m. The cavalry advance struck the enemy's pickets within a mile and continued skirmishing until they came upon a rifle pit near the railroad. The pit was lined with infantry and supported with a light battery near Baylor's Farm. Kautz reported the enemy's position to Smith and told him that he was unable to dislodge them. Smith ordered Kautz to withdraw and get into position by moving left.[6]

Hinks immediately made a personal reconnaissance and found that the enemy was positioned in Baylor's field, which commanded the road. The Confederate works were atop a rise overlooking an open field of fire 300 to 400 yards in width. The Federal attack would need to move through fallen timbers and a thick thicket as well as a swampy woods, all difficult, particularly for inexperienced soldiers. Having reported this to Smith, Hinks was ordered to deploy his command in two lines of battle with skirmishers in front and assault the works; Hinks completed his arrangements by 6:00 a.m. To attack the enemy works, Colonel Samuel A. Duncan's brigade, in advance, and Colonel John Holman's brigade, in support, had to pass through a swamp and some thick woods. The greenness of Hinks' cavalry delayed the move, but finally his advance began. They came under heavy artillery and infantry fire along the whole line. The main Confederate force consisted of 400 troopers of the Fourth North Carolina Cavalry supported by two artillery pieces, with supports, upon the crest of a hill on the right. Despite the fire from these works, Hinks' men emerged from the woods and moved swiftly over the 400 yards of open, rising ground between the woods and the works. Tragically, two of the regiments left the cover of the woods prematurely and suffered serious causalities. Meanwhile, Colonel Joseph Kiddoo, commanding the Twenty-Second United States Colored Troops, on his own accord ordered his regiment to charge the rifle pits in his front. Some of his men shouting "Remember Fort Pillow" dashed across the open ground. In the face of this assault, the Confederates fled towards Petersburg, leaving one gun in Federal hands. This line was carried a little after 8:00 a.m. Needing time to reorganize his troops after this unexpected affair, Smith delayed his advance until about 9:00 a.m.[7]

Hinks renewed his march via a route from the City Point Road to the Jordan Point Road. Having reached the Jordan Point Road, he turned to the right and again met the enemy's pickets on Bailey's Creek near Bryant's House. Deploying Holman's command, Hinks drove them beyond the woods surrounding Ruffin's House. Hinks immediately advanced his command into position in front of the enemy's works, covering his troops with a line of skirmishers from beyond the junction of the Jordan Point Road and Suffolk Stage Road on the left, to beyond Peebles' House on the right. He directed the skirmishing line to keep up a constant fire upon the gunners in the enemy's works.

Nevertheless, the crossfire from the enemy batteries prevented Hinks from placing his guns into position to bombard the enemy works until later in the day, when he pushed a section into position to the right of Peebles' House and another section to the left of the house. Duncan's brigade was pushed five hundred yards forward to the crest in Jordan's field. Hinks battery helped protect this advanced position. In the early afternoon, Baldy rode to Hinks' front and, along with Colonel Holman and a staff officer, reconnoitered the Confederate line. Musketry fire in their direction caused Holman to jump aside, but Baldy was unmoved, impressing an observer with his bravery under fire. At about 2:00 p.m., under Smith's direction, Hinks' line was extended to the right to connect with Brooks' line.[8]

Finding that the enemy had enough troops to defend works nearly two miles before their main line, Smith at once ordered Brooks to make the rest of his march in line of battle. Brooks deployed his line and moved forward on the City Point Railroad and wagon road. At the intersection of the railroad and the road, Brooks' advance came upon Stannard's brigade, which Martindale had sent to connect the Second and First Division. Martindale had advanced steadily forward against the enemy skirmishers, who were supported by artillery. Brooks and Martindale arranged to make the City Point Railroad the line of direction and connection of the two divisions. Brooks used Burnham's line of skirmishers to maintain the connection. This line soon engaged enemy skirmishers occupying heavy woods and drove them into a field, where they had small French rifle pits covered by their main works. The works consisted of a line of batteries connected by rifle pits extending from Brooks' right to his left. A sharp and continuous fire of artillery was kept up from these works and the riflemen in the pits. This firing gave every indication of a large force. An effort was made to get some artillery in position but finding a place that was not commanded by the enemy was difficult. Brooks finally was able to place one section in position, but this proved ineffectual.[9]

Martindale's division also suffered from the fire of the enemy works on Jordan's Hill but resolutely maintained its ground. Martindale sent Stedman's brigade to the right and extended his skirmishers to the Appomattox. Stedman moved his right forward more than eight hundred yards and came within reach of the enemy's works on Harrison's Creek. They were now ready to move forward, but their front was entirely commanded by the enemy guns on Jordan's Hill.[10]

Smith's skirmishers were halted in the edge of the woods nearest to the works. Baldy came to the front, in view of the works, about noon with the leading troops of Brooks' command. This line of earthworks, called the Dimmock Line, ran east-southeast from the Appomattox River over low ground to the City Point Railroad; then, turning sharply, it mounted the high ground and ran south along a series of crests for about a mile and a half from Confederate Battery Number Five to Battery Number Twelve. It was finally drawn back so as to surround Petersburg and meet the Appomattox again south of the city. These works presented a very formidable obstacle to the troops. They were situated on commanding crests, and the forest was felled in their front to expose advancing lines to enemy fire for half a mile or more.[11]

Based upon Butler's information, Smith expected to see a weak line of enemy works that was lightly manned. Instead, the line was very strong, and from the number of guns and the pertinacity of the skirmishers on the outside, Smith believed the works must be sufficiently manned. Also, the hills occupied by Martindale were too far off to command the works in his front. They were also lower than those held by the enemy. Since Butler's information was erroneous, Smith was obliged to get correct information and began to reconnoiter the position. Despite his request, no engineer officer was ordered to report to him. Therefore, Smith was obliged to make the reconnaissance in person. The reconnaissance was necessarily slow; Smith was sometimes forced on his hands and knees. An engineer officer could have done the work more quickly than Smith, who was frequently interrupted by the necessity of attending to his proper duties. Smith was also slowed by the ill effects of drinking bad water at Cold Harbor and a relapse of malaria. He found that Brooks' command was at the salient of the enemy line, which consisted of a strongly profiled work heavily flanked on the left by redoubts. These flanking works also faced Hinks' lines. Smith completed his reconnaissance in front of Hinks and Brooks shortly after 3:00 p.m.[12]

He then went to Martindale's division to examine its front, arriving around 4:00 p.m. Martindale's front faced a broad valley that had several deep ditches and ravines and was completely covered by the enemy artillery fire. Beyond this valley, the enemy occupied a strong line of works open in the rear and connected by heavily profiled rifle pits. While Smith was with Martindale, the Confederates got two guns in position on Archer's Hill, on the west side of the Appomattox, and immediately opened fire on Stedman's lines. Stedman suffered severely from this fire, against which Martindale had nothing to interpose. Stedman was compelled to retire about eight hundred yards. Smith completed his reconnaissance of Martindale's front and returned to the center of his line about 5:00 p.m.[13]

Smith's reconnoitering was necessarily slow. While he had been anxious to lose no time, he was also determined to take no step that would get his command badly repulsed before such works. Very little infantry could be seen, but that did not prove the Confederates were not there, and it was improbable that the number of guns at work would be there without strong support. In light of his reconnoitering, Smith concluded that the wide-open space in his front and the scope of the enemy artillery prevented any chance of success by a column of assault. Instead, Smith would try a heavy line of skirmishers with his artillery massed upon the salient to keep down the fire of its guns while the infantry advanced. Baldy's reconnaissance also indicated the point of his attack. Ravines carved in front of the Confederate Batteries Five through Seven provided relatively safe approaches for his men. He would be able to launch his attack close to the Confederate lines and thus minimize the time his men would be under fire. There was a particularly large ravine in front of the primary focus of the attack, Battery Five, on top of Jordan Hill.[14]

In compliance with this plan, division commanders on the right and left were ordered to conform to the movements of the center division. The skirmish line was doubled, and the line of battle held in readiness to move forward when the skirmishers had reached the works. The disposition of troops took about a half hour. Upon ordering up the artillery, it was found that the chief of artillery, Captain Frederick M. Follett, had, upon his own responsibility, taken everything to the rear and unhitched the horses to water them. Smith deemed it impossible to dispense with the artillery, and there was nothing to do but wait. This detained the movement for an hour.[15]

Meanwhile, far to the left of Smith's line, Kautz was making his attack. Kautz had pushed the enemy pickets back into the main entrenchments and came in sight of the lines about noon. Several miles of entrenchments were in view, and the ground in front was comparatively level and afforded little or no cover from the enemy's artillery. The enemy opened with artillery from five redoubts as soon as the cavalry appeared in view, and subsequently two more redoubts were discovered on the extreme right. The works were not strongly defended with infantry, and Kautz decided to make a demonstration to get through the line. A general advance was ordered, and the skirmishers pushed forward to within 500 yards of the entrenchments. Since only a portion of the men were armed with carbines and so many men were required to take care of the horses, Kautz's attacking force was actually weaker than the enemy's line, and the skirmishers could not be advanced any farther. Kautz held on until 5:30 p.m. when, becoming short of ammunition and receiving information that the enemy was reinforcing its position, he ordered the withdrawal of his entire command to the Jordan Point Road and bivouacked there. The cavalry commander neglected to notify Smith or any of his infantry commanders of his retreat. Perhaps this was a result of Butler's instruction to Kautz to report directly to him during the offensive without going through Smith.[16]

Between 6:30 and 7:00 p.m., Smith ordered his skirmishers to advance, and Captain Follett opened all the batteries upon the bastioned salient, which made no response. The long and heavy line of Brooks' skirmishers advanced gallantly under sharp infantry fire. The skirmish lines of Burnham's and Bell's brigades plunged into the ravine forty feet below the parapet of the salient work of Battery Number Five and scaled the fort under heavy artillery and musket fire. Some of the soldiers used their bayonets as steps or grasped weeds for balance as they climbed up. They gained the rear of the enemy's line, entered the redoubt, routed or captured the garrison, and seized the enemy guns. In carrying the work, they took between three hundred and four hundred prisoners and four pieces of artillery double-shotted with canister. These guns had been kept waiting for Smith's columns of assault. The pieces were quickly turned on the retreating foe. Smith rode up, and one of his men proposed three cheers for "Old Baldy Smith." A mouthful of hoecake did not prevent one sergeant of the Third New York from cheering him. Smith took off his hat and smiled from ear to ear but calmed his men down "by waiving his hand gently, as does an orchestra leader when he means 'pianissimo.'" Brooks soon joined Smith, and the two officers gained control of the celebrating soldiers. In the meantime, the lines of battle were moved forward to occupy the works. Brooks' command was formed to resist a possible counterattack, while Martindale on the right and Hinks on the left were following up the advantage. Brooks' entire division front extended some 800 yards, from around Battery Number Six northwest to Martindale's position.[17]

Four redoubts on the left commanded Brooks' position and kept up a galling artillery fire. Hinks' skirmishers, closely followed by the columns in support, swept towards these works and gained complete possession of them from Confederate Battery Number Six on Hinks' right to Battery Number Eight near his left. Holman's brigade with the assistance of Bells' brigade took Number Six, and Duncan's brigade captured Number Seven. Duncan reformed his force and assaulted Number Eight, a strong work that was well posted on a considerable elevation behind a difficult ravine. This battery was turned and carried in the face of strong resistance and with considerable loss.[18]

Holman's brigade then moved to take Battery Number Nine in the front while Duncan's brigade moved on its flank. Duncan advanced through a deep ravine and marched five hundred yards but arrived after Holman's brigade had charged the battery's front in the face of artillery fire and carried the battery. The Confederates retired to Number Ten, a more commanding and formidable work. Duncan's force immediately assaulted

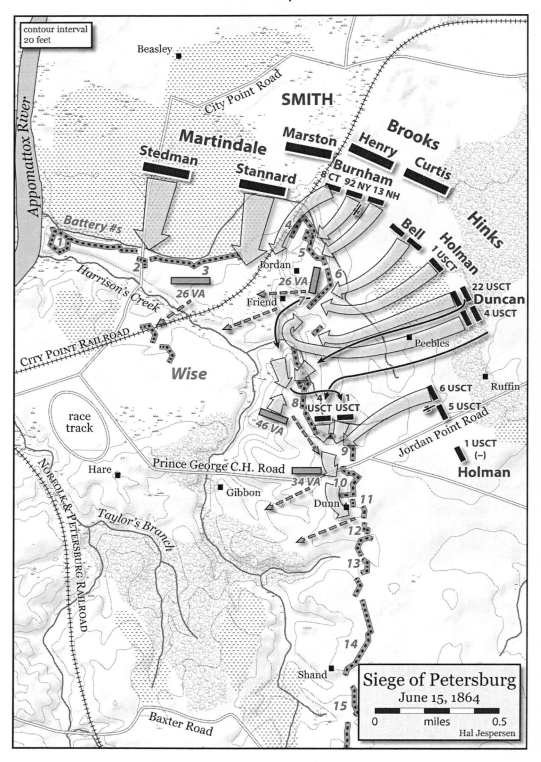

contour interval
20 feet

Appomattox River

Beasley

City Point Road

SMITH

Martindale

Marston

Brooks

Stedman

Henry

Curtis

Stannard

Burnham

8 CT 92 NY 13 NH

Hinks

Battery #s

1

Bell

Holman
1 USCT

2

4

5

Jordan

6

22 USCT

Duncan

3

26 VA

26 VA

4 USCT

Harrison's Creek

Friend

7

Peebles

City Point Railroad

Wise

race
track

8

4   1
USCT USCT

6 USCT

Ruffin

5 USCT

46 VA

9

Jordan Point Road

1 USCT
(–)

Hare

Prince George C.H. Road

34 VA

10

Holman

Gibbon

Dunn

11

Norfolk & Petersburg Railroad

Taylor's Branch

12

13

14

Shand

Siege of Petersburg
June 15, 1864

15

Baxter Road

0   miles   0.5

Hal Jespersen

Siege of Petersburg, June 15, 1864.

this battery and, after a sharp conflict, carried it slightly before 9:00 p.m. When Number Ten was captured, the enemy abandoned Battery Number Eleven still further to the left, though prisoners stated that the Forty-Second North Carolina regiment was close at hand to reinforce it.[19]

While the two brigades were moving against the Confederate works, Smith came onto that part of the field and ordered Hinks' two reserve regiments to assure the capture of Batteries Nine, Ten, and Eleven. These two regiments moved in front of the works in partial support of Holman's frontal assault on Number Nine and Duncan's flank attacks. They advanced over six hundred yards of ground much obstructed by stumps, piles of wood, fallen timber, bushes, and pools. Their only guide was the flash of the enemy guns whose fire, however, was much diverted by the flanking parties. As Duncan carried Number Ten, the regiments approached and assured the capture of the redoubt.[20]

At this time, Smith received a report that Martindale had carried the enemy works between Jordan's House and the Appomattox. This report overstated the Second Division's accomplishment. Martindale's command had advanced about a mile. He directed Stannard to move along the railroad and Stedman along the City Point and Petersburg highway. This afforded some protection against incessant fire from Archer's Hill. In this advance, Stannard captured Battery Number Three and took two pieces of artillery; Stedman reached the enemy's fortified position at Harrison's Creek. By this time, Martindale determined that it was too dark to make a practical advance on the east side of the City Point highway. To attack the enemy position, he would have had to cross an eight-foot-deep ditch behind which the Confederates had constructed a one hundred-yard-long parapet. Martindale later reported that these obstacles would have certainly caused disorder in the line of attack. Rather than continue the attack in the darkness, Smith ordered Martindale to withdraw his command to the Spring Hill Road and form behind Brooks on the heights.[21]

Smith had succeeded in breaking through the strong line of Confederate works from Battery Number Three to Battery Number Eleven inclusive. By 9:00 p.m., his forces were unable to advance further because of darkness, and Smith suspended the attack. In part, this suspension came from Smith's general opposition to night attacks. His own military principles and experiences led him to oppose assaults after dark. Smith wrote that a military command was a unit only as long as the intelligence that directed it had perfect control of it and could move it according to the exigencies of the situation. It became disorganized exactly in the proportion to which this control was lost. For a large body of men to march in line of battle at night and maintain an effective organization was impossible. The general in command simply stepped down from his position and commanded what was in his immediate front, leaving all other operations entirely to chance. He could neither estimate the force against him nor the obstacles to overcome. Because he could not know the details, he was powerless to repair disaster or take intelligent advantage of success. Any operation which produced such results was militarily unsound.[22]

Smith's own experiences justified his principles. In the autumn of 1861, he had been ordered to make a night reconnaissance. His men were not veterans but were not entirely raw either. He had taken every precaution that suggested itself, but his men began to fire into each other before they were within three miles of the enemy. In a similar incident, during the Peninsula campaign, he was ordered at sunset to form his division for an assault on Fort Magruder. The lines were formed as directed. The men needed to advance through a narrow wood to attack the fort. In moving through the wood, the wings lost their direction and were marching towards each other. They would have soon collided, but Smith happened to be in front and halted the command. He rectified the lines and threw out pickets for the night, simply reporting what he had done. Smith remembered Longstreet's unsuccessful night attack on Hooker at Wauhatchie in October 1863. He knew he was not alone in his opposition to night attacks. At Missionary Ridge, Sherman did not attack Bragg on the night of November 25, and Grant approved this halt.[23]

In addition, Smith decided to suspend the assault because some hours before he had heard that Lee's army was rapidly crossing at Drewry's Bluff. From 2:00 p.m., the Confederates were crowding trains to Petersburg. As early as 6:50 p.m., a report came of two trains—totaling thirty-six cars of Confederate troops—passing towards Petersburg. The enemy appeared to be sending troops on the roads west of Petersburg. At 7:30 p.m., another train of thirteen cars had been seen en route to the city, and Confederates were observed marching to the city's defense. An hour later, two more trains were reported on their way toward Petersburg. At 9:30 p.m., Butler wrote Smith that the sum of Confederates sent to Petersburg had not yet equaled ten thousand. But significant numbers had indeed arrived.[24]

The Confederates defended their lines with Brigadier General Henry Wise's and Brigadier General James Dearing's brigades totaling between 3,600 and 4,300 men. During the day, General Beauregard had requested reinforcements, and General Hoke's division had been sent. Before sunset, Brigadier General Johnson Hagood's brigade arrived. During the next few hours, the rest of Hoke's division arrived, adding approximately 6,000 more Confederates to retain the lines not captured by Smith and establish new lines closer to Petersburg. After Hoke's arrival, the Confederates numbered more than 9,000 men while Smith's infantry force was estimated to be between 10,000 and 14,000 men. Considering that Beauregard had the defensive works, it seems extremely unlikely that Baldy could have successfully advanced his force over unknown and very difficult terrain in the dark and captured and held Petersburg during the night of June 15–16, 1864. In response to Hinks' suggestion to continue the attack after 9:00 p.m., Smith told Hinks that he believed that Beauregard was marching upon Petersburg with a larger force than Smith had at his command and would probably enter the town before Baldy could possibly reach it. Smith considered that the risk to the advantages won by his command was too great to warrant any further movement that night, and that they would do well if they succeeded in holding all that they had gained. Smith later reported that he thought it prudent "to hold what we had than by attempting to reach the bridges to lose what we had gained, and have the troops meet with a disaster."[25]

Smith's decision to halt the attack was also influenced by word of Federal reinforcements. The previous day when Grant had told Butler to order Smith to attack Petersburg, he offered reinforcements from the Army of the Potomac. But when Butler gave Baldy his orders, he failed to share this critical information with him. Around 4:30 p.m., Smith received a note from Grant stating that Hancock's corps was marching towards Petersburg. If Smith needed Hancock's force, he could ask for it. Smith requested that Hancock support his assault by attacking the enemy lines in the vicinity of the Norfolk and Petersburg Railroad. At about 6:30 p.m., Smith repeated this request to Hancock's chief of staff, Lieutenant Colonel Charles H. Morgan.[26]

Hancock's march from City Point had been delayed, waiting for promised rations that never did arrive. To avoid further delay, Hancock decided to march without them. At 10:30 a.m., he left City Point with orders to march to Harrison's Creek. Hancock's map from headquarters proved erroneous, and the designated creek happened to be behind enemy lines. He decided to move to a point where he believed his orders meant him to go. About 5:30 p.m., Grant informed Hancock of Smith's attack on Petersburg and ordered him to assist in the attack. Shortly after this, Smith's request for aid arrived. Hancock was shocked by these messages. These two notes were the first and only communications informing him that Petersburg was to be attacked that day. Had Grant told him earlier of the day's objective, Hancock would not have delayed his march for rations and would have moved directly toward Petersburg, arriving early in the afternoon. As soon as he received the notes, Hancock sent word to Smith of his position and assured him of his support. At 6:30 p.m., the head of Birney's division arrived at the Bryant House on Bailey's Creek, about one mile behind Hinks' division.[27]

At about 8:00 p.m., Hinks met with Birney and proposed two possible uses for his division. Birney could move up the road on the left, past Bryant's House, to the Norfolk and Petersburg Road, and by that road strike and capture the enemy's works further to the left. If Birney did not choose this option, he could move his division behind Hinks and deploy to the left, thereby prolonging the line and capturing the remaining works. Hinks suggested that by either of these movements, the two corps could easily enter Petersburg. Birney objected to both suggestions, stating that he would not move his troops at night in the enemy's presence upon unfamiliar ground. Since Birney outranked Hinks, Hinks did not press his advice but instead returned to his command.[28]

After Hinks' command had taken Battery Number Eleven, Smith gave orders to form a defensive line. Duncan's brigade was reformed and rested for the night near Battery Number Ten. Details were set at work cutting down the reverse slopes of the fortifications as a precaution against possible attack. On his way back to headquarters, Smith met Hancock, who said he was bringing up two divisions and asked about the condition of affairs. Smith told him what had been done, pointed out his lines as well as he could in the darkness, and gave him a description of the country in front. Considering the darkness, the character of the country, and enemy reinforcements, Smith did not repeat his request for Hancock to assault on his left but asked the Second Corps commander to relieve his troops in the front line of works that he had carried, so that the enemy would encounter fresh troops should the Confederates attempt to recapture their works. Smith did not think his men were in condition to resist a strong attack because they had had no sleep the previous night. Hancock complied with Smith's request, sending two divisions into the works that Hinks and Brooks had taken. They started around 11:00 p.m. and completed the relief about 3:00 a.m. Hancock reported that by the time this movement was completed, it was too late and dark for any immediate advance.[29]

Hancock received a dispatch from Grant about 11:00 p.m. It stated that if Petersburg did not fall that night, Hancock and Smith were to take up a defensive position and maintain it until all the forces came up. Smith's suggestions for the disposition of Hancock's troops satisfied Grant's directive. The earthworks captured by Baldy were turned against the enemy, artillery was brought up and placed in them, and all preparations were made to prevent their recapture.[30]

During the evening, Hancock and Smith also received word from General Butler. While admitting "they are crowding troops down from Richmond" and ignoring the problems of darkness and unknown terrain, Butler pressed both corps commanders to continue the attack on Petersburg during the night.[31] He wanted to put the Appomattox between them and Lee's army. Instead, Smith decided that it would be wiser to wait until daybreak to resume the offensive with Hancock's corps. This would eliminate the problems of darkness and unknown terrain and reduce the advantages of Beauregard's reinforcements. Because of the commanding positions that Smith and Hancock believed they occupied, an attack at daybreak had a much greater chance of success. Thus, at midnight, Smith wrote to Butler, "It is impossible for me to go farther to-night, but, unless I misapprehend the topography, I hold the key to Petersburg."[32] Hancock also wrote Butler endorsing Smith's view stating, "General Smith and myself have examined the country but cannot determine the exact position of the enemy ... having arrived at this point after dark, I can determine little about the features of the country, and I cannot tell what the morning will bring forth; but I think we cover all of the commanding points in front of Petersburg."[33]

Despite Smith's accomplishment, the battle of Petersburg was later considered as a missed golden opportunity to capture the Cockade City. Three major criticisms were offered to explain this failure. First, Smith was faulted for unnecessarily delaying his attack on the main works from noon until about 7:00 p.m. Civil War officer and historian George Bruce believed that Smith should not have spent any time reconnoitering the enemy works or waiting for the artillery. An attack at noon would have been as successful as the one made at 7:00 p.m. Bruce insisted that nothing was learned by Smith's reconnaissance, and artillery was ineffectual in aiding Civil War assaults. Historian Edward Longacre agrees: "Had Smith composed himself to strike in midafternoon, even through use of conventional assault tactics, it seems likely he would have overwhelmed every major work in his front before darkness fell" and taken Petersburg before reinforcements stopped him. In his July 1865 report, General Grant also criticized the time that Smith spent prior to his assault. One modern Grant biographer accused Smith of being timid.[34]

Second, Smith was criticized for not following up his advance after 9:00 p.m., especially with Hancock's two divisions within supporting distance. Grant stated in his 1865 report that the night "was clear, the moon shining brightly, and favorable to further operations."[35] He mistakenly believed that the Confederates were without a military force to prevent an easy occupation of Petersburg. Grant charged that Smith "stopped at the works he captured, and gave the enemy time to get in a garrison and intrench it."[36] Butler also pointed to the "night as bright and clear as a nearly full moon could make it" and believed that Smith should have captured Petersburg that evening.[37] Butler pointed to his directives during the fifteenth to press to the Appomattox. Civil War officer and historian Thomas Livermore believed that despite the risk to the Eighteenth Corps, the prize of Petersburg was worth the gamble. General Hinks wrote, "I have now no doubt that, with prompt movement and the cooperation of Birney, we could easily have entered Petersburg at any time before twelve o'clock on the night of the fifteenth of June."[38] Colonel Henry also believed the Corps should have advanced further. General Beauregard, noting his weakly defended lines, stated, "Petersburg was clearly at the mercy of the Federal commander, who had all but captured it, and only failed of final success because he could not realize the fact of the unparalleled disparity between the two contending forces."[39]

Third, Hancock's failure to arrive at the battlefield until after dark was blamed for denying the Federals reinforcements certain to assure a victorious assault on the city.

Hancock's delay waiting for rations and the errors in his orders and map were blamed on poor arrangements among the staffs of Grant, Butler, and Meade. But Hancock reported his late arrival was due to not receiving positive orders or information on the Petersburg assault. Grant kept both Hancock and Meade in the dark about Smith's attack. In his memoirs, Grant admitted that had he informed Hancock earlier, the Second Corps would have joined Smith prior to his attack. Thus, Grant bears the sole responsibility for Hancock's failure to assist Smith during daylight and for any failure in the battle that resulted from Hancock's delay. As Historian Gordon Rhea noted, Grant's failure profoundly influenced the outcome of the Petersburg offensive, for there is little doubt that a joint attack by Hancock and Smith during the afternoon or evening of June 15 would have overrun the Dimmock Line and Petersburg as well.[40]

As to the views that Smith unnecessarily delayed the attack during the day or unjustifiably suspended the attack at night, much evidence stands contrary to those criticisms. The time spent prior to the attack was necessary to determine both the place and the method of Smith's attack. His reconnaissance was necessary because of Butler's incorrect information regarding the enemy's works and, as Grant stated in his memoirs, if the works "had been properly manned they could have held out against any force that could have attacked them."[41] General Brooks agreed: "The works of the enemy were very strong earthworks. The attack was therefore made at the very earliest practicable moment."[42] The failure to make similar thorough reconnaissances less than two weeks earlier at Cold Harbor had resulted in the severe Federal losses. Noting this, historian Richard Bache stated, "With the frightful experience of recent attacks on entrenchments without previous thorough reconnaissance of the ground, Smith personally made a careful one as preliminary to advancing."[43]

In making the reconnaissance by himself, Smith was "so sick that I could barely ride my horse, was dragging myself around on the picket line exposed in every possible way that, when I did strike the blow I might make no failure and murder no men."[44] This concern for his men was shown in a later note that stated, "The lives of the soldiers were intrusted to me with the command of them and were not to be wasted uselessly. During the war I had made it a rule never to order soldiers into a fight without knowing what was in front of them."[45] General Hinks praised the innovative plan that resulted from Smith's reconnaissance. He believed that had Smith assaulted at noon with columns of assault, his command would have met disaster. Smith's inventive tactic of assaulting with heavy skirmish lines completely surprised the enemy and won the works with little loss. Even one modern critic admitted, "Smith's skirmish-line tactics succeeded by robbing the defenders of the opportunity to use close quarters ammunition such as canister. As Smith had hoped, this precaution prevented great loss of life."[46] As another noted, Baldy "was not rash; the last thing he wanted was another Cold Harbor."[47] Thus, the strength of the earthworks at Petersburg, the recent results of poor reconnaissances, and Smith's concern for his command mandated his reconnoitering work, which led to his careful and innovative plan that resulted in a noteworthy victory.[48]

Some of the delays that occurred during the day actually found more tolerance from Grant than Smith. The time spent prior to the attack was the subject of a conversation between Brooks and Grant a day or two after the battle. Grant fully appreciated the difficulties and especially the delay caused by the absence of the artillery horses. He derived consolation from the idea that during the war, the enemy also had many such unexpected and unavoidable mishaps. Commenting on these mishaps shortly after the battle, Smith wrote, "If my artillery officer had been hung the day before, and [Butler] had given me an engineer officer, I should have had the bridges before dark."[49]

Smith also squarely faced the critics who advocated continuing his attack after dark. Not only did Smith's own experiences and principles oppose a night attack, but, as he reported, the enemy reinforcements and the unknown terrain prevented his advance. He was not alone in this assessment. Ropes and Livermore both show that Beauregard's view of the two armies underestimated his own force and overestimated Smith's command. Historian A. Wilson Greene also noted that Smith's concerns about Confederate reinforcements were legitimate. Hancock agreed with Baldy that the darkness and terrain prevented a further advance.[50]

Subordinates of Smith also endorsed his cessation of hostilities because of the darkness and ground. Martindale believed continuing the attack at night "would have been unwise. The complications of obstructions on the ground were too numerous."[51] Major Henry Noyes wrote that, after the fighting ceased, "I was unable to discover with accuracy the enemy's line although but a short distance from there. A further movement was arrested by a sudden volley of musketry induced by our near approach. The ground in our front was traversed by deep ditches and was so uncertain as to make a forward movement of our troops at the late hour of the night a doubtful experiment and unadvisable."[52] Colonel Stedman agreed with Noyes' view. Lieutenant G.W. Kelley commented, "Beyond the captured lines, the country was still new to us.... Although the moon was at its full, much of the country beyond us was deeply wooded, and further—moonlight, while furnishing a very pretty ray to hang a criticism upon, is not of much dependence to hang the fate of an army upon."[53] Colonel Duncan reported the difficulty of advancing in the dark. Even General Hinks and Colonel Henry supported Smith's caution. While Hinks endorsed a night attack, he doubted if Smith could have held Petersburg and wondered if temporarily holding the city was worth the risk to the corps. Hinks wrote, "I believe that nothing was lost by Smith's caution."[54] Henry considered that "the want of daylight, unknown topography of the ground, and of the enemy's force, formed sufficient grounds for our delay."[55]

The failure of the Federals to capture Petersburg on June 15 continues to be viewed as a missed great opportunity. The nearly ten months of war that followed elevated its importance as a strategic victory unrealized. Baldy was criticized for not moving swiftly enough against the Confederate defenders and then not taking full advantage of his initial victory. Smith and other observers provide reasonable rebuttals to these critiques. There were several good reasons for his careful preparations for the final attack and the decision to not pursue an attack in the night over unknown terrain. What he may not have realized at the time was the strategic nature of the offensive and the risk that it required. In that regard, his outlook as an independent commander on that day was limited. At the same time, his superiors must bear even greater responsibility, for none of the army commanders or the general-in-chief shared with him and General Hancock the full picture of the battle's true objective and its strategic importance in time for them to plan an effective operation. Even during the day, the lack of engagement by Baldy's superiors was crucial to the outcome. One can reasonably question whether Baldy should have been able to overcome the challenges he faced and both capture and retain Petersburg during the day or evening of June 15. However, had there been full communication with the two corps commanders who were on the field that day, there is no doubt that the Cockade City would have been securely in Federal hands and able to resist Confederate reinforcements that evening.[56]

On the morning of June 16, much to Smith's regret, no order came for him to renew the assault. Instead, Grant, finding the enemy in force, decided to delay the attack until the Ninth Corps arrived. He sent Smith an order at 10:30 a.m. to reconnoiter his front with the objective of ascertaining the best point and manner of advancing that evening at 6:00 p.m., if such an advance were to be ordered. Smith was to make all preliminary preparations for such an advance, and at the same time, to ready his reserve force to support the left in case it was attacked. Hancock would be placed in command of all forces until Meade arrived.[57]

In his reconnaissance, Martindale found the enemy strengthening its position and expressed concern that in an advance, he would again receive the reverse and enfilading fire that Stedman had suffered. The Confederate artillery at Archer's Hill made an attack along the river impractical, and so he would move toward the railroad. He hoped to get some cover on the south side of the railroad. Brooks held the ground he had gained the previous day. Hinks' command was withdrawn to a point near the junction of the Spring Hill and City Point roads on the right. Hinks directed Holman to picket the river from Martindale's right to the gunboats. Duncan's brigade was employed to construct batteries along the crest of the bluff near Walthall's Farm; this eventually enabled the Federals to silence the guns on Archer's Hill.[58]

Meade came on the field about 2:00 p.m. and took command. Smith wrote to him, "I have in the neighborhood of 8,000 men for an attack, in good fighting trim and good spirits, and will be ready to make an attack in my front at any hour which may be indicated by your order."[59] At 4:00 p.m., Meade sent a circular calling for the Second Corps to make an attack at 6:00 p.m. Smith was ordered to support Hancock's attack by taking advantage of any success that resulted and by threatening the enemy and drawing his attention.[60]

At 6:00 p.m., Brooks' and Martindale's divisions moved forward to fulfill Meade's order. Two brigades of the First Division and one brigade of the Third Division made a demonstration in Brooks' front near Friend's House. Martindale advanced to divert the enemy. He moved Stannard's and Stedman's brigades over the same ground they had traversed the previous night. The division again advanced close to the enemy's entrenched lines. The enemy's battery on Archer's Hill reopened on Martindale's command as he advanced, but the Federal guns in the fort at Jordan's Hill soon silenced them. Martindale stayed in this position until the Federal assault ceased. His command then withdrew to its position of the morning. Smith had sent Colonels Henry's and Bell's brigades to assist the Second Corps in their attack, which captured additional Confederate batteries.[61]

During the day of the sixteenth, Dana, Grant, and engineer officers examined the lines the Eighteenth Corps had carried on the previous day. Grant told Smith that he was perfectly satisfied with what he had done under the obstacles he had met. Dana wrote to Stanton:

> The success of Smith last night was of the most important character. He carried these heights, which were defended by works of the most formidable character, and this gives us perfect command of the city and railroad.... The works are of the very strongest kind, more difficult even to taken than was Missionary Ridge at Chattanooga.[62]

Rawlins wrote to his wife:

> The attack of General W.F. Smith on Petersburg last night was very successful, resulting in the capture of the entire left of its main defenses. These defenses were very formidable and

had the enemy succeeded in throwing a sufficient number of troops into the place, we would not have been able to carry these works except by siege. They command the city of Petersburg, which lies in a flat below them.

While the captured lines were important gains, the earthworks did not quite command the city. Evidently, Dana and Rawlins were unfamiliar with the terrain.[63]

Smith also rode along the lines. He went to Hinks' African American soldiers and told them that he was proud of their courage and spirited performance in battle. Smith's pride in his men was exhibited in a general order announced the next day. He expressed "his appreciation of the soldierly qualities which have been displayed during the campaign of the last seventeen days."[64] Smith noted the hardships of the marches in the hot sun, watchful nights in the trenches, and seven battles that they had fought. He cited particularly "the crowning point of honor" of capturing the Confederate earthworks before Petersburg. He called special attention to Hinks' command, which displayed "all the qualities of good soldiers."[65] Baldy shared with Assistant Secretary of War Charles Dana that Hinks' division could not be exceeded as soldiers and that going forward, he would send them into difficult places as readily as his best white troops. Smith similarly expressed his pride to his wife, stating, "God gave me a great victory yesterday and with very small loss and I was very thankful for it."[66]

On June 17, 1864, Meade intended to have the Sixth Corps and Ninth Corps relieve the Eighteenth Corps' lines and send the corps to Butler at Bermuda Hundred. Neill's division of the Sixth Corps relieved Brooks' division, and Hancock returned Henry's and Bell's brigades. Brooks' entire division and the two brigades of the Third Division under Bell moved back to Bermuda Hundred during the night. Meade decided, however, to retain the remainder of the Eighteenth Corps so that it could participate in an attack the next day. With Smith leading Brooks' division, Martindale was left in command of his division and Hinks' command. Meade also placed Neill's division under Martindale.[67]

On the morning of June 18, the three divisions under Martindale advanced to Harrison's Creek. Hinks' newly constructed batteries silenced the Confederate guns on Archer's Hill. The enemy was strongly posted on the opposite bank of the creek at Page's House. Martindale formed his command for the assault. Neill was placed on the left with his left resting on the City Point highway. Martindale's own division was placed on the right extending to the river with Stedman in the first line. Duncan's brigade would advance in supporting distance of Martindale's division.[68]

At noon, the whole Federal line, consisting of Martindale on the right, Hancock in the center, and Burnside on the left, was ordered forward. Martindale's line advanced rapidly and immediately carried the crest at Page's House. This advance required that his line be extended to the right. Duncan was brought to the second line as Stannard joined Stedman on the first line. When Martindale found that the Second Corps did not advance, he directed Neill to advance in echelon to keep up his connection with the forces on his left and right. By this means, a farther advance was gained.[69]

At 3:00 p.m., Martindale received an order from Meade to advance without regard to his connection on his left. Under this order, Neill advanced fifty paces, and Martindale's division advanced two hundred yards. When Martindale advanced beyond the Second Corps, however, his command became exposed to a severe flank fire. Upon the requests of his brigade commanders, Martindale asked Meade to suspend his advance. At 5:00 p.m., Meade permitted Martindale to suspend the attack because the Second

Corps had failed in their attack. The result of Martindale's advance was the capture of seventy-eight prisoners and possession of important points, including the ridge on which Page's House was situated and the peninsula on the north side of Harrison's Creek. From this peninsula, Federal artillery fire could easily reach the railroad bridges crossing the Appomattox in the center of Petersburg.[70]

Martindale's command held its position until the morning of June 20, when the remainder of the Eighteenth Corps was relieved and sent to Bermuda Hundred. At Bermuda Hundred, the corps was reorganized. The Third Division was reassigned to the Tenth Corps and became the Second Division, Tenth Corps, under the command of General Turner. Hinks' division became the Third Division of the Eighteenth Corps. There were also some command changes. General Brooks became the commander of the Tenth Corps; General Stannard replaced Brooks as First Division commander.[71]

On June 21, the Eighteenth Corps returned to the lines they had previously occupied in front of Petersburg. Martindale's division spent the time in late June and in July strengthening the lines and advancing them gradually. Hinks' division did picket and fatigue duty in late June. In July, the division continued its duty in the trenches and on picket on the Appomattox River. Stannard's division also busily engaged in remodeling and rebuilding its lines. Covered ways, connecting the front with the rear, and earthworks were constructed. A strong abatis was also constructed along his whole front.[72]

The First Division was the only one of Smith's divisions that saw noteworthy action after the corps' return to the trenches. At daylight on the twenty-fourth, the enemy's batteries opened with unusual severity on both Stannard's front and right flank. After more than a half hour of this heavy artillery fire, Brigadier General Johnson Hagood's brigade attacked Stannard's lines. Stannard quietly withdrew his pickets. Stannard's division's fire along the line was reserved until the enemy had come up to the point previously occupied by the pickets. A rapid fire was then opened along Stannard's whole line. The enemy found themselves entrapped. They were unable to hold the abandoned skirmish line, to carry Stannard's works, or to retreat, except with the certainty of being cut to pieces. A large number of them dropped their arms and surrendered—sixty-one to Henry's brigade and 134 to Colonel Edgar M. Cullen's brigade. A portion of the enemy endeavored to escape to their lines but were shot down in the attempt. In all, their loss was estimated at four hundred.[73] Stannard's total loss was sixty-eight.[74]

A day earlier, Butler temporarily assigned Turner's division to Smith's command. Turner arrived early on the morning of the twenty-fourth. His command relieved a division of the Ninth Corps and occupied the lines connecting Martindale's left and the Ninth Corps' right. Turner's position was in front of Hare's House. During the day Smith decided to send Turner's division to capture the enemy's advanced position on a hill in Turner's front. Smith ordered Turner to make necessary preparations and commence the attack at 7:30 p.m. Later in the afternoon, Smith told Turner that he should not make the attack until Smith had seen Grant, but Turner misunderstood Smith and suspended his preparations. When Smith arrived on the ground, he found that it would be too dark for his artillery to be effective in clearing the enemy rifle pits and that Turner had in position only 2,800 of the 3,500 men intended for the attack. Smith also determined that his forces in the lines would be too weakened by sending out the assaulting column. Facing these developments, he decided to postpone the offensive. The next day, Captain Farquhar, the corps chief engineer, examined the enemy's line in Turner's front and found it so well covered that Smith had Turner's assault postponed indefinitely.[75]

During the night of June 29, 1864, Bell's brigade dislodged the enemy's pickets in a wood some one hundred yards in front of Turner's left and secured a position that enabled forty sharpshooters to enfilade part of the enemy's line. On the thirtieth, Smith sent Turner instructions to try again to carry the enemy's position in his front. Barton's brigade was selected as the principal assaulting column. Barton would be supported on the right by Curtis and on the left by Bell. The attack was planned for 5:00 p.m.[76]

The success of the assault depended on surprise. Unfortunately, Barton frustrated the surprise by forming his lines in full view of the enemy. This error drew sharp fire that temporarily stopped the formation of his troops. To divert the enemy from Barton, Turner immediately ordered Bell to commence his attack, but Barton still had not moved by 5:20 p.m. The Confederates, alerted by Bell's attack, reinforced the position that Smith desired to be taken. Seeing that all chance of surprise was gone, Turner acted upon the discretion left to him by Smith and suspended the attack. Later in the evening, Turner reported to Smith his extreme regret for the failure of the movement. Turner relieved Barton of his command for his carelessness in revealing the whole movement to the enemy and his inexcusable failure to form his line at the specified time.[77]

In late June, General Barnard, the chief engineer of the Army of the Potomac, visited Smith to talk over the situation. Smith's and Burnside's corps lay in the trenches accomplishing nothing; in fact, they were losing men every day to heat and enemy sharpshooters. Smith told Barnard that on June 15 he had broken a continuous line. The enemy had reformed their lines in Smith's front by connecting the untaken portions of their old lines with a new line. Smith suggested that where the new line joined a portion of the old one was probably a place for an assault. The two generals rode over the lines to this point. The point was defended by low rifle pits at the bottom of an open slope. Only a few soldiers could occupy the pits. The Federal artillery and infantry fire commanded the slope. Smith looked over the ground and told Barnard that he would agree to take the pits and deploy his force on the slope, provided Grant would make the main assault with the Army of the Potomac. While Smith's suggestion was not put into action, Barnard did forward Smith's advice. In a memorandum dated July 2, Barnard suggested that they "assault the salient of the enemy's position near where our front line intersects the old line of works." He continued, "We are now close up to the plateau, or ridge, over which the Jerusalem road enters Petersburg. If we can gain that plateau, I do not believe Petersburg can be held any longer."[78]

The breakthrough of the Dimmock Line at Petersburg showed the capabilities Smith had exhibited more dramatically at Brown's Ferry. Yet Smith's distrust of Butler and his recent experience at Cold Harbor limited his eagerness to snatch Petersburg, the long-sought prize. Nonetheless, Grant praised Baldy for his efforts and was soon to consider him for even higher command. But, Smith's character as an engineer of victory was consumed by his criticism of defeat. Such criticism would lead to Smith's removal rather than promotion.

CHAPTER XIV

The Critic of Defeat Is Removed

After the battles at Petersburg, professional and personal differences between Smith and Butler increased. Their main policy conflict occurred over the Army's use of African American soldiers. Smith had no ideological stake in proving that Black men would make good soldiers—he judged his Black soldiers by the same standards as other new soldiers. When they performed well, he was the first to praise them. When he found them deficient in drill and discipline, Smith reported it. As he told one reporter, "There is material in the Negroes to make the best troops in the world if they are properly trained."[1] Always concerned about his men, Smith realized that untrained soldiers could not be relied on in battle; it endangered the new soldier to be put into action before he was fully trained. Butler misunderstood Smith's opposition to using Black troops by attributing it to a prejudice against African Americans. Butler's long dedication to the idea that Black soldiers were equal to their white counterparts aggravated his hostility to Smith's determination to hold the Blacks to the standards that he held the other soldiers.[2]

On June 23, in reaction to a report by his chief of artillery, Smith requested that Butler send Captain Francis C. Choate's Black battery to Bermuda Hundred for more training or have its members replaced by better trained artillerists and transfer the present members to the infantry. Three days later, the situation of the Black troops became more critical. Suffering from illness and an unhealed wound, General Hinks, their division commander, requested to be relieved of command and have another general officer discharge his duties. On the same day, Smith wrote Rawlins that Hinks' relief would leave the division without a proper officer to command it. Hinks' second in command was unfit for duty and was presently under arrest for insubordination.[3]

In this note, Baldy also expressed his views on the Third Division's condition. Hinks' division numbered 5,000 men. Four regiments, totaling about 2,200 men, still had not been drilled in loading their muskets. Therefore, Hinks reported them unfit for service in the field. Smith recommended that these men be sent to a camp of instruction so they could later be relied on to resist enemy attacks on the Federal lines. This would leave Hinks with 2,800 men. Smith understood that Brigadier General Edward Ferrero, commanding a Black division in the Ninth Corps, had about 4,000 men. Smith suggested that the two divisions be consolidated under the command of Ferrero and assigned either to the Ninth or Eighteenth Corps as Grant might judge best. Smith also repeated his suggestions about Choate's battery to Rawlins.[4]

Later that day, Butler challenged most of Smith's views on Hinks' division. In a letter to Rawlins, Butler dismissed Smith's chief of artillery's report on Choate's battery. He

also discounted Smith's charges against Hinks' untrained regiments. While acknowl-
edging Hinks' fine service, he did not consider the Third Division commander's relief as
a cause for dispersing the Black soldiers. Butler did not object, however, to Smith's suggestion to have all the Black troops consolidated under Ferrero's command.[5]

On June 28, Smith sent another letter to Rawlins. Smith argued that his assessment
was based not only on Captain Samuel S. Elder's report, but also upon General Hinks'
and Captain Choate's reports and upon his own observation. He enclosed reports by
Hinks and Choate to support his suggestions. Hinks reported that Choate's battery
proved "inefficient and unserviceable" and that Choate had applied for replacements
for his incompetent gunners.[6] Hinks reported that his three dismounted cavalry regiments were unskilled in the use of muskets and entirely unfit for operations in the field
because they lacked training. Two infantry regiments that had been recently recruited,
the Tenth and Thirty-Seventh, had little opportunity for drill and were far from effective. In contrast, the conduct of the Fourth, Fifth, Sixth, and Twenty-Second Regiments
of Duncan's brigade and the First Regiment of Holman's brigade in the battles of Petersburg gave conclusive evidence that "colored men, when properly officered and drilled,
will not only make soldiers, but the best of soldiers of the line."[7] Hinks warned, however,
that the success of the project of using Black soldiers was imperiled "by assuming that
the Negro was a soldier ready made, rather than that he would make a soldier by patient,
persistent, and intelligent drill and instruction."[8]

Choate reported on the dismal situation he faced. The enlisted men were former
plantation slaves, and, with one exception, unable to read or write. It had been found
impossible to teach the gunners how to point a piece with even tolerable correctness or
to obtain a man who could cut fuses or fit them correctly. In the shelling that was done,
it had been necessary for an officer to point and elevate each piece and to superintend
the cutting and fitting of the fuses.[9]

With the relief of Hinks on July 1, the situation became more critical. Smith wrote
to Grant on July 5 asking if he had been shown Smith's letters to Rawlins. Smith urged
Grant to take some steps to make the division as effective as possible. The Black men
were capable of being excellent soldiers, but they needed effective officers. Baldy also
wrote to Weitzel asking whether his reports to Butler had been forwarded to Grant.[10]

On July 9, Butler wrote to Smith that he had not forwarded Smith's suggestions
"from a belief that the interest of the service required a little delay." Butler had found in
conferring with Grant that one of Smith's suggestions had been adopted. Choate's battery had been withdrawn and sent to a camp of instruction. Butler admitted that Smith's
ideas were "valuable" and permitted him to send them directly to Grant.[11]

Smith's and Butler's professional differences were aggravated by personal conflicts. Both generals were proud men and were quick to find fault with the other. This led
to strained relations. Even minor issues, such as the manner of the Eighteenth Corps'
march to the Petersburg trenches, led to major eruptions between the two generals. At
7:30 p.m. on June 20, Butler sent Smith an order to ready his corps to cross the Appomattox River at daylight the next day. That evening, Smith sent notice to his three division
commanders to ready their commands. He also gave the commanders marching orders.
They could not all cross the single bridge over the river at once, so Smith directed Stannard to start at 4:00 a.m., Hinks at 5:30 a.m., and Martindale at 7:30 a.m. Staggering the
marching orders would prevent confusion and save the men from the fatigue that came
from standing about heavily loaded with knapsacks. All three divisions would arrive at

Petersburg long before dark, which was the earliest they could take their places in the entrenchments.[12]

The next morning, the divisions moved as Smith ordered. About 9:00 a.m., Martindale's division happened to be passing Butler's headquarters. Butler believed Martindale's division's presence at this time meant the division commander was guilty of a "very gross dereliction of duty in not moving when ordered."[13] Accordingly, he wrote Smith a note. While noting Smith's merit and ability and his respect for him, Butler complained that Smith's column "which was ordered to move at daylight in the cool of the morning is now just passing my headquarters in the heat of the day for a ten-mile march."[14] Butler then stated "the great fault of all our movements is dilatoriness and if this is the fault of your division commanders let them be very severely reproved therefore."[15] He justified this sanction: "I have found it necessary to relieve one general for this among other causes, where it took place in a movement of vital importance and in justice to him you will hardly expect me to pass in silence a like fault where of less moment."[16]

As there had been no order that the column should move at daybreak, and as the corps was moving as he had ordered it, Smith felt that Butler was actually criticizing him. At 3:40 p.m., Smith sternly replied to Butler's complaints. While giving due respect to Butler's rank and experience, Smith wrote that a reprimand could only come from the sentence of a court martial. He observed that his experience in marching troops was superior to Butler's. He then refuted Butler's charge of slowness: "Your accusation of dilatoriness on my part this morning or at any other time since I have been under your orders is not founded on fact, and your threat of relieving me does not frighten me in the least."[17]

Smith wrote to his wife that day, "Butler has written an insulting letter today & you can imagine the style in which I answered it."[18] He expected to be relieved and be home with her in a few days. Smith exclaimed, "What a lying beast Butler is."[19] Smith later admitted that the irritation exhibited in his reply was excessive, but he completely distrusted Butler. Butler had just relieved Gillmore from command of the Tenth Corps, which Smith thought unjust. Doubting Butler's honesty and integrity, Smith saw Butler's complimentary phrases as hypocritical and so even these phrases angered Baldy. He considered Butler's letter a direct threat. He yielded to his wrath and sent a letter that was admittedly not in accordance with military discipline.[20]

At 5:30 p.m. and 5:45 p.m. respectively, Butler wrote two apologetic and unofficial notes to Smith. Butler told Smith that his first note contained neither an accusation nor a threat. He claimed that he never believed that Smith could be frightened. Butler only suggested that if some of his division commanders were at fault, they should be corrected. He claimed that he never thought that the slowness of the movement was Smith's fault. Despite the apologies, Smith felt that he could be of no real service under Butler. He sent Rawlins copies of Butler's letter and his reply with a request to be relieved from duty in Butler's department.[21]

Smith's request for relief was not honored. Instead, on June 29, Grant and Butler conferred with him in an attempt to solve any differences between Smith and Butler. Butler was very friendly, and Smith admitted they gave him everything he had requested. Nevertheless, Smith believed this reconciliation was of no use. Smith wrote his to wife, "I can stand as much as most men but I cannot live under this man [Butler] much longer and so I am going home on a sick leave for I really am not fit to stay here in this hot sun."[22] Despite his illness, Smith was probably willing to stay if he felt he could perform some service. But he did not think this was possible under Butler. Accordingly, the next day Smith wrote to Rawlins. He enclosed a certificate from the medical director of the corps and asked for a leave of absence of twenty days. He explained how the exposure to the hot sun prevented him from doing his work. He requested that someone be placed in command who could stay in the saddle during the day. Privately, Baldy had also become concerned about the health of his wife and wanted to be with her at their summer home in Goshen, Vermont.[23]

Smith also wrote a confidential note to Rawlins. Baldy told Rawlins he had seen Grant drink excessively the previous day at Smith's headquarters. For some time, Rawlins, as Grant's chief of staff and close friend, had been trying to rid the lieutenant general of his drinking problem. He thanked Baldy for the "friendly forethought and the interest you manifested in his behalf. Yet 'tis only what one knowing your friendship for him might have expected. Being thus advised of the slippery ground he is on, I shall not fail to use my utmost endeavors to stay him from falling." Rawlins mentioned that he would forward Smith's request for leave to Grant, but Rawlins knew that Grant "will be loath to part with you from the field, even for a few days."[24]

Grant was fully aware of the professional and personal problems between Smith and Butler. He had told Dana that in the quarrel between the two generals, Butler was in the wrong. On July 1, 1864, Grant wrote to Halleck requesting his evaluation of the problem. Grant had no personal difficulty with Butler, who always understood and promptly obeyed his instructions, but Butler lacked the knowledge to execute his orders properly. There was also a prejudice against him that limited his usefulness. Grant feared that it would become necessary to separate him and Smith. The lieutenant general believed that Smith was "one of the most efficient officers in service, readiest in expedients, and most skillful in the management of troops in action."[25] He did not want to remove Smith from his present position unless the Eighteenth Corps commander was promoted to a higher command. However, Grant recognized that if Butler remained, Smith might have to be relieved, and he suggested Butler's transfer to a department command that did not require field service. He would feel better if Smith, Franklin, or Joseph J. Reynolds commanded the right wing of the army. Nonetheless, Grant was unwilling to recommend Butler's retirement.[26]

During the next day, Smith received Grant's reply to his request for leave. Grant stated that unless it was absolutely necessary, he preferred that Smith would not go. He told Smith it was not necessary to expose himself to the hot sun, and if it should become necessary, Grant could temporarily attach Humphreys to Smith's command. Dana also wrote to Smith that he must not leave because Dana had prospects for Smith that were very flattering and needed to be discussed. Smith wrote to Rawlins that with the reorganization to be done in his command, he would stay and hope for a change in the weather.[27]

Later in the day (July 1), Smith wrote a long letter to Grant explaining his position. Smith stated that his troubles with his head had driven him three times from the Southern climate and that he was unable to visit his lines during the day. Thus, he felt his duty as corps commander was not properly fulfilled. Moreover, Smith believed the differences between Butler and himself made it necessary to replace Smith with someone who was not hostile to Butler. Since a replacement would assist Butler better, Smith felt there was no sufficient reason for him to remain and risk permanent disability.[28]

Smith had felt in late May that Butler had too many troops and so he had gladly joined the Army of the Potomac "with the most hearty goodwill and intentions."[29] While there, Smith felt Meade had snubbed him and made false charges against him. Smith returned to the department, thinking Grant's presence would prevent Butler's blunders. Butler's letters to Smith made him feel that someone else would be of far more service than he. Smith offered to use his request for relief on account of ill health as the means to remove himself as an obstacle to harmony in the army and as a cause for the lack of success in the campaign.[30]

Smith turned finally to advising Grant on Butler's department. He asked how Grant could entrust two corps to Butler, whom he described "as helpless as a child on the field of battle and as visionary as an opium eater in council," when Grant had men like Franklin and Wright available to replace Butler.[31] He urged Grant to let his good sense, and not his heart, decide the question.[32]

Dana visited Smith the next day. Dana told him that Grant had written to the secretary of war and recommended that Butler be relieved, and Smith put in command of the right wing of the army. Dana insisted that Smith continue in command at all hazards and not go on leave. Dana said Grant was relieving Butler because he could not be trusted with the command of troops in the movements about to be made. Grant told Dana that next to Sherman, he had more confidence in Smith's ability than in any other general in the field.[33]

During the day, Halleck replied to Grant's July 1 letter. Halleck wrote, "It was foreseen from the first that you would eventually find it necessary to relieve General B. on account of his total unfitness to command in the field and his generally quarrelsome character."[34] Halleck suggested that Butler be left in local command of his department and Grant make a new corps of Smith's command. This would leave Butler under Grant's immediate control and relieve Butler of his field command.[35]

Partially using Halleck's suggestion, Grant wrote to Halleck on July 6. He asked Halleck to obtain an order assigning the troops serving in the field in Butler's department to Smith's command and ordering Butler, commanding the department, to his headquarters at Fort Monroe. Grant also told Smith that he intended to give him the command of the troops in the field belonging to the department. In effect, Smith would be given command of the Army of the James while Butler was left as an administrative figurehead. The next day, in General Order Number 225, the president directed that the troops of the Department of North Carolina and Virginia serving with the Army of the Potomac in the field under Smith would constitute the Eighteenth Corps, and Smith would command this corps. Butler would command the remainder of the department troops, having his headquarters at Fort Monroe.[36]

On July 8, Rawlins wrote Smith that he had permission to go home, for there would be no movements for a week or ten days. Rawlins told Smith to inform Butler of the leave. Baldy was torn between staying and receiving what he expected would be a new command and going on leave. When he received "alarming reports" about Mrs. Smith's health, he became "desperately anxious" and decided to use the leave. The next night, Smith told Butler that he was going on a ten-day leave of absence that Grant had given him. He had turned over the command to Martindale.[37]

Early during the evening of July 9, Grant and Butler had a confidential conference, and Grant treated him with the utmost cordiality.[38] Despite Grant's friendliness, Grant never told Butler about Order Number 225, and it did not come up in the conversation. Butler found out about the order shortly after this meeting.[39]

That same night, Smith and General Franklin, who was visiting his army friends at City Point for a few days, went to Brigadier General Rufus Ingalls' quarters. There, the three generals talked and drank. Not long afterwards, Grant came in and, after greeting everyone, had a couple of drinks. Smith was surprised and exasperated by Grant's drinking. As the evening progressed, Grant and Smith became engaged in an acrimonious talk on Cold Harbor.[40]

On the morning of July 10, immediately after breakfast, Butler went to Grant to inquire about Order 225.[41] He had received a copy of it from a friend in the War Department. Butler showed the order to Grant and told him he did not understand it. According to Butler, Grant replied, "Oh—I did not mean you should have seen that order. It is a mistake. I suppressed all the copies that were transmitted through me…. I don't want this at all. I want Smith to report to you—you to have the full command. I was going to add the 19th Corps to your department, and I shall when it comes here from Washington."[42]

Butler then gave Grant his view of his differences with Smith and urged Grant to remove Smith from command of the Eighteenth Corps. Butler told Grant that Smith's refusal to obey orders to push on to Petersburg during the night of June 15 was enough cause for his removal. Butler admitted that Baldy was brave enough when left to his separate command, but he claimed that Smith wasted his time making reconnaissances when he was ordered to make assaults. Butler also claimed that Smith was obstinate and insubordinate. Smith was never satisfied in accepting suggestions that he did not recommend. According to Butler's account, Grant assured Butler that he would remedy the problem.[43]

While Butler was talking to Grant, Smith came to Grant's headquarters. Smith went to Rawlins and told him that Grant had been drinking at Ingalls' the previous night. Rawlins expressed distress and promised to continue his efforts to stop Grant's drinking. Smith added that he had given up a life-long friendship, presumably with McClellan, because he saw him as no longer able to bring victory and would not support anyone in the future who could not win the war. He realized later that this impolitic comment was uncalled for and may have cooled Rawlins' feelings for him. After Butler left, Smith visited Grant. Baldy elaborated on the blunders of the recent campaign and its terrible waste of life. He believed a deficiency of Meade's generalship caused those blunders. Among other instances, Smith referred to the fearful slaughter at Cold Harbor on June 3. Smith pointed to Meade's order to the corps commanders to attack along the line without reference to any other corps as "unprofessional in the highest degree and a murderous one when the lives of the soldiers and the 'cause' were put in jeopardy."[44] Grant went into the discussion defending Meade stoutly, but finally acknowledged "that he [Grant] had said nothing about it because it could do no good."[45] Nothing was said about Smith's right to criticize Meade, and Smith never suspected that Grant was offended.[46]

Actually, Smith's comments about Meade and the overland campaign outraged the lieutenant general. After Smith left, Grant told Comstock that he never came so near to relieving a man as he did Smith on account of what Baldy said to him. Grant believed that Smith's condemnation of Meade's generalship and the Virginia campaign was simply an indirect attack on him and his generalship.[47]

In the afternoon at 1:30 p.m., Grant wrote Halleck that he was suspending the order respecting Smith and Butler. In his note of July 6, Grant had requested an order that would relieve Butler of the department's field duty and give it to Smith. Order Number 225 failed to accomplish this end. It created the Eighteenth Corps as an independent command and gave the corps to Smith. This created a third army in the field at a time when Grant wanted to consolidate his forces. The order also left Butler with considerable field duty because the Tenth Corps was still in his command.[48] For the present, Grant decided to leave Smith in command of the Eighteenth Corps and, if there was no objection to a brigadier general holding the position, Brooks in command of the Tenth Corps. Both corps would be left in the department as before. He also wished to have the Nineteenth Corps added to the department and General Franklin assigned to field duty under Butler.[49]

The introduction of Franklin into the Army of the James may have been Grant's last attempt to retain both Butler and Smith. Grant's request for Franklin to presumably resume command of the Nineteenth Corps under Butler would have made Franklin senior corps commander and a possible buffer between Butler and Baldy. Considering Franklin's close relationship with Smith, he was the best possible choice for such a role. But, since Butler intended to retain field command over all three corps in his department, much of Smith's criticism would probably go unaddressed. The administration's swift response through General Halleck on July 12, indicating that Franklin would not be restored to field service with the Nineteenth Corps, made this idea moot. In fact, the president was determined to keep Franklin from any field service. With the conflict between Butler and Smith still unresolved, Grant took the next few days to arrive at a solution. Grant finally resolved the conflict by leaving Butler as the field commander of the department and by issuing orders on July 18 relieving Smith as the commander of the Eighteenth Corps. Much controversy still surrounds Grant's resolution of this conflict.[50]

Grant may have seen in Order Number 225 a reluctance on the part of the administration to give Grant the power to relieve Butler of field duty. Despite the clarity of Grant's July 6 letter, the order only partially fulfilled his request and created another undesirable independent command. Grant probably knew that Butler's appointment had been a political necessity and realized that the same political forces that got him appointed must have wanted him to remain. Butler had had many influential Republican backers. Party leaders had sounded him out about the possibility of being Lincoln's running mate. He had strong supporters in the Senate and a considerable popular following. With the presidential election less than four months away, the administration was probably quite sensitive to Butler's position. Comstock wrote, "It was practically decided in Washington that Butler should not be removed from his department, and Gen. Grant had accepted the decision."[51]

While the attitude of the administration probably determined Grant's decision, the lieutenant general also looked kindly on Butler. Grant attempted to keep Butler by requesting Franklin's appointment as a corps commander in the Army of the James and using Franklin's skill to compensate for Butler's lack of military training. Moreover, Grant never advocated Butler's retirement and had repeated in his letter to Halleck on July 1 that Butler had always been prompt in obeying Grant's orders and clear in his understanding of them. Grant acknowledged Butler's inability to execute his orders but figured that his presence in Butler's department could prevent any mistakes resulting from the department commander's inexperience.[52]

Other explanations for Grant retaining Butler in command have been advanced.

Smith had received reports that Butler threatened Grant with the disclosure of his drinking problem if he did not revoke the order. It was also reported that Butler exploited rumors that he was to be nominated by the Democrats as a way of pressuring Grant into revoking the order. These reports certainly were circulating at the time. Dana believed that Butler "cowed" Grant into revoking the order. But all of these reports fail to explain Grant's decisions. Grant's drinking problem was so well known that publicizing it would probably have had little effect on his position. It was also unlikely that Butler made any threat against the administration. He already had promised to support Lincoln. The reports about Butler's nomination from the Chicago convention were inaccurate, and Butler realized that the Peace Democrats hated him more than Lincoln. If he ever entertained the belief that he could win the nomination, he must have realized that his influence was based on his support for the administration and would have evaporated as soon as he sought the nomination.[53]

The other side of the question was why Grant decided to relieve Smith from command of the Eighteenth Corps. In his letter to Halleck on July 1, Grant stated that if Butler remained, Smith would have to be relieved. In addition, Grant's conferences with Butler and Smith, and Smith's letters to Grant, showed that Smith and Butler could no longer work together in the department. But Smith's criticisms, which had in part created the conflict between Butler and Smith, had also escalated in reference to Meade and the Virginia campaign. Comstock's entry in his diary on July 17 revealed how Smith alienated Grant. For some time, Smith had criticized the campaign "in his ex cathedra way" as a succession of useless slaughters. Grant had heard about this and told Comstock that he was unable to decide between relieving Smith or talking to him. Subsequently, Baldy carried the works at Petersburg, and this pleased Grant. After this, Smith constantly talked against Meade and pushed for Franklin to replace him. During the night before he left on leave, Smith insisted that Grant remove Meade and asked in the most offensive way if Grant expected to defeat Lee with Meade in command. Smith also declared he would not serve with Butler, and this helped to force Grant's hand.[54]

Though Grant had been willing to tolerate Smith's earlier views on Butler's generalship and the superiority of either the North Carolina or James River campaign strategies over the overland campaign, he would not allow himself or his generalship to be questioned. Grant had come to believe that Smith's severe condemnations of Meade and the tactics used in Virginia were actually directed at him. Wilson believed that Meade and Butler helped instill and escalate this belief in Grant. Smith's conference with Grant on July 10 exhausted Grant's tolerance. Grant also came to realize, as Smith mentioned in his July 2 letter, that Butler's department would function far better with corps commanders who got along with Butler, and that disharmony in the command undermined the success of the campaign. After thinking over the situation, Grant published Order Number 61 on July 18 relieving Smith from duty and placing Martindale in temporary command of the Eighteenth Corps.[55]

While on leave, Baldy had gotten some indication of these developments. On July 10, he had gone by sea to New York, thinking the ocean air would benefit his head troubles. He hurried to his wife's side to find her very ill but improving. Dr. George Suckley, the Eighteenth Corps medical director and a devoted friend, visited the Smiths. The doctor told the general that there were some intriguing happenings going on at headquarters with reference to Smith, and that Butler and some high officers in the Army of the Potomac were involved.[56]

On July 19, Smith returned from his leave of absence, and Grant sent for him. Grant told Smith that he "could not relieve General Butler," and that as Smith had so severely criticized Meade, Grant determined to relieve Baldy of command of the Eighteenth Corps and order him to New York City to await orders.[57] In their discussion that day and in one the following morning, Grant narrated Smith's long-time opposition to the Virginia campaign and its generals. In the discussion, Grant cited two of Smith's letters to two of Grant's friends written before the campaign began. These letters urged Grant's friends to discourage Grant from making the overland campaign. Smith told Grant that the letters were sent to his friends for his consideration and were motivated only by a sincere desire to serve him and the country. Grant insisted that Smith had been condemning the campaign and its generals since March, and Baldy's criticism had become endemic and indiscreet. Grant also cited a letter that he had recently received from Old Point that mentioned Smith's criticisms of Meade. The charge was accurate, for Smith had told Colonel Shaffer, Butler's chief of staff, that Meade was responsible for the blunders of the campaign and should be relieved. Smith realized later that Shaffer had repeatedly asked Smith about Meade to elicit just that response. Grant also charged Smith with being responsible for a *New York Tribune* article on June 27 that blamed Hancock for the failure to capture Petersburg because he refused to cooperate with Smith. This charge was unjustified. While Smith knew William Kent, the correspondent who wrote the article, Smith never stated that Hancock failed to cooperate with him. Smith wrote to Hancock on July 8 expressing his deep regret for the article and assuring him that he never made such an accusation. Finally, Grant got to the main cause for Smith's relief. Grant told Smith that he had come to the conclusion that Smith "had intended to whip him over Meade's shoulders," and that he thought Cold Harbor "was a very good battle anyhow."[58] Smith could only deny this charge, but Grant had made up his mind. The lieutenant general closed the meeting, exclaiming to Baldy, "You talk too much."[59]

Despite this conference, Smith still did not realize that Grant was directly responsible for his relief. In a letter to Wilson, Baldy insisted that the criticisms he expressed to Grant had not caused his removal. He believed that Butler and Meade had misrepresented his views to Grant. They had changed Smith's criticism of their generalship into a condemnation of Grant. Smith pointed to this deception as the reason for Grant suspending Order Number 225 and relieving him. Wilson agreed that those whom Smith criticized (Butler and Meade) "were doubtless ingenious enough to make it appear that his shafts were aimed at the chief commander."[60] Smith also wrote to Senator Solomon Foot of Vermont, on July 30, alleging that Butler had used his political influence and his knowledge of Grant's drunkenness to force Grant into removing Smith.[61]

Grant and Rawlins also stressed the conflict between Smith and Meade and Butler as the cause for Baldy's removal. On the day of Smith's relief, Grant told Wilson, "No man in the army, not Genl. Smith himself regrets this matter more than I do, for no man appreciates the General's great abilities better than I do—or is more anxious to use them in this war, but he is at outs with too many men—and some whom I can't overthrow."[62] Grant explained that these men included Meade, Butler, and Burnside. Grant had "thought of putting [Smith] in command at Washington over everything in that direction but I have already recommended Franklin."[63] After the war, Grant wrote to Smith that Baldy was not relieved for participating in any anti-Grant cabal, but because of his inability to serve under Butler. Rawlins seconded Grant's statements and believed the removal was justified. Although Rawlins knew Smith was an honest, able, and good friend to Grant, he felt Smith's criticism was actuated by disappointment and selfish ambition. He wrote to his wife that Smith was relieved "because of his spirit of criticism of all military movements and men, and his failure to get along with anyone he is placed under, and his disposition to scatter the seeds of discontent throughout the army."[64]

Others also cited the conflict between Butler and Smith as the reason for Butler remaining and Smith leaving. Meade attributed Smith's relief to Butler's remaining in command. Meade, in a letter to his wife, denied that he ever had any quarrel with Smith. Colonel Theodore Lyman, of Meade's staff, wrote, "Woe to those who stand up to him [Butler] in the way of diplomacy! Let the history of 'Baldy' Smith be a warning to all."[65] Lyman had heard from camp rumors that Smith, relying on his reputation with Grant, had ideas of "shelving Butler" and "giving Meade a tilt overboard."[66] The general impression was that Order Number 225 would put Butler away. But Butler had a long conference with Grant, which Lyman believed led to Butler's reinstatement and Smith's relief. Lyman recounted, "Thus did Smith the Bald try the Macchiavelli [sic] against Butler the crossed-eyed, and got floored at the first round!"[67] William Russell, a staff officer in the Eighteenth Corps, wrote to Smith that it was generally believed that he had been relieved "on account of difficulty" with Butler.[68] The New York Tribune supported the belief that Smith's relief came from his impatience at being subordinate to Butler, whom the paper referred to as a "distinguished volunteer officer."[69]

While Smith's differences with Butler and Meade may have provided enough justification for Grant's decision, the main reason for Smith's removal was that Grant became convinced that Smith's attacks were directed at him. Comstock described to Wilson how furious Grant was with Smith over their July 10 conference and how it led to Smith's removal. General Humphreys also correctly understood that Smith's relief was a result of a conflict between Grant and Smith. Provost Marshal Marsena Patrick wrote in his journal, on July 22, that Grant was disgusted by Smith's intrigues against Butler. After Cold Harbor, Smith "has quarreled with Meade & everyone else ending in an attempt to thrash Grant over Meade's shoulders for which Grant shut him up."[70] Patrick accused Smith of plotting against Grant, which Patrick felt caused Smith's relief.[71]

Perhaps, the most correct assessment of Smith's retirement was given in a Rochester Democrat article that was reprinted by the New York Times on August 3. The universal impression, said the Democrat, was that Grant had the highest opinion of "the natural ability and professional acquirements of Gen. Smith, and that their relations partook of the utmost intimacy and mutual confidence and trust." The correspondent, claiming to know Smith very well, denied charges that his removal came from Smith's "spirit of fault-finding" and selfish attempts to secure higher command. Smith did believe that Meade and Butler needed to be removed in order to bring the campaign to a victorious conclusion. But this belief arose only from a "conscientious conviction."[72]

The writer also admitted that Smith did have troubles with Generals Butler and Meade. His troubles with the former were seen as official in character, those with the latter as personal in nature. The correspondent insisted that Smith's differences arose from an "ardent zeal for the good of his country and the thorough overthrow of the military power of the rebellion." The correspondent conceded, "That zeal may have led him into indiscretions but if he did commit them, they should be judged by his motive. The natural independence of thought and expression of Gen. Smith—a virtue which becomes often a fault when exercised within the necessary restraints of military life, no doubt had also something to do with bringing on his official difficulties." The newspaper concluded that Grant's determination to remove Smith indicated that the former corps commander would be lost for future operations and would unlikely be given another command.[73]

While Grant was responsible for relieving Smith, Baldy's critical nature led to his erstwhile friend's action. Dana pointed this out to Smith:

> I regret more even than you do perhaps, that you are consigned to inaction. But yet I think you are somewhat responsible for it yourself, and it seems to me a pretty grave responsibility…. I won't scold about what is after all a constitutional peculiarity; but you will at least let me tell you of it in all friendship and frankness. If instead of running athwart the idiosyncrasies of those in controlling places, you had held your tongue and flung away your pen, I am sure your friends would have not cherished you with any warmer affection, but all your power of usefulness would have been in constant action and the country would have been immensely the gainer.[74]

Dana told Wilson that Smith's relief "was very much his own fault, and that if he had no tongue, and had never known how to write, I had no doubt he would now be commanding one of the large armies."[75]

Smith expressed mixed feelings about his relief. He was glad to get away from the army controversies and the hostilities of Butler and Meade. On the night of July 19, General Martindale visited him. Martindale assured his former corps commander that he would make everything right in two hours if Smith would consent to serve under Butler as before. Baldy replied that no commission was worth such a price. However, he did regret the manner in which he was relieved. He had offered to be relieved from the department on account of his ill health. Instead, Grant humiliated him by having him return to Virginia only to be removed from command because of his critique of the campaign. Smith thought that his duty to Grant as his friend and chief required him to give Grant an honest assessment of the war. Smith believed that besides Rawlins, he was Grant's most faithful supporter. Consequently, Baldy felt betrayed that his outspokenness had resulted in his relief.[76]

Smith also regretted leaving his men, who were sources of love, loyalty, and confidence. On July 20, he published his farewell address to his corps. "Since I have been your commander," he said, "I have tried to share with you your dangers and have rejoiced with you in your gallant deeds. During this time your record has been bright and unsullied."[77] Smith stated that any shortcomings in the campaign could not be blamed on either the corps or its commander. He concluded, "May God Bless and always crown your efforts with victory."[78]

Some were pleased about Smith's departure. Butler's reaction was understandable. He wrote to his wife, "Smith has gone home on sick leave, not to come back again for the present at least. Sick or well, I have made a mistake in him, he is dishonest, intriguing, and selfish to the last degree."[79] Butler blamed Smith and Halleck for originating Order Number 225. Butler correctly foresaw that Smith "will not be employed by Grant again during the campaign."[80] Sylvanus Cadwallader of the *New York Herald* also believed Smith's opposition to his superiors made his retention "incompatible with the interests of the service."[81] He charged Smith with "a restless ambition that was continually overleaping itself."[82]

However, most expressed genuine sadness about Smith's departure. His men expressed this regret. As one recalled, "He was a brave and accomplished general, distinguished for his strategic grasp, military foresight, and fearless spirit. He was the embodiment of soldierly qualities, and the idol of his troops."[83] Wilson wrote to Smith, "I have talked with officers of every grade, and have heard nothing but regret expressed that you should have been taken away."[84] General Franklin congratulated Smith for getting away from Butler but was sad that Smith was not given a new command. General McClellan wrote to Franklin that he had heard that Smith was relieved and without a command. He stated, "I do not comprehend this sudden change of plans and the retention of such a man as Butler in place of Smith—it does not augur at all well for success when such a choice is made. Can it be that Grant thinks Butler to be capable of high command—or is some miserable political intrigue at the bottom of it?"[85] Assistant War Secretary Dana told Wilson that he deeply regretted that Smith was not permitted to serve, both on his account and that of the country which "now so much needs the assistance of clear heads and willing arms—but all he can do now is wait and study; his turn will come."[86] John Brady of the *New York Herald* wrote that Smith's relief was a "severe blow to the troops of this command, who almost adore the General."[87] On July 23, the *New York Times* and *Philadelphia Daily Evening Bulletin* also expressed sadness about Smith's relief. Both wrote, "The country will certainly feel that in Gen. Smith it loses the services of one of the ablest soldiers of the army. It is to be hoped that a new field for his distinguished talent will speedily be found."[88]

Baldy eagerly awaited a field command in another theater of operations. He had been extremely successful at Chattanooga and had worked well with General Sherman. Dana wrote Wilson about the possibility of Smith serving under Sherman. But Dana soon realized that Smith would not regain a field command until Grant changed his view of Smith's critical nature. Unbeknownst to Smith, Grant had determined not to reinstate him to a field command. Smith's last war duties would be of a far different kind.[89]

CHAPTER XV

The Conclusion of Smith's Army Service

Smith's critique of the war in the East had convinced General Grant that Baldy's service in the field would have to end. Baldy sincerely desired to return to field command, but the problems in the East restricted his possible area for service to the West. But even there, Grant would ultimately prevent Smith's field service. Smith's wartime army service concluded, not on the battlefield, but in the fight for justice in addressing the corruption found in the Department of the Gulf.[1]

By August 1, 1864, Smith had returned home to his wife at College Point on Long Island to await orders. In January 1865, Brigadier General James Harrison Wilson, Baldy's former student and close friend, wrote to Smith expressing regret that Baldy had not been given a command. He still insisted that Grant was not responsible for Smith's relief. Wilson believed that Butler and Meade provoked Grant, by "improper means," into relieving Baldy. Nevertheless, it was Smith's difficulties with those two that also led to his removal. Wilson thought these difficulties were illustrated by Smith's admission that Sherman and Franklin were the only two generals under whom he could serve without showing disgust and contempt. Wilson determined that "insubordination rather than neglect of duty or failure in any enterprise was the cause ostensibly of your removal—at the time it took place."[2]

Wilson also told Baldy about a discussion between Sherman and Grant that had occurred the previous October. Sherman asked for Smith's services, but Grant suggested that he request someone else. Sherman stressed his desire for Smith but indicated that he would accept an alternative. Wilson had talked with Sherman and Thomas in January, and both expressed their admiration for Smith. Sherman in particular was unreserved in his remarks about Smith's "talents and fertility of resource as a military man."[3] If a command suitable to Baldy's rank and skill became available, Sherman would be willing to give it to Smith.[4]

Wilson urged Smith to say nothing against Grant and avoid bringing the controversy surrounding his removal as Eighteenth Corps commander before the politicians. Wilson told his friend to bide his time. He assured Baldy that Stanton would ultimately obtain substantial justice for him. Wilson still hoped that Smith would join him in one more campaign before the war ended. In late February 1865, Wilson wrote another encouraging letter to Smith. Noting Butler's removal, Wilson felt Smith would soon be restored to a command equal to his rank and capacity. But Smith came to realize that Grant, and not Butler, was responsible for his failure to return to the field.[5]

Grant's feelings became clear when Major General Edward R.S. Canby, commander of the Military Division of West Mississippi, requested Smith's services on February 13, 1865. Canby had asked Smith if he would become a corps commander in his army. Smith had known Canby for years and had a high regard for his character; he therefore considered the offer a great compliment. Smith immediately accepted the assignment but told Canby that he did not think Grant would approve the application. Canby expressed hope for success and wrote to Halleck requesting Smith. Canby wanted Smith because he believed that the War Department and Grant had confidence in him. Canby believed that Smith could control the general conduct of the campaign and carry out the plan of operations in case of his absence. Unfortunately, Smith proved correct in his assessment of Grant. Grant wrote to Halleck, "It will not do for Canby to risk Smith with any military command whatever. The moment Canby should differ with him in judgment as to what is to be done, and he would be obliged to differ or yield to him entirely, he would get no further service out of him, but on the contrary, he would be a clog."[6] Respecting Grant's opinion in this case, Halleck wrote to Canby that Grant refused his request on the grounds that "Baldy would either command you or thwart all your operations."[7] Thus, Grant's hostility to Smith kept him from any field command for the remainder of the war.[8]

In November 1864—after Smith had been relieved of command and before Canby approached him—Smith had received a new assignment. On November 23, by direction of President Lincoln, Smith was appointed a special commissioner to inspect and report upon the condition of affairs in the Military Division of West Mississippi. This investigation would include the review of the condition and supplies of the troops, the operations of the staff departments, and all matters connected with contraband trade. Lincoln authorized Smith to take depositions of any citizen in the investigation. Smith was also permitted to request from any officer such reports or statements as he might deem necessary. An aide-de-camp and an officer of the Judge Advocate's Department would accompany and assist Smith. The judge advocate officer, under Smith's direction, would summon the witnesses, administer the oaths, and take down testimony. Smith would periodically report to the adjutant general of the army, recommending the removal, dismissal, or trial of officers found to be unworthy of their positions. In each case, Smith was to provide the reasons for the recommendation and the testimony upon which it was based.[9]

The president formally assigned Smith to this commission on December 10, 1864. Smith would serve with another special commissioner, Henry Stanberry. The assignment did not significantly differ from the earlier one except that the two commissioners would also report to the secretary of war "upon matters as they may deem of importance to the public interests."[10]

During December 1864, Smith collected his staff for the trip to New Orleans. Lieutenant Colonel Nicolas Bowen, Smith's longtime adjutant general, was appointed the judge advocate of the commission. On account of an accident to the steamer *Guiding Star*, Smith's departure was delayed until December 21. Arriving in New Orleans on January 2, 1865, he started at once to establish his quarters and offices with the aid of General Canby. Smith presided alone on the commission for three months. Stanberry had declined the appointment as special commissioner on January 13. In his place, Lincoln appointed James T. Brady of New York on March 14. Brady was a distinguished trial lawyer and influential War Democrat. Brady joined Smith in New Orleans on April 8.[11]

Smith started taking testimony on January 26. The investigations were conducted in a desultory manner. When a particular issue was found, it was fully investigated before the next subject was touched. There was significant difficulty in discovering the practices of the various departments since most of the witnesses were unwilling and often implicated in corrupt transactions. Despite the difficulties, Smith made periodic reports to the adjutant general, informing him of his progress in revealing guilty public officials and military officers. Smith discovered that the Military Division had the "greatest want of system and conformity to the acts of Congress and orders of the government." Moreover, "many of the officials had been engaged during all their term of office in gross misconduct."[12]

On April 12, Brady joined Smith in making one of the commission's most important reports to the secretary of war. The commissioners put Smith's earlier correspondence in narrative form and presented significant evidence to show that Major General Stephen A. Hurlbut, commander of the Department of the Gulf, and his provost marshal general, Colonel Harai Robinson, had used their offices for "oppression, speculation and plunder." By their example, this corruption "pervaded the department generally."[13]

Soon after starting his duties as commissioner, Smith had discovered, through reliable information, that Robinson had in several instances accepted money for procuring trade permits. In February, Smith examined the bank president, cashier, and clerk of the National Bank of New Orleans where Robinson deposited his money. This inquiry showed that Robinson had attempted to hide his funds under the name of the clerk. Robinson was then examined. He made statements Smith knew were false, and Smith had Canby place him under arrest for perjury and taking bribes.[14]

Smith also obtained reliable testimony from J.S. Clark, of Clark & Fulton, a respectable commercial house in New Orleans, and from Charles A. Weed, of Weed & Company of New Orleans, that each firm had paid Robinson $10,000 for special trade permits. William Courtenay, an agent of the Star line of steamers, had also given Robinson a bribe of $1,000.[15]

Robinson tried to cover up this bribe by writing a letter to Hurlbut dated January 2, 1865, stating his outrage at Courtenay's offer of the bribe and mentioning that the bribe was retained only for moral motives. This letter was written on paper with a printed heading in which blanks were left for the month and day, and the year was printed. It was proven clearly that no paper thus imprinted reached Robinson's office until February 16. This letter helped prove Hurlbut's involvement in Robinson's transactions.[16]

Hurlbut was called to testify on this bribe and the other illegal payments. Hurlbut testified that he received Robinson's letter on March 14 and did not know how he received it. But W.W. Rowley, an acquaintance of Hurlbut, testified that he delivered the letter to him at 3:00 p.m. on March 13. This led the commissioners to charge Hurlbut with an official falsehood: endorsing the letter as being received on March 14 whereas it was received on the thirteenth. Hurlbut was also charged with a similar falsehood when he denied all knowledge of how the letter reached him.[17]

On March 19, the revelation of this cover-up led Robinson to volunteer to testify on the practices in the department. His testimony, collaborated by other sources, led the commissioners to charge Hurlbut with complicity with Robinson in receiving bribes or gratuities from Clark & Fulton and C.A. Weed. Robinson also aided Smith in proving Hurlbut's further guilt. Robinson went to Hurlbut to get a letter that sanctioned the reception of the payments from Clark & Fulton and C.A. Weed. On April 2, Robinson visited Hurlbut and told him that they would be cleared if he got a letter of instructions from Hurlbut dated back to the proper time covering the whole business. Robinson also agreed to take the entire burden of receiving the payments if Hurlbut returned his share. Hurlbut agreed to write the letter but told Robinson it would take a couple of days to get the money. Robinson then reported this agreement to Smith. Smith tested Robinson's information by allowing him to return to Hurlbut. On April 4, Robinson visited Hurlbut to get the money and the letter. Hurlbut produced most of the money. He also wrote the letter and antedated it to November 19, 1864. Hurlbut made a mistake in this cover-up by starting the date with an "A." Not having the foresight to obliterate the mistake or take a fresh sheet, Hurlbut wrote an "N" directly over the "A" in the abbreviation of "Nov." Immediately after this, Robinson took the money and this letter to Smith. Consequently, the commission charged Hurlbut with writing the letter on April 4, 1865, and antedating it to November 19, 1864, in order to create false testimony in his favor regarding the taking of bribes.[18]

Further testimony led to additional charges of corruption against Hurlbut. Hurlbut granted permits for trade to his brother-in-law, L.L. Crandell. Although the department commander found that Crandell had received $5,000 for one of these permits, he neither reproved him nor took any cognizance of the act as illegal or unjust. Hurlbut was charged with granting a permit so that Crandell could receive the bribe. Hurlbut also faced perjury charges for denying knowledge of the bribe to Crandell and for denying that he antedated the letter to Robinson. The department commander was also charged with conniving with his provost marshal general to prevent the detection of offenses that Robinson had perpetrated. Finally, Hurlbut was charged with "willfully interfering to obstruct and hinder this commission in the discharge of its duties, so as to prevent the discovery of fraud and injustice practiced in this Department by officers in the service or employment of the Government."[19]

Considering these charges, Smith and Brady wrote to Canby requesting that Hurlbut be arrested and confined. They also requested that Hurlbut's General Order Number 35, which restricted the commission's powers and denied the commission's authority prior to Brady's arrival, be revoked. Canby endorsed the commission's charges by requesting a court to consider the allegations as soon as possible. On April 19, Canby published a general order stating that the commission's power was based on the highest authority and any restrictions or denial of its authority by Hurlbut was revoked.[20]

On April 13, the commissioners also wrote to Stanton urging Hurlbut's arrest and confinement. They felt that "in visiting General Hurlbut with the treatment he seems so well to deserve, they strike at once the root of the corrupt system which has wrought so much mischief with this department."[21] The commissioners' recommendations were initially sustained by their superiors. Grant wrote to Stanton that he agreed with Canby that Hurlbut be brought to trial. Judge Advocate General Joseph Holt, in a Military Bureau report on May 22, concurred with the opinion of the special commission that "Maj. Gen. S.A. Hurlbut has been guilty of heinous crimes and should be forthwith brought to trial."[22]

The corruption that the commission found in the Department of the Gulf did not begin under Hurlbut. The commission found illegal activity dating back to Butler's tenure. Evidence showed that Butler forced someone to sell a steamer to him. Butler then overcharged the government $300 per day for the steamer's use and later made a $17,000 profit by selling the ship. Testimony also showed that the Department commander approved of his brother, Colonel Andrew J. Butler, trading with the enemy.[23] Major

General N.P. Banks replaced Butler but only increased the illegal trade activities. Federal rules and regulations that directed all captured property to be turned over to the area's Treasury agents were ignored and openly violated. Cotton taken from Texas and the Teche River expeditions was not given to the Treasury Department. Instead, Banks' assistant quartermaster, Captain Jacob Mahler, sold the cotton to New Orleans merchants. Under orders from the department commander, Colonel Samuel B. Holabird, Banks' quartermaster, also violated Federal law by taking the cotton captured at Port Hudson and selling it to fund Black Louisiana regiments. Holabird also approved the sale of cotton to Colonel G.W. Guess of Texas, a Confederate officer. Holabird not only traded with Confederates but also cheated the loyal governor of Louisiana, James Madison Wells. Wells testified that Holabird overcharged him for transportation, charged him for duties not done, and held back refunds for undisclosed fees. Holabird forced Wells to sell his cotton under the market price. Wells lost $150,000 due to this sale. Holabird also made Wells pay excessive fees amounting to over $50,000.[24]

The Department of the Gulf commanders and their staffs were not alone in the corruption. Major General Francis J. Herron's administration in Texas ignored the laws and regulations in respect to captured and abandoned property. Brigadier General Mason Brayman, in charge at Natchez, J.F. Richardson, assistant special Treasury agent, and J.H. Stevens, local agent, were engaged "in outrageous violations of the Treasury Regulations in the matters of allowing supplies to go out and cotton to come in." Brayman sent parties outside the lines to capture cotton; Richardson would then go beyond the lines to meet with the owners of the captured cotton to negotiate the price that he would pay for the seized property. Richardson and Stevens used the steamer *Winona* to facilitate this trade. Brayman was also guilty of taking cotton from at least one loyal owner. The commissioners concluded that Brayman conducted his administration with a reckless disregard of the law, and his trade with the enemy made him unfit for his office.[25]

Other officers in the area were guilty of corruption. The custom house agents in New Orleans refused to approve legitimate requests for permits until either a third party in league with the agents was paid a certain percentage of the invoice or the custom officials were given gifts. In one case, the present amounted to $1,000. Taking a percentage of the invoices, accepting bribes and gifts, and allowing the fraudulent trade in cotton were regular occurrences in the custom house. In another case, the local government officials shut down the stores in Vicksburg and extorted money for their reopening. The testimony before the commission showed all the officers in charge were cognizant or connected with "these nefarious transactions."[26]

The commission's investigations also showed corruption in the establishment of Lincoln's Ten-Percent Plan in Louisiana. According to this plan, a civilian state government would be established in Louisiana as soon as ten percent of those who voted in 1860 took an oath of future loyalty. Banks registered many ineligible voters and manipulated both the state election and elected convention. The commission termed the attempt to carry out the reorganization of Louisiana "a complete failure."[27] It also showed great waste in the new government. Two members of the convention alone charged over $6,000 of cigars and brandy to the state treasury. The printing bill for the convention was $150,000. This government "blocked true democracy and return to loyal government."[28]

Political corruption was more than matched by the pervasive illegal commercial activities in the region. The commissioners concluded that the government program of regulating trade within districts to prevent the Confederates from receiving contraband was thwarted by the misconduct of several officials: "Grand schemes for trading in cotton had been arranged in New Orleans with a view to make foreign capital useful in furnishing pecuniary aid to the Rebels."[29]

Despite the overwhelming evidence collected by the Smith-Brady commission showing widespread corruption in the Military Division of West Mississippi, little was done to correct the situation or punish the guilty officials and military officers. The commissioners recommended that Hurlbut and Robinson be tried. They also recommended that Banks' assistant quartermaster, Captain Mahler, be tried for defrauding the government in a purchase of coal, for perjury, and for tampering with witnesses. Despite these well-founded requests, Hurlbut was honorably mustered out without any trial in June 1865.[30]

On August 4, the frustrated commissioners wrote to Judge Advocate General Holt, who was responsible for determining who would be tried for these alleged crimes. They suggested that if Hurlbut escaped prosecution, Robinson should not be tried or called as a witness. They also urged that Clark & Fulton be released from their bonds if they would not be used as government witnesses.[31]

Five days later, the commissioners' frustration must have turned to exasperation. Holt wrote that Hurlbut would not be tried. He stated that he would not prosecute Robinson either, since Robinson volunteered to describe the corrupt practices in the department. Holt then proposed that Robinson give the government all the money he and Hurlbut had received as bribes or compensation from Clark, Weed, Courtenay, and others. After these funds were collected, Robinson would be dishonorably discharged from the service without a trial. Before this was done, however, Holt requested Smith's opinions.[32]

Smith had agreed with an earlier position held by Holt to treat Robinson better than Hurlbut if he testified against the department commander. Smith believed it was far more likely that Hurlbut corrupted Robinson than the reverse case scenario. "As corruption can only be done away with by striking at the foundation head when the impurity is there," Smith felt "the conviction of a Major General of far more importance to the government than that of a colonel." Smith and Brady joined together to reply to Holt's proposal. The commissioners felt Robinson should be released and discharged because Hurlbut was allowed to escape. It would be unjust to dishonorably discharge Robinson when Hurlbut was honorably discharged. The commissioners stated, "In our judgment, each of them is at least equally guilty and no reason appears to us why the government should treat them differently in reference to their official positions."[33]

The commissioners also objected to making Robinson pay for all the funds received as bribes. The whole amount corruptly received was $23,000. Hurlbut received $14,000 of this amount. He gave $8,000 of this to Robinson who delivered it to Smith. Smith turned it over to the War Department. This meant Robinson would have to pay $9,000 and Hurlbut $6,000. Smith seized Robinson's bank account in New Orleans of $7,702.25 of gold valued at $2.25 per greenback dollar. This had been retained under Canby's orders. If the gold value was considered, Robinson's account would cover his obligation and leave a balance in his favor.[34]

The commission's final report was delayed until September 23, 1865. The delay, in part, was a result of a serious accident to Smith's knee that confined him to his room for over a month. Smith and Brady still pressed for Hurlbut's trial and were shocked to hear of Mahler's acquittal, "a result for which they are wholly unable to account because in the judgment of the commission the documentary evidence very plainly established his guilt."[35]

The commissioners' work was further undermined by Canby. In October, he wrote to the adjutant general that some of the officers scheduled to be tried had already resigned and he thought it was "too late to investigate the conduct of the other officers implicated with any benefit to the government."[36] On November 11, Stanton approved Canby's views.[37]

The commission's work raised serious questions about the reconstruction government in Louisiana. On April 23, 1866, the House of Representatives requested that President Andrew Johnson turn over the report to Congress. Stanton convinced Johnson to refuse this request since "its publication would not in my opinion be consistent with the public interest." Thus, the Johnson administration essentially nullified the thorough and revealing work of Smith and Brady.[38]

While the special commissioners were completing their final report, Smith was given additional duty. In March 1865, Congress had passed a resolution directing Stanton to inspect the quartermaster department and compare the reports of the officers in charge of the quartermaster's depots in several cities with the articles on hand. On June 16, the adjutant general assigned Smith to preside over a commission to investigate the depot at Cincinnati. Between June 20 and August 16, the commissioners took inventories of all property on hand. They found clothing and camp and garrison equipment in nineteen warehouses located in different parts of the city. The result of the inspection showed that, for most articles, the numbers recorded in the inventories of property on hand were greater than the report of the officers. The excesses and deficiencies were noted in the commissioners' report. Their report also noted the quality of the supplies, stating, "Inspection of clothing manufactured at the Depot, and comparison with standard samples, showed in most instances a compliance with the requirements made." The commissioners concluded with "no opinion either favorable or unfavorable, in regard to the results of their investigation, or in regard to the manner in which the officers stationed at the post have performed their duties." The Adjutant General received their report on November 8, 1865.[39]

Having completed the duties of both commissions, feeling there was no further need of his services as major general of volunteers after the war was over, and unwilling to wait to be mustered out, Smith tendered his resignation as major general of volunteers on November 4, 1865. This left him as major of engineers in the regular army. On November 1 and 6, he accepted the regular army brevets of lieutenant colonel for White Oak Swamp, colonel for Antietam, and brigadier general for the battles around Chattanooga. He later accepted the regular army rank of brevet major general for his services in the field during the war.[40]

Meanwhile, Smith's injured knee had still not healed. On December 6, from his home in New York, Smith wrote to the Adjutant General enclosing a medical certificate and requesting approval of the doctor's recommendations. Dr. John F. Hammond recommended a six-week leave of absence and transfer from New York, where the cold weather had had an ill effect on the injury, to the coast of Florida, where a milder climate prevailed, so that Smith's injured knee would properly recover. On December 30, 1865, the leave was approved.[41] But, Smith's desire to visit Florida was not based strictly on medical reasons. Baldy had a new career opportunity awaiting him there.

Months earlier, three men, including a former Smith aide-de-camp, had visited Smith. They proposed to create a company for laying a telegraph cable from Florida to the Spanish colony of Cuba and offered Smith the presidency. When Smith's good friend, Alexander Hamilton, a grandson of the treasury secretary of the same name, offered his name and influence to the undertaking, Smith accepted the position. The company was incorporated and called the International Ocean Telegraph Company.[42]

Smith's first duty as company president was to get the exclusive privilege to run the cable from Florida. He had served in Florida before the war and had many friends there. During January 1866, Smith visited Florida and attended the meeting of the legislature. A pleasant month spent in Tallahassee secured a binding, seventeen-year franchise from the legislature for a cable between Cuba and Florida. The next step was to get the same privilege from Congress. This was a tougher job because the Western Union Telegraph Company opposed Smith's company and the obvious competition it posed. With the help of Congressman Elihu Washburne of Illinois, an exclusive seventeen-year franchise for the cable was finally granted by Congress.[43]

Smith applied to the adjutant general on January 16 for a six-month leave starting on February 1 and for permission to leave the United States and visit Europe. The next day, the secretary of war approved Smith's requests. Smith made arrangements to travel to Spain to get the final exclusive franchise for connecting the United States with Cuba. Smith was treated kindly by Secretary of State William Seward, who provided letters of reference to the American minister in Madrid extolling Smith's virtues as a citizen and his services as a soldier.[44]

After some delay, Smith left for England on the *Fulton* in April 1866. He was accompanied by his wife on their first overseas outing together. Their passage across the Atlantic took two weeks. While in England, they visited Exeter and London; they then travelled to Paris, southern France, and over the Basque Pyrenees into Spain. Smith delivered his letters from Seward to the United States minister in Madrid.[45]

The secretary of the legation, Horatio Perry was very friendly to Smith. Perry arranged for Smith to meet with the prime minister, General Leopoldo O'Donnell. A colonel of the staff was ordered to report to Smith every morning to ascertain if he wanted to visit any garrisons and have the troops turned out for drill. Smith was also to have every military courtesy extended to him throughout the kingdom. Colonel Prendergast, the staff officer, spoke English perfectly and was most attentive to Smith during his entire visit. Smith was always pleased to see the Spanish infantry drill since the men "seemed so light and active and moved as though they had springs in their heels."[46]

Smith also visited the home of former prime minister General Ramon Narvaez in Madrid. The Smiths were invited to Sunday receptions at the home of the mother of Empress Eugenie but declined to attend "not having yet shaken off the Puritan Sunday habits of our own country." Smith also decided not to attend the bull fights during his visit since he "had no fancy for such cruel exhibitions."[47]

With Perry's help, Smith's petition for the exclusive right of laying a telegraph cable between Cuba and the United States was presented to the minister for the Colonies, Canovas del Castillo. The government moved slowly in its review of Smith's petition. This delay forced Smith to write the adjutant general to ask for a two-and-a-half month extension so that he could conclude his business. Smith wrote, "As I am here negotiating with reference to telegraphic communications with Europe via the West India Islands and Brazil I trust the National importance of the business will aid in obtaining for me the required extension."[48] The secretary of war approved Smith's request on June 13.[49]

After waiting two months for some action, Smith decided to leave the matter in the charge of the secretary of the legation and return home. A few days before his planned departure, Smith watched the engineer troops at Aranjuez construct a bridge across the Tagus in his honor. The following day, the Smiths attended a private reception given by the queen. Shortly thereafter, the Smiths left for the United States and arrived in New York on the Fourth of July.[50]

On October 24, 1866, Smith applied for an additional leave of six months and permission to return to Europe. On November 12, the adjutant general replied that Grant had disapproved any additional leave. On November 24, Smith tendered his resignation as major of engineers in the regular army. He decided to leave the army because he could not expect advancement or recognition in the smaller reorganized army under Grant. Baldy believed that Grant's actions in blocking his promotion under Canby showed that Grant had lost little of his animosity toward him. His resignation was accepted on March 21, 1867.[51]

Smith spent his last years of military service in the familiar role of criticizing military misdeeds. The Smith and Brady Commission discovered widespread corruption and much military involvement in the illicit wartime cotton trade. Once again, Smith's old nemesis, Secretary Stanton, saw that these findings were not revealed nor were the guilty parties prosecuted. Thus, this last episode ended like many of Baldy's other conflicts, with Smith's efforts being frustrated. Undoubtedly this helped to convince Smith that other pursuits would be more fruitful. His recently initiated overseas efforts as a telegraph company president would continue and become his first civilian endeavor.

Chapter XVI

Smith's Postwar Civilian Life

Now as a civilian, Smith continued as president of the International Ocean Telegraph Company. He wrote to Admiral David Dixon Porter on November 5, 1867, inquiring about Porter's view of laying a telegraph wire to the Dry Tortugas. Porter replied, "In time of war the Tortugas would be almost useless without a telegraph line, and it would cost so little to run one there from Key West that I only wondered why it had not been done before." While Porter encouraged Smith's telegraph work in the United States, Baldy's work to gain Spanish sanction for the telegraph connection between Florida and Cuba had not yet met with success. When a revolution toppled the monarchy of Queen Isabella in September 1868, Smith decided to visit Spain again and make a second attempt. He presented the renewed petition to the acting regent, Marshal Serrano, and this time he was successful. Spain granted the company a forty-year exclusive franchise.[1]

Armed with its three franchises, the company had no difficulty in raising the money for the cable. The company then contracted for the cables from Cuba to Key West and from Key West to the mainland of Florida at Puerto Rasa. Since the Western Union Telegraph Company would not extend their land line to Puerto Rasa, the company was obliged to construct one, and finally the system was opened for business.[2]

The company also sent an agent to the West India islands and British Guiana and obtained promises of annual subsidies. These subsidies would be paid as soon as the telegraph line was extended to those areas. Possessing these pledges, Smith travelled to England and organized a company to lay cables from British Guiana to Cuba and from Cuba through Jamaica to Panama. This company bound itself to exclusive business relations with the International Ocean Telegraph Company.[3]

The International Ocean Telegraph Company came under severe pressure from Western Union and the Cable Telegraph Company. After a struggle of some years, Smith returned to England to find a purchaser for the company's line and franchises, which were paying well. Smith "hated falling into the clutches of these companies and determined to sell out the control to Englishmen."[4] Nonetheless, Edward Sanford, who served both as a vice president of the Western Union Company and as a member of the board of the directors of the International Ocean Telegraph Company, advised Western Union to buy Smith's company. In April 1873, International Ocean Telegraph sold its controlling interest, $125 a share for the preferred shares and $100 per share for the common shares, to Western Union. This ended Smith's interest in telegraph matters, and he was glad to be relieved of the business. As long as he was engaged in getting franchises or making contracts for laying cables, he was interested, but the full work of administration bored him.[5]

After getting out of the telegraph business, Smith decided to go on a European trip for a rest. The Smiths traveled first to Antwerp and then to Brussels, where the American minister to Belgium gave them a dinner. In Hamburg, they saw Emperor William. The emperor was fond of children and one day stopped and chatted with Smith's five-year-old daughter Clara Farrar. From Germany, the Smiths travelled to Austria, Italy, France, and finally to England, where they stayed with friends, including United States Minister to Great Britain, General Robert Schenck. The Smiths were blessed in England with the birth of Stuart Farrar, who was to be their only surviving son.[6]

Smith's presidency in the telegraph company and his trips to Europe led to his interest in foreign affairs. In May 1870, he wrote to General Wilson, "I am very sorry that Grant is beaten on the Santo Domingo business for it would have helped us if that Island had come under our flag. A good many men in Congress think there is a big steal in it which is most undoubtedly true." Smith's interest in gaining Caribbean franchises for his company undoubtedly led him to support Grant's attempt to annex Santo Domingo.[7]

Smith's involvement in the Caribbean continued after he left the telegraph business. Since 1868, Cuba had been suffering from a civil war between Cuban rebels and the Spanish colonial government. In 1877, a junta of rich and influential citizens from Cuba, who had been authorized by the rebel leaders to negotiate with Spain for peace, approached Smith in an attempt to end the fighting. Smith agreed to serve as their agent to treat with Spain for peace. Smith was empowered to offer $100,000,000 in bonds for the sale of Cuba to the Cubans. There was a strong chance that these bonds would be endorsed by the United States.[8]

Smith's main task was to gain Spanish approval for the sale of Cuba. He wrote to Louis Philippe, Comte de Paris, on October 28, 1877, seeking his advice and support. He

had known the count as a member of General McClellan's staff during the Peninsula Campaign. The count was the Orleanist claimant to the French throne and related both by blood and marriage to King Alfonso XII of Spain and his intended wife.[9]

At the outset of the letter, Smith wrote that he lacked official sanction from Washington and had never belonged to the Republican party. Nonetheless, Smith had known Secretary of State William Evarts for several years. Through many social and political friends that the two men had in common, Smith had been assured that his views about Cuba were "expressing the opinions of the Gov't."[10]

Smith told the count that the United States' interest in Cuba was based on a strong desire to see slavery abolished. The secretary of state reported that the United States had no desire to annex Cuba. Based on

William F. Smith after the Civil War (G.H. Houghton, Civil War Photograph Album, Vermont Historical Society).

Evart's position, Baldy then proposed his plan for peace. The administration would ask Congress, at the request of Madrid, to authorize the American endorsement of $100,000,000 in Cuban government bonds payable to the Spanish king to buy out his title to the island. The United States would require the right to intervene with force whenever Cuban independence was threatened by a foreign power. The United States would also insure protection of the loyal population in Cuba. The Cuban leadership had agreed to suspend its attempts to gain Congressional support until Smith's efforts for peace had concluded.[11]

Smith had involved himself in this matter to stop the waste of life and treasure. He hoped to serve the young king by gaining this settlement for him. Smith also had many acquaintances in Havana and for their sake hoped for a peaceful resolution of the conflict. He thought the entire crisis could be settled by April 1878.[12]

Shortly after writing this letter, Smith decided to return to Europe to seek support for his plan. Before traveling to Madrid, he visited Paris and sought the advice of the Comte de Paris. Louis Philippe said, "I do not think you will succeed, but I will give you a letter to my uncle the Duke de Montpensier, and he will be able to give you good advice on the subject." Smith wrote to the duke, enclosing the count's letter and asking his advice. The duke advised Smith to make no mention of his plan because it would not be favorably received by the Spanish government. The duke also invited Smith to visit him. Smith thanked him for the advice but declined the invitation.[13]

During Smith's visit to Madrid, the American minister, without consulting Smith, arranged for an interview with the Spanish king. Smith's correspondence with the Duke de Montpensier, and information derived from other sources, revealed that Marshal Arsenio Martinez-Campos, captain general of Cuba, had promised the king a pacified Cuba as a wedding present. With the wedding imminent, Smith's visit in January 1878 was particularly ill-timed. Smith, therefore, never broached the subject in his conversation with the monarch. Subsequently, Martinez-Campos ended hostilities in Cuba by the Peace of El Zanjón, which gave Cuba a degree of self-government.[14]

The inability of Spain to sustain genuine reform in Cuba brought the revolution that ultimately ended Spanish rule in Cuba. Smith believed that had Martinez-Campos' pledges been kept, or had Smith's proposition been made and accepted, Spain, Cuba, and the United States would have been saved from a costly war. He believed that the declaration of war against Spain was "uncalled for."[15]

He was also critical of the American policy in the Philippines. After the Filipinos had assisted the Americans in defeating the Spanish, Smith believed that the United States was obligated to treat them as allies and protect their liberties. Instead, President William McKinley decided to colonize the Philippines. The American determination to subjugate the islands led to an unsuccessful three-year Filipino revolution for independence. If the United States had treated the Filipinos justly, "we might at this day have a friendly people under our protection which would keep us with zeal, the Eastern door open to our convenience." Smith wondered, "Can it be that greed among our countrymen and the political ambition of individuals have stifled our old love for liberty and our old worship of justice? If so, we shall, before many years act so as to bring a combination of great powers against us, not to defend liberty or justice but to protect themselves from an arrogant, warlike, and rapacious horde."[16]

The Smiths' European tour, which began after Baldy's retirement from the telegraph business, came to an end during the winter of 1874-1875. Owing to some bad investments, Smith was forced to return to America and seek new employment. When Smith arrived in New York, the mayor sent for him and asked him to take the position of police commissioner. Mayor William H. Wickham hoped that Smith would accept the position so that he could also be elected president of the board of police commissioners. Some of Smith's New York friends, including Alexander Hamilton and John Jacob Astor, urged him to accept the appointment as a duty to his adopted city. Smith finally agreed and was appointed on May 1, 1875, to serve for a six-year term.[17]

With Governor Samuel Tilden's approval, Wickham replaced the other three members of the board. With the support of the replacements, Smith was elected president of the board on December 31. This board of four police commissioners governed the city police force subject only to guidelines provided by the state legislature. All rules, regulations, appointments, and promotions were made through and by the board. They were also in charge of street cleaning and the Bureau of Elections, which at election time employed over 2,000 people as inspectors of elections and poll clerks. As president, Smith presided over the board, held a position on the Health Board, and was paid $8,000 annually for his service. Each of the other board members was paid $6,000 annually and was assigned one of the board's duties. Tammany Democrat Sidney P. Nichols directed the street cleaning bureau, Republican DeWitt Wheeler had charge of the board treasury, and Joel Erhardt served as chairman of the Committee on Rules, which formed the executive of the police force.[18]

Smith believed the board would have done a good job except for an inherent defect in the personnel of the police force. He observed, "Dishonesty permeated the force." The police, from inspectors to the lowest policeman, were corrupt. Captains would send their detectives to assess and collect a monthly tax on all businesses that were chronic violators of state or municipal laws in their precincts. If the blackmail were not paid promptly, the place would be raided. Another corrupt practice of the detectives accounted for much of their work. Each police officer had a "nest of thieves" that he protected. He would on occasion warn them of an imminent raid or aid his thieves when they required evidence to help them circumvent conviction. For this protection, these criminals would inform their police protector about crime in the precinct unless they or their allies perpetrated it. Smith believed that the policemen in general had no esprit de corps and found little or no risk in taking bribes.[19]

Smith reasoned that one way to reduce such corruption was to raise the standards of admission to the police force, but this was not done. Instead, the four commissioners equally divided the appointments among themselves. Each applicant was called before the full board and examined. Applicants were rarely rejected. Considering that many of these applicants were nominated by ward politicians, who were eager to see their henchmen on the force, it was not surprising that the new policeman was "ready for his share of plunder as soon as he pinned on his shield." Blocked by the existing patronage system, Smith had control only over his appointments. He hunted about for soldiers with good discharge papers and found many to appoint. Baldy never heard of any of these appointees being charged with corrupt practices. He divided as fairly as possible the remainder of his appointments on the police force, as well as his share of the patronage in the street cleaning bureau, between the Tammany and anti-Tammany factions of the Democratic party. Unfortunately, some of these appointments turned out to follow the endemic pattern of corruption in the force. In one case, Smith promoted a policeman to sergeant because his work showed courage and honesty. Shortly afterwards, this sergeant was caught participating in a blackmailing affair. Disgusted by this crime, Smith sent for the sergeant and told him that he would be dismissed, whereupon the blackmailer offered Baldy a bribe. Smith then became convinced that many of the force were so enmeshed in corruption that they had "no idea that there was such a word as honesty in the language."[20]

Smith participated in one reform in police organization that became part of the police manual in 1875. The four inspectors and several captains in the police force had no set duties or responsibilities and merely waited at police headquarters until some work turned up. The board divided the city into four districts and made each inspector responsible for one of the districts. The captains were prohibited from coming to headquarters unless they needed to discuss important matters with the commissioners or the superintendent. The results were beneficial. With greater responsibility, the inspectors markedly increased the closing of illicit businesses.[21]

In 1878, Smith found himself pulled into the growing conflict between the anti-Tammany Democrats, who were allied with the Republican machine, and the Tammany Democrats. Edward Cooper, the head of the anti-Tammany Democrats, pressured Smith to transfer a certain captain for political reasons. Smith told Cooper that during his board membership, he had divided patronage equally between the two factions and had refused to ally with either one. He was a loyal National Democrat and nothing more. He refused to transfer the captain because it would involve him in the factional fight. Cooper warned Smith that he would have to choose sides. Smith replied that he would not ally with Cooper. Cooper's victory in the mayoral election of 1878 made Smith wonder how long he would remain as commissioner.[22]

In the meantime, bitter personal feelings developed among the commissioners. The political machines created this ill feeling by publicizing false and slanderous stories about the commissioners and tricking them into believing their colleagues were responsible. The machines caused the discord within the board to prevent it from concentrating on its efforts to keep machine politics out of the police administration. This trouble injured the efficiency of the board's services, allowing the mayor to charge the street cleaning bureau with dereliction of duty. That bureau was the weakest point in the administration. The employees were selected on political grounds without the slightest reference to honesty or efficiency. Smith had tried to have the work done by contractors, but a court decision prevented the police board from contracting out the work.[23]

On January 21, 1879, Erhardt proposed a resolution, blaming carelessness and inebriety among the board members for creating a damaging influence on the department. He criticized the board for not stopping widespread corruption. Politicians had influenced board members to prevent just punishment and to transfer captains for personal reasons. The *New York Times* believed that Erhardt's resolution, which included a call for Mayor Cooper's investigation of the board, was in part directed at Smith because he refused to permit necessary half-pay retirements from the force. Smith wrote to Cooper on March 11 denying Erhardt's allegations.[24]

Nonetheless, Cooper decided to accept Erhardt's view. Without any serious investigation, Cooper presented four charges against Erhardt, Nichols, and Smith. Cooper maintained that the police government and discipline had become lax, leading the police to become more inefficient and demoralized. The streets were not thoroughly cleaned, and daily garbage removals were not done. The commissioners were guilty of feuding with one another and of conduct unbecoming their offices. Smith wrote Cooper merely denying all of his charges. He could not be more specific since Cooper's charges did not cite any examples.[25]

During a hearing held by the mayor, all the commissioners presented notes asserting that unless evidence proved that the individual commissioners neglected their duties, they could not be removed. Cooper contended that if the board's obligations went unfulfilled, the members could be removed for that failure alone. But his only evidence was that some streets were dirty. In protest against any proceedings for his removal that failed to present specific allegations supported by evidence, Baldy refused to communicate with Cooper except through counsel. Cooper refused to hear Smith's attorneys. After the hearing, Smith charged that Cooper had no specific charges and had run a prejudiced investigation.[26]

On April 5, 1879, Cooper asked the governor to approve the removal of Erhardt, Nichols, and Smith. Cooper may have sought a new police board for the sake of the public good, but he possibly also made the request to gain control of the board's important election machinery. The importance of this machinery cannot be exaggerated, especially in close state or national elections. Erhardt's term had expired, and the selection of his successor ended his tenure. An alliance of the Tammany Democrats and Republicans in the Board of Aldermen selected Republican Stephen B. French. On April 17, Governor Lucius Robinson, an anti-Tammany Democrat, approved Nichols' removal, and Cooper replaced him with an anti-Tammany Democrat.[27]

Governor Robinson delayed dismissing Smith. The governor finally complied with Cooper's request, and Smith was removed on August 5, 1879. The *New York Times* admitted that Smith's removal was the result of anti-Tammany partisan politics. City Controller John Kelly, head of Tammany Democracy, charged the governor and mayor with unjust political tactics. Smith was replaced by an anti-Tammany Democrat. Despite Robinson's actions, Smith wrote to Wheeler and French on August 30 that he was ready to perform his duties as police commissioner. After Nichols successfully challenged his removal in the courts and was reinstated on February 7, 1880, Smith began legal proceedings to challenge his dismissal. Smith asked Judge Charles Daniels of the Supreme Court to reverse Cooper's actions. On July 2, the New York Supreme Court reinstated Smith because Cooper had denied Smith counsel and the charges against Smith were without evidence.[28]

Smith resumed his seat on the board on July 10, 1880. The presidency of the board had gone to French. John Voorhis, who held Smith's old seat, attempted to block Smith's return, but an injunction to stop Voorhis' removal was set aside in Superior Court. The court ruled that Smith's removal was illegal and in law he "never really ceased to be a police commissioner."[29] Smith took his seat despite Voorhis' protests.[30]

Back in September 1879, Baldy also had served as a Tammany delegate at the state Democratic convention. At the convention, he gave the seconding speech for his old army colleague, General Slocum, who was the Tammany Hall choice for governor. After Robinson defeated Slocum for the nomination, many Tammany delegates seceded to pick a Tammany candidate. Tammy Hall boss John Kelly offered this nomination to Smith, but he refused because he believed an additional Democratic candidate would only help elect a Republican. The Tammany convention nominated Kelly, and in the gubernatorial election of 1879, the Republican won.[31]

Smith was also active in the 1880 campaign for the National Democratic presidential nomination. He decided to work strenuously for the nomination of his old comrade-in-arms, General Hancock. Baldy argued that Hancock's administration in Louisiana and Texas had been eminently satisfactory to all conservative men, and his prestige in the North would undermine the bloody shirt tactics of the Republicans. Smith went to Vermont and secured a solid delegation from his native state for Hancock. Smith persuaded General Franklin to go to the National Convention in Cincinnati with him, though Franklin was rather pessimistic about Hancock's chances.[32]

On their way to Cincinnati, they met William Scott of Erie. He offered to spend $100,000 to defeat Senator Thomas Bayard of Delaware in the convention. While Smith was fond of Bayard, he did not think Bayard could be elected. When Smith and Franklin arrived in Cincinnati, they had about $150,000 subscribed to the Hancock campaign. On the first ballot, no candidate received the necessary two-thirds vote. The vote for Hancock was so large, however, that the other leaders passed a motion to adjourn for the day to forestall his nomination. That night, Senator William A. Wallace of Pennsylvania joined the Hancock ranks and brought funds for the depleted treasury. The next day, Hancock was nominated on the second ballot. The Indiana delegation, which solidly backed Thomas Hendricks, refused to support a unanimous vote. To reduce their hostility to the nominee, Smith asked them if they wished to name the vice-presidential candidate. They agreed and named William H. English. After working so hard for Hancock's nomination, Smith was understandably disappointed when Hancock lost the presidential election to Republican nominee James A. Garfield.[33]

In the city election of 1880, Democrat William R. Grace was elected mayor. Smith told the new mayor that he had remained as police commissioner only to prevent Cooper from filling his place. Smith asked Grace to seek a replacement and offered to resign as soon as the mayor found someone. After some delay, Grace made his selection, and Smith resigned on March 11, 1881. Grace was grateful for Baldy's support during his campaign and offered him the prestigious position of city chamberlain. Smith thanked Grace for his offer but declined it because he wanted to leave municipal government.[34]

Three years after leaving New York City politics, Smith sought new employment. His friend General John Newton was then chief of engineers. Newton's engineers were carrying forward numerous internal improvements, and many officers and civil engineers were needed for the supervision of various river and harbor works. Because of his wide experience and due to Newton's influence, Smith was appointed a United States agent by the secretary of war and placed in charge of the works on the peninsula between the Delaware and Chesapeake bays with his headquarters at Wilmington, Delaware. Smith's compensation would be $3,000 per annum plus travelling expenses. Over the next seventeen years, Smith closely supervised the works on the peninsula and administered the duties "with such economy and skill as I have been possessed of by Providence."[35] He retired from this post on July 1, 1901.[36]

In July 1888, Democratic Congressman Richard Townshend of Illinois proposed that Baldy be appointed to the position of major general in the regular army and placed on the retired list at that rank. Townshend believed that Smith's volunteer rank and war service justified this request. Townshend noted that Smith's service included devising the operations that saved the Army of the Cumberland "from starvation and capture at Chattanooga."[37] Smith, well past the age of retirement, "was fully entitled to that favor at the hands of the Government, for a lifetime of hard and conspicuous service in which he has always displayed the most incorruptible honesty, the most outspoken patriotism and devotion, and the highest ability."[38] There was stern opposition to Townshend's proposal, for Smith had never held the rank in the regular army and had resigned rather than retired from the army. Opponents pushed for an amendment that would put Baldy on the retirement list at the regular army rank that he held when he resigned. Townshend was forced to accept this change but misinformed his fellow members that Smith had resigned as a colonel in the regular army rather his actual rank of major of engineers. Unaware of the mistake, the House accepted the amended version of Townshend's proposal and passed a bill on July 20, 1888, to put Baldy on the retired list as a colonel.[39]

The Senate amended the House bill by placing Smith on the retired list as major of engineers. This conformed to the uniform rule of the Committee on Military Affairs that placed officers on the retired list at the grade that they held when they left the service. Republican Senator Charles F. Manderson of Nebraska defended the Senate version of the House bill against objections that aimed to keep Smith off the retired list. On August 7, the Senate bill passed overwhelmingly. The Senate directed its conferees to insist on its version.[40]

Townshend spoke on behalf of the House bill. However, threats by fellow members to return the bill to committee made Townshend agree to the Senate bill. On February 5, 1889, the House voted unanimously for the Senate bill. Congress passed the bill on February 7. The adjutant general and secretary of war approved the bill, and the president signed it on February 19.[41] Smith was officially retired at his actual rank of major of engineers.

Smith did not instigate Townshend's bill and delayed accepting the appointment of major of engineers on the retired list. He feared that he would have to surrender his United States agent position if he accepted the retired major commission. On March 7, Smith asked War Secretary Redfield Proctor not to relieve him as United States agent since he had not as yet accepted the commission. On April 1, Proctor asked the attorney general to decide whether Smith could hold both his civil position in the Corps of Engineers and his commission. On April 13, Attorney General William H. Miller ruled that from earlier precedents and decisions, a retired officer could draw the pay of a civil office provided he fulfilled the duties of that office. Accordingly, Smith accepted the commission of major of engineers on the retired list on April 13.[42]

In the postwar years, Smith renewed or maintained prewar and wartime friendships with fellow Civil War generals. General Franklin remained his closest friend. General J.H. Wilson also was close to Smith, actively corresponding with his former West Point professor. Smith renewed his friendship with his old Topographical Engineer commander, Confederate General Joseph E. Johnston, and the two men frequently exchanged visits. They often discussed the events of the war, such as the Peninsula Campaign, which had found them on opposite sides of the battle line, and the Atlanta Campaign. Smith considered Johnston "a profound student of military history. I never knew a more thorough soldier and gentleman."[43]

Baldy also corresponded with Fitz John Porter, who spent much of his time after the war trying to overturn the court martial verdict that blamed him for the Federal defeat at Second Bull Run. Like many of Porter's friends, Smith believed that Porter had been unjustly convicted and congratulated him when he was finally cleared. Smith wrote of his old West Point classmate, "Brave, patriotic, ambitious, he was a model in his life for soldiers and gentlemen to imitate, and the Military Academy furnishes no higher example than his."[44]

Smith also worked to serve the memory and the families of old friends. After General Hancock died in 1886, Smith helped to raise money for Hancock's widow and children. The contributions were collected through J.P. Morgan, who acted as treasurer of the funds. Smith also served as president of the General George B. McClellan Memorial Association.[45]

He was also an active member of the first generation of Civil War historians. He continued to express his opinions about the war and challenge those popular and official views that he believed to be incorrect. In doing so, he sought to set the record straight in order to uncover mistakes whenever they crossed his path. His wartime animosity toward or admiration of certain generals did not decline after the war. He still believed Generals Pope and Burnside were "beneath contempt," and continued to admire Generals Don Carlos Buell and Thomas.[46] He believed that Halleck had some good administrative qualities and that his skillful administration in Missouri probably saved "that state after the fool Fremont had nearly wrecked our chances there."[47] His feelings toward McClellan and Grant remained mixed. He felt McClellan could have won a great victory in 1862 by attacking Petersburg after Malvern Hill but that he lacked the initiative. Smith did not know that McClellan advised such an attack, and that Halleck vetoed it. But Smith also believed that interference from Washington generally undermined McClellan's efforts. Smith thought that Grant had ordinary ability and was unaccomplished in directing movements and conducting battles.[48]

Smith began his refutation of popularly-held Civil War views in the summer of 1868 when he wrote a series of articles in the *New York World* under the name "Volunteer." These challenged the view that Grant was a superior general. Smith suggested that the popular view that a great general would make a good president was unfounded in Grant's case since he had failed miserably in the Virginia Campaign of 1864. Smith elaborated on the battles of the Wilderness, Spotsylvania Court House, and North Anna to argue that Grant had needlessly wasted the lives of his men without making substantial gains.[49]

Smith, in a book review in the *Washington Evening Star* in October 1887, next challenged John A. Logan's evaluation of the United States Military Academy. Logan, in *The Volunteer Soldier in America*, asserted that West Point had not turned out superior generals. Smith refuted Logan's charges by pointing out that the best generals of both sides were graduates of West Point. Logan conveniently ignored West Pointers, such as Generals Grant and Sherman, who left the prewar service but returned in 1861. According to Smith, the training that the Federal army and corps commanders had received at West Point played a significant role in the final Union victory.[50]

Smith then used the review to critique the roles that military education and political influence played in the South and the North. He contended that when the Confederate armies were successful, it was because they "were organized on the principle that military education was too important a factor to be neglected and the armies were led by West Point men and to its graduates were always given the highest subaltern command." Furthermore, said Smith, they were directed "without the intermeddling of politicians or bureau magnates." With this system of command, the Confederates, even with their ports blockaded and without proper finances and necessary supplies, maintained the war for four years and "brought in doubt the view of a single American nationality."[51]

In contrast, asserted Smith, the North, with its great superiority in numbers and material wealth, allowed itself to be governed by political considerations rather than military principles. He pointed out that some of the first general field commissions in the volunteer service were given to those who had political influence but lacked military knowledge. Campaigns were also ordered for political reasons, and men were appointed to command armies because of political clout. The actions of the Committee on the Conduct of the War and some cabinet officers "procrastinated the war and made demagoguism the direct road to preferment." In spite of this system, the West Pointers were finally able to defeat the Confederacy. Smith concluded, "Four years of war were enough to test the value of an academic military education, and no one is more competent to give an opinion as to that value than the volunteer soldier of America."[52]

To revise popular beliefs, Smith also wrote articles for *Century Magazine*, which were later collected and re-published in R.U. Johnson's *Battles and Leaders of the Civil War*, and presented papers before the Military History Society of Massachusetts. In "Franklin's Left Grand Division," Smith strongly defended Franklin's performance at the battle of Fredericksburg. Using an affidavit he wrote in February 1863 for the Committee on the Conduct of the War, Baldy attacked the Committee's report that blamed Franklin for the Federal defeat. Baldy argued that Burnside should have been held responsible for the battle's outcome. Smith showed that before the battle, he and Franklin presented the only plan that offered the Federals any chance of success.[53]

Smith wrote "Butler's Attack on Drewry's Bluff" and "The Eighteenth Corps at Cold Harbor" to show the incompetence of Generals Butler, Meade, and Grant. Smith blamed Butler for blocking able suggestions of his corps commanders and leading his army to defeat at Drewry's Bluff. Baldy treated Cold Harbor as the climax of a failed campaign and placed responsibility for the heavy casualties on the shoulders of Grant and Meade.[54]

In "The Military Situation in Northern Virginia," Smith attempted to show that McClellan's removal had a crippling effect on the Union campaign in the autumn of 1862. He pointed out that the Federals at the time of McClellan's relief were in a vastly superior position in relation to the divided Confederate army, and that this advantage was surrendered by Burnside's move towards Fredericksburg. He wrote the paper particularly to show that Stanton did not give McClellan a fair chance. In a paper on the Chattanooga campaign, Baldy showed the great Federal victories around Chattanooga did not occur as Grant had planned. He described the events of November 1863 to assert that Thomas's plan to have Hooker attack the Confederate left flank while Thomas advanced in the center was responsible for the Union victory. Grant's plan to have Sherman make the major attack on the Confederate right never succeeded. In "The Movement Against Petersburg," Baldy defended his performance at Petersburg on June 15, 1864, against charges that Grant made in his official report. He refuted Grant's charges that he unnecessarily delayed the attack and did not attack with his entire force.[55]

In 1892, General Butler published his autobiography, which also attacked Smith's actions as Eighteenth Corps commander. Smith was blamed for undermining Butler's plans and for failing to capture Petersburg. A year later, Baldy countered with his own memoir, *From Chattanooga to Petersburg*. He denied Butler's charges and placed the blame for any failure at Drewry's Bluff and Petersburg on Butler and Grant. Opponents and friends alike praised his book.[56]

Smith also became involved in two official controversies with battlefield parks. The Antietam Board invited Generals Smith and Franklin to indicate where the various units of the Sixth Corps were located during the battle. They gladly complied with this request. In 1897, Smith, Franklin, Colonel Thomas Hyde, and historian John C. Ropes visited the field. They were in full agreement as to the unit positions and events during the battle. In front of the Dunkard Church, they found park tablets stating that Smith's division had been checked in an assault. As Smith had not ordered any assault and placed the Third Brigade precisely where he had intended, the tablets were in error. Smith wrote to Major George Davis, head of the Antietam Commission, expressing the view that since Colonel Irwin's brigade reached their designated position, the Confederates were not responsible for stopping their advance. On July 29, 1897, Davis responded by citing the battle reports to show that at least two regiments of the brigade had been checked by stern enemy fire; consequently, the park would not alter the plaques. Smith replied that the tablets' assertion that his division was "checked" implied that his troops failed to go where they were ordered. Smith contested this viewpoint and insisted the brigade remained where it was placed until Lee retired. Moreover, the staggering of two regiments should not be characterized by a check of a division. Eventually, the controversial tablets were removed.[57]

The outcome of the other official controversy was more important to Smith. Unfortunately, in this one, he was unsuccessful. The Chickamauga and Chattanooga Park, in one of its maps, asserted that General Rosecrans devised the successful plan that relieved the Army of the Cumberland at Chattanooga in October 1863. General Henry V. Boynton, the historian of the park, had served with Rosecrans and insisted that his old commander was responsible for the plan. After the war, Rosecrans also took credit for the plan. Smith, who had been breveted brigadier general for his work at Chattanooga and had been praised for his work by Generals Thomas and Grant, asserted that he was responsible for the short line plan that climaxed with the Brown's Ferry expedition and Hooker's move through Lookout Valley. He wrote two pamphlets and several newspaper columns supporting his position. J.C. Ropes assisted him in his efforts. Boynton countered Smith's arguments with letters and newspaper articles.[58]

In 1897, Baldy wrote to Secretary of War Russell A. Alger asking that an engineer officer be appointed to examine the question. Colonel Henry M. Duffield was assigned to the task in January 1898. Smith presented papers to Duffield but found that Duffield had succeeded Boynton as park historian when Boynton was promoted to park commission president. Smith was demoralized by the secretary's choice but tried his best to convince Duffield of his position. As expected, Duffield's report in January 1900, sustained the park's position. In March, Smith appealed to Secretary of War Elihu Root to appoint an independent board to study the controversy. A board of three army officers was convened in August to consider the question. The head of the board, Major General John R. Brooke, was a friend of Boynton. The second board member was Brooke's adjutant general, Colonel Michael V. Sheridan. Colonel George L. Gillespie was the third member. Smith attempted to convince the board through his papers, and through the arguments of his counsel, Anthony Higgins, when he was ill. But on February 1, 1901, the board sustained the park's position. He wrote to Secretary of War Elihu Root to disapprove the board's report but to no avail. Smith hoped that the president might set aside Root's approval, but Theodore Roosevelt failed to overturn the secretary's decision. Nevertheless, Smith continued to write in support of his position until his death.[59]

Despite this setback on the Brown's Ferry controversy, Baldy was still widely respected. Civil War veterans and newspapers wrote favoring him in the controversy as well as supporting moves to put him on the retired list as major general. The *Army and*

Navy Journal on February 15, 1902, wrote, "We have always supposed that (Smith) was entitled to the credit of the Brown's Ferry affair."[60] General Wilson wrote his old friend that he would attempt to talk to President Roosevelt on the Brown's Ferry and retired major general commission issues. Smith was also honored in his native state. General Wistar and other officers presented Vermont with a plaque honoring Smith for his war service. The tablet is now located next to the entrance of the State House of Representatives. The Vermont legislature also passed a resolution petitioning Congress to put Smith on the retired list as major general in the regular army. The governor and the *Montpelier Daily Journal* endorsed this resolution.[61]

Smith's health declined in the autumn of 1902. His wife had died in 1899, but he still had the comfort of his daughter, Clara. He was visited frequently by his son, Stuart, who had graduated first in his class at the United States Naval Academy and was then an assistant naval constructor. On February 28, 1903, at 6:30 p.m., Brevet Major General William Farrar Smith died at the age of seventy-nine. The cause of death was chronic diabetes and nephritis. His funeral was held at St. Stephen's Church in Philadelphia on March 3. He was buried in Arlington National Cemetery.[62]

Smith's life was a series of controversies, most of which were caused by his insistence on expressing his opinions, regardless of the consequences. His decision to speak out about the blundering generals and meddlesome politicians who undermined the Northern war effort led to his removal as Eighteenth Corps Commander in 1864. That action ended his combat career, although it certainly did nothing to silence him.

Smith's subsequent career indicates that to the very end, he remained an outspoken critic of ineptitude and vice. As special commissioner, he condemned the Department of the Gulf as thoroughly corrupt. In civilian life, he was not deterred either from demanding of others the high standards of honesty, integrity, and competence that he demanded of himself. As a police commissioner, he fought to establish efficiency and honesty in a police force burdened by widespread corruption. In foreign affairs, he advocated a peaceful settlement in Cuba and participated in efforts to find an equitable solution. He condemned the McKinley administration for its unnecessary and despotic use of military force to end the Spanish possession of Cuba and the Filipino war for independence.

Yet, William Farrar Smith reserved most of his criticisms for his writings on the Civil War. Recounting his Brown's Ferry expedition and assault on Petersburg, he explained how inventiveness and initiative could bring victory. He also showed how the Republican politicians had mishandled the war effort. As ever, Baldy was condemned for his views. But, his determination to offer sensible alternatives to official policy and to speak out against incompetence and corruption, whatever the consequences, makes him an author of an unforgettable critique of politics and war.

Chapter Notes

Chapter I

1. James Harrison Wilson, *Life and Service of William Farrar Smith* (Wilmington, Delaware: John M. Rogers Press, 1904),14; Typed Autobiography of General Smith,1–2, William Farrar Smith Papers, Vermont Historical Society, Barre, Vermont. This manuscript will hereafter be cited as Smith Memoir. Unless otherwise indicated, all Smith Papers come from the Vermont Historical Society.

2. Smith Memoir, 3, Smith Papers.

3. Smith Memoir, 3–4, Smith Papers.

4. *Ibid.*

5. *Ibid.*

6. Smith Memoir, 5, Smith Papers.

7. Smith Memoir, 5–6, Smith Papers; William Langer, *An Encyclopedia of World History*, fourth ed. (Boston: Houghton Mifflin, 1968), 833; Wilson, 16–17.

8. Smith Memoir, 5, Smith Papers; Wilson, 14.

9. J.R. Poinsett to John Smith, 5 December 1839, John Smith to J.R. Poinsett, 9 December 1840, John Smith to J.G. Totten, 20 January 1841, W.F. Smith to J.R. Poinsett, 30 January 1841, United States Military Cadet Application Papers, 1805–1866, Record Group 94, National Archives, Washington, D.C. (Washington, D.C.: National Archives Trust Fund Board, Microcopy no. 688); Wilson, 14.

10. Almon Lawrence to J.R. Poinsett, 25 November 1839 and 17 November 1840, United States Military Academy Cadet Application Papers, 1805–1866.

11. Smith Memoir, 6, Smith Papers.

12. Smith Memoir, 7, Smith Papers; James L. Morrison, *"The Best School in the World": West Point, the Pre-Civil War Years, 1833–1866* (Kent: Kent State University Press, 1986), 71, 101.

13. United States Military Catalog 1841–1842, Register of Delinquencies volume 3 Classes of 1845 and 1846 United States Military Academy, 96, United States Military Academy Library, West Point, New York; Smith Memoir, 8, Smith Papers.

14. United States Military Academy Catalog 1842–1843, United States Military Academy Library; Morrison, 66; Smith Memoir, 8, 14 Smith Papers; Charles G. Downing and Roy L. Swift, "Howard, Richard Austin," Handbook of Texas Online, accessed May 2, 2021, https://www.tshaonline.org/handbook/entries/howard-richard-austin.

15. The "persecution" refers to the army's court martial of Fitz John Porter for his performance at Second Bull Run in August 1862. Porter was made the scapegoat for that Union defeat and was not reinstated until 1886 (Mark Boatner, *Civil War Dictionary* [New York: David McKay Co., 1959], 661–662.)

16. Smith Memoir, 8, 262, Smith Papers.

17. United States Military Academy Catalog 1843–1844, Register of Delinquencies, 96, United States Military Academy Library.

18. Register of Delinquencies, 96, United States Military Academy Library.

19. Smith Memoir, 9, Smith Papers; United States Military Academy Catalog 1844–1845, Register of Delinquencies, 96, United States Military Academy Library; Smith received the nickname "Baldy" because his hair was thinner than normal and to distinguish him from other Smiths at the Academy. Wilson, 17; Boatner, 776. Of the class of 1845, seven would serve in the Confederate army while fifteen would serve in the Federal army, including one southerner who stayed loyal to the Union. Morrison, 183.

20. W.F. Smith to J.J. Abert, 19 July 1845, 15 October 1845 and 2 November 1845, Register of Letters Received by the Topographical Bureau of the War Department 1824–1866 (hereafter cited as RLRTB), Record Group 77, National Archives (Washington, D.C.: National Archives Trust Fund Board, Microcopy no. 505); J.J. Abert to W.F. Smith, 11 July 1845 and 5 November 1845, Letters Sent by the Topographical Bureau of the War Department and by Successor Divisions in the Office of the Chief of Engineers, 1829–1870 (hereafter cited as LSTB), Record Group 77, National Archives (Washington, D.C.: National Archives Trust Fund Board, Microcopy no. 66); W.F. Smith to R. Jones, 21 July 1845, Letters Received by the Office of the Adjutant General (Main Series), 1822–1860 (hereafter cited as LROAG), Record Group 94, National Archives (Washington, D.C.: National Archives Trust Fund Board, Microcopy no. 567); Smith Memoir, 9–10, Smith Papers.

21. Smith Memoir, 11, Smith Papers; W.F. Smith to J.J. Abert, 18 May 1846, RLRTB; W.F. Smith to R. Jones, 6 August 1847 and 25 October 1847, LROAG.

22. Smith Memoir, 11, Smith Papers; W.F. Smith to R. Jones, 10 August 1848 and endorsement by A.E. Church, 1 September 1848, LROAG; J.J. Abert to W.F. Smith, 7 September 1848, 24 October 1848 and 2 December 1848, LSTB; W.F. Smith to J.J. Abert, 23 October 1848, RLRTB; W.F. Smith to J.J. Abert, 7 October 1858, Letters Received by the Topographical Bureau of the War Department 1824–1865 (hereafter cited as LRTB), Record Group 77, National Archives (Washington, D.C.: National Archives Trust Fund Board, Microcopy no. 506).

23. Smith Memoir, 12–14, Smith Papers; J.E. Smith to R. Jones, 10 August 1848 and endorsement by A.E. Church, 1 September 1848, LROAG; J.J. Abert to W.F. Smith, 7 September 1848, 24 October 1848 and 2 December 1848, LSTB; W.F. Smith to J.J. Abert, 23 October 1848, RLRTB; Charles G. Downing and Roy L. Swift, "Howard, Richard Austin," Handbook of Texas Online, accessed May 2, 2021, https://www.tshaonline.org/handbook/entries/howard-richard-austin.

24. Smith Memoir, 15, Smith Papers; Charles G. Downing and Roy L. Swift, "Howard, Richard Austin," Handbook of Texas Online, accessed May 2, 2021, https://www.tshaonline.org/handbook/entries/howard-richard-austin.

25. Johnston et al., 4–7; Smith Memoir, 15, Smith Papers.

26. Johnston et al., 4–7; Smith Memoir, 16, 18, 19, Smith Papers; William Goetzmann, Army Exploration in the American West 1803–1863 (New Haven: Yale University Press, 1959), 228.

27. Smith Memoir, 20, Smith Papers.

28. Smith Memoir, 21–24, Smith Papers.

29. Smith Memoir, 25–26, Smith Papers.

30. Smith Memoir, 30–32, Smith Papers.

31. Johnston et al., 26; Smith Memoir, 34, 36, Smith Papers; Goetzmann, 230.

32. Johnston et al., 26; Smith Memoir, 276–278, Smith Papers; Goetzmann, 231–232; Rudi R. Rodriguez, "Rodriguez, José Policarpio," Handbook of Texas Online, accessed May 2, 2021, https://www.tshaonline.org/handbook/entries/rodriguez-jose-policarpio.

33. Johnston et al., 13–14, 26–28.

34. Smith Memoir, 279, Smith Papers; W.F. Smith to R. Jones, 16 January 1850, LROAG.

35. Johnston et al., 39–40; Goetzmann, 236–237.

36. J.E. Johnston to J.J. Abert, 7 January 1851, and W.F. Smith to J.E. Johnston, 26 October 1850, LRTB.

37. J.E. Johnston to J.J. Abert, 7 January 1851, and W.F. Smith to J.E. Johnston, 26 October 1850, LRTB.

38. Smith Memoir, 44–45, Smith Papers; J.J. Abert to W.F. Smith, 31 March 1851, LSTB; W.F. Smith to R. Jones, 25 September 1850 and endorsed by J.E. Johnston and J.J. Abert, LROAG; J.E.

Johnston to J.J. Abert, 17 February 1851, LRTB; John R. Bartlett, Personal Narrative of Explorations and Incidents in Texas, New Mexico, California, Sanora, and Chihuahua connected with the United States and Mexican Boundary Commission during the Years 1850, '51, '52, and '53, 2 vols. (New York: D. Appleton & Co., 1854), 1:348; see also Senate Document No. 119, 32nd Congress 1st session.

39. Boatner, 265; Dictionary of American Biography, 20 vols. and Index (1928–43), 6:153.

40. W.H. Emory to W.F. Smith, 15 December 1851, W.F. Smith to W.H. Emory, 22 December 1851, 24 December 1851 and 20 January 1852, LROAG; Senate Executive Document No. 6, 33rd Cong., Special Session (1853), 109.

41. W.F. Smith to W.H. Emory, 2 February 1852, and W.H. Emory endorsement, undated, LROAG.

42. W.H. Emory to W.F. Smith, 15 January 1852 and 16 January 1852, LROAG; Frank N. Schubert, Vanguard of Expansion: Army Engineers in the Trans-Mississippi West (Washington, D.C.: Chief of Engineers, 1980), 60–61.

43. W.H. Emory to W.F. Smith, 16 January 1852, W.F. Smith to W.H. Emory, 20 January 1852, LROAG.

44. W.H. Emory to W.F. Smith, 21 January 1852, LROAG.

45. W.F. Smith to W.H. Emory, 22 January 1852, LROAG.

46. W.H. Emory to W.F. Smith, 22 January 1852, W.H. Emory to A.H. H. Stuart, 24 January 1852, and W.F. Smith to W.H. Emory, 22 January 1852 and 23 January 1852, LROAG.

47. W.H. Emory to W.F. Smith, 23 February 1852, and W.F. Smith to W.H. Emory, 2 March 1852, LROAG.

48. W.H. Emory to W.F. Smith, 7 March 1852, LROAG.

49. W.F. Emory to W.F. Smith, 31 March 1852, 12 May 1852 and 9 June 1852, and W.F. Smith to S. Cooper, 6 December 1852, LROAG; J.J. Abert to W.F. Smith, 8 June 1852, LSTB.

50. W.F. Smith to J.J. Abert, 1 December 1852 and 13 December 1852, LRTB; J.J. Abert to W.F. Smith, 4 December 1852, 11 December 1852, 14 December 1852 and 28 December 1853, LSTB; Smith Memoir, 50, Smith Papers.

51. Smith Memoir, 50–51, Smith Papers; M.L. Smith to J.J. Abert, 22 August 1853, LRTB, W.F. Smith to S. Cooper, 1 May 1853, LROAG.

52. Smith Memoir, 51, Smith Papers; W.F. Smith to J.J. Abert, 7 October 1858, LRTB; J.J. Abert to W.F. Smith, 14 January 1854 and 7 October 1853, LSTB; W.F. Smith to J.J. Abert, 1 May 1854, and W.F. Smith to S. Cooper, 30 October 1853, LROAG; S. Cooper to W.F. Smith, 7 November 1853, Letters Sent by the Office of the Adjutant General Main Series 1800–1890 (hereafter cited as LSOAG), Record Group 94, National Archives (Washington, D.C.: National Archives Trust Fund Board, Microcopy co. 565).

53. The boxes' contents show the type of instruments that Smith used as an engineer officer. This

first box contained one sextant, artificial horizon, box of chronometer, pocket chronometer, small Calder compass, surveying chain and pins, reconnoitering glass, one nautical almanac (1854), table of Logarithms, Leu's tables, set of drawing instruments, six sheets of antiquarian drawing paper, six sheets Double Elephant paper, twelve sheets of drawing paper, twelve yards of tracing linen, ten quires letter paper, twelve notebooks, three dozen pencils, twelve cards steel pens, four pieces of Indian rubber, twelve pieces of mouth glue, and two cards fine mapping pens. The second box contained one portable transit and stand. J.J. Abert to W.F. Smith, 1 June 1854, LRTB.

54. J.J. Abert to W.F. Smith, 1 June 1854, LSTB; W.F. Smith to J.J. Abert, 23 December 1853, 16 June 1854, 8 July 1854, 3 August 1854 and 17 August 1854, LRTB.

55. J.J. Abert to W.F. Smith, 3 August 1854, 22 August 1854 and 7 September, LSTB.

56. W.F. Smith to J.J. Abert, 1 October 1854, LRTB.

57. Smith Memoir, 51–53, Smith Papers; W.F. Smith to J.J. Abert, 3 August 1854, 17 August 1854 and 1 October 1854, LRTB.

58. W.F. Smith to J.J. Abert, 27 November 1854, LRTB; J.J. Abert to W.F. Smith, 14 December 1854, LSTB.

59. Smith Memoir, 54, Smith Papers.

60. Smith Memoir, 56, Smith Papers; W.F. Smith to J.J. Abert, 5 May 1855, LRTB; L.H. Holden medical certificate, 20 May 1855, enclosed with W.F. Smith to S. Cooper, 6 June 1855, LROAG; Wilson, 22.

61. Smith Memoir, 56–58, Smith Papers.

62. W.F. Smith to S. Cooper, 30 August 1855, and Jefferson Davis endorsement, undated, LROAG; Smith Memoir, 57–58, Smith Papers.

63. Smith Memoir, 58–59, Smith Papers; Wilson, 22–23.

64. S. Moore Medical Certificate, 2 August 1856, enclosed with W.F. Smith to J.B. Long, 28 August 1856, and Military Academy Superintendent and War Secretary endorsements, undated, C.H. Smith Medical Certificate, 27 September 1856, enclosed with W.F. Smith to S. Cooper, 2 October 1856, and W. Edgar Medical Certificate, 24 November 1856, LROAG. Smith's partial paralysis at this time does not suggest a symptom of the malaria he had first suffered a year earlier and would suffer periodically throughout his army career. Instead, a modern diagnosis of Smith's illness suggests that he suffered from transient ischemic attacks. Such attacks came from poor circulation and may have reoccurred later in Baldy's life. He would be able to recover fully from each attack. Interview with Alexander V. Rubino, M.D., 19 October 1984.

65. Smith Memoir, 59, Smith Papers; J.J. Abert to W.F. Smith, 15 April 1858, I.C. Woodruff to W.F. Smith, 24 February 1859, and I.C. Woodruff to W.F. Smith, 26 February 1859, LSTB; W.F. Smith to J.J. Abert, 7 October 1858, and W.F. Smith to I.C. Woodruff, 1 March 1859, LRTB; W.F. Smith to S.

Cooper, 12 July 1859, and J.B. Floyd to W.F. Smith, 2 November 1859, LROAG: This is the last citation for Microcopy 567.

66. Smith Memoir, 60–62, Smith Papers; Wilson, 21–22.

Chapter II

1. Smith Memoir, 61, 68–69; Smith Papers; *Dictionary of American Biography*, 6:136–137.

2. 2 Smith Memoir, 69–70, 272–273, Smith Papers.

3. Smith Memoir, 63–64, Smith Papers.

4. Smith Memoir, 64–65, Smith Papers; Wilson, 20–21.

5. J.A. Dix to J.B. Floyd, 9 February 1861, Letters Received by the Office of the Adjutant General (Main Series), 1861–1870, Record Group 94, National Archives (Washington, D.C.: National Archives Trust Fund Board, Microcopy no. 619): hereafter cited LROAG; Smith Memoir, 65, Smith Papers.

6. Smith Memoir, 65–67, Smith Papers; Wilson, 21–22; *Annual Report of the Lighthouse Board to the Secretary of the Treasury for the Fiscal Year Ended June 30, 1884.* (Washington, D.C.: Government Printing Office, 1884), 134.

7. W.F. Smith to L. Thomas, 22 April 1861 and 18 May 1861, LROAG; Smith Memoir, 70–71, Smith Papers.

8. Smith Memoir, 71–72, Smith Papers; Wilson, 30–31; J.A. Rawlins to M. Rawlins, 2 April 1864, Wilson Papers. For further information on the Smith's surviving children, see chapter XVI.

9. Smith Memoir, 71–72, Smith Papers; Wilson, 30–31.

10. W.B. Franklin to L. Thomas, 8 May 1861, LROAG.

11. H. Bache to L. Thomas, 18 May 1861 and 1 June 1861, W.F. Smith to S.P. Chase, 29 April 1861, and W.B. Franklin to L. Thomas, 8 May 1861, LROAG; Smith Memoir, 73–74, Smith Papers; George Benedict, *Vermont in the Civil War*, 2 vols. (Burlington, Vermont: Free Press Association, 1886–1888), 1:131.

12. Smith Memoir, 74–75, Smith Papers.

13. Smith Memoir, 76–77, Smith Papers.

14. Smith Memoir, 77–78, Smith Papers; H. Bache to L. Thomas, 18 July 1861, LROAG; Wilson, 31–32.

15. E. Fairbanks to W.F. Smith, 19 July 1861, and Smith Memoir, 78–79, Smith Papers; Benedict, 1:131.

16. "The Army of the Potomac," *Report of the Joint Committee on the Conduct of the War*, 37th Congress, 3rd Session, part I, 1863, 188–189 Cited hereafter as JCCW.

17. General Order no 5, 1 August 1861, George B. McClellan Papers, Division of Manuscripts, Library of Congress, Washington, D.C.; Benedict, 1:131; Robert N. Scott, Chief Compiler, *The War of the Rebellion: A Compilation of the Official Records*

of the Union and Confederate Armies (Washington, 1880–1901), Series I, volume 5:15. Cited hereafter as *OR*. All references will be to Series I; Stephen Sears, *George B. McClellan: The Young Napoleon* (New York: Ticknor and Fields, 1988), 68, 95.

18. General Order no. 1, 4 August 1861, General Orders and Standing Orders (Smith's Brigade, Army of the Potomac), Record Group 393, Inventory vol. 2, Entry no. 4534, National Archives.

19. General Order no. 1, 4 August 1861, and General Order no. 6, 5 August 1861, General Orders and Standing Orders (Smith's Brigade, Army of the Potomac).

20. General Order no. 6, 5 August 1861, General Orders and Standing Orders (Smith's Brigade, Army of the Potomac); W.F. Smith to S. Williams, 28 August 1861, Letters and Telegrams Received (Smith's Brigade, Army of the Potomac), Record Group 393, Inventory vol. 2, Entry no. 4532, National Archives.

21. Smith Memoir,194, Smith Papers; G.B. McClellan to W.F. Smith, 7 August 1861 and 7 August 1861, Letters and Telegrams Received (Smith's Brigade, Army of the Potomac).

22. Smith Memoir, 85, 86, 194, 195, Smith Papers.

23. Smith Memoir, 85, 86, 194, 195, R. Proctor to W.F. Smith, 30 January 1892, and clipping of L.E. Chittenden, "Recollections of President Lincoln," 265, Smith Papers; W.F. Smith to S. Williams, 9 September 1861, and S. Williams to W.F. Smith, 9 September 1861, McClellan Papers.

24. Presidential Order, 13 August 1861, LROAG; George B. McClellan, *McClellan's Own Story: The War for the Union* (New York: C.L. Webster, 1886), 95.

25. *OR*, 5:168–169.

26. *OR*, 5:169–170.

27. *OR*, 5:170, 171, 173, 175, 177, 183.

28. *OR*, 5:168–180, 216; Benedict, 1:134. For Stuart's involvement in the engagement, see Emory M. Thomas, *Bold Dragoon: The Life of J.E.B. Stuart* (New York: Harper & Row, 1986), 86.

29. *OR*, 5:215–216

30. McClellan, 92, 95; W.F. Smith to Charles Mundee, 26 September 1861, William Farrar Smith Papers, James William Eldridge Collection, Huntington Library, San Marino, California; S. Williams to W.F. Smith, 27 September 1861, McClellan Papers; Boatner, 775; *OR*, 5:218–219; Russel H. Beatie, *Army of the Potomac: McClellan Takes Command, September 1861-February 1862*, Volume II (Boston: DaCapo Press, 2004), 16–21. Stephen W. Sears, *Lincoln's Lieutenants: The High Command of the Army of the Potomac* (New York: Houghton Mifflin Harcourt, 2017), 87, 92, 109.

Chapter III

1. Smith Memoir, 79–80, Smith Papers; Wilson, 33; Benedict, 1:235, *OR*, 5:17; General Order no. 20, 24 October 1861, Standing Order no. 71, 22 October

1861, Standing Order no. 93, 16 November 1861 and Standing Order no 155, 21 February 1862, General Orders and Standing Orders (Smith's Division, Army of the Potomac), Record Group 393, Inventory vol. 2, Entry no. 4523, National Archives.

2. Benedict, 1:240; General Order no. 17, 13 October 1861, and Standing Order no. 55, 5 October 1861, General Orders and Standing Orders (Smith's Division, Army of the Potomac), Record Group 393, Inventory vol. 2, Entry no. 4534, National Archives.

3. *JCCW*, 37th Congress, 3rd Session, Part I, 187.

4. *JCCW*, 37th Congress, 3rd Session, Part I, 186–187.

5. Hancock, as temporary division commander in December, furthered Smith's intentions by ordering the relief of the sentinels every two hours and permitted brigade commanders to relieve them every hour in severe weather. Fires would be allowed for support pickets, 200 paces behind the sentinels, with special permission. Standing Order no. 108, 12 December 1861, General Orders and Standing Orders (Smith's Division, Army of the Potomac), Record Group 393, Inventory vol. 2, Entry no. 4534, National Archives.

6. W.F. Smith to J. Brannan, 17 November 1861, Letters Sent (Smith's Division, Army of the Potomac). Record Group 393, Inventory vol. 2 Entry no. 4526, National Archives; Benedict, 1:96, 97, 136–137; W.T. H. Brooks to De Lorma Brooks, 18 February 1862, William T.H. Brooks Papers, U.S. Army Heritage and Education Center, Carlisle Barracks, Pennsylvania; *JCCW*, 37th Congress, 3rd Session, Part I, 186–187; General Order no. 38, 16 November 1861, General Order no. 45, 23 November 1861, and Standing Order no. 108, 12 December 1861, General Orders and Standing Orders (Smith's Division, Army of the Potomac), Record Group 393, Inventory vol. 2, Entry no. 4534, National Archives; W.S. Hancock to R. Marcy, 8 December 1861, McClellan Papers.

7. J. Brannan to W.S. Hancock, 23 December 1861, Letters Sent and Reports of Operations (Third Brigade, Smith's Division, Army of the Potomac) Record Group 393, Inventory vol. 2, Entry no. 4622, National Archives.

8. Benedict, 1:96, 97, 137.

9. W.F. Smith to G.B. McClellan, 14 October 1861 and 21 November 1861, McClellan Papers.

10. W.S. Hancock to R. Marcy, 21 October 1861, W.T. H. Brooks to S. Williams, 25 November, and W.F. Smith to R. Marcy, 23 October 1861 and 24 October 1861, McClellan Papers; McClellan, 180; Benedict, 1:98; Frank Moore, ed., *The Rebellion Record*, 11 vols. (New York: G.P. Putnam, 1861–1863; D. Van Nostrand, 1864–1868), 3:54.

11. General Order no. 46, 26 November 1861 and General Order no. 54, 30 December 1861, General Orders and Standing Orders (Smith's Division, Army of the Potomac) Record Group 393, Inventory vol. 2, Entry no. 4534, National Archives; Sears, *Lincoln's Lieutenants*, 146; F.J. Porter to G.B. McClellan, 30 November 1861, W.S. Hancock to R.

Marcy, 17 December 1861, W.S. Hancock to G.B. McClellan, 20 December 1861, McClellan Papers.

12. *JCCW*, 37th Congress, 3rd Session, Part I, 186–193.

13. "Ball's Bluff," *JCCW* 37th Congress, 3rd Session, Part II, 9, 256, 260, 264–265.

14. Alfred Castleman, *Army of the Potomac* (Milwaukee: Strickland and Co., 1863), 70.

15. *OR*, 51, Part I, 526.

16. *OR*, 5:504–508.

17. *OR*, 5:504–508; W.F. Smith to S. Williams, 7 February 1862, McClellan Papers.

18. W.F. Smith to G.B. McClellan, 22 February 1862, McClellan Papers: *OR*, 5:509–510.

19. Smith Memoir, 81–83, Smith Papers; William E.S. Whitman, *Maine in the War for the Union* (Lewiston: N. Dingley Jr., and Co., 1965), 138,168.

20. W.T. H. Brooks to D. Brooks, 18 February 1862, Brooks Papers; George G. Meade, *The Life and Letters of George Gordon Meade*, 2 vols. (New York: C. Scribner's Sons, 1913), 1:248; Stephen Sears, *Lincoln's Lieutenants*, 170.

21. *JCCW*, 37th Congress, 3rd Session, Part I, 10; Warren Hassler, *George B. McClellan: Shield of the Union* (Baton Rouge: Louisiana State University Press, 1957), 54, 56; Stephen Sears, *Lincoln's Lieutenants*, 157–158.

22. War Council Meeting, 1862, Edwin M. Stanton Papers, Division of Manuscripts, Library of Congress.

23. *Ibid.*

24. *Ibid.*

25. Sears, *Lincoln's Lieutenants*, 159.

26. Smith Memoir, 196–198, and W.F. Smith manuscript autobiographical account of his Civil War experiences, written for his daughter on 4 July 1883 and 1 February 1887, Smith Papers. This latter account has been edited and published. See Herbert M. Schiller, ed., *The Autobiography of Major General William F. Smith, 1861–1864* (Dayton, Ohio: Morningside, 1990), 32.

27. W.F. Smith to H.V. Boynton, 26 February 1887, Ezra Carman Papers, Manuscripts and Archives Division, New York Public Library, New York, New York.

28. Smith Memoir, 196–198, Smith Papers; Schiller, ed., 32; W.F. Smith to H.V. Boynton, 26 February 1887, Carman Papers; Wilson, 47.

29. Smith Memoir, 196–198, Smith Papers; Schiller, ed., 31–32; W.F. Smith to H.V. Boynton, 26 February 1887, Carman Papers.

30. *OR*, 5:751.

31. Benedict, 1:137, 161, 242–243; *OR*, 5:751; *OR*, 11, Part III, 31, 37; General Order, 22 March 1862, Miscellaneous Letters and Orders Received (Second Division, Fourth Army Corps), Record Group 393, Inventory vol. 2, Entry no. 4629, National Archives.

Chapter IV

1. Smith Memoir, 200, Smith Papers.

2. Smith Memoir, 200, Smith Papers; *OR*, 5:42, 47.

3. Smith Memoir, 201; *OR*, 11, Part I, 300.

4. *OR*, 11, Part I, 300.

5. *OR*. 11, Part I, 300, 301, 306.

6. George Stevens, *Three Years in the Sixth Corps* (New York: D. Van Nostrand, 1870), 37–38.

7. *OR*, 11, Part I, 301, 308–309; Smith Memoir, 203, Smith Papers; Schiller, ed., 34; W.F. Smith to J.C. Ropes, 26 November 1893, John Codman Ropes Papers, Boston University Library, Boston, Massachusetts; Stephen Sears, *To the Gates of Richmond: The Peninsula Campaign* (New York: Ticknor and Fields, 1992), 42; Russel H. Beatie, *The Army of the Potomac: McClellan's First Campaign, March 1862-May 1862*, Volume III (New York: Savas Beatie LCC, 2007), 327–328, 364.

8. *OR*, 11, Part I, 301, 308–309; Smith Memoir, 202–203, Smith Papers; W.F. Smith to J.C. Ropes, 26 November 1893, Ropes Papers; Glenn Tucker, *Hancock the Superb* (Dayton, Ohio: Morningside Bookshop, 1980), 78; Sears, *To the Gates,* 42.

9. *OR*, 11, Part I, 301, 306, 359–360; W.F. Smith to Charles Suydam, 14 April 1862, Letters Sent (Second Division, Fourth Army Corps) Record Group 393, Inventory vol. 2, Entry no. 4526, National Archives.

10. *OR*, 11, Part I, 18, 363; G.B. McClellan to W.F. Smith, 15 April 1862, McClellan Papers; McClellan, 284–285; Sears, *To the Gates*, 55.

11. *OR*, 11, Part I, 18; *JCCW*, 37th.Congress, 3rd Session, Part I, 599.

12. *OR*, 11, Part I, 364, 372; Benedict, 1:251.

13. *OR*, 11, Part I, 364–365; *New York Herald*, 30 April 1862.

14. *OR*, 11, Part I, 364–366, 372, 375; *New York Herald*, 30 April 1862; Schiller, ed., 35; Sears, *To the Gates*, 56.

15. *OR*, 11, Part I, 364–366, 371–373, 378; for more detail about the Vermont Brigade at Lee's Mill, see Benedict, 1:249–261.

16. *OR*, 11, Part III, 103.

17. *OR*, 11, Part I, 363–365 and 11, Part III, 102–103; G.B. McClellan to Sarah Lyons Smith, 16 April 1862, and E.M. Stanton to G.B. McClellan, 17 April 1862, McClellan Papers.

18. *OR*, 11, Part I, 364–365 and 11, Part 3, 107; W.F. Smith to G.B. McClellan, [16 April 1862], and E.D. Keyes to R. Marcy, 20 April 1862, McClellan Papers.

19. *OR*, 11, Part I, 381 and 11, Part III, 119–120.

20. Edward P. Alexander, "Sketch of Longstreet's Division—Yorktown and Williamsburg," *Southern Historical Papers*, 10, No. 1 (1882):35.

21. Smith Memoir, 203, Smith Papers; Schiller, ed., 35; Wilson, 43; Alexander, 35; Louis Philippe Albert d'Orléans, Comte de Paris, *History of the Civil War in America*, 4 vols. (Philadelphia: Porter & Coates, 1875–1888), 2:10–11; John C. Ropes, *The Story of the Civil War*, 4 vols. (New York: G.P. Putnam's Sons, 1894–1913), 2:106–107.

22. W.T. H. Brooks to D. Brooks, 22 April 1862, Brooks Papers.

23. W.T.H. Brooks to D. Brooks, 22 April 1862,

Brooks Papers; *JCCW*, 37th Congress, 3rd Session, Part I, 600; McClellan, 312.

24. Clipping of the *Vermont Standard*, 25 April 1862, Smith Papers; U.S. Congress, House, 37th Congress, 2nd Session, 22 April 1862 and 2 May 1862, *Congressional Globe*, 1766, 1930–1931, 1933. H.L. Suydam probably referred to Hiram Lloyd Suydam, a businessman from Geneva, New York. He served for four months as regimental quartermaster of the 33rd New York, one of Smith's regiments, starting on May 15, 1861, but resigned after four months of service. Lewis Cass Aldrich., *History of Ontario County*, edited by George S. Conover (Syracuse: D. Mason & Co., 1893), 162.

25. An exception was the *Burlington, Vermont Free Press* on April 25, which suspected from evidence it acquired from letters and reports that the charges were true. By May 9, the *Free Press* had accepted the position that Smith was not drunk. While the *New York Herald* correspondent on April 29 believed the assaults "gained us no additional advantage, and resulted only in disaster," he still felt the charge of intoxication was false. Clippings of the *Burlington, Vermont Free Press*, 25 April 1862 and 9 May 1862, Smith Papers; *New York Herald*, 29 April 1862.

26. *New York Tribune*, 23 April 1862.

27. *New York Tribune*, 24 April 1862.

28. *Ibid.*

29. *New York Tribune*, 29 April 1862.

30. *New York Times*, 25 April 1862, 26 April 1862 and 2 May 1862; *New York Tribune*, 29April 1862 and 30 April 1862.

31. *Philadelphia Daily Evening Bulletin*. 24 April 1862, 25 April 1862 and 29 April 1862; *Burlington Sentinel* cited in clipping of *Burlington, Vermont Free Press*, 9 May 1862, Smith Papers.

32. G.B. McClellan to W.F. Smith, 24 April 1862, G.B. McClellan to Abraham Lincoln, 25 April 1862, and G.B. McClellan to S.L. Smith, 26 April 1862, Smith Papers.

33. E.D. Keyes to W.F. Smith, 26 April 1862, and W.T. H. Brooks to W.F. Smith, 26 April 1862, Smith Papers.

34. *New York Times*, 2 May 1862.

35. C.H. Chapman to J. Morrill, 26 April 1862, F. Daniels to J. Morrill, 1 May 1862, Smith Papers; U.S. Congress, House, 37th Congress, 2nd Session, 2 May 1862 *Congressional Globe*, 1930.

36. L.A. Grant to J. Morrill, 26 April 1862, Smith Papers.

37. L.A. Grant to J. Morrill, 26 April 1862, and J.B. McKean to J. Morrill, 25 April 1862, Smith Papers; U.S. Congress, House, 37th Congress, 2nd Session, 2 May 1862, *Congressional Globe*, 1930.

38. U.S. Congress, House, 37th Congress, 2nd Session, 2 May 1862, *Congressional Globe*, 1930–1931. Not all interpreted Morrill's statement as a retraction. The *Philadelphia Public Ledger* on May 3 called on Morrill to retract the slander upon Smith. But Biddle wrote to Smith that he considered the matter resolved in Smith's favor.

Philadelphia Public Ledger, 3 May 1862; C. Biddle to W.F. Smith, undated, Smith Papers.

39. U.S. Congress, House, 37th Congress, 2nd Session, 2 May 1862, *Congressional Globe*, 1933.

40. James Van Alen to W.F. Smith, 7 May 1862, Smith Papers; *New York Tribune*, 25 April 1862 and 14 May 1862; *Philadelphia Public Ledger*, 12 May 1862.

41. W.F. Smith to Charles Suydam, 29 April 1862, Letters Sent (Second Division, Fourth Army Corps) Record Group 393, Inventory vol. 2, Entry no. 4526, National Archives; *OR*, 11, Part I, 389–392; *New York Tribune*, 3 May 1862; Castleman, 128.

42. *New York Tribune*, 3 May 1862; *OR*, 11, Part I, 392–393.

43. Standing Order no. 231, 28 April 1862, and Standing Order no. 238, 2 May 1862, General Orders and Standing Orders (Second Division, Fourth Army Corps) Record Group 393, Inventory vol. 2, Entry no. 4534, National Archives; Castleman, 125, 128; *OR*,11, Part I, 390.

44. *OR*, 11, Part I, 526.

45. *Ibid.*

46. *OR*, 11, Part I, 526, 534–535.

47. *OR*, 11, Part I, 526–527, 535.

48. Sears, *Lincoln's Lieutenants*, 197–201.

49. *OR*, 11, Part I, 527, 535.

50. *OR*, 11, Part I, 527, 535; Sears, *Lincoln's Lieutenants*, 201; Smith Memoir, 207–208, and C. Stewart to W.F. Smith, 13 October 1883 and 3 November 1883, Smith Papers. Stewart asserts that he, and not the African American man, found the enemy redoubts empty while on a reconnaissance ordered by Sumner. C. Stewart to W.F. Smith, 13 October 1883, Smith Papers.

51. *OR*, 11, Part I, 535–536; Sears, *To the Gates*, 74.

52. *OR*, 11, Part I, 536–537.

53. *OR,* 11, Part I, 537–538.

54. *OR,* 11, Part I, 527; G.B. McClellan to Ellen McClellan, 6 May 1862, McClellan Papers.

55. *OR*, 11, Part I, 548.

56. *OR*, 11, Part I, 538.

57. *OR*, 11, Part I, 546.

58. Smith Memoir, 209, Smith Papers; G.B. McClellan to E. McClellan, 6 May 1862, McClellan Papers; W.T. H. Brooks to D. Brooks, 7 May 1862, Brooks Papers; Benedict, 1:273; *OR*, 11, Part I, 528, 546.

59. OR, 11, Part I, 538–539; Sears, *To the Gates*, 80; Tucker, 86.

60. *OR*, 11, Part I, 539–540; Tucker, 86–87; Sears, *To the Gates*, 80–81; for Confederate views of the battle, see *OR*, 11, Part I, 604–605, Alexander, 43–44, and Douglas S. Freeman, *Lee's Lieutenants, A Study in Command*, 4 vols. (New York: C. Scribner's Sons, 1946),1: 180–188.

61. *OR*, 11, Part I, 540–541.

62. *OR*, 11, Part I, 528, 541; Benedict, 1:274.

63. W.F. Smith to J.C. Ropes, 13 February 1898, Ropes Papers.

64. G.B. McClellan to E. McClellan, 6 May 1862, McClellan Papers.

65. Robert U. Johnson and Clarence C. Buell, eds. *Battles and Leaders of the Civil War*, 4 vols. (New York: The Century Company, 1887–1888), 2:198–199; hereafter cited as *Battles and Leaders*; W.F. Smith to J.C. Ropes, 13 February 1898, Ropes Papers; McClellan, 322; G.B. McClellan to E. McClellan, 6 May 1862, McClellan Papers; Wilson, 45–46; Beatie, 3:364; David M. Jordan, *Winfield Scott Hancock: A Soldier's Life* (Bloomington: Indiana University Press, 1988), 45; Stephen Sears also criticizes McClellan for his late arrival on the field to address Smith's requests. The army commander was first alerted to the need to be at the front at 1:00 P.M. Sears, *Lincoln's Lieutenants*, 203.

66. Standing Order no. 149, 17 May 1862, Register of Letters Received and Endorsement (Second Division, Sixth Provisional Corps) Record Group 393 Inventory vol. 2, Entry no. 4529, National Archives; *OR*, 11, Part III, 168, Benedict, 1:275.

67. Schiller, ed., 39; W.B. Franklin to W.F. Smith, 29 September 1892, Smith Papers; Mark A. Snell, *From First to Last: The Life of Major General William B. Franklin* (New York: Fordham University Press, 2002), 69.

68. *OR*, 11, Part I, 655; W.F. Smith to E. Purdy, 26 May 1862, LROAG.

69. *OR*, 11, Part I, 656; Stevens, 65–66; Thomas Hyde, *Following the Greek Cross* (New York: Houghton Mifflin, 1894), 61.

70. Benedict, 1:280.

71. Stevens, 73, 75; Standing Order nos. 293–295, 5 June 1862, and General Order no. 172, 21 June 1862, General and Standing Orders (Second Division, Sixth Provisional Corps) Record Group 393, Inventory vol. 2, Entry no. 4534, National Archives; Benedict, 1:281; *OR*, 11, Part III, 669; Louis Philippe D'Orléans to G.B. McClellan, 8 June 1862, McClellan Papers.

72. W.F. Smith to E. Purdy, 3 June 1862, Letters Sent (Second Division, Sixth Provisional Corps) Record Group 393, Inventory vol. 2, Entry no. 4526, National Archives.

73. W.F. Smith to E. Purdy, 24 May 1862 and 3 June 1862, Letters Sent (Second Division, Sixth Provisional Corps) Record Group 393, Inventory vol. 2, Entry no. 4526, National Archives; W.F. Smith to R. Marcy, 11 June 1862, McClellan Papers.

74. General Order no. 109, 13 April 1862, General and Standing Orders (Second Division, Fourth Army Corps) Record Group 393, Inventory vol. 2, Entry no. 4534, National Archives, W.F. Smith to R. Marcy, 11 June 1862, McClellan Papers.

Chapter V

1. Hassler, 138–139, 141–142; Sears, *Lincoln's Lieutenants*, 236, 241.

2. Schiller, ed., 41; Sears, *To the Gates*, 203.

3. *OR*, 11, Part II, 429, 462–463.

4. *OR*, 11, Part II, 429, 462–463, 466.

5. R. Marcy to W.F. Smith, 27 June 1862, McClellan Papers.

6. *OR*, 11, Part II, 318, 463; A.V. Colburn to W.B. Franklin and W.F. Smith, 27 June 1862, and R. Marcy to W.F. Smith, 27 June 1862, McClellan Papers; Benedict, 1:283.

7. *OR*, 11, Part II, 467–468; Sears, *To the Gates*, 247.

8. *OR*, 11, Part II, 467, 476, 480–481; Sears, *To the Gates*, 249–250.

9. *OR*, 11, Part II, 463, 473–474, 481; Whitman, 175; R.F. Taylor Report, 9 July 1862, William B. Franklin Papers, Division of Manuscripts, Library of Congress; Sears, *To the Gates*, 258; For a discussion of this abortive Confederate attack, see Freeman, 1:544–546, and *OR*, 11, Part II, 661, 690, 706.

10. Smith Memoir, 133, Smith Papers; *OR*, 11, Part II, 430–431, 463–464; Sears, *To the Gates*, 259, 266; Samuel P. Bates, *History of Pennsylvania Volunteers*, 5 vols. (Harrisburg: B. Singerly, 1869), 1:1237; Paris, 2:119.

11. *OR*, 11, Part 2, 477–479; Benedict, 1:294–298; Sears, *To the Gates*, 272; Benedict, 294.

12. Benedict, 1:298–299; Freeman,1:555.

13. Smith Memoir, 134, Smith Papers.

14. *OR*, 11, Part II, 464; Smith Memoir, 135–136, Smith Papers.

15. *OR*, 11, Part II, 77, 561; Smith Memoir, 136, Smith Papers; Benedict, 1:304; Whitman, 147.

16. Smith Memoir, 137–138, Smith Papers; *OR*, 11, Part II, 464–465, 469, 561; Benedict, 1:305, 307; Whitman, 177; Hyde, 75; Stevens, 105.

17. Smith Memoir, 137–138, Smith Papers; *OR*, 11, Part II, 464–466, 469, 477, 481, 561; Benedict, 1:304–305, 307; Whitman, 177; Hyde, 75; Stevens, 104–105.

18. *OR*, 11, Part II, 557, 627; Benedict, 1:305 307; Sears, *To the Gates*, 281, 287–288; Freeman, 1:575,578. Douglas Southall Freeman believed Jackson could have turned Smith's right flank but remained uncharacteristically inactive. Freeman, 1:578–580. Stephen Sears believes that the Union force was strong enough to deter Jackson, but the Confederate general could have done more to prevent Franklin from reducing the rear guard later in the day and sending four brigades to reinforce the Federals at Glendale. Sears also suggests that Jackson's physical exhaustion could also explain his unusual lack of initiative. Sears, *To the Gates*, 287–289.

19. Smith Memoir, 139, Smith Papers; *OR*, 11, Part II, 431, 464, 469; *Battles and Leaders*, 2:381. Kenneth P. Williams, *Lincoln Finds a General*, 5 vols. (New York: Macmillan, 1950), 1:238.

20. Smith Memoir, 139–140, Smith Papers.

21. Smith Memoir, 142–143, Smith Papers.

22. *OR*, 11, Part II, 431, 464, 469, 481; Hyde, 78.

23. *OR*, 11, Part II, 431, 464, 469, 481.

24. Castleman, 176–177.

25. *OR*, 11, Part II, 464, 469, 481; Benedict, 1:310; Castleman, 176–177.

26. Smith Memoir, 145–146, Smith Papers; *OR*, 11, Part II, 464.

27. Smith Memoir, 146, Smith Papers.

28. *OR*, 11, Part II, 464; Smith Memoir, 146, 149–150, Smith Papers; Castleman, 177; Benedict, 1:311.

29. Freeman,1:640–641; *OR*, 11, Part II, 464; W.F. Smith to J.C. Ropes, 21 March 1895, Ropes Papers; Smith Memoirs, 147, 150, Smith Papers; *Philadelphia Public Ledger*, 8 July 1862.

30. Freeman, 1:640–641; *OR*, 11, Part II, 464; W.F. Smith to J.C. Ropes, 21 March 1895, Ropes Papers; List of Brevets, [2 August 1862], McClellan Papers.

31. W.F. Smith's leave approval, 16 July 1862, Register of Letters Received and Endorsement Sent (Second Division, Sixth Corps) Record Group 393, Inventory vol. 2, Entry no. 4529, National Archives; R. Sattorlee to [L. Thomas], 29 July 1862, and W.F. Smith to L. Thomas, 4 August 1862, LROAG; G.B. McClellan to E. McClellan, 18 July 1862, McClellan Papers; Bates, 1:1237; Benedict, 1:311; Stevens, 114; Snell, 149.

32. *New York Times*, 10 July 1862; Smith Memoir, 151–152, Smith Papers; Schiller, ed., 50; Sears, *Lincoln's Lieutenants*, 272, 284; W.F. Smith to J.C. Ropes, 21 March 1895, Ropes Papers; G.B. McClellan to E. McClellan, 18 July 1862, McClellan Papers.

33. E.P. Townsend to W.F. Smith, 5 August 1862, LSOAG; Smith Memoir, 151–152, Smith Papers; W.F. Smith to L. Thomas, 4 August 1862 and 4 August 1862, LROAG; W.F. Smith returned to camp on August 12. General and Standing Orders (Second Division, Sixth Army Corps) Record Group 393, Inventory vol. 2, Entry no. 4534, National Archives; Sears, *Lincoln's Lieutenants*, 284; Snell, 154.

34. Hassler, 183–195.

Chapter VI

1. G.B. McClellan to E. McClellan, 22 August 1862, McClellan Papers.

2. *Ibid.*

3. *OR*, 19, Part I, 24–25; G.B. McClellan to E. McClellan, 22 August 1862, and G.B. McClellan to H.W. Halleck, 27 August 1862, McClellan Papers; William Love, *Wisconsin in the War of the Rebellion* (New York: Sheldon & Co., 1866), 315–316; Bates, 1:1237–1238.

4. James M. McPherson, *Battle Cry of Freedom: The Civil War Era* (New York: Ballantine Books, 1988), 528–529, 531–533.

5. Smith Memoir, 154, Smith Papers.

6. James M. McPherson, *Ordeal by Fire: The Civil War and Reconstruction* (New York: Alfred A. Knopf, 1982), 280–281.

7. Snell, 173.

8. *OR*, 19, Part I, 25–26; Snell, 173; McPherson, *Ordeal*, 281.

9. *OR*, 19, Part I, 26–27; R. Marcy to W.B. Franklin, 12 September 1862, and W.F. Smith to W.B. Franklin, 13 September 1862, McClellan Papers; McPherson, *Ordeal*, 281.

10. *OR*, 19, Part I, 28, 401, 407–408; Charles Slocum, *Life and Services of Major General Henry Warner Slocum* (Toledo: Slocum Pub. Co., 1903), 46; Benedict, 1:322; *Battles and Leaders*, 2:594.

11. *OR*, 19, Part I, 28, 401, 407–408; Slocum, 46; Benedict, 1:322; *Battles and Leaders*, 2:594.

12. *OR*, 19, Part I, 28, 401, 407–408; Slocum, 46; Benedict, 1:322; *Battles and Leaders*, 2:594.

13. *Battles and Leaders*, 2:596; Williams, 1:381; Snell, xii, 187, 189.

14. *OR*, 19, Part I, 376, 406; Whitman, 149–150; *OR*, 19, Part II, 296; Williams, 1:381; D. Scott Hartwig, *To Antietam Creek* (Baltimore: Johns Hopkins University Press, 2012), 577–578.

15. Stephen W. Sears, *Landscape Turned Red: The Battle of Antietam* (New Haven: Ticknor & Fields, 1983), 173, 178, 256; McPherson, *Ordeal*, 281, 283, 285; Timothy H. Donovan et al., *The American Civil War* (Wayne, New Jersey: Avery Publishing Group, 1987), 59–60.

16. Smith Memoir, 176, Smith Papers.

17. McPherson, *Ordeal*, 281; Boatner, 21; Smith Memoir, 176, Smith Papers; Schiller, ed., 53–54; *OR*, 19, Part I, 30, 61, 376–377, 402, 406–407, 409.

18. Smith Memoir, 176, Smith Papers; Schiller, ed., 54; *OR*, 19, Part I, 30, 61, 376–377, 402, 406–407, 409; *JCCW*, 37th Congress, 3rd Session, Part I, 626; Stevens, 149; Luther Stevenson, "The Maryland Campaign and the Battle of Antietam," 22, Loyal Legion Collection, U.S. Army Heritage and Education Center; Irwin later praised Smith for his order to advance the Third Brigade to the position that they held. W.H. Irwin to W.F. Smith, 2 May 1878, Smith Papers.

19. Smith Memoir, 177, Smith Papers; Benedict, 1:328; *OR*, 19, Part I, 61, 402–403, 408.

20. Smith Memoir, 177–178, Smith Papers; *OR*, 19 Part I, 61; Hassler, 284; Sears, *McClellan*, 314.

21. Smith Memoir, 179, Smith Papers.

22. Ropes, 2:370.

23. Smith Memoir, 178–79, and Clipping of the *New Orleans Times-Democrat*, 20 December 1896, Smith Papers; Schiller, ed., 55; Ropes, 2:370; Hassler, 284; Williams, 2:452–453; Sears, *McClellan*, 315; Sears, *Lincoln's Lieutenants*, 405.

24. Schiller, ed., 56; Hassler, 285–289.

25. *OR*, 19, Part I, 409–410.

26. *OR*, 19, Part I, 410–413, 910; for more details on the Seventh Maine at Antietam, see Hyde, 95–97.

27. *OR*, 19, Part I, 377; Luther Stevenson, "The Maryland Campaign and the Battle of Antietam," 30, Loyal Legion Collection; William Swinton, *Campaigns of the Army of the Potomac* (New York: C. Scribner's Sons, 1882), 222–224; Ropes, 2:370; W.F. Smith to W.B. Franklin, 10 December 1900, Smith Papers; Williams, 2:461; Sears, *Landscape*, 303.

28. Sears, *Lincoln's Lieutenants*, 411; Smith Memoir, 179, Smith Papers; R. March to W.B. Franklin, 18 September 1862 and 19 September 1862, and W.B. Franklin to G.B. McClellan, 18 September 1862, McClellan Papers.

29. For a discussion of Lincoln and the policy of emancipation, see J.G. Randall and David Donald, *The Civil War and Reconstruction*, 2nd ed. (Lexington, Massachusetts: D.C. Health and Co., 1969), 279–298, and McPherson, *Ordeal*, 293–294.

30. Smith Memoir, 268–269, Smith Papers; Boatner, 694, 765.

31. Smith Memoir, 269–270. McClellan wrote to his wife on September 25: "The President's late proclamation, the continuation of Stanton and Halleck in office, render it almost impossible for me to retain my commission and self-respect at the same time." McClellan, 615.

32. Clipping of "Was McClellan a Traitor?" *Harper*, 20 November 1914, Smith Papers; see also Tyler Dennett, *Lincoln and the Civil War in the Diaries and Letters of John Hay* (Westport: Negro University Press, 1972), 216–218.

33. Smith Memoir, 269–270 Smith Papers.

34. Smith Memoir, 269–270 Smith Papers.

35. Smith Memoir, 269–270, and Clipping of "Was McClellan a Traitor?" *Harper*, 20 November 1914, Smith Papers; Dennett, 216–218; J.H. Franklin, *The Emancipation Proclamation* (Garden City, New York: Doubleday, 1963), 79; Hassler, 300, 302–303; Sears, *McClellan*, 326; Sears, *Lincoln's Lieutenants*, 423; *OR*, 19, Part II, 395–396; McClellan, 655; General Jacob Cox mentioned that McClellan also asked Generals Burnside, John Cochrane, and Cox about opposing the Proclamation. The three generals urged McClellan not to act against the Proclamation. Jacob D. Cox, *Military Reminiscences of the Civil War*, 2 vols. (New York: C. Scribner's Sons, 1900), 1;359–363

36. *OR*, 19, Part I, 379; Stevens, 156, 158; C. Mundee to brigade commanders, 30 September 1862, Letters Sent (Second Division, Sixth Army Corps) Record Group 393, Inventory vol. 2, Entry no. 4526, National Archives.

37. W.F. Smith to O.D. Greene, 6 October 1862, Letters Sent (Second Division, Sixth Army Corps) Record Group 393, Inventory vol. 2, Entry no. 4526, National Archives.

38. *Ibid.*

39. G.B. McClellan to W.B. Franklin, 27 October 1862, Endorsements Sent (Sixth Army Corps) Record Group 393, Inventory vol. 2, Entry no 4409, National Archives.

40. G. Ruffles to W.B. Franklin, 7 November 1862, Franklin Papers; Standing Order no. 436, 30 October 1862, General and Standing Orders (Second Division, Sixth Army Corps) Record Group 393, Inventory vol. 2, Entry no. 4534, National Archives; *OR*, 51, Part I, 942; Stevens, 158–159, 164; G.B. McClellan to A. Lincoln, 5 November 1862, and W.B. Franklin to R. Marcy, 13 October 1862, 29 October 1862 and 30 October 1862, McClellan Papers.

41. Schiller, ed., 33.

42. W.F. Smith to J.C. Ropes, 29 December 1896, Ropes Papers.

43. Schiller, ed., 33; W.F. Smith to G.O. Shattuck, 1 November 1892, Smith Papers; W.F. Smith to H.V. Boynton, 26 February 1887, Carman Papers; W.F. Smith to J.C. Ropes, 26 November 1893 and 29 December 1896, Ropes Papers.

44. *OR*, 19, Part II, 583.

Chapter VII

1. *OR*, 21:59–61.

2. *Battles and Leaders*, 3:128; Schiller, ed., 58–59; W.F. Smith, "The Military Situation in Northern Virginia from the 1st to the 14th of November 1862," *Military Historical Society of Massachusetts Papers* 3 (1903): 105–107, 118–121.

3. McPherson, *Ordeal*, 303; Francis W. Palfrey, *The Antietam and Fredericksburg* (New York: Charles Scribner's Sons, 1883), 138; Mason Tyler, *Recollections of the Civil War* (New York: G.P. Putnam's Sons, 1912), 58; Newton Curtis, *From Bull Run to Chancellorsville* (New York: G.P. Putnam's Sons, 1906), 219; Francis Augustin O'Reilly *The Fredericksburg Campaign: Winter War on the Rappahannock* (Baton Rouge: Louisiana State University Press, 2006), 47, 49.

4. Smith Memoir, 184, Smith Papers.

5. Palfrey, 138; Smith Memoir, 183–184, Smith Papers; *Battle and Leaders*, 3:128–129.

6. O'Reilly, 51–52; Joseph Newell, ed., *"Ours." Annals of 10th Regiments, Massachusetts Volunteers, in the Rebellion* (Springfield: C.A. Nichols & Co., 1875), 159, 161; Tyler, 58; Curtis, 219; Benedict, 1:337; Morning Report, First Brigade, Second Division, Sixth Army Corps, 10 December 1862, Letters and Orders Received (Sixth Army Corps), Record Group 393, Inventory vol. 2, Entry no. 4434, National Archives.

7. Smith Memoir, 184, Smith Papers.

8. *Ibid.*

9. Smith Memoir, 184, Smith Papers; *Battles and Leaders*, 3:129–130.

10. O'Reilly, 52; Smith Memoir, 184, Smith Papers; *Battles and Leaders*, 3:129–130; McPherson, *Ordeal*, 304.

11. Smith Memoir, 185–186; Smith Papers; *Battles and Leaders*, 3:131.

12. *Battles and Leaders*, 3:131; Smith Memoir, 186, Smith Papers; *OR*, 21:449, 523, 534–535; A. Burnside to W.B. Franklin, 11 December 1862, Franklin Papers; Williams, 2:525; O'Reilly, 100.

13. *OR*, 21:449, 523, 535; *Battles and Leaders*, 3:131.

14. *OR*, 21:449, 523, 535; *Battles and Leaders*, 3:131.

15. Smith Memoir, 187, and W.F. Smith's affidavit on the battle of Fredericksburg for the Joint Committee on the Conduct of the War, 14 February 1863 (cited hereafter as Smith Affidavit), Smith Papers; *Battles and Leaders*, 3:132–133; *OR*, 21:109; O'Reilly, 117.

16. W.B. Franklin, *Reply of Major General William B. Franklin to the Report of the Joint*

Committee of Congress on the Conduct of the War on the Battle of Fredericksburg (New York: D. Van Nostrand, 1867), 1–2; *Battles and Leaders*, 3:133–134; Smith Affidavit, and Smith Memoir, 188, Smith Papers; Wilson, 54–55; O'Reilly, 117–118, 135.

17. J.A. Hardie to A. Burnside, 12 March 1863, James A. Hardie Papers, Division of Manuscripts, Library of Congress.

18. Franklin, 2.

19. *Battles and Leaders*, 3:134–135; Smith Memoir, 187–188, Smith Papers; Franklin, 2; Wilson, 55; Snell, 218.

20. O'Reilly, 137–138.

21. Smith Memoir, 188, Smith Papers.

22. Smith Affidavit, and Smith Memoir, 188, Smith Papers; *JCCW*, 37th Congress, 3rd Session, Part I, 698, 709; *Battles and Leaders*, 3:135; Franklin, 2; O'Reilly, 138.

23. *OR*, 21:450–451, 523; O'Reilly, 141.

24. *OR*, 21:359–360, 450, 535; Smith Affidavit, Smith Papers; Swinton, 247–248; *JCCW*, 37th Congress, 3rd Session, Part I, 661.

25. Benedict, 1:344; *JCCW*, 37th Congress, 3rd Session, Part I, 709; *OR*, 21:451, 523, 526, 530, 533; Franklin, 5; *New York Times*, 21 December 1862; O'Reilly, 356–362; Edward J. Stackpole, *The Battle of Fredericksburg* (Harrisburg, PA: Historical Times, 1965), 23, 32.

26. *Battles and Leaders*, 3:137.

27. Franklin, 4–5; *JCCW*, 37th Congress, 3rd Session, Part I, 698–699, 709; *OR*, 21:449; Stevens, 173; Snell, 223.

28. *OR*, 21:530.

29. *OR*, 21:451, 456, 523–524; *Battles and Leaders*, 3:138.

30. Smith Affidavit, Smith Papers.

31. *Battles and Leaders*, 3:137–138; Smith Affidavit, Smith Papers.

32. Smith Affidavit, Smith Papers; *Battles and Leaders*, 3:138.

33. *Battles and Leaders*, 3:138; Smith Affidavit, Smith Papers.

34. Franklin, 10; *JCCW*, 37th Congress, 3rd Session, Part I, 656, 661–662; Snell, 228–231, 235.

35. Snell, 229; *OR*, 21:868–869.

36. *OR*, 21:869.

37. *Ibid.*

38. *Ibid.*

39. Roy Basler, ed., *The Collected Works of Abraham Lincoln*, 9 vols. (New Brunswick: Rutgers University Press, 1953), 6:15.

40. Baldy was away on leave to be with his wife, who was pregnant and having complications. Franklin wrote his wife that Sarah Smith was "threaten with miscarriage being very nervous & troubled by our late repulse." Snell, 238.

41. Basler, ed., 6:15n–16n.

42. Snell, 236–240; *OR*, 21:868. William Farrar Smith, "Burnside Relieved," *Magazine of American History* 15 (1885), 197. On June 23, 1865, Smith wrote a letter to Burnside that included the subject of Baldy's letter to Lincoln. Smith claimed in his letter to Burnside that the letter "to the President which you saw and from which I did not understand you to dissent." Yet, Smith does not indicate the timing of either Burnside's review of the letter or evidence of Burnside's support, and there is no record that Burnside replied to Smith's letter. Smith, "Burnside Relieved," 200.

43. *New York Herald*, 26 December 1862.

44. Morning Report, First Brigade, Second Division, Sixth Corps, 26 December 1862, Letters and Orders Received (Sixth Army Corps), Record Group 393, Inventory vol. 2, Entry no. 4434, National Archives.

45. Morning Report, First Brigade, Second Division, Sixth Corps, 26 December 1862, Letters and Orders Received (Sixth Army Corps) Record Group 393, Inventory vol. 2, Entry 4434, National Archives; *New York Herald*, 26 December 1862; Tyler, 68.

46. Morning Reports, First Brigade, Second Division, Sixth Corps, 28 December 1862 and 29 December 1862, Letters and Orders Received (Sixth Army Corps) Record Group 393, Inventory vol. 2, Entry 4434, National Archives.

47. *OR*, 51, Part I, 973; Newell, ed., 173; Smith Memoir, 155, Smith Papers, McPherson, *Ordeal*, 317.

48. *JCCW*, 37th Congress, 3rd Session, Part I, 711–712, 732, 735, 737, 738, 741, 743, 745.

49. Cutler Andrews, *The North Reports the Civil War* (Pittsburgh: University of Pittsburgh Press, 1955), 338.

50. *OR*, 51, Part I, 975; Andrews, 338.

51. Smith Memoir, 155–156, Smith Papers; Schiller, ed., 64; Smith, "Burnside Relieved," 197; O'Reilly, 476; Ironically, Colonel Charles S. Wainwright accused Franklin and Smith of spreading anti-Burnside by private comments against the army commander and his plan. If Wainwright was correct, at least Smith tried to correct his error. See Allan Nevins, ed., *A Diary of Battle: The Personal Journals of Colonel Charles S. Wainwright 1861–1865* (New York: Harcourt & World, 1962), 157–159.

52. Smith Memoir, 156, Smith Papers.

53. Smith Memoir, 156, Smith Papers; A. Burnside to W.B. Franklin, 20 January 1863, Smith Papers.

54. *OR*, 21:991.

55. Love, 348; *New York Tribune*, 23 January 1863 and 24 January 1863; Tyler, 71; Newell, ed., 188–190; *OR*, 21:991; Smith Memoir, 157, Smith Papers.

56. Smith Memoir, 157–158, Smith Papers; Wilson, 56; Love, 348; *New York Tribune*, 27 January 1863; Tyler, 72; Newell, ed., 188–190.

57. Smith Memoir, 157–158, Smith Papers; Smith, "Burnside Relieved," 198.

58. W.T. H. Brooks to D. Brooks, 22 June 1862, Brooks Papers.

59. W.T. H. Brooks to D. Brooks, 2 October 1862, Brooks Papers.

60. Basler, ed., 6:74–75; *OR*, 21:998–999; W.T. H. Brooks to D. Brooks, 22 June 1862, 2 October 1862 and 17 February 1863, Brooks Papers; *JCCW*, 37th Congress, 3rd Session, Part I, 735–738, 743–745; W.B. Franklin to W.F. Smith, 4 March 1863, Smith Papers.

61. *OR*, 21:998–999.

62. *OR*, 21:998–999, W.F. Smith to A. Burnside, 27 February 1863 and 13 April 1863, and A. Burnside to W.F. Smith, 23 January 1865, Smith Papers; Smith, "Burnside Relieved," 199.

63. Smith Memoir, 158, 360, Smith Papers; Snell, 250–251; O'Reilly, 490–491; Ludwell Johnson, *Division and Reunion: America 1848–1877* (New York: John Wiley & Sons, 1978), 100–102; *OR*, 21:1004–1005; Paris, 2:605; *Philadelphia Public Ledger*, 27 January 1863.

64. *New York Times*, 6 February 1863.

65. *New York Times*, 6 February 1863; *OR*, 25, Part II, 15, 52–53; W.F. Smith to L. Thomas, 3 February 1863, LROAG.

66. Meade, 1:353.

67. Schiller, ed., 66; Smith was not alone in having an ill view of Hooker. Generals Darius Couch, O.O. Howard, and Meade were all privately critical. Nevins. ed., *Diary of Battle*, 155.

68. Meade, 1:353; Schiller, ed., 66; W.B. Franklin to W.F. Smith, 28 May 1863, Smith Papers; *OR*, 25, Part II, 52., Williams, 2:561.

69. *New York Times*, 9 February 1863.

70. *New York Times*, 15 February 1863; Stevens, 187.

71. Hyde, 117.

72. *OR*, vol. 25, Part II, 44.

73. *OR*, 18:149, 536.

74. J.M. Loving, ed., *Civil War Letters of George Washington Whitman* (Durham: Duke University Press, 1975), 86–88; Henry S. Burrage, *History of the Thirty-Sixth Regiment Massachusetts Volunteers* (Boston: Rockwell & Churchill, 1894), 34; E.O. Lord, ed., *History of the Ninth Regiment New Hampshire* (Concord: Republican Press Association, 1895), 295; William Todd, *The Seventy-Ninth Highlanders, New York Volunteers in the War of Rebellion, 1861–1865* (Albany: Press of Brandow, Barton & Co., 1886), 274.

75. *OR*, 18:539.

76. *OR*, vol. 51, Part I, 989; Smith Memoir, 88, 361, Smith Papers.

77. W.F. Smith to A. Lincoln, 10 March 1863, Abraham Lincoln Papers (on microfilm), Swem Library, William and Mary, Williamsburg, Virginia; Basler, ed., 6:129–130.

78. *New York Tribune*, 14 March 1863; E.M. Stanton endorsement, 19 March 1863, LROAG; W.F. Smith to A. Lincoln, 10 March 1863, Abraham Lincoln Papers, Swem Library, William and Mary, Williamsburg, Virginia; Smith Memoir, 88, 361, Smith Papers; A. Lincoln memo, 9 March 1863, Stanton Papers.

79. Wilson, 57–58.

80. Smith Affidavit, Smith Memoir, 87, 266–267, 362, and W.F. Smith to G.O. Shattuck, 1 November 1892, Smith Papers; Johnson, 100; Schiller, ed., xiv; Wilson, 58–59.

81. Bruce Tap, *Over Lincoln's Shoulder: The Committee on the Conduct of the War* (Lawrence: University of Kansas Press, 1998), 160; *JCCW*, 37th Congress, 3rd Session, Part I, 698–699, 707–712, 723–725; W.B. Franklin to W.F. Smith, 4 March 1863, Smith Papers; Meade, 1:361–362; Franklin, 1–11; Snell, 254–255, 261.

82. Tap, 161; Smith Affidavit, Smith Papers; Franklin, 12; Meade, 1:362; Snell, 254–256.

83. Swinton, 254.

84. Paris. 2:764.

85. Ropes, 2:461.

86. Ropes, 2:463.

87. *Ibid.*

88. *Battles and Leaders*, 3:128–138; Swinton, 245, 247–248, 254; Ropes, 2:460–468; Paris, 2:763–764.

89. O'Reilly, 138, 495–496, 501; Snell, 225–226.

90. Snell, 225–226.

91. Smith Memoir, 87, Smith Papers.

92. W.F. Smith to L. Thomas, 20 April 1863, LROAG; Smith Memoir, 87, 215; Wilson, 58–59.

93. R.S. Sattelee and J.F. Hammond Medical Certificate, 27 May 1863, LROAG.

94. R.S. Sattelee and J.F. Hammond Medical Certificate, 27 May 1863, and J.C. Kelley to E. Townsend, 24 May 1863, LROAG; E. Townsend to W.F. Smith, 2 June 1863, LSOAG; Smith Memoir, 87, 215, Smith Papers; *OR*, 26, Part I, 506; Wilson, 58–59.

95. Smith Memoir, 216, Smith Papers.

Chapter VIII

1. Smith Memoir, 89, Smith Papers.

2. L. Thomas to W.F. Smith, 7 June 1863, LROAG; Smith Memoir, 89, 215–216; Freeman Cleaves, *Meade of Gettysburg* (Dayton, Ohio: Morningside Bookshop, 1980), 118.

3. Cleaves, 118; Tucker, 124–125.

4. *OR*, 27, Part II, 220 and 27, Part III, 240, 330; Smith Memoir, 89, Smith Papers; Edwin B. Coddington, *The Gettysburg Campaign: A Study of Command* (New York: Charles Scribner's Sons, 1968), 146.

5. *OR*, vol. 27, Part II, 223–224.

6. *OR*, 27, Part II, 220, 224, 443, 551–552; J.C. Schultze to E.C. Wilson, 28 June 1863, Letters Sent (Department of the Susquehanna) Record Group 393, Inventory vol. 1, Entry no. 4606, National Archives; Neil Boyd, "The Confederate Invasion of Central Pennsylvania and the Battle of Sporting Hill," https://web.archive.org/web/20030304185356im_/http://campcurtin.org/campcurtin/reenact/5.gif ; Joseph Cress, "Civil War150: Union Veteran recalls fight at Oyster Point," June 26, 2013, The Sentinel, https://cumberlink.com/news/local/history/civil-war-union-veteran-recalls-fight-at-oyster-point/article_8f1654ca-decd-11e2-9ab6-001a4bcf887a.html.

7. Smith Memoir, 90–91, Smith Papers; *OR*, 27, Part II, 213, 220, 235, 443, 551–552; Randall and Donald, 401; Cleaves, 132–133; Neil Boyd, "The Confederate Invasion of Central Pennsylvania and the Battle of Sporting Hill" https://web.archive.org/web/20030304185356im_/http://campcurtin.org/campcurtin/reenact/5.gif; Joseph Cress, "Civil War150: Union Veteran recalls fight at Oyster Point," June 26, 2013, The Sentinel,   https://cumberlink.com/news/local/history/civil-war-union-veteran-recalls-fight-at-oyster-point/article_8f1654ca-decd-11e2-9ab6-001a4bcf887a.html.

8. *OR*, 27, Part II, 220, 236.

9. *OR*, 27, Part II, 220 and 27, Part III, 476; Smith Memoir, 90, Smith Papers.

10. *OR*, 27, Part II, 220–221; Smith Memoir, 90, Smith Papers.

11. *OR*, 27, Part II, 224, 696–697.

12. *OR*, 27, Part II, 221, 224, 236, 697; Smith Memoir, 91, Smith Papers; Freeman, 3:137–138.

13. Smith Memoir, 92, Smith Papers.

14. *OR*, 27, Part II, 221, 224, 237; Smith Memoir, 91–92, Smith Papers; Freeman, 3:138; Coddington, 202.

15. *OR*, 27, Part II, 221; Diary of Isaac Harris, 1 July 1863, Isaac Harris Papers, United States Army Military History Institute.

16. Smith Memoir, 92, and Merkel Landis, "Civil War Times in Carlisle" (1931), Smith Papers.

17. *OR*, 27, Part II, 221, 224–225.

18. *OR*, 27, Part II, 213 and 27, Part 3, 508, 549.

19. Cleaves, Chapters 11–12; Randall and Donald, 401–405.

20. *OR*, 27, Part III, 526.

21. *OR*, vol. 27, Part III, 577.

22. *OR*, 27, Part II, 238 and 27, Part III, 526, 548, 577, 593, 677; D. Couch to W.S. Ketchum, 16 August 1863, Letters Sent (Department of the Susquehanna), Record Group 393, Inventory vol.1, Entry no. 4606, National Archives; *New York Tribune*, 9 July 1863 and 13 July 1863; Coddington, 542; Eric J. Wittenberg, J. David Petruzzi and Michael F. Nugent, *One Continuous Fight: The Retreat from Gettysburg and the Pursuit of Lee's Army of Northern Virginia, July 4–14, 1863* (New York: Savas Beatie, 2008), 45.

23. *OR*, 27, Part II, 221, 225; Coddington, 542.

24. *OR*, 27, Part II, 221–223 and 27, Part III, 579–580.

25. Smith Memoir, 95, Smith Papers; *OR*, 27, Part II, 222 and 27, Part III, 531, 578–579, 584–585; Coddington, 543.

26. *OR*, 27, Part III, 580.

27. *OR*, 27, Part III, 611.

28. *OR*, 27, Part III, 611; Coddington, 562; Wittenberg, Petruzzi, and Nugent, 257.

29. Wittenberg, Petruzzi, and Nugent, 200.

30. *OR*, 27, Part I, 968 and 27, Part II, 222, 226.

31. Meade 2:366; *OR*, 27, Part I, 147 and 27, Part II, 222–223, 226 and 27, Part III, 698.

32. *OR*, 27, Part II, 227, 920–921, 925–926.

33. Smith Memoir, 97, 211–212, Smith Papers.

34. Smith Memoir, 211–213, Smith Papers; *OR*, 27, Part II, 920–921, 925–926.

35. Basler, ed., 6:327–328.

36. *OR*, 27, Part III, 680.

37. *OR*, 27, Part III, 651.

38. *OR*, 27, Part II, 238.

39. *OR*, 27, Part I, 119 and 27, Part II, 238 and 27, Part III, 579, 651, 680.

40. *OR*, 27, Part III, 705, 715–716.

41. *OR*, 27, Part III, 757–758.

42. *OR*, 27, Part III, 747–749, 757–758; D. Couch to H.H. Lockwood, 23 July 1863, Letters Sent (Department of the Susquehanna) Record Group 393, Inventory vol. 1, Entry no. 4606, National Archives.

43. *OR*, 27, Part III, 771.

44. *OR*, 27, Part III, 764, 765, 771, 774.

45. Montgomery Blair to W.F. Smith, 10 August 1863, Smith Papers.

46. W.F. Smith to M. Blair, 23 August 1863, Smith Papers.

47. Meade, 2:144; M. Blair to W.F. Smith, 10 August 1863, 13 August 1863 and 19 August 1863, and W.F. Smith to M. Blair, 11 August 1863 and 23 August 1863, Smith Papers.

48. W.F. Smith to M. Blair, 23 August 1863, Smith Papers.

49. W.F. Smith to Capt. Melvin, 23 August 1863, Smith Papers.

50. *OR*, 29, Part II, 102; Meade, 2:144; Standing Order no.108, 26 August 1863 and W.F. Smith to L. Thomas, 31 August 1863, LROAG; Smith Memoir, 363 and W.F. Smith to Capt. Melvin, 23 August 1863, Smith Papers.

Chapter IX

1. Smith Memoir, 218, 220, Smith Papers; *OR*, 30, Part III, 362 and 30, Part IV, 62.

2. U.S. Board of Officers upon the Claim of Major General William F. Smith, *Brown's Ferry, 1863* (Philadelphia: F. McManus, Jr. & Co., 1901), 62; cited hereafter as *Brown's Ferry*.

3. *Brown's Ferry*, 55, 62, 110; W.F. Smith, "An Historical Sketch of the Military Operations around Chattanooga, Tenn., September 22 to November 27, 1863," *Military Historical Society of Massachusetts Papers* 8 (1910): 154–155.

4. *Brown's Ferry*, 135, 217–218; Peter Cozzens, *The Shipwreck of Their Hopes: The Battles for Chattanooga* (Urbana: University of Illinois Press, 1994), 18. Also see David A. Powell, *Battle Above the Clouds: Lifting the Siege of Chattanooga and the Battle of Lookout Mountain, October 16-November 24, 1863* (El Dorado Hills, CA: Savas Beatie LLC, 2017), 19.

5. *Brown's Ferry*, 72–74; Smith, "Historical Sketch," 163; Cozzens, 19–20; Powell, 22–23.

6. *Brown's Ferry*, 72–74; Smith, "Historical Sketch," 163.

7. *Brown's Ferry*, 80.

8. *Brown's Ferry*, 46, 75–8, 96; *OR*, 30, Part IV, 348–349; Livermore, 303; Powell, 4.

9. *Brown's Ferry*, 79.

10. *Brown's Ferry*, 79, 81; Smith, "Historical Sketch," 195; Thomas Livermore, "The Siege and Relief of Chattanooga," *Military Historical Society of Massachusetts Papers* 8 (1910):303.

11. *Brown's Ferry*, 71, 78–79, 82; Wilson, 64–65.

12. *Brown's Ferry*, 78–79, 94–95.

13. *Brown's Ferry*, 55; Schiller, ed., 72; Cozzens, 40–41.

14. A flying ferry is a raft used as a ferry and held by an anchor cable fastened upstream from a ferry site.

15. Smith, "Historical Sketch," 161–162; Smith Memoir, 223, Smith Papers.

16. *OR*, 30, Part I, 208.

17. *OR*, 30, Part I, 208, 216–217.

18. *Brown's Ferry*, 55–58, 67, 86; Smith, "Historical Sketch," 164.

19. Smith, "Historical Sketch," 168–169; *Brown's Ferry*, 55–56.

20. Smith, "Historical Sketch," 169–170; *Brown's Ferry*, 56; *OR*, 31, Part I, 77.

21. *Brown's Ferry*, 56.

22. Smith, "Historical Sketch," 170.

23. Smith, "Historical Sketch," 170; *Brown's Ferry*, 57.

24. Smith, "Historical Sketch," 170; *Brown's Ferry*, 46, 48, 51, 56–57, 64, 72, 73, 88, 105, 183, 194, 195; Livermore, 292–293, 303, 312–313, 324, 328; Wilson, 65–71. The view that Smith was primarily responsible for the plan that restored the short line is not universally held. The controversy over the authorship of the plan between Smith and his critics began in the postwar years. See this discussion in Chapter XVI. Modern historians still debate the issue. For an interpretation that supports Rosecrans's authorship of the specific plan, see William M. Lamers, *The Edge of Glory: A Biography of General William S. Rosecrans* (New York: Harcourt Brace & World, 1961), 389–400. Nevertheless, historian James L. McDonough credits Smith with the specific plan for the restoration of the short line. See James L. McDonough, *Chattanooga: A Death Grip on the Confederacy* (Knoxville: University of Tennessee Press, 1984), 55, 57–58, 74. A more recent assessment suggests that Baldy was the author of the specific plan that used the Brown's Ferry location for the Federal attack from Chattanooga. Cozzens, 41–43, 425–426.

25. *Brown's Ferry*, 57; Fairfax Downey, *Storming the Gateway: Chattanooga, 1863* (New York: David McKay Co., 1960), 135.

26. *Brown's Ferry*, 57; W.F. Smith to J.C. Ropes, 13 February 1898, and Preston West to J.C. Ropes, 28 November 1889, Ropes Papers; Smith Memoir, 235, Smith Papers; Smith, "Historical Sketch," 156, 166. Downey, 140–141.

27. *Brown's Ferry*, 58–59; *OR*, 31, Part I, 42 and 31, Part II, 27.

28. *OR*, 31, Part I, 77 and 31, Part II, 27; Cozzens, 51–53.

29. *Brown's Ferry*, 59.

30. Ulysses S. Grant, *Personal Memoirs of U.S. Grant*, 2 vols. (New York: C.L. Webster & Co., 1885), 2:35; *Brown's Ferry*, 59; *OR*, 31, Part II, 27.

31. Cozzens, 53,56; *OR*, 31, Part I, 77.

32. *OR*, 31, Part I, 77–78.

33. *OR*, 31, Part I, 78–80, 136.

34. Cozzens, 63–64; *OR*, 31, Part I, 49, 50, 78, 80, 84–87, 136.

35. *OR*, 31, Part I, 52, 78; *New York Tribune*, 18 November 1863.

36. *OR*, 31, Part I, 78; for a modern account of the battle, see McDonough, 76–85.

37. *Brown's Ferry*, 36; Smith, "Historical Sketch," 172; *OR*, 31, Part I, 56, 58 and 31, Part II, 28.

38. Cozzens, 73–74; William F. Smith to Dennis H. Mahan, December 7, 1863, William Farrar Smith Collection, Division of Manuscripts, Library of Congress.

39. *Brown's Ferry*, 110.

40. Cozzens, 100; Smith, "Historical Sketch," 175–176; *Brown's Ferry*, 110.

41. *OR*, 31, Part I, 72.

42. *OR*, 31, Part I, 68, 72; Downey, 146.

43. *Brown's Ferry*, 60.

44. *OR*, 31, Part III, 122.

45. *OR*, 31, Part III, 201.

46. *Brown's Ferry*, 59–60; *OR*, 31, Part III, 122, 123, 201.

Chapter X

1. Smith, "Historical Sketch," 189; *OR*, 31, Part I, 137; Smith Memoir, 105, Smith Papers; W.F. Smith to the officer of the day, 26 October 1863, W.F. Smith to W.E. Merrill, 29 October 1863, W.F. Smith to G. Burroughs, 31 October 1863, W.F. Smith to W. Hazen, 2 November 1863, and W.F. Smith to W.E. Merrill, 4 November 1863, Records of the Chief Engineer, Department of the Cumberland (cited hereafter as RCEDC), Record Group 393, Inventory vol. 1, Entry no. 1041, National Archives; in this order book, the orders from the Chief Engineer were generally unsigned or written by the command of Smith. But since Smith gave all the orders, he is cited here and will be cited hereafter as the author of the directives.

2. Smith, "Historical Sketch," 189–190, 192–193; McDonough, 106–107 Cozzens, 106–107.

3. Smith, "Historical Sketch," 193.

4. *Ibid*.

5. Smith, "Historical Sketch," 193–194; Andrews, 476; McDonough, 107; Cozzens, 108.

6. Smith, "Historical Sketch," 194–195; William T. Sherman, *Memoirs of General W.T. Sherman*, 2 vols. (New York: C.L. Webster, 1891), 1:390, 400.

7. W.F. Smith to A.D. Bache, 7 December 1863, William F. Smith Papers, Division of Manuscripts, Library of Congress; Wilson, 74–77; Henry Villard, *Memoirs of Henry Villard*, 2 vols. (Boston: Houghton Mifflin, 1904), 2:233; Smith, "Historical Sketch," 195–196, 198; Wilson, 71, 74–76; Downey, 152–153; McDonough, 108–109; Cozzens, 112.

8. W.F. Smith to A.D. Bache, 7 December 1863, William F. Smith Papers, Division of Manuscripts, Library of Congress; Wilson, 74–77; Smith, "Historical Sketch," 196, 198; Downey, 152–153; McDonough, 108–109.

9. *OR*, 31, Part II, 73.

10. *OR*, 31, Part II, 73–74.

11. John Y. Simon, ed., *The Papers of Ulysses S. Grant*, 18 vols. (Carbondale: Southern Illinois University Press, 1967–1991), 9:432–433; *OR*, 31, Part II, 74.

12. Smith, "Historical Sketch," 200–201; *OR*, 31, Part II, 74–75; Wilson, 76.

13. Smith, "Historical Sketch," 201; *OR*, 31, Part II, 66, 74–75.

14. Smith, "Historical Sketch," 197.

15. Smith, "Historical Sketch," 199–200; Wilson, 77; Downey, 153–154; McDonough, 114.

16. Smith, "Historical Sketch," 201–209, 212; for more detail on General Cleburne's defense of Missionary Ridge, see *OR*, 31, Part II, 706, 726, 735, 739, 745–753, 758; Downey, 154–155.

17. Smith, "Historical Sketch," 207–210; Downey, 168–172 McDonough, 156–157.

18. Smith, "Historical Sketch," 213–215; McDonough, 130–142.

19. Smith, "Historical Sketch," 216–218; McDonough, 182–183, 211–212.

20. Smith, "Historical Sketch," 212, 216, 222–245; Cozzens, 241.

21. *OR*, 31, Part II, 573; This quote can also be found in Sherman, 1:402.

22. Simon, ed., 9: 565–566.

23. *OR*, 31, Part III, 277.

24. *OR*, 31, Part II, 572–573 and 31, Part III, 277; Simon, ed., 9:565–566.

25. *OR*, 31, Part III, 414.

26. Simon, ed., 9:650n; W.F. Smith to W.G. Eaton, 29 November 1863, and W.F. Smith to H.S. Dean, 29 November 1863, RCEDC; *OR*, 31, Part II, 75 and 31, Part III, 404, 414; W.F. Smith to I.C. Woodruff, 10 December 1863, LRTB; I.C. Woodruff to W.F. Smith, 22 December 1863, 3 February 1864, 11 February 1864, and 12 February 1864, LSTB.

27. Comstock Diary, 14 December 1863, Cyrus Comstock Papers, Division of Manuscripts, Library of Congress; W.F. Smith to P. O'Connell, 2 January 1864, W.F. Smith to the commander of the Twenty First Michigan Volunteers, 2 January 1864, and W.F. Smith to D. Ennis, 3 January 1864, RCEDC.

28. W.F. Smith to G.O. Shattuck, 4 August 1892, Smith Papers; W.F. Smith to C. Dana, 15 January 1864, Stanton Papers.

29. W.F. Smith to C. Dana, 15 January 1864, Stanton Papers.

30. *Ibid.*

31. Comstock Diary, 18 January 1864, Comstock Papers; Simon, ed., 10:39, 40, 41n, 45–46; *OR*, 33:394–395.

32. *OR*, 31, Part III, 457–458; Wilson, 80.

33. J. Tucker to W.F. Smith, 31 January 1864, Smith Papers; Simon, ed., 10:232n-233n; *OR*, 31, Part III, 571 and 32, Part II, 79–80; Grant, 2:97–98.

34. *OR*, 32, Part II, 468.

35. Comstock Diary, 11 March 1864, Comstock Papers; Simon, ed., 10:142n; *OR*, 32, Part II, 468; Walter Hebert, *Fighting Joe Hooker* (New York: Bobs Merrill, 1944), 268–270.

36. C. Mundee to W.F. Smith, 10 January 1864, Smith Papers.

37. J.H. Wilson to W.F. Smith, 10 February 1864, James Harrison Wilson Papers, Division of Manuscripts, Library of Congress.

38. J.H. Wilson to W.F. Smith, 14 February 1864, Wilson Papers.

39. C. Mundee to W.F. Smith, 10 January 1864, Smith Papers; O.E. Babcock to W.F. Smith, 9 February 1864, Letters Received (Eighteenth Army Corps), Record Group 393, Inventory vol. 2, Entry no. 6890, National Archives; J.H. Wilson to W.F. Smith, 10 February 1864, 14 February 1864 and 27 February 1864, Wilson Papers; Simon, ed., 10:142n.

40. Schiller, ed., 83.

41. *New York Herald*, 17 March 1864.

42. *Ibid.*

43. *New York Herald*, 17 March 1864, *New York Times*, 12 March 1864 and 14 March 1864; *New York Tribune*, 12 March 1864; *Boston Daily Evening Transcript*, 5 March 1864 and 12 March 1864.

44. *New York Times*, 24 March 1864.

45. G. Gray to W.F. Smith, 5 February 1886, Smith Papers; *New York Times*, 24 March 1864 and 25 March 1864; *OR*, 33:861 and 36, Part II, 348; *Battles and Leaders*, 4:104–106, 106n; Wilson, 81.

46. W.F. Smith to J.H. Wilson, 16 March 1864, Wilson Papers.

47. *Ibid.*

48. *Ibid.*

49. Simon, ed., 10:39–41, 110n; *OR*, 32, Part II, 411–413; Wilson, 82–84.

50. J.A. Rawlins to Mary Rawlins, 13 April 1864, Wilson Papers.

51. One possible reason for the renewed administration confidence in Meade was reported in the *New York Times*, 25 March 1864. The paper reported that political pressure on Lincoln from Pennsylvania was enough to block any change in command.

52. J.A. Rawlins to M. Rawlins, 13 April 1864, Wilson Papers; Wilson, 40–41, 81–84; Comstock Diary, 11 March 1864, Comstock Papers; *New York Times*, 24 March 1864 and 25 March 1864; Sears, *Lincoln's Lieutenants*, 619.

53. *Brown's Ferry*, 54; *OR*, 33:861; *Battles and Leaders*, 4:104.

Chapter XI

1. *OR*, 33:861; J.A. Rawlins to M. Rawlins, 2 April 1864, Wilson Papers; a typed review by W.F. Smith of B.F. Butler, *Autobiography and Personal Reminiscences of Major General Benjamin F. Butler*, Smith Papers; cited hereafter as Smith Review.

2. John Rawlins to M. Rawlins, 6 March 1864, Wilson Papers; Diary Entry 7 March 1864, Cyrus Ballou Comstock Diary,1863–67; W.F. Smith to W.B. Franklin, 28 April 1864, Franklin Papers; W.B. Franklin to W.F. Smith, 29 June 1864, Smith Papers; Snell, 325.

3. *Battles and Leaders,* 4:206n; Schiller, ed., 84; Smith Review, Smith Papers.

4. *Battles and Leaders,* 4:206; Smith Review, Smith Papers; *OR,* 33:794–795; William Glenn Robertson, *Back Door to Richmond: The Bermuda Hundred Campaign; April-June 1864* (Newark: University of Delaware Press, 1987), 25.

5. W.F. Smith, *From Chattanooga to Petersburg under Generals Grant and Butler* (Boston: Houghton Mifflin, 1893), 117n.

6. B.F. Butler, *Autobiography and Personal Reminiscences of Major General Benjamin F. Butler* (Boston: A.M. Thayer & Co., 1892) 637–638, 1053–1054; Smith, *From Chattanooga,* 117, 117n; *OR,* 33:828; George W. Wolfson, "Butler's Relations with General Grant and the Army of the James in 1864," *South Atlantic Quarterly,* vol. X, no. 4 (October 1911): 379.

7. Smith, *From Chattanooga,* 117n.

8. Smith, *From Chattanooga,* 114, 115, 116, 116n, 117, 117n; *Battles and Leaders,* 4:206; clippings of articles written by W.F. Smith under the name "Volunteer" in the *New York World,* 1868 (cited hereafter as "Volunteer" articles), and W.F. Smith to G.O. Shattuck, undated, Smith Papers; Smith's view that Grant failed to stress Petersburg is largely sustained by at least one modern historian. See Robertson, 31.

9. Smith Review, Smith Papers; Schiller, ed., 85, 90; *Battles and Leaders,* 4:206–207.

10. Schiller, ed., 85; Butler, 636–637; Alfred P. Rockwell, "The Tenth Army Corps in Virginia May 1864," *Military Historical Society of Massachusetts Papers* 9 (1912):271; *OR,* 33:885–886.

11. *OR,* 33:916, 961.

12. *OR,* 33:1019; see Robertson, 20.

13. W.F. Smith to S.L. Smith, 24 April 1864, Smith Papers.

14. W.F. Smith to S.L. Smith, 30 April 1864, Smith Papers.

15. W.F. Smith to S.L. Smith, 24 April 1864, 26 April 1864, 30 April 1864, Smith Papers; W.F. Smith to W.B. Franklin, 28 April 1864, Franklin Papers; *OR,* 33:1019.

16. W.F. Smith to W.B. Franklin, 28 April 1864, Franklin Papers; See also T. Harry Williams, *Lincoln and His Generals* (New York: Alfred Knopf, 1952), 293.

17. W.F. Smith to W.B. Franklin, 28 April 1864, Franklin Papers.

18. *OR,* 33:1019 and 36, Part II, 327, 349; Butler, 638.

19. *OR,* 33:916; Rockwell, 268; I.J. Wistar, *Autobiography of Isaac Jones Wistar, 1827-1905* (Philadelphia: The Wistar Institute of Anatomy and Biology, 1937), 446–448; Butler, 639; Smith, *From Chattanooga,* 173.

20. *Battles and Leaders,* 4:207–208; Butler, 640; Rockwell, 273; *OR,* 36, Part II, 430; Robertson, 59.

21. *Battles and Leaders,* 4:207–208; Rockwell, 274.

22. Smith Review, and W.F. Smith to J.H. Wilson, 19 July 1864, Smith Papers; *Battles and Leaders,* 4:208; Smith, *From Chattanooga,* 117; At least one later-day historian sustains Smith's view of the certainty and the need of capturing Petersburg in early May. See Wolfson, 380–382.

23. *OR,* 36, Part II, 475; Robertson, 80.

24. Rockwell, 274–275; George Bruce, "General Butler's Bermuda Campaign," *Military Historical Society of Massachusetts Papers* 9 (1912): 316–317; Butler, 642–643; *OR,* 36, Part II, 154, 475; Jessie A. Marshall, ed., *Public and Private Correspondence of Gen. Benjamin F. Butler during the Period of the Civil War,* 5 vols. (Norwood, Massachusetts: privately published, 1917), 4:167–169. For a modern account of this battle, see Robertson, 79–82.

25. Marshall, 4:167–169.

26. *OR,* 36, Part II, 124, 519–522.

27. *OR,* 36, Part II, 124–125, 522–523.

28. *OR,* 36, Part II, 154–155; for a modern account that is critical of Brooks' limited gains, see Robertson, 85–89.

29. Butler, 645; Marshall, 4:175; Rockwell, 277; Bruce, 322.

30. Marshall, ed., 4:179–180; Joseph Denny, *Wearing the Blue in the Twenty-fifth Massachusetts Volunteer Infantry* (Worcester: Putnam & Davis, 1879), 276; Rockwell, 278; *OR,* 36, Part II, 126, 149, 589; Robertson, 112; for a modern account of the battle of Swift Creek, see Robertson, 110–116.

31. *OR,* 36, Part II, 126–127, 148–149.

32. *OR,* 36, Part II, 133–134; S.M. Thompson, *Thirteenth Regiment of New Hampshire Volunteer Infantry in the War of the Rebellion, 1861-1865* (Boston: Houghton Mifflin, 1888), 265.

33. *OR,* 36, Part II, 593; Butler, 645; Smith, *From Chattanooga,* 183; *Battles and Leaders,* 4:208.

34. *Battles and Leaders,* 4:208; Smith, *From Chattanooga,* 118–119, 183.

35. Smith, *From Chattanooga,* 181–182; In his autobiography, Baldy states that Butler told his staff that he did not propose to build a bridge for West Point men to retreat across. Schiller, ed., 86; Historian George Wolfson said, "Butler's neglect to take the advice of his subordinates was due not only to a poor grasp of the situation but to his peculiar headstrong character which impelled him to refuse any advice not in accord with his own point of view." Wolfson, 384.

36. Smith, *From Chattanooga,* 181–182; Rockwell, 278–283; Wolfson, 383–384.

37. Rockwell, 280.

38. Smith, *From Chattanooga,* 183.

39. Smith, *From Chattanooga,* 183–184; Rockwell, 280.

40. Butler, 648; *Battles and Leaders,* 4:208; *OR,* 51, Part I, 1260; Rockwell, 285.

41. W.F. Smith to S.L. Smith, 2 May 1864, and Smith Review, Smith Papers; Smith, *From Chattanooga,* 150–152.

42. Smith, *From Chattanooga*, 148–155; Schiller, ed., 90; Wilson, 103.

43. Smith, *From Chattanooga*, 149.

44. Smith, *From Chattanooga*, 148–155; Butler, 648–649; *OR*, 36, Part II, 149, 619.

45. *Battles and Leaders*, 4:208–209; Rockwell, 286–287; Marshall, 4:194–195; Robertson, 142–143.

46. *OR*, 36, Part II, 113–114, 122–123, 650, 692; *Battles and Leaders*, 4:209.

47. *OR*, 36, Part II, 114.

48. *OR*, 36, Part II, 114–115, 123.

49. *OR*, 36, Part II, 115.

50. Smith Review, Smith Papers.

51. OR, 36, Part II, 115; Smith Review, Smith Papers.

52. *OR*, 36, Part II, 115, 134.

53. *OR*, 36, Part II, 115, 127, 806.

54. *OR*, 36, Part II, 115, 776–777, 805–806; G. Weitzel to N. Bowen, 15 May 1864, Smith Papers; Robertson, 170.

55. *OR*, 36, Part II, 116, 150–152; *Battles and Leaders*, 4:210.

56. *OR*, 36, Part II, 116, 127, 150–152; *Battles and Leaders*, 4:210; F.W. Farquhar to W.F. Smith, 27 May 1864, Register of Letters Received (Eighteenth Army Corps), Record Group 393, Inventory vol. 2, Entry no. 6886, National Archives; William Derby, *Bearing Arms in the Twenty-Seventh Massachusetts Regiment of Volunteer Infantry during the Civil War, 1861–1865* (Boston: Wright & Potter Printing Co., 1883), 269. There is some controversy over Heckman's failure to put wire in front of his lines. Butler claims there were nine miles of wire for use, but Heckman claims that he was unable to procure any when he requested it on the fifteenth. Butler, 658; Derby, 290.

57. *OR*, 36, Part II, 116. 123: Bruce, 334.

58. A.A. Humphreys, *The Virginia Campaign of '64 and '65* (New York: C. Scribner's Sons, 1883), 149, 152; Denny, 289–290; *OR*, 36, Part II, 129–130, 144, 152, 199–200; Derby, 272–273, 291; Bruce, 334; Rockwell, 290–291; Robertson, 174, 180–181.

59. *OR*, 36, Part II, 108–109, 116–117, 151–152; Freeman, 3:488.

60. *OR*, 36, Part II, 116, 128, 135, 137; Thompson, 296–298; Smith Review, Smith Papers.

61. *OR*, 36, Part II, 128, 135, 137.

62. Martin Haynes, *A History of the Second Regiment, New Hampshire Volunteer Infantry* (Manchester, New Hampshire: C.F. Livingston, Printer, 1865), 170.

63. Wistar, 452–453; Haynes, 170; *OR*, 36, Part II, 108–109.

64. *OR*, 36, Part II, 38–39, 43, 94–95; For the Tenth Corps at Drewry's Bluff, see Robertson, 198–208.

65. *OR*, 36, Part II, 116–117, 153; Humphreys, 153.

66. *OR*, 36, Part II, 117, 144, 152–153, 162–163; Wistar, 453–454; Haynes, 170–171; Thompson, 298–299; Bruce, 342–343; Robertson, 193–194.

67. *OR*, 36, Part II, 38–39, 95, 116–117, 135, 139, 144, 152–153, 162–163, 834–835; Bruce, 342–343;

Wistar, 453–454; Haynes, 170–171; Thompson, 298–299; Robertson, 193–194.

68. *OR*, 36, Part II, 95, 116–117, 123, 128, 135, 152; J.W. Shaffer to W.F. Smith, 16 May 1864, Smith Papers; Humphreys, 154; Robertson, 204.

69. W.F. Smith to S.L. Smith, 16 May 1864, Smith Papers.

70. Smith Review, and W.F. Smith to S.L. Smith, 7 May 1864 and 16 May 1864, Smith Papers; Derby, 288.

71. Butler, 644; B.F. Wilson to H. Wilson, 7 May 1864, Henry Wilson Papers, Division of Manuscripts, Library of Congress; no further reference to this collection will be made. Rockwell, 295–297; Smith, *From Chattanooga*, 119; W.F. Smith to S.L. Smith, 26 April 1864, and Smith Review, Smith Papers.

72. J.H. Wilson, *Under the Old Flag*, 2 vols. (New York: D. Appleton & Co., 1912), 1:417–418; *Battles and Leaders*, 4:212; *OR*, 36, Part III, 43.

73. *OR*, 36, Part III, 43.

74. J.A. Rawlins to M. Rawlins, 13 April 1864, Wilson Papers.

75. *OR*, 36, Part III, 43; J.A. Rawlins to M. Rawlins, 13 April 1864, and W.F. Smith to J.H. Wilson, 16 March 1864, Wilson Papers; *Battles and Leaders*, 4:212; Wilson, 1:417–418, 423.

76. *OR*, 36, Part III, 43.

77. *OR*, 36, Part III, 68–69, 141, 178.

78. *OR*, 36, Part III, 178.

79. Smith, *From Chattanooga*, 20–21, 116.

80. Smith Review, Smith Papers; Robertson, 242.

81. *OR*, 36, Part II, 861–862, 903 and 36, Part III, 32–33, 108–110, 182.

82. *OR*, 36, Part III, 108–109, 180–181.

83. *OR*, 36, Part III, 41–42, 74, 109–110.

84. Smith Review, Smith Papers.

85. *OR*, 36, Part II, 145, 903 and 36, Part III, 104, 144, 204 and 51, Part I, 1248, 1252; Smith Review, Smith Papers.

86. *OR*, 36, Part II, 145 and 36, Part III, 204 and 51, Part I, 1248, 1252; Smith Review, Smith Papers; *New York Times*, 30 May 1864.

87. Marshall, 4:261.

88. Smith Review, Smith Papers; *OR*, 36, Part I, 7–8; Marshall, 4:261.

Chapter XII

1. Smith Review, Smith Papers; *OR*, 36, Part I, 8 and 36, Part III, 236, 245; Marshall, ed., 4:268.

2. Smith Review, Smith Papers; W.F. Smith's report on the battle of Petersburg, 9 August 1864, Benjamin F. Butler Papers, Division of Manuscripts, Library of Congress; this report will hereafter be cited as Smith Report.

3. Smith Report, Butler Papers.

4. Smith Review, Smith Papers; Smith Report, Butler Papers; *OR*, 36, Part III, 285–286, 288, 410; Smith, *From Chattanooga*, 121.

5. *OR*, 36, Part I, 998 and 36, Part III, 289; Smith Report, Butler Papers.

6. *OR*, 36, Part I, 998; General Order no. 39, 30 May 1864, General Orders (Eighteenth Army Corps), Record Group 393, Inventory vol. 2, Entry no. 6891, National Archives; Charles Devens' report on the battle of Cold Harbor, 6 June 1864, Smith Papers.

7. *OR*, 36, Part I, 998 and 36, Part III, 261, 278, 288.

8. *OR*, 36, part I, 998.

9. *Battles and Leaders*, 4:222; *OR*, 36, Part I, 999 and 36, Part III, 410.

10. *OR*, 36, Part I, 999.

11. *Ibid.*

12. *OR*, 36, Part I, 999–1000; *Battles and Leaders*, 4: 222–223; Gordon C. Rhea, *Cold Harbor: Grant and Lee, May 26-June 3, 1864* (Baton Rouge: Louisiana State University Press, 2002), 227, 233–234: McPherson, *Ordeal*, 411.

13. Charles Devens report, 6 June 1864, Smith Papers; *OR*, 36, Part I, 997, 1018–1020 and 51, Part I, 1266–1267; William Hyde, *History of the One-Hundred-and-Twelfth Regiment N.Y. Volunteers* (Fredonia, N.Y.: W. McKinstry & Co., 1866), 82–83; Rhea, 247–248.

14. Charles Devens report, 6 June 1864, Smith Papers; *OR*, 36, Part I, 996–997, 1000, 1018–1020 and 51, Part I, 1266–1267; William Hyde, 82–83; Rhea, 248–249, 254–255.

15. *OR*, 36, Part I, 996–997, 1000, 1005, 1007–1009, 1012 and 51, Part I, 1248; Rhea, 250–252.

16. *OR*, 51, Part I, 1253.

17. Charles Devens report, 6 June 1864, Smith Papers; *OR*, 36, Part I, 1000, 1005–1006 and 51, Part I, 1248–1249.

18. *OR*, 36, Part I, 1000.

19. *Ibid.*

20. *OR*, 36, Part I, 1000–1001; W.F. Smith to A.A. Humphreys, 5 June 1864, and W.F. Smith endorsement, 24 September 1864, Press copies of telegrams sent (Eighteenth Army Corps), Record Group 393, Inventory vol. 2, Entry no. 6882, National Archives.

21. *OR*, 36, Part I, 1001.

22. *OR*, 36, Part I, 1001–1002 and 36, Part III, 505.

23. *OR*, 36, Part I, 1002 and 36, Part 3, 506, 508, 509, 563; *Battles and Leaders*, 4:226; Wilson, *Smith*, 91, 93–94.

24. *OR*, 36, Part I, 1002 and 36, Part III, 493, 494, 507, 508; Noah A. Trudeau, *Bloody Roads South: The Wilderness to Cold Harbor, May-June 1864* (Boston: Little, Brown, 1989), 281–282.

25. Rhea, 308, 348.

26. *OR*, 36, Part I, 1006, 1009, 1012–1013 and 51, Part I, 1249.

27. *OR*, 36, Part I, 1002 and 51, Part I, 1254, 1260, 1264.

28. *OR*, 36, Part I, 1002; *New York Herald*, 7 June 1864; *Battles and Leaders*, 4:228.

29. *OR*, 36, Part I, 1002–1003 and 51, Part I, 1249, 1264; Rhea, 352.

30. *OR*, 36, Part III, 508 and 51, Part I, 1254, 1261–1262.

31. *OR*, 36, Part I, 1003 and 51, Part I, 1254, 1262.

32. Rhea, 358–360; *OR*, 36, Part I, 1003.

33. *OR*, 36, Part I, 1003 and 36, Part III, 554.

34. *OR*, 36, Part III, 555.

35. *OR*, 36, Part I, 1003–1004 and 36, Part III, 555; *Battles and Leaders*, 4:226.

36. *OR*, 36, Part I, 1004 and 36, Part III, 545, 556.

37. *OR*, 51, Part I, 1249; *Battles and Leaders*, 4:227.

38. *Battles and Leaders*, 4:227.

39. *OR*, 36, Part I, 301.

40. *Battles and Leaders*, 4:227; *OR*, 36, Part I, 301–302, 1004; Comstock Diary, 3 June 1864, Comstock Papers.

41. *OR*, 36, Part I, 88, 194, 195, 1004; Schiller, ed., 94–95; Grant, 2:272; *Battles and Leaders*, 4:227.

42. *OR*, 36, Part I, 1004–1005 and 36, Part III, 541, 557; *Battles and Leaders*, 4: 227–228.

43. Derby, 302.

44. *OR*, 36, Part I, 178–180, 194–195; Derby, 302.

45. Rhea, 390.

46. *Battles and Leaders*, 4:229–230; Rhea, 390.

47. *Battles and* Leaders, 4:229–230; Freeman sustains Smith's hypothesis. Freeman believes that had Smith not been misdirected by Grant's orders, he would have been able to join in an attack with the Sixth Corps on the morning of June 1, which could have shattered the Confederate right wing. Freeman, 3:506–507. Rhea agrees that critics rightly fault Grant for neglecting to take advantage of the gap between Lee's right flank and the Chickahominy River. Rea, 392.

48. W.F. Smith memo, undated, William F. Smith Papers, U.S. Army Heritage and Education Center; *Battles and Leaders*, 4:225, 229.

49. W.F. Smith memo, undated, Smith Papers, U.S. Army Heritage and Education Center; *Battles and Leaders*, 4:225, 229.

50. Marshall, ed., 4:362; "Volunteer" articles, Smith Papers.

51. W.F. Smith to R.E. Lee, 6 July 1868, Robert E. Lee Papers, Virginia Historical Society, Richmond, Virginia; R.E. Lee to W.F. Smith, 27 July 1868, W.B. Franklin to W.F. Smith, 29 June 1864 and 4 August 1868, and "Volunteer" articles, Smith Papers.

52. Thomas Livermore, "Grant's Campaign Against Lee," *Military Historical Society of Massachusetts Papers* 4 (1905): 430.

53. Livermore, "Grant's Campaign," 430, 434; J.H. Wilson and C.A. Dana, *Life of U.S. Grant* (Springfield, Massachusetts: Burdon Bill & Co., 1868), 229, 231–233, 235, 236; Wilson, *Under the Old Flag*, 1:401–404.

54. Peter Michie, *The Life and Letters of Emory Upton* (New York: D. Appleton & Co., 1885), 108.

55. Swinton, 494.

56. Swinton, 491.

57. Swinton, 491, 494; Michie, 108–109; J.C. Ropes, "Grant's Campaign in Virginia in 1864,"

Military Historical Society of Massachusetts Papers 4 (1905): 396. 403, 413; Grant, 2:276; William S. McFeely, *Grant* (New York: W.W. Norton, 1981), 171.

58. Theodore Lyman, *Meade's Headquarters, 1863–1865* (Boston: The Atlantic Monthly Press, 1922), 149.

59. Lyman, 148–149; *OR*, 36, Part I, 1005 and 36, Part III, 572, 588, 603, 617, 618, 622, 624–625.

60. *Battles and Leaders*, 4:228; *Philadelphia Daily Evening Bulletin*, 6 June 1864; *OR*, 36, Part III, 623–624; Nicolas Bowen Diary, 4 June 1864, Smith Papers.

61. *OR*, 36, Part III, 656, 660, 689.

62. *Battles and Leaders*, 4:228; *OR*, 36, Part III, 600, 638–639, 666–667. For scholarly criticism of Grant's delay in arranging a truce to permit care for the Federal wounded on the field, see McFeely, 171, 173.

63. *OR*, 36, Part III, 687–688; Army of the Potomac Circular, 6 June 1864, Letters Received (Eighteenth Army Corps), Record Group 393, Inventory vol. 2, Entry no. 6890, National Archives.

64. *OR*, 36, Part III, 666–667, 679, 687–688, 716; Army of the Potomac Circular, 7 June 1864, Letters Received (Eighteenth Army Corps), Record Group 393, Inventory vol. 2, Entry no. 6890, National Archives.

65. Thompson, 369; *OR*, 36, Part I, 1005.

66. *OR*, 36, Part I, 1005 and vol. 36, Part III, 748, 754, 755.

67. W.F. Smith, "The Movement Against Petersburg June 1864," *Military Historical Society of Massachusetts Papers* 5 (1906):108.

68. Smith Report, Butler Papers; Smith, "The Movement," 108–109; *OR*, 40, Part II, 17; A. Wilson Greene, *A Campaign of Giants: The Battle of Petersburg* (Chapel Hill: University of North Carolina Press, 2018), 51.

69. Smith, "The Movement," 109; Smith Report, Butler Papers; W.F. Smith to S.L. Smith, 13 June 1864, Smith Papers.

70. P. West to W.F. Smith, undated, Smith Papers; Schiller, ed., 97–98; *Battles and Leaders*, 4:206; Smith, *From Chattanooga*, 176–178.

Chapter XIII

1. I.J. Wistar to J.H. Wilson, 13 May 1903, Wilson Papers.

2. Marshall, 4:364; Greene, 61.

3. *OR*, 36, Part III, 754–755 and 40, Part II, 17, 43–44; Smith, "The Movement," 109; Smith Report, Butler Papers; P. West to W.F. Smith, undated, Smith Papers; Greene, 75, 85.

4. Greene, 85–86; Smith Report, Butler Papers; *OR*, 40, Part I, 700 and 51, Part I, 1247; Nicolas Bowen Diary, 14 and 15 June 1864, Smith Papers.

5. Smith Report, Butler Papers; Humphreys, 206–207; Greene, 85.

6. Smith Report, Butler Papers; *OR*, 40, Part I, 705.

7. Greene, 88–89, 94; E. Hinks to W.F. Smith, 1 January 1866, Ropes Papers; *OR*, 40, Part I, 721.

8. *OR*, 40, Part I, 721–722; S.A. Duncan report on the battle of Petersburg, 25 June 1864, Ropes Papers; Greene, 97.

9. W.T. H. Brooks to W.F. Smith, 3 March 1866, Smith Papers; Smith Report, Butler Papers; Smith, "The Movement," 86; *OR*, 51, Part I, 1256.

10. *OR*, 51, Part I, 1256.

11. Thomas Livermore, "The Failure to Take Petersburg June 15, 1864," *Military Historical Society of Massachusetts Papers* 5 (1906): 52–53; Smith Report, Butler Papers; Smith, "The Movement," 88–89.

12. Smith Report, Butler Papers; Smith, "The Movement," 88–89, 96; Smith Review, and W.F. Smith to G. Shattuck, 2 September 1892, Smith Papers; Schiller, ed., 102; Livermore, "The Failure," 53; *OR*, 40, Part III, 20.

13. J. Martindale to W.F. Smith, 11 December 1865, Smith Papers; *OR*, 51, Part I, 1256; Smith Report, Butler Papers; Smith, "The Movement," 89–90.

14. Smith Report, Butler Papers; Smith, "The Movement," 89–90; W.F. Smith to G. Shattuck, 2 September 1892, Smith Papers; Gordon C. Rhea, "Baldy Smith: The Scapegoat of Petersburg," *North & South* 14, no. 3 (May 2012): 23.

15. New Hampshire, *Report of the Adjutant General of the State of New Hampshire* (1866), 2:795; Smith Report, Butler Papers; Smith, "The Movement," 90; W.T. H. Brooks to W.F. Smith, 3 March 1866, Smith Papers; *OR*, 40, Part I, 722 and Part II, 84; E. Hinks to W.F. Smith, 1 January 1866, Ropes Papers.

16. *OR*, 40, Part I, 729; Smith Report, Butler Papers; A.V. Kautz, "Reminiscences of the Civil War," 76–77, A.V. Kautz, "Report of the Military Services of August V. Kautz," 11, and A.V. Kautz Diary, 14 to 16 June 1864, August V. Kautz Papers, U.S. Army Heritage and Education Center; A.V. Kautz to W.F. Smith, 16 June 1864, Letters Received (Eighteenth Army Corps), Record Group 393, Inventory vol. 2, Entry number 6890, National Archives; Greene, 76, 97.

17. *OR*, 40, Part I, 715 and 51, Part I, 1247–1248; Smith Report, Butler Papers; Livermore, "The Failure," 59; Thompson, 382–402; Moore, ed., 11:571; Kautz, "Reminiscences of the Civil War," 77, Loy Papers; New Hampshire, *Report of the Adjutant General of the State of New Hampshire* (1866), 2:794–795; Edward Longacre, ed., "The Roughest Kind of Campaigning: Letters of Sergeant Edward Wightman, Third New York Volunteers, May–July 1864," *Civil War History* 28 (1982):337–339; Greene, 103, 105.

18. J. Holman report of the battle of Petersburg, 20 June 1864, S.A. Duncan report, 25 June 1864, and E. Hinks to W.F. Smith, 1 January 1866, Ropes Papers; *OR*, 40, Part I, 722; Greene, 107; Rhea, "Baldy Smith: The Scapegoat of Petersburg," 25.

19. J. Holman report, 20 June 1864, S.A. Duncan report, 25 June 1864, and E. Hinks to W.F. Smith, 1 January 1866, Ropes Papers.

20. S.A. Duncan report, 25 June 1864, Ropes Papers.

21. *OR*, 40, Part I, 705, 719 and 51, Part I, 1256; J. Martindale to W.F. Smith, 11 December 1865, Smith Papers.

22. Smith, "The Movement," 96–97; Smith Report, Butler Papers. Thomas J. Howe, *The Petersburg Campaign: Wasted Valor, June 15–18, 1864* (Lynchburg, Virginia: H.E. Howard, Inc. 1988), 35–36.

23. Smith, "The Movement," 97–98.

24. Smith Report, Butler Papers; *OR*, 40, Part II, 53, 83, 88; William F. Smith, "General W.F. Smith at Petersburg," *The Century Magazine* 54 (May-October 1897): 637; Although Smith did not remember receiving it, General Butler may have also sent a message between 7:00 P.M. and 8:00 P.M., ordering Baldy to cease firing and entrench. Thomas Baird to W.F. Smith, 24 June 1897, and Smith Memoirs, 283–292, Smith Papers; Schiller, ed.,143–155; Wilson, *Smith*, 109; Edward G. Longacre, "The Army of the James, 1863–1865: A Military, Political, and Social History," Ph.D. diss., Temple University, 1988, 429–430. The veracity of the Butler's message to entrench is debated. Greene questions the existence of the message. See Greene, 116–117, 540; Gordon Rea believes the message to be true. See Gordon C. Rhea, "Baldy Smith: The Scapegoat of Petersburg," 25–26.

25. Frank Peabody, "Crossing of the James and First Assault upon Petersburg, June 12–15, 1864," *Military Historical Society of Massachusetts Papers* 5 (1906):136–137; Livermore, "The Failure," 61–62, 65–66; J.C. Ropes, "The Failure to Take Petersburg on June 16–18, 1864," *Military Historical Society of Massachusetts Papers* 5 (1906):185–186; Smith Report, Butler Papers; E. Hinks to T. Livermore, 21 February 1878, Ropes Papers; Smith Review, Smith Papers; Smith, "The Movement," 88; Humphreys, 207, 210; Marshall, 4:374; Smith, *From Chattanooga*, 65–67; Wilson, *Smith*, 109; Freeman, 3:529–530; Gordon C. Rhea, *On to Petersburg, Grant and Lee, June 4–15, 1864* (Baton Rouge: Louisiana University Press, 2017), 245, 392; Greene, 85.

26. Smith, *From Chattanooga*, 80; *OR*, 40, Part II, 59, 73 and 51, Part I, 270–271; Rhea, "Baldy Smith: The Scapegoat of Petersburg," 19, 23.

27. Humphreys, 210; *OR*, 40, Part I, 303–306 and 40, Part II, 63; Greene, 80.

28. E. Hinks to W.F. Smith, 1 January 1866, Ropes Papers; E. Hinks to W.F. Smith, 7 March 1892, 12 March 1892 and 31 December 1892, Smith Papers; *OR*, 40, Part II, 644.

29. *OR*, 40, Part I, 305–306, 366, 404, 700 and 51, Part I, 1248; S.A. Duncan report, 25 June 1864, Ropes Papers; N. Bowen Diary, 15 and 16 June 1864, and Smith Review, Smith Papers; Smith Report, Butler Papers; Greene, 115.

30. *OR*, 40, Part I, 306; Simon, 11:53

31. *OR*, 40, Part II, 60.

32. *OR*, 40, Part II, 83.

33. *OR*, 40, Part II, 60, 83; Smith Review and W.G. Mitchell to W.S. Hancock, 9 December 1865, Smith Papers; Smith, *From Chattanooga*, 106.

34. George Bruce, "Petersburg, June 15—Fort Harrison, September 29: A Comparison," *Military Historical Society of Massachusetts Papers* 14 (1918):108–111; *OR*, 36, Part I, 21–25; Peabody, 140–141; Denny, 346–347; Charles Coffin, *Four Years of Fighting* (Boston: Ticknor & Fields, 1866), 357; Longacre, 463; McFeely, 39. See also Sears, *Lincoln's Lieutenants*, 702–703. For other contemporary criticisms of Smith's failure, see Greene, 117–119.

35. *OR*, 36, Part I, 25.

36. Simon, ed., 12:35.

37. Butler, 690.

38. E. Hinks to T. Livermore, 21 February 1878, Ropes Papers.

39. Howe, 35–37; *OR*, 36, Part I, 21–25; E. Hinks to T. Livermore, 21 February 1878, Ropes Papers; *Battles and Leaders*, 4:541; G.T. Beauregard to C.M. Wilcox, 9 June 1874, *Military Historical Society of Massachusetts Papers* 5 (1906): 119–123; Humphreys, 210; E. Hinks to W.F. Smith, 12 March 1866, Smith Papers; Butler, 689–690; Simon, ed., 12:35; Rhea, *Petersburg*, 315–317.

40. Wilson, *Under the Old Flag*, 1:454; Wilson, *Smith*, 110; *OR*, 40, Part I, 303–306, 315; Grant, 2:298; Swinton, 506; Richard Bache, *Life of General George Gordon Meade* (Philadelphia: H.T. Coates & Co., 1897), 461; Derby, 334; Clarence MacCartney, *Grant and His Generals* (New York: McBridge Co., 1953), 207; T. Harry Williams, 320; Howe, 29–30; Longacre, 431–432; McFeely, 39; Rhea, *Petersburg*, 243, 264, 313.

41. Grant, 2:295.

42. W.T. H. Brooks to W.F. Smith, 3 March 1866, Smith Papers.

43. Smith, "The Movement," 77–115; Smith Report, Butler Papers; Grant, 2:295; Bache, 463; W.T. H. Brooks to W.F. Smith, 3 March 1866, Smith Papers; W.F. Smith memo, undated, Smith Papers, U.S. Army Heritage and Education Center.

44. Smith, "The Movement," 96.

45. Schiller, ed., 94.

46. Longacre, 423.

47. Rhea, "Baldy Smith: The Scapegoat of Petersburg," 23.

48. Smith, "The Movement," 95–96; Schiller, ed., 94; E. Hinks to W.F. Smith, 1 January 1866, Ropes Papers; Wilson, *Smith*, 109; Longacre, 423; Rhea, *Petersburg*, 281–315.

49. W.T. H. Brooks to W.F. Smith, 3 March 1866, Smith Papers; Smith, "The Movement," 95–96.

50. Smith. "The Movement," 97–98; Smith Report, Butler Papers; Ropes, "The Failure," 185–186; Livermore, "The Failure," 65–66, 101–102; *OR*, 40, Part II, 61, 83; Greene, 120–122.

51. J. Martindale to W.F. Smith, 11 December 1865, Smith Papers.

52. H. Noyes to W.F. Smith, 12 December 1865, Smith Papers.

53. G. Kelley to W.F. Smith, 2 July 1898, Smith Papers.

54. E. Hinks to T. Livermore, 21 February 1878, Ropes Papers.

55. J. Martindale to W.F. Smith, 11 December

1865, H. Noyes to W.F. Smith, 12 December 1865, G.W. Kelley to W.F. Smith, 2 July 1898, and G.V. Henry to W.F. Smith, 12 March 1866, Smith Papers; S.A. Duncan report, 25 June 1864, and E. Hinks to T. Livermore, 21 February 1878, Ropes Papers; *OR*, 40, Part I, 714, 718.

56. Rhea, *On to Petersburg*, 312–317; Cleaves, 269; Greene, 119–120.

57. Smith, *From Chattanooga*, 106; *OR*, 36, Part I, 21–25 and 40, Part II, 112; T. Harry Williams, 320; Greene, 133.

58. *OR*, 40, Part I, 714–715, 722, 40, and Part II, 113–114 and 51, Part I, 1246–1248; Howe, 55.

59. *OR*, 40, Part II, 113.

60. *OR*, 40, Part II, 89, 113.

61. *OR*, 40, Part I, 318, 700, 714–715, and 40, Part II, 114 and 51, Part I, 1246–1248, 1256–1257; Howe, 57.

62. *OR*, 40, Part I, 21.

63. *OR*, 40, Part I, 21–22; J.A. Rawlins to M. Rawlins, 16 June 1864, Wilson Papers; W.F. Smith to J.C. Ropes, 16 March 1887, Smith Papers, U.S. Army Heritage and Education Center.

64. General Order, 17 June 1864, Edward W. Hinks Papers, Boston University Library.

65. *Ibid.*

66. *OR*, 40, Part I, 21; General Order, 17 June 1864, Hinks Papers; Greene, 110; W.F. Smith to S.L. Smith, 16 June 1864, Smith Papers.

67. *OR*, 40, Part I, 214, 700, 714–715, and 40, Part II, 118–119, 133–134, 141–143, 153–155, 203 and 51, Part I, 1246–1248, 1257.

68. *OR*, 51, Part I, 1257.

69. *OR*, 40, Part II, 176, 204 and 51, Part I, 1258.

70. *OR*, 40, Part II, 205–206 and 51, Part I, 1258; Howe, 124.

71. *OR*, 40, Part II, 224–225, 228, 267 and 51, Part I, 1250, 1258.

72. *OR*, 40, Part I, 214–215, 696–697, 710–712, 715–716, and 40, Part II, 266 and 51; Part I, 1250, 1251, 1259.

73. The Confederates estimated their losses more conservatively: 25 killed, 72 wounded, and 209 missing. *OR*, 40, Part II, 804.

74. *OR*, 40, Part I, 710–711, 716 and 40, Part II, 401, 797 and 51, Part I, 1250–1252; J.A. Rawlins to M. Rawlins, 24 June 1864, Wilson Papers.

75. *OR*, 40, Part I, 213, 696–697 and 40, Part II, 362, 366, 369, 400, 426, 428, 449.

76. *OR*, 40, Part I, 697–698 and 40, Part II, 539; J.W. Turner to W. Barton, 30 June 1864, J.W. Turner to L. Bell, 30 June 1864, John W. Turner Papers, U.S. Army Heritage and Education Center.

77. *OR*, 40, Part I, 698, 703–704 and 40, Part II, 538–539; Greene, 343.

78. *OR*, 40, Part II, 584; Schiller, ed., 107–108.

Chapter XIV

1. *Boston Commonwealth*, 29 July 1864.

2. General Order, 17 June 1864, Hinks Papers; *OR*, 40, Part I, 21, and 40, Part II, 202–203, and 40, Part III, 118; Butler, 493–495, 578–579; *Boston Commonwealth*, 29 July 1864.

3. *OR*, 40, Part II, 202–203, 371, 459–460 and 40, Part III, 18.

4. *OR*, 40, Part II, 202–203.

5. *OR*, 40, Part II, 459.

6. *OR*, 40, Part II, 490.

7. *OR*, 40, Part II, 491.

8. *OR*, 40, Part II, 460, 489–491; E. Hinks to W. Russell, 26 June 1864, and E. Hinks to W.F. Smith, 27 June 1864, Smith Papers.

9. F.C. Choate to W. Russell, 27 June 1864, Smith Papers.

10. *OR*, 40, Part III, 27.

11. *OR*, 40, Part III, 58.

12. *OR*, 40, Part II, 264–266, 288; Smith, *From Chattanooga*, 155–160; W.F. Smith to S.L. Smith, 21 June 1864, Smith Papers.

13. Butler, 694.

14. Smith, *From Chattanooga*, 187.

15. *Ibid.*

16. Smith, *From Chattanooga*, 155–156, 186–187; Butler, 694; *OR*, 40, Part II, 299–300.

17. Smith, *From Chattanooga*, 155–156, 187–188; Smith Review, Smith Papers; *OR*, 40, Part II, 300.

18. W.F. Smith to S.L. Smith, 21 June 1864, Smith Papers.

19. *Ibid.*

20. Smith, *From Chattanooga*, 156; W.F. Smith to S.L. Smith, 21 June 1864 and 22 June 1864, Smith Papers.

21. *OR*, 40, Part II, 300–301; Smith, *From Chattanooga*, 188.

22. W.F. Smith to S.L. Smith, 29 June 1864, Smith Papers.

23. W.F. Smith to S.L. Smith, 29 June 1864, Smith Papers; *OR*, 40, Part II, 538; Schiller, ed., 111.

24. Smith, *From Chattanooga*, 53–54.

25. *OR*, 40, Part II, 559.

26. *OR*, 40, Part I, 32 and 40, Part II, 558–559; Smith, *From Chattanooga*, 29–30.

27. *OR*, 40, Part II, 595; Smith, *From Chattanooga*, 34; W.F. Smith to S.L. Smith, 2 July 1864, Smith Papers.

28. Smith, *From Chattanooga*, 35–37; *OR*, 40, Part II, 595.

29. *OR*, 40, Part II, 595.

30. Smith, *From Chattanooga*, 35–37; *OR*, 40, Part II, 595.

31. *OR*, 40, Part II, 595.

32. Smith, *From Chattanooga*, 35–37; *OR*, 40, Part II, 595.

33. W.F. Smith to S.L. Smith, 3 July 1864, Smith Papers; Smith, *From Chattanooga*, 175.

34. *OR*, 40, Part II, 595.

35. Smith, *From Chattanooga*, 2–4; *OR*, 40, Part II, 598.

36. *OR*, 40, Part III, 31, 69; Smith, *From Chattanooga*, 175.

37. *OR*, 40, Part III, 88, 119; Schiller, ed., 111–112.

38. This conference may have occurred on July

8. The letter used to describe this evening leaves the exact date indefinite. Marshall, 4:481.

39. Marshall, 4:481.

40. *OR*, 40, Part III, 83–84; W.F. Smith to G. Shattuck, 5 January 1893; Smith Review, W.B. Franklin to W.F. Smith, 4 February and 9 February 1887, and Clipping of W.F. Smith's reply to C. Comstock's review of *From Chattanooga to Petersburg* in an article entitled "Grant and Butler," *New York Evening Post*, 12 June 1893, Smith Papers.

41. This meeting may have occurred on July 9. A dispatch indicates Butler had the meeting by 6 p.m. July 9. But the dispatch also notes the reception of a letter sent on July 10 leading Jessie Marshall to suggest the dispatch was incorrectly dated. A letter written on July 10 from Butler to his wife could be interpreted to date the conference either on July 9 or July 10. In his autobiography, Butler gives July 10 as the date of the conference. *OR*, 40, Part III, 114; Marshall, 4:481–483; Butler, 699.

42. Marshall, 4:481.

43. Butler, 695–696.

44. W.F. Smith manuscript on why he was relieved from command, undated, Smith Papers.

45. Smith, *From Chattanooga*, 176.

46. Schiller, ed., 112–113; W.B. Franklin to W.F. Smith, 9 February, W.F. Smith manuscript on why he was relieved from command, undated, Smith Review, and W.F. Smith to G. Shattuck, 5 January 1893, Smith Papers; W.F. Smith to George Suckley, 2 August 1864, Ferdinand Dreer autograph collection [0175], Historical Society of Pennsylvania, Philadelphia, Pennsylvania; *Battles and Leaders*, 4:229; Smith, *From Chattanooga*, 175–176.

47. Clipping of Cyrus Comstock's review of *From Chattanooga to Petersburg* in an article entitled "Grant and Butler," *New York Evening Post*, 12 June 1893, and J.H. Wilson to W.F. Smith, 19 May 1893, Smith Papers.

48. Grant may have been incorrect about the Tenth Army Corps. Dana telegraphed Rawlins on July 11: "We were wrong at City Point about the Tenth Corps—that has never been assigned to Butler's command and was only temporarily under his orders when it was sent into his dept. and he was senior to Gillmore.—When Butler was sent to Fort Monroe, it was for Genl. Grant to dispose of the Tenth as he chose." Simon, 11:210n.

49. *OR*, 40, Part III, 122–123; Clipping of C. Comstock review in the *New York Evening Post*, 12 June 1893, Smith Papers.

50. Bruce Catton, *Grant Takes Command* (Boston: Little, Brown, 1969), 328–329, 332–333; Snell, 330–331; *OR*, 40, Part III, 175, 313, 360; Clipping of C. Comstock review in the *New York Evening Post*, 12 June 1893, Smith Papers.

51. Rockwell, 297–298; Butler, 713; Wilson, *Smith*, 84; Wolfson, 390, 392; Marsena Patrick Journal, 24 July 1864, Marsena R. Patrick Papers, Division of Manuscripts, Library of Congress; Clipping of C. Comstock review in *New York Evening Post*, 12 June 1893, Smith Papers; T. Harry Williams, 323–324; MacCartney, 213; Sears,

Lincoln's Lieutenants, 715; The Patrick Diary can be found in published form in David S. Sparks, ed. *Inside Lincoln's Army: The Diary of Marsena Rudolph Patrick, Provost Marshal General, Army of the Potomac* (New York: Thomas Yoseloff, 1964); Thomas J. Goss, *The War within the Union Command and Politics and Generalship during the Civil War* (Lawrence: University Press of Kansas, 2003), 181.

52. *OR*, 40, Part II, 558 and 40, Part III, 123; Grant's presence failed in preventing Butler's blunders. When Butler's violation of orders in December cost Grant the capture of Fort Fisher, Grant asked for Butler's removal. After his reelection in November, Lincoln was less constrained by Butler's political influence and approved Grant's request. MacCartney, 218; Smith, *From Chattanooga*, 5–6; Clipping of C. Comstock review in the *New York Evening Post*, 12 June 1893, Smith Papers; *OR*, 40, Part II, 44–45.

53. Butler, 712–713; S. Cadwallader to J.H. Wilson, 17 September 1904, and J.H. Wilson to S. Cadwallader, 24 September 1904, Wilson Papers; Smith, *From Chattanooga*, 178, 193; Marsena Patrick Journal, 20 July 1864, Patrick Papers; Longacre, "The Army," 517; Greene, 366. In mid-July, some of Butler's friends wrote to him about the possibility of the War Democrats and Fremont supporters uniting and nominating him for president, but there is no evidence that he seriously considered such a candidacy. William Zornow, *Lincoln and the Party Divided* (Norman: University of Oklahoma Press, 1954), 110–112; T. Harry Williams, 323; Sparks, ed. 415.

54. *OR*, 40, Part II, 558; Smith, *From Chattanooga*, 29; Cyrus Comstock Diary, 17 July 1864, Comstock Papers; Greene, 366–367.

55. *OR*, 40, Part II, 558, 595 and 40, Part III, 313; J.H. Wilson, *Life of John A. Rawlins* (New York: Neale Pub. Co., 1916), 250; Clipping of Comstock review in *New York Evening Post*, 12 June 1893, Clipping of J.H. Wilson, "General 'Baldy' Smith: The Story of a Misjudged Man," *New York Sun*, 22 May 1893, and J.H. Wilson to W.F. Smith, 19 May 1893, Smith Papers; Wilson, *Smith*, 107–108, 115.

56. Schiller, ed., 115–116.

57. Smith, *From Chattanooga*, 176–177.

58. *Battles and Leaders*, 4:229.

59. *Battles and Leaders*, 4:229; Smith, *From Chattanooga*, 46–47, 176–177; *OR*, 40, Part III, 89; W.F. Smith to J.H. Wilson, 23 April 1870, Wilson Papers; Smith manuscript on why he was relieved, undated, and W.F. Smith to G. Shattuck, 29 July 1892, Smith Papers; Andrews, 551; Schiller, ed., 116; Greene, 367.

60. Wilson, *Rawlins*, 250.

61. Smith, *From Chattanooga*, 174–179; W.F. Smith to J.H. Wilson, 20 May, Wilson Papers; W.F. Smith to E. Hinks, 13 January 1866, Hinks Papers; Wilson, *Smith*, 107–108; Wilson, *Rawlins*, 250.

62. J.H. Wilson to W.F. Smith, 4 August 1864, Smith Papers.

63. J.H. Wilson to W.F. Smith, 4 August 1864,

Smith Papers; for Grant's recommendation to have Franklin command the troops at Washington, see *OR*, 37, Part II, 374.

64. J.H. Wilson to W.F. Smith, 4 August 1864, and Clipping of J.H. Wilson, "General 'Baldy' Smith: The Story of a Misjudged Man," Smith Papers; J.A. Rawlins to M. Rawlins, 19 July 1864, Wilson Papers; Wilson, *Rawlins*, 250; Wilson, *Smith*, 105; Smith, *From Chattanooga*, 58.

65. Lyman, 192.

66. *Ibid.*

67. Lyman, 193.

68. W. Russell to W.F. Smith, 2 August 1864, Smith Papers.

69. Meade, 2:214–215; Lyman, 192–193; W. Russell to W.F. Smith, 2 August 1864, Smith Papers; *New York Tribune*, 27 July 1864.

70. Marsena Patrick Journal, 22 July 1864, Patrick Papers.

71. Clipping of C. Comstock review in *New York Evening Post*, 12 June 1893, A.A. Humphreys to W.F. Smith, 24 November 1883, and J.H. Wilson to W.F. Smith, 19 May 1893, Smith Papers; Marsena Patrick Journal, 22 July 1864, Patrick Papers.

72. *New York Times*, 3 August 1864.

73. *Ibid.*

74. MacCartney, 220.

75. MacCartney, 219–220; J.H. Wilson, *The Life of Charles A. Dana* (New York: Harper & Brothers, 1907), 343. Though Dana reproved Smith for his indiscreet censure of his superiors, he entirely agreed with Baldy's opinions. After Grant notified Halleck that he was suspending Order no. 225, Dana telegraphed Rawlins on July 11: "I see that the General has backed down on Butler but I hope that he will fix it so that that military lawyer will not be able to ruin the end of the campaign as he has ruined and foiled the beginning— Nullifying all its vast cost and awful bloodshed." Four days later, Dana wrote Rawlins, "at least 20,000 men have been slaughtered by Meade's blind, unconsidered, fragmentary assaults at Cold Harbor and Petersburg, assaults even more deficient in all the elements of generalship than Burnside's infamous massacre at Fredericksburg." Simon, 11:210n, 253n.

76. W.F. Smith to G. Suckley, 2 August 1864, Dreer Collection; Smith, *From Chattanooga*, 56–58; Wilson, *Smith*, 115–116; W.F. Smith to J.H. Wilson, 23 April 1870 and 29 April 1870, Wilson Papers.

77. *OR*, 40, Part III, 359.

78. W.F. Smith to G. Suckley, 2 August 1864, Dreer Collection; *OR*, 40, Part III, 359.

79. Marshall, 4:493.

80. Marshall, 4:513.

81. *New York Herald*, 22 July 1864.

82. Marshall, 4:484, 493, 513; *New York Herald*, 22 July 1864.

83. Derby, 359.

84. J.H. Wilson to W.F. Smith, 4 August 1864, Smith Papers.

85. W.B. Franklin to W.F. Smith, 25 July 1864,
Smith Papers.

86. J.H. Wilson to W.F. Smith, 20 August 1864, Wilson Papers.

87. *New York Herald*, 23 July 1864.

88. Derby, 358–359; W.B. Franklin to W.F. Smith, 25 July 1864, and J.H. Wilson to W.F. Smith, 4 August 1864, Smith Papers; J.H. Wilson to W.F. Smith, 20 August 1864, Wilson Papers; Wilson, *Dana*, 343; *New York Herald*, 23 July 1864; *New York Times*, 23 July 1864; *Philadelphia Daily Evening Bulletin*, 23 July 1864.

89. Wilson, *Dana*, 345–346, 348; W.F. Smith to G. Shattuck, 22 June 1893, Smith Papers.

Chapter XV

1. W.F. Smith to G. Suckley, 2 August 1864, Dreer Collection; *OR*, 48, Part I, 917.

2. J.H. Wilson to W.F. Smith, 4 January 1865, Wilson Papers.

3. J.H. Wilson to W.F. Smith, 4 January 1865, Wilson Papers.

4. J.H. Wilson to W.F. Smith, 29 October 1864 and 4 January 1865, Wilson Papers.

5. J.H. Wilson to W.F. Smith, 4 January 1865 and 25 February 1865, Wilson Papers; W.F. Smith to E. Hinks, 6 December 1865, Hinks Papers.

6. *OR*, 48, Part I, 917.

7. *OR*, 48, Part I, 1002.

8. *OR*, 48, Part I, 830, 917, 1001, 1002, 1092; Simon, ed., 13: 397n, 450; Smith Memoir, 293–294, Smith Papers.

9. *OR*, 41, Part IV, 634, 653, 817.

10. *OR*, 41, Part IV, 817.

11. H. Stanberry to E.M. Stanton, 13 January 1865, Stanton Papers; *OR*, 48, Part I, 1165–1166; W.F. Smith to E. Townsend, 3 December 1864 and 17 December 1864, W.F. Smith to J. Hardie, 1 December 1864, and War Department Memorandum, 12 December 1864, LROAG; E. Townsend to W.F. Smith, 3 December 1864, R. Williams to W.F. Smith, 5 December 1864, and War Department Memorandum, 16 March 1865, LSOAG; *Dictionary of American Biography*, 2:583–584; Smith-Brady Commission Report, 23 September 1865, 1–5, Records of the Adjutant General's Office, Record Group 94, Entry no. 737, National Archives; cited hereafter as *SBCR*.

12. *SBCR*, 1–5, 274–283, 304–305.

13. *Report of Maj.-Gen. Wm. F. Smith and Hon. James T Brady on the Official Conduct of General S.A. Hurlbut, and others, at New Orleans, April 12, 1865* (Chicago: Evening Journal Book and Job Printing House, 1876), 3; this report, which is a published portion of *SBCR*, will hereafter be cited as *RSB*.

14. *RSB*, 3–4.

15. *RSB*, 4–5.

16. *RSB*, 5–7.

17. *RSB*, 7, 23.

18. *RSB*, 8–10, 12–18, 23.

19. *RSB*, 20–24.

20. *SBCR*, 283–286; *OR*, 48, Part II, 61–62.

21. *RSB*, 24.

22. Military Bureau Report, 22 May 1865, Register of Letters Received, Office of the Adjutant General, Record Group 94, National Archives (Washington, D.C.: National Archives Trust Fund Board, Microcopy no.711); *RSB*, 24.

23. *SBCR*, 145–149, 157–158; Ludwell Johnson, *Red River Campaign* (Baltimore: Johns Hopkins Press, 1958), 52.

24. *SBCR*, 26–27, 34, 38–42, 52–54, 56–57, 129–136.

25. *SBCR*, 159–161, 164, 172, 179, 182, 184, 279, 280.

26. *SBCR*, 58–59, 68–69, 77, 173.

27. *SBCR*, 6.

28. Benjamin Thomas and Harold Hyman. *Stanton* (New York: Knopf, 1962), 461; *SBCR*, 5–13.

29. *SBCR*, 13–14.

30. *SBCR*, 306–307; *Dictionary of American Biography*, 9:426.

31. *SBCR*, 288.

32. *SBCR*, 288–295.

33. *Ibid.*

34. *SBCR*, 289–295; War Department Memorandum, 19 May 1865, Register of Letters Received, Office of the Adjutant General, Record Group 94, National Archives (Washington, D.C.: National Archives Trust Fund Board, Microcopy no. 711).

35. *SBCR*, 306–307; W.F. Smith to E. Townsend, 5 August 1865 and 15 September 1865, LROAG.

36. E. Canby to E. Townsend, 4 October 1865, LROAG.

37. E. Canby to E. Townsend, 4 October 1865 and T. Eckert endorsement, 11 November 1865, LROAG.

38. E.M. Stanton to A. Johnson, 30 April 1866, Letters Sent by the Secretary of War to the President and Executive Departments, 1863–70, Record Group 107, National Archives (Washington, D.C.: National Archives Trust Fund Board, Microcopy no. 421). Smith commented that the special commission "caught several criminals none of whom were punished; and some promoted." W.F. Smith note, undated, Smith Papers.

39. Report of the Special Commission of Inspection Quartermaster Department, Cincinnati, Ohio, received by the Adjutant General's Office, 8 November 1865, LROAG; E. Townsend to W.F. Smith, 16 June 1865, LSOAG.

40. Smith Memoir, 293, Smith Papers; W.F. Smith to E. Townsend, 4 November 1865, W.F. Smith acceptance of the appointment of brevet ranks of lieutenant colonel, colonel, and brigadier general, 1 and 6 November 1865, Letters Received by the Commission Branch of the Adjutant General's Office 1863–1870, Record Group 94, National Archives (Washington, D.C.: National Archives Trust Fund Board, Microcopy no. 1064); cited hereafter as LRCBAGO. Smith's acceptance of the rank of brevet major general is not present in LRCBAGO. Adjutant General reports dated April 20, 1888, however, do cite Smith's appointment to the ranks of brevet lieutenant colonel through brevet major general and mention the service for which Smith was breveted. LRCBAGO.

41. W.F. Smith to E Townsend, 6 December 1865, J.F. Hammond medical certificate, 5 December 1865, and E. Townsend endorsement, 30 December 1865, LROAG.

42. Smith Memoir, 294–295, Smith Papers; W.F. Smith to G.W. Cullum, 15 January 1879, G.W. Cullum File, United States Military Academy Library.

43. Smith Memoir, 295–296, Smith Papers.

44. Smith Memoir, 296, Smith Papers; W.F. Smith to E. Townsend, 16 January 1866, and E. Townsend endorsement, 17 January 1866, LROAG.

45. Smith Memoir, 296–300, Smith Papers; W.F. Smith to E. Townsend, 21 May 1866, LROAG.

46. Smith Memoir, 300–302; Smith Papers; Harold Livermore, *History of Spain* (New York: Farrar, Straus & Cudahy, 1958), 385.

47. Smith Memoir, 301–302, Smith Papers.

48. W.F. Smith to E. Townsend, 21 May 1866, LROAG.

49. Smith Memoir, 302, Smith Papers; W.F. Smith to E. Townsend, 21 May 1866, and War Department endorsement, 13 June 1866, LROAG.

Chapter XVI

1. Smith Memoir, 312, 317–318, Smith Papers; David D. Porter to W.F. Smith, 6 November 1867, Smith Papers, Charles Thomas Harbeck Collection, Huntington Library.

2. Smith Memoir, 318, Smith Papers.

3. Smith Memoir, 319, Smith Papers.

4. Smith Memoir, 318, Smith Papers.

5. Smith Memoir, 318–319, Smith Papers; W.F. Smith to G.W. Cullum, 15 January 1879, Cullum File.

6. Smith Memoir, 319–332, Smith Papers.

7. W.F. Smith to J.H. Wilson, 17 May 1870, Wilson Papers.

8. Smith Memoir, 314, Smith Papers.

9. Langer, 669, 680; Smith Memoir, 314, Smith Papers; W.F. Smith to Louis Philippe, Comte de Paris, 28 October 1877, Smith Papers.

10. *Ibid.*

11. *Ibid.*

12. *Ibid.*

13. Smith Memoir, 313–314, Smith Papers.

14. Rhea Smith, *Spain* (Ann Arbor: University of Michigan Press, 1965), 369; Harold Livermore, 400; Smith Memoir, 314–315, Smith Papers.

15. Smith Memoir, 303, 315, Smith Papers.

16. Smith Memoir, 299, Smith Papers. In the revolution, the Philippines lost sixteen thousand soldiers, and the United States suffered over seven thousand casualties. Leon Wolff, *Little Brown Brother: How the U.S. Purchased and Pacified the Philippines Islands at the Century's Turn* (New York: Kraus Reprint Co., 1970), 356–360.

17. Smith Memoir, 332–333, Smith Papers; A.E. Costello, *Our Police Protectors* (New York: C.F. Roper & Co., 1884), 266, 286.

18. Costello, 269–270; Smith Memoir, 335, Smith Papers; W.F. Smith to G.W. Cullum, 15 January 1879, Cullum File; *New York Times*, 31 August 1879; Joel Erhardt, S.P. Nichols, and W.F. Smith, *Proceedings in Relation to the Removal of Police Commissioners: Erhardt, Nichols, and Smith* (New York: privately printed, 1879), 22, 29, 43.

19. Smith Memoir, 336–337, 344–345, Smith Papers.

20. Smith Memoir, 337, 345, Smith Papers.

21. Smith Memoir, 345–346, Smith Papers; Costello, 266–267, 269, 277.

22. Smith Memoir, 346–347, Smith Papers.

23. Smith Memoir, 347–350, Smith Papers.

24. Erhardt, Nichols, and Smith, 43, 46; *New York Times*, 29 December 1879.

25. Erhardt, Nichols, and Smith, 1, 2, 11, 12, 14.

26. Erhardt. Nichols, and Smith, 16, 18, 53, 77–78.

27. Erhardt, Nichols, and Smith, 67–72; *New York Times*, 29 December 1879.

28. *New York Times,* 22 March 1879, 7 August 1879, 19 March 1880, and 20 July 1880; Costello, 286, 454.

29. *New York Times*, 11 July 1880.

30. *New York Times*, 9 July 1880, 11 July 1880 and 13 July 1880.

31. Smith Memoir, 351, Smith Papers; *New York Times*, 11 September 1879, 12 September 1879 and 5 November 1879.

32. Smith Memoir, 354, Smith Papers; Jordan, 268.

33. Smith Memoir, 354–355, Smith Papers; Wilson, *Smith*, 123–124; *Congressional Quarterly, Guide to U.S. Elections* (Washington, D.C.: Congressional Quarterly, 1975), 48, 136.

34. Smith Memoir, 356, Smith Papers; Costello, 464; *New York Times*, 3 November 1880, 4 November 1880, 5 November 1880 and 12 March 1881.

35. W.F. Smith to J.M. Wilson, 17 April 1901, Smith Papers.

36. J.H. Wilson, *Smith*, 124–125; J.M. Wilson to W.F. Smith, 15 July 1884, Chief of Engineers to W.F. Smith, 30 April 1901, and W.F. Smith to J.M. Wilson, 17 April 1901, Smith Papers.

37. U.S. Congress, House, 50th Congress, 1st Session, 19 July 1888, *Congressional Record*, 19:6543.

38. *Ibid.*

39. U.S. Congress, House, 50th Congress, 1st Session, 19 July 1888, *Congressional Record*, 19:6543–6546, 6556; U.S. Congress, House, 50th Congress, 1st Session, 20 July 1888, *Congressional Record*, 19:6581.

40. U.S. Congress, Senate, 50th Congress, 1st Session, 7 August 1888, *Congressional Record*, 19:7275–7276, 7282.

41. J.C. Kelton endorsement, 12 February 1889 and W.C. Endicott to Grover Cleveland, 13 February 1889, LRCBAGO: U.S. Congress, House, 50th Congress, 1st Session, 9 August 1888, *Congressional Record*, 19:7400; U.S. Congress, House, 50th Congress, 1st Session, 13 August 1888, *Congressional Record*, 19:7492; U.S. Congress, House, 50th

Congress, 1st Session, 26 September 1888, *Congressional Record*, 19:8967; U.S. Congress, House, 50th Congress, 2nd Session, 5 February 1889, *Congressional Record*, 20:1518; U.S. Congress, Senate, 50th Congress, 2nd Session, 7 February 1889, *Congressional Record*, 20:1601; U.S. Congress, House, 50th Congress, 2nd Session, 19 February 1889, *Congressional Record*, 20:2066.

42. Smith Memoir, 359, Smith Papers; W.F. Smith to R. Proctor, 7 March 1889, and Clipping of *Army and Navy Journal*, 7 September 1889, LRC-BAGO; W.F. Smith to J.H. Wilson, 14 January, Wilson Papers.

43. Smith Memoir, 280–282, Smith Papers; W.F. Smith to J.E. Johnston, 5 October 1890, Joseph E. Johnston Papers, Swem Library, College of William and Mary.

44. Smith Memoir, 262–267, Smith Papers; Otto Eisenschiml, *The Celebrated Case of Fitz John Porter* (Indianapolis: Bobbs Merrill, 1950), 304.

45. Petition, undated, Winfield S. Hancock Papers, U.S. Army Heritage and Education Center; E. McClellan to Oliver [E. McClellan], 19 January ____, Claude W. Unger Collection [1860A], Historical Society of Pennsylvania.

46. W.F. Smith to G. Shattuck, 25 October 1892, Smith Papers.

47. *Ibid.*

48. W.F. Smith to G. Shattuck, 25 October 1892, Smith Memoir, 197–198, and Smith Memoir Appendix, Smith Papers; Hassler, 189.

49. "Volunteer" Articles, and W.B. Franklin to W.F. Smith, 4 August 1868, 12 August 1868 and 14 August 1868, Smith Papers.

50. Clipping of W.F. Smith review of J.A. Logan, *The Volunteer Soldier of America* in the *Washington Evening Star*, 9 October 1887, Smith Papers.

51. *Ibid.*

52. *Ibid.* At least one historian supports Smith's view of the negative political influence in Northern strategy. Ludwell Johnson pointed out that between November 1862 and March 1864, the two highest ranking Union generals were Massachusetts politicians Nathaniel Banks and Benjamin Butler, "whose martial accomplishments had ranged from disasters to fiascos." Johnson, *Division*, 90.

53. Smith Affidavit, Smith Papers; *Battles and Leaders*, 3:128–138; W.F. Smith to J.C. Ropes, 9 March 1895, and W.F. Smith to T. Dwight, 17 April 1895, Ropes Papers.

54. W.F. Smith, "Butler's Attack on Drewry's Bluff," *Battles and Leaders*, 4:206–212; W.F. Smith, "The Eighteenth Corps at Cold Harbor," *Battles and Leaders*, 4:221–230.

55. W.F. Smith, "Military Situation"; W.F. Smith, "Historical Sketch"; W.F. Smith, "The Movement"; Clipping of W.F. Smith letter to the editor in *Philadelphia Times*, 30 January 1892, Smith Papers; W.F. Smith to J.C. Ropes, 9 February 1892, Ropes Papers.

56. For the complete citations for Smith's and Butler's published autobiographies, see chapter XI,

notes 5 and 6 respectively; H.V. Boynton to J.H. Wilson, 23 May 1893, Wilson Papers; Clipping of J.H. Wilson, "General 'Baldy' Smith," *New York Sun*, 22 May 1893, and J.H. Wilson to W.F. Smith, 19 May 1893, Smith Papers.

57. Smith Memoir, 174–176, W.F. Smith to G. Davis, 9 May 1897 and 31 July 1897, and G. Davis to W.F. Smith, 29 July 1897, Smith Papers; David Lilley to writer, 4 November 1983.

58. W.F. Smith to J.C. Ropes, 3 February 1896, 30 January 1898, 10 February 1898, 15 March 1898 and 19 March 1898, and J.H. Wilson to J.C. Ropes, 14 September 1895 and 25 September 1895, Ropes Papers; *Brown's Ferry.*

59. *Brown's Ferry*; H.M. Duffield to W.F. Smith, 10 March 1898, Smith Papers, U.S. Military Academy Library; W.F. Smith to J.H. Wilson, 28 March 1901, 12 April, 28 January, undated, 16 December 1902, and J.H. Wilson to W.F. Smith, 27 January 1902, Wilson Papers; W.F. Smith to Mr. Williams, 18 September 1901, Simon Gratz autograph collection [0250A], Historical Society of Pennsylvania.

60. Clipping of the *Army and Navy Journal*, 13 November 1902, Smith Papers.

61. J.H. Wilson, *Smith*, 126–127; clipping of the *Montpelier Daily Journal*, August 22, 1901, T.C. Cheney to W.F. Smith, 13 November 1902, Smith Papers.

62. Clipping of the *Philadelphia Times*, 2 March 1903, S.F. Smith to the Adjutant General, 1 March 1903, and S.F. Smith to the Assistant Adjutant General, 7 April 1903, LRCBAGO.

Bibliography

Manuscripts

William T.H. Brooks Papers, United States Army Heritage and Education Center.

Benjamin F. Butler Papers, Division of Manuscripts, Library of Congress.

Ezra Carman Papers, Manuscript and Archives Division, New York Public Library, Astor, Lenox, and Tilden Foundations.

Cyrus Comstock Diary, Cyrus B. Comstock Papers, Division of Manuscripts, Library of Congress.

G.W. Cullum File, United States Military Academy Library.

Ferdinand J. Dreer Autograph Collection, Historical Society of Pennsylvania, Philadelphia, Pennsylvania.

William B. Franklin Papers, Division of Manuscripts, Library of Congress.

Simon Gratz Autograph Collection, Historical Society of Pennsylvania.

Winfield Scott Hancock Papers, United States Army Heritage and Education Center.

James A. Hardie Papers, Division of Manuscripts, Library of Congress.

Isaacs Harris Diary, Isaac Harris Papers, United States Army Heritage and Education Center.

Edward W. Hinks Papers, Boston University Library.

Joseph E. Johnston Papers, Swem Library, College of William and Mary.

August V. Kautz Papers, United States Army Heritage and Education Center.

Robert E. Lee Papers, Virginia Historical Society.

Abraham Lincoln Papers (microfilm copies), Swem Library, College of William and Mary.

Loyal Legion Collection, United States Army Heritage and Education Center.

George B. McClellan Papers, Division of Manuscripts, Library of Congress.

Marsena Patrick Journal, Marsena R. Patrick Papers, Division of Manuscripts, Library of Congress.

Records of the Adjutant General's Office (Record Group 94), National Archives: (a) Letters Received by the Commission Branch of the Adjutant General's Office, 1863–1870. (b) Letters Received by the Office of the Adjutant General, 1822–1860 and 1861–1870. (c) Letters Sent by the Office of the Adjutant General, 1800–1890. (d) Register of Letters Received by the Office the Adjutant General. (e) Smith-Brady Commission Report. (f) United States Military Academy Cadet Application Papers.

Records of the Office of the Chief of Engineers (Record Group 77), National Archives: (a) Letters Received by the Topographical Bureau of the War Department, 1824–1865. (b) Letters Sent by the Topographical Bureau of the War Department and by Successor Divisions in the Office of the Chief of Engineers, 1829–1870.

Register of Letters Received by the Topographical Bureau of the War Department, 1824–1866.

Records of the Office of the Secretary of War (Record Group 107), National Archives: Letters Sent by the Secretary of War to the President and Executive Departments, 1863–1870.

Records of the United States Army Continental Commands (Record Group 393), National Archives. Included are the records of the following commands: Smith's Brigade and Smith's Division, Army of the Potomac; Second Division, Fourth Army Corps; Second Division, Sixth Army Corps; Sixth Army Corps; Department of the Susquehanna; Department of the Cumberland; and Eighteenth Army Corps.

Register of Delinquencies, volume 3, Classes of 1845 and 1846, United States Military Academy, United States Military Academy Library.

John Codman Ropes Papers, Boston University Library.

William Farrar Smith Papers, Charles Thomas Harbeck Collection, The Huntington Library.

William Farrar Smith Papers, Division of Manuscripts, Library of Congress.

William Farrar Smith Papers, James William Eldridge Collection, The Huntington Library.

William Farrar Smith Papers, United States Army Heritage and Education Center.

William Farrar Smith Papers, United States Military Academy Library.

William Farrar Smith Papers, Vermont Historical Society.

Edwin M. Stanton Papers, Division of Manuscripts, Library of Congress.

John Turner Papers, United States Army Heritage and Education Center.

Claude W. Unger Collection, Historical Society of Pennsylvania.
United States Military Academy Catalogs, 1841–1845, United States Military Academy Library.
Henry Wilson Papers, Division of Manuscripts, Library of Congress.
James Harrison Wilson Papers, Division of Manuscripts, Library of Congress.

Congressional Documents

House. 50th Congress, 1st Session. 19 July 1888, 20 July 1888, 9 August 1888, 13 August 1888 and 26 September 1888. *Congressional Record* 19.
House. 50th Congress, 2nd Session. 5 February 1889 and 19 February 1889. *Congressional Record* 20.
House. 37th Congress, 2nd Session. 22 April 1862 and 2 May 1862. *Congressional Globe. Report of the Joint Committee on the Conduct of the War,* 37th Congress, 3rd Session, Part I: "Army of the Potomac," and Part II: "Bull Run. Ball's Bluff." 1863.
Senate. 50th Congress, 1st Session. 7 August 1888. *Congressional Record* 19.
Senate. 50th Congress, 2nd Session. 7 February 1889. *Congressional Record* 20.
Senate. 32nd Congress, 1st Session. Senate Document No. 119.
Senate Executive Document 6, 33rd Cong., Special Session. 1853.
Senate Executive Document 64, 31st Congress, 1st Session, J.E. Johnston et al. "Reports of Secretary of War with Reconnaissances of Routes from San Antonio to El Paso."1850.

State Documents

New Hampshire, *Report of the Adjutant General of the State of New Hampshire,* vol. 2 (1866).

Newspapers

Boston Commonwealth, April 1861–August 1864.
Boston Daily Evening Transcript, April 1861–August 1864.
New York Herald, April 1861–August 1864.
New York Times, April 1861–August 1864; August 1879–March 1881.
New York Tribune, April 1861–August 1864.
Philadelphia Daily Evening Bulletin, April 1861–August 1864.
Philadelphia Public Ledger, April 1861–August 1864.

Books and Articles

Primary Sources

Alexander, E.P. "Sketch of Longstreet's Division—Yorktown and Williamsburg." *Southern Historical Society Papers* 10 (1882): 32–45.

Annual Report of the Lighthouse Board to the Secretary of the Treasury for the Fiscal Year Ended June 30, 1884. Washington, D.C.: Government Printing Office, 1884.
Bartlett, John R. *Personal Narrative of Explorations and Incidents in Texas, New Mexico, California, Sonora, and Chihuahua Connected with the United States and Mexican Boundary Commission During the Years 1850, '51, ''52, and '53.* Two vols. New York: D. Appleton & Co., 1854.
Basler, Roy, ed. *The Collected Works of Abraham Lincoln.* Nine vols. Brunswick: Rutgers University Press, 1953.
Bates, Samuel P. *History of Pennsylvania Volunteers.* Five vols. Harrisburg: B. Singerly, 1869.
Benedict, George. *Vermont in the Civil War.* Two vols. Burlington: Free Press Association, 1886–1888.
Bruce, George. "General Butler's Bermuda Campaign." *Military Historical Society of Massachusetts Papers* 9 (1912): 303–345.
_____. "Petersburg, June 15-Fort Harrison, September 29: A Comparison." *Military Historical Society of Massachusetts Papers* 14 (1918): 83–115.
Butler, Benjamin F. *Autobiography and Personal Reminiscences of Major-General Benjamin F. Butler.* Boston: A.M. Thayer & Co., 1892.
Castleman, Alfred. *Army of the Potomac.* Milwaukee: Strickland & Co., 1863.
Coffin, Charles. *Four Years of Fighting.* Boston: Ticknor & Fields, 1866.
Costello, A.E. *Our Police Protectors.* New York: C.F. Roper & Co., 1884.
Cox, J.D. *Military Reminiscences of the Civil War.* Two vols. New York: C. Scribner's Sons, 1900.
Curtis, Newton. *From Bull Run to Chancellorsville.* New York: G.P. Putnam's Sons, 1906.
Dennett, Tyler. *Lincoln and the Civil War in the Diaries and Letters of John Hay.* Westport: Negro University Press, 1972.
Denny, Joseph. *Wearing the Blue in the Twenty-fifth Massachusetts Volunteer Infantry.* Worcester: Putnam & Davis, 1879.
Derby, William. *Bearing Arms in the Twenty-Seventh Massachusetts Regiment of Volunteer Infantry during the Civil War, 1861–1865.* Boston: Wright & Potter Printing Co., 1883.
Erhardt, Joel, S. Nichols, and W.F. Smith. *Proceedings in Relation to the Removal of Police Commissioners: Erhardt, Nichols, and Smith.* New York: privately printed, 1879.
Franklin, William B. *Reply of Major General William B. Franklin to the Report of the Joint Committee of Congress on the Conduct of the War on the Battle of Fredericksburg.* New York: D. Van Nostrand, 1867.
Grant, Ulysses S. *Personal Memoirs of U. S. Grant.* Two vols. New York: C. L Webster & Co., 1885.
"G.T. Beauregard to C.M., 9 June 1874." *Military Society of Massachusetts Papers* 5 (1906): 119–123.
Haynes, Martin. *A History of the Second Regiment, New Hampshire Volunteer Infantry.* Manchester: C.F. Livingston, printer, 1865.

Humphreys, A.A. *The Virginia Campaign of '64 and '65*. New York: C. Scribner's Sons, 1883.

Hyde, Thomas. *Following the Greek Cross*. New York: Houghton Mifflin, 1894.

Hyde, William. *History of the One Hundred and Twelfth Regiment New York Volunteers*. Fredonia: W. McKinstry & Co., 1866.

Johnson, Robert U., and Clarence C. Buell, eds. *Battles and Leaders of the Civil War*. Four vols. New York: The Century Company, 1887–1888. W.F. Smith wrote three articles and one postscript that appear in this work.

Livermore, Thomas. "The Failure to Take Petersburg June 15, 1864." *Military Historical Society of Massachusetts Papers* 5 (1906): 35–73.

_____. "Grant's Campaign against Lee." *Military Historical Society of Massachusetts Papers* 4 (1905): 407–459.

_____. "The Siege and Relief of Chattanooga." *Military Historical Society of Massachusetts Papers* 8 (1910): 273–339.

Longacre, Edward, ed. "The Roughest Kind of Campaigning: Letters of Sergeant Edward Wightman, Third New York Volunteers, May-July 1864." *Civil War History* 28 (1982): 324–350.

Lord, E.O., ed. *History of the Ninth Regiment New Hampshire*. Concord: Republican Press Association, 1895.

Love, William. *Wisconsin in the War of the Rebellion*. New York: Sheldon & Co., 1866.

Loving, J.M., ed. *Civil War Letters of George Washington Whitman*. Durham: Duke University Press, 1975.

Lyman, Theodore. *Meade's Headquarters, 1863–1865*. Boston: The Atlantic Monthly Press, 1922.

Marshall, Jessie A., ed. *Public and Private Correspondence of Gen. Benjamin F. Butler during the Period of the Civil War*. Five vols. Norwood, Massachusetts: privately published, 1917.

Massachusetts Infantry. 36th Regiment. *History of the Thirty-Sixth Regiment Massachusetts Volunteers*. Boston: Rockwell & Churchill, 1894.

McClellan, George B. *McClellan's Own Story: The War for the Union*. New York: C.L. Webster, 1886.

Meade, George G. *The Life and Letters of George Gordon Meade*. Two vols. New York: C. Scribner's Sons, 1913.

Michie, Peter. *The Life and Letters of Emory Upton*. New York: D. Appleton & Co., 1885.

Moore, Frank, ed. *The Rebellion Record: A Diary of American Events*. Twelve vols. New York: D. Van Nostrand, 1862–1871.

Nevins, Allan, ed. *A Diary of Battle: The Personal Journals of Colonel Charles S. Wainwright 1861–1865*. New York: Harcourt, Brace & World, 1962.

Newell, Joseph, ed. *"Ours" Annals of 10th Regiment, Massachusetts Volunteers in the Rebellion*. Springfield: C.A. Nichols & Co., 1875.

Paris, Comte de Louis Philippe Albert d' Orleans. *History of the Civil War in America*. Four vols. Philadelphia: Porter and Coates, 1875–1888.

Palfrey, Francis W. *The Antietam and Fredericksburg*. New York: Charles Scribner's Sons, 1881–1883.

Peabody, Frank. "Crossing of the James and First Assault upon Petersburg, June 12–15, 1864." *Military Historical Society of Massachusetts Papers* 5 (1906): 124–145

Report of Maj.-Gen. Wm. F. Smith and Hon. James T. Brady on the Conduct of General S. A. Hurlbut, and others, at New Orleans, April 12, 1865. Chicago: Evening Journal Book and Job Printing House, 1876.

Rockwell, Alfred P. "The Tenth Army Corps in Virginia May 1864." *Military Historical Society of Massachusetts Papers* 9 (1912): 267–299.

Ropes, John C. "The Failure to Take Petersburg, June 12–15, 1864." *Military Historical Society of Massachusetts Papers* 5 (1906): 157–186.

_____. "Grant's Campaign against Lee." *Military Historical Society of Massachusetts Papers* 4 (1905): 363–405.

_____. *The Story of the Civil War*. Four vols. New York: G.P. Putnam's Sons, 1894–1913.

Scott, Robert N., chief compiler. *The War of the Rebellion: A Compilation of the Official Records of the Union and Confederate Armies*. Washington, D.C.: Government Printing Office, 1880–1901. Seventy vols. in 128 books. The *Official Records* are supplemented by the *Official Atlas of the Civil War*.

Sherman, William T. *Memoirs of General W. T. Sherman*. Two vols. New York: C.L. Webster & Co., 1891.

Simon, John Y., ed. *The Papers of Ulysses S. Grant*. Twelve vols. Carbondale: Southern Illinois University Press, 1967–1984.

Smith, William F. *From Chattanooga to Petersburg under Generals Grant and Butler*. Boston: Houghton Mifflin, 1893.

_____. "An Historical Sketch of the Military Operations around Chattanooga, Tenn., September 22 to November 27, 1863." *Military Historical Society of Massachusetts Papers* 8 (1910): 149–246.

_____. "Burnside Relieved." *Magazine of American History* 15 (1885): 197–201.

_____. "The Military Situation in Northern Virginia from the 1st to the 14th of November 1862." *Military Historical Society of Massachusetts Papers* 3 (1903): 104–121.

_____. "The Movement against Petersburg June 1864." *Military Historical Society of Massachusetts Papers* 5 (1906): 77–115.

Sparks, David S., ed. *Inside Lincoln's Army: The Diary of Marsena Rudolph Patrick, Provost Marshal General, and Army of the Potomac*. New York: Thomas Yoseloff, 1964.

Stevens, George. *Three Years in the Sixth Corps*. New York: D. Van Nostrand, 1870.

Swinton, William. *Campaigns of the Army of the Potomac*. New York: C. Scribner's Sons, 1882.

Thompson, S.M. *Thirteenth Regiment of New Hampshire Volunteer Infantry in the War of the Rebellion, 1861-1865*. Boston: Houghton Mifflin, 1888.

Todd, William. *The Seventy-Ninth Highlanders,*

New York Volunteers in the War of Rebellion, 1861–1865. Albany: Press of Brando, Barton, & Co., 1886.

Tyler, Mason. *Recollections of the Civil War.* New York: G.P. Putnam's Sons, 1912.

U.S. Board of Officers upon the Claim of Major General William F. Smith. *Brown's Ferry, 1863.* Philadelphia: F. McManus, Jr. & Co., 1901.

Villard, Henry. *Memoirs of Henry Villard.* Two vols. Boston: Houghton Mifflin, 1904.

Whitman, William. *Maine in the War for the Union.* Lewiston: N. Dingley Jr. & Co., 1865.

Wilson, James Harrison. *Life and Service of William Farrar Smith.* Wilmington, Delaware: John Rogers Press, 1904.

_____. *Life of Charles A. Dana.* New York: Harper & Brothers, 1907.

_____. *Life of John A. Rawlins.* New York: Neale Pub. Co., 1916.

_____. *Under the Old Flag.* Two vols. New York: D. Appleton & Co., 1912.

Wilson, J.H., and Charles Dana. *Life of U. S. Grant.* Springfield, Massachusetts: Gurdon Bill & Co., 1868.

Wistar, I.J. *Autobiography of Isaac Tones Wistar, 1827–1905.* Philadelphia: The Wistar Institute of Anatomy and Biology, 1937.

Secondary Sources

Aldrich, Lewis Cass. *History of Ontario County.* Edited by George S. Conover. Syracuse: D. Mason & Co., 1893.

Andrews, J. Cutler. *The North Reports the Civil War.* Pittsburgh: University of Pittsburgh Press, 1955.

Bache, Richard. *Life of General George Gordon Meade.* Philadelphia: H.T. Coates & Co., 1897.

Beatie, Russel H. *The Army of the Potomac: McClellan Takes Command, September 1861-February 1862.* Volume II. Boston: DaCapo Press, 2004.

_____. *The Army of the Potomac: McClellan's First Campaign, March 1862- May 1862.* Volume III. New York: Savas Beatie, 2007.

Boatner, Mark. *Civil War Dictionary.* New York: David McKay Co., 1959.

Boyd, Neil Boyd. "The Confederate Invasion of Central Pennsylvania and the Battle of Sporting Hill." https://web.archive.org/web/20030304185356im_/http://campcurtin.org/campcurtin/reenact/5.gif.

Cleaves, Freeman. *Meade of Gettysburg.* Dayton, Ohio: Morningside Book Shop, 1980.

Coddington, Edwin B. *The Gettysburg Campaign: A Study of Command.* New York: Charles Scribner's Sons, 1968.

Congressional Quarterly. *Guide to U. S. Elections.* Washington, D.C.: Congressional Quarterly, 1975.

Cozzens, Peter. *The Shipwreck of Their Hopes: The Battles for Chattanooga.* Urbana: University of Illinois Press, 1994.

Cress, Joseph. "Civil War 150: Union Veteran recalls fight at Oyster Point." June 26, 2013, *The Sentinel,* https://cumberlink.com/news/local/history/civil-war-union-veteran-recalls-fight-at-oyster-point/article_8f1654ca-decd-11e2-9ab6-001a4bcf887a.html.

Dictionary of American Biography. Twenty vols. New York: Charles Scribner's Sons, 1928–1937.

Donovan, Timothy H. *The American Civil War.* Wayne, New Jersey: Avery Publishing Group, 1987.

Downey, Fairfax. *Storming the Gateway: Chattanooga, 1863.* New York: David McKay Co., 1960.

Downing, Charles G., and Roy L. Swift. "Howard, Richard Austin." Handbook of Texas Online, https://www.tshaonline.org/handbook/entries/howard-richard-austin.

Eisenschiml, Otto. *The Celebrated Case of Fitz John Porter.* Indianapolis: Bobbs-Merrill, 1950.

Franklin, John Hope. *The Emancipation Proclamation.* Garden City, New York: Doubleday, 1963.

Freeman, Douglas. *Lee's Lieutenants: A Study in Command.* Four vols. New York: C. Scribner's Sons, 1946.

Goetzmann, William. *Army Exploration in the American West 1803–1863.* New Haven: Yale University Press, 1959.

Greene, A. Wilson. *A Campaign of Giants: The Battle of Petersburg.* Chapel Hill: University of North Carolina Press, 2018.

Gross, Thomas J. *The War within the Union Command: Politics and Generalship during the Civil War.* Lawrence: University Press of Kansas, 2003.

Hartwig, D. Scott. *To Antietam Creek.* Baltimore: Johns Hopkins University Press, 2012.

Hassler, Warren. *George B. McClellan: Shield of the Union.* Baton Rouge: Louisiana State University Press, 1957.

Hebert, Walter. *Fighting Joe Hooker.* New York: Bobbs-Merrill, 1944.

Howe, Thomas J. *The Petersburg Campaign: Wasted Valor, June 15-1 8, 1864.* Lynchburg, Virginia: H.E. Howard, Inc., 1988.

Johnson, Ludwell. *Division and Reunion: America 1848–1877.* New York: John Wiley & Sons, 1978.

_____. *Red River Campaign.* Baltimore: Johns Hopkins Press, 1958.

Jordan, David M. *Winfield Scott Hancock: A Soldier's Work.* Bloomington: Indiana University Press, 1988.

Lamers, William M. *The Edge of Glory: A Biography of General William S. Rosecrans.* New York: Harcourt, Brace & World, 1961.

Langer, William, ed. *An Encyclopedia of World History.* 4th ed. Boston: Houghton Mifflin, 1968.

Livermore, Harold. *History of Spain.* New York: Farrar, Straus and Cudahy, 1958.

Longacre, Edward G., "The Army of the James, 1863–1865: A Military, Political, and Social History." Ph.D. diss., Temple University, 1988.

MacCartney, Clarence. *Grant and His Generals.* New York: McBridge Co., 1953.

McDonough, James L. *Chattanooga—A Death Grip on the Confederacy.* Knoxville: University of Tennessee Press, 1984.

McPherson, James. *Battle Cry of Freedom: The Civil War Era.* New York: Ballantine Books, 1988.

_____. *Ordeal by Fire: The Civil War and Reconstruction.* New York: Alfred Knopf Co., 1982.

McFeely, William S. *Grant.* New York: W.W. Norton 1981.

Morrison, James L. *"The Best School in the World": West Point, The Pre-War Years, 1833–1866.* Kent: Kent State University Press, 1986.

O'Reilly, Francis A. *The Fredericksburg Campaign: Winter War on the Rappahannock.* Baton Rouge: Louisiana State University Press, 2006.

Powell, David A. *Battle Above the Clouds: Lifting the Siege of Chattanooga and the Battle of Lookout Mountain, October 16–November 24, 1863.* El Dorado Hills, CA: Savas Beatie, 2017.

Randall, J.G., and David Donald. *The Civil War and Reconstruction.* 2nd ed. Lexington, Massachusetts: D.C. Health and Co., 1969.

Rhea, Gordon C. "Baldy Smith: The Scapegoat of Petersburg." *North & South* 14, no. 3 (May 2012): 18–29.

_____. *Cold Harbor: Grant and Lee, May 26–June 3, 1864.* Baton Rouge: Louisiana State University Press, 2002.

_____. *On to Petersburg: Grant and Lee, June 4–15, 1864.* Baton Rouge: Louisiana State University Press, 2017.

Robertson, William Glenn. *Back Door to Richmond: The Bermuda Hundred Campaign, April June 1864.* Newark: University of Delaware Press, 1987.

Rodriguez, Rudi R. "Rodriguez, José Policarpio." Handbook of Texas Online, https://www.tshaonline.org/handbook/entries/rodriguez-jose-policarpio.

Sears, Stephen W. *George B. McClellan: The Young Napoleon.* New York: Ticknor & Fields, 1988.

_____. *Landscape Turned Red: The Battle of Antietam.* New York: Ticknor & Fields, 1983.

_____. *Lincoln's Lieutenants: The High Command of the Army of the Potomac.* New York: Houghton Mifflin Harcourt, 2017.

_____. *To the Gates of Richmond: The Peninsula Campaign.* Ticknor & Fields, 1992.

Schubert, Frank W. *Vanguard of Expansion: Army Engineers in the Trans-Mississippi West, 1819–1877.* Washington, D.C.: Historical Division, Chief of Engineers, 1980.

Slocum, Charles. *Life and Services of Major General Henry Warner Slocum.* Toledo: Slocum Pub. Co., 1903.

Smith, Rhea. *Spain.* Ann Arbor: University of Michigan Press, 1965.

Snell, Mark A. *From First to Last: The Life of Major General William B. Franklin.* New York: Fordham University Press, 2002.

Stackpole, Edward J. *The Battle of Fredericksburg.* Harrisburg, Pennsylvania: Historical Times, 1965.

Tap, Bruce. *Over Lincoln's Shoulder: The Committee on the Conduct of the War.* Lawrence: University of Kansas Press, 1998

Thomas, Benjamin, and Harold Hyman. *Stanton.* New York: Knopf, 1962.

Thomas, Emory M. *Bold Dragoon: The Life of J.E.B. Stuart* New York: Harper & Row, 1986.

Trudeau, Noah A. *Bloody Roads South: The Wilderness to Cold Harbor, May-June 1864.* Boston: Little, Brown, 1989.

Tucker, Glenn. *Hancock the Superb.* Dayton, Ohio: Morningside Book Shop, 1980.

Williams, Kenneth P. *Lincoln Finds a General.* Five vols. New York: Macmillan, 1950.

Williams, T. Harry. *Lincoln and His Generals.* New York: Alfred Knopf, 1952.

Wittenberg, Eric J., J. David Petruzzi, and Michael F. Nugent. *One Continuous Fight: The Retreat from Gettysburg and the Pursuit of Lee's Army of Northern Virginia, July 4–14, 1863.* New York: Savas Beatie, 2008.

Wolff, Leon. *Little Brown Brother: How the U.S. Purchased and Pacified the Philippine Islands at the Century's Turn.* New York: Kraus Reprint Co., 1970.

Zornow, William. *Lincoln and the Party Divided.* Norman: University of Oklahoma Press, 1954.

Index

Numbers in **bold italics** indicate pages with illustrations